THE SOUL OF
JADE MOUNTAIN

The Soul of Jade Mountain

Husluman Vava

translated by
Terence Russell

Literature from Taiwan Series
in collaboration with
the National Museum of Taiwan Literature and
National Taiwan Normal University

CAMBRIA
PRESS

Amherst, New York

TABLE OF CONTENTS

Foreword vii

Translator's Preface ix

Author's Preface: Memories of a Change of Key 1

Part I: 5

Chapter One: At the Beginning 7

Chapter Two: A Place Called Lumah 25

Chapter Three: Festival to Open New Land 43

Chapter Four: The Sowing Ceremony 75

Chapter Five: The Bird-Chasing Season 95

Chapter Six: Taro Skin in the Wind 115

Chapter Seven: The Stars that Never Fall from the Sky 135

Chapter Eight: Oh Millet! We Welcome You to Our Homes 157

Chapter Nine: The Road to Maturity 179

Chapter Ten: The Ear-Shooting Festival 199

Part II: 219

Chapter 1: The One Nearest to the Ancestors 221

Chapter 2: An Appointment with Food 243

Chapter 3: A Gift from the Gods 259

Chapter 4: The Hunt 277

Chapter 5: A Hunter Named Black Bear 303

Chapter 6: Cina's Loom 323

Chapter 7: The Lost Village of Women 337

Chapter 8: The Woman Who Came From Afar 355

Chapter 9: The Season for Tying Sogon Grass Knots 379

Chapter 10: The Ritual of Birth 395

About the Author and the Translator 417

FOREWORD

Taiwanese literature, like its history, reflects the island's hybrid ethnic diversity and unique culture. Due to its geographical proximity to the Chinese Empire, Taiwanese literature has been greatly influenced by the ancient tradition of classical Chinese literature.

In 1895, Taiwan's fifty-one years of Japanese colonial rule began. During this period, the groundwork for the development of modern Taiwanese literature was laid. The end of World War II also meant the end of Japanese rule, but it was not a time of peace for Taiwan, which found itself caught in the escalation of the Cold War. The result of this was thirty-eight years of martial law. However, through political activism and the persistent efforts of the Taiwanese people who sought to revolutionize and refine the island's political system, martial law ended in 1987 and the island was transformed into Asia's most liberal country, and one with a strong, democratic political system. The struggle for democracy also set the tone for increased responsiveness and acceptance in the literary sphere.

As such, it is important that the world learns about the distinctive brand into which Taiwan literature has evolved. This book is part of the Literature from Taiwan Series, which comprises a varied selection of literary works showcasing exemplary Taiwan literature. It is part of a systematic and measured attempt to introduce Taiwan's distinctiveness to the rest of the world.

All the literary creations featured in the series have been composed by writers who were afflicted or confined by the societal pressures of their time. If one reads a single work of Taiwanese literature, one can easily sense the exuberance of Taiwan's literary masters. However, when one reads a collection, one can experience the force that is driving Taiwan forward.

Since the Taiwan Ministry of Culture's launch of its promotional project, "Books From Taiwan (BFT)" in 2016, the Taiwanese Ministry of Culture has taken on a proactive role in establishing an international copyright information platform and has been an active presence at international book fairs. The Ministry of Culture, furthermore, has been inviting international translators to Taiwan and assisting in the facilitation of translations of Taiwanese books into various languages, measures which have proven fruitful thus far. The National Museum of Taiwan Literature (NMTL) is affiliated with the Ministry of Culture and its structural organization/structural mechanism aligns with that of the BFT, with both parties focusing on the promotion of important Taiwan literary creations.

In addition to this book series, the NMTL has been working on creating a long-term database of translators of Taiwanese literature. It has also conducted a Taiwanese literary survey in various countries with the aim of promoting Taiwanese literature internationally as well as raising awareness for Taiwan's literary excellence, thus giving it a well-deserved voice on the international stage of world literature.

—Su Shuo-Bin,
Director,
National Museum of Taiwan Literature

Translator's Preface

The ancestors of Taiwan's Austronesian Indigenous peoples migrated to the island from areas in southern China and Southeast Asia more than five thousand years ago. Over the course of the millennia, they developed unique ways of thriving in the rich, diverse semitropical ecospheres of the island. Rugged mountain terrain, fertile coastal plains, and an ocean teeming with life encouraged a tremendous diversity of cultural responses, leading to the formation of at least twenty-nine Indigenous nations with their own distinct identities and languages. Then, beginning some three thousand years ago, these enterprising people established trade routes all over the South Pacific. Those trade routes also served as conduits of cultural influence that saw Austronesian language and ways of life come to dominate in the archipelagos of the southern Pacific, including the Philippines, Indonesia and Polynesia. Today, speakers of Austronesian languages, believed to have first developed in Taiwan, live in areas as widely dispersed as Hawai'i, New Zealand, Easter Island, and Madagascar.

Yet, the story of the original Austronesian peoples of Taiwan is seldom told. After their initial migrations to the island, they settled in the fertile coastal plains, located mostly in the west. There they sustained themselves by hunting and gathering, as well as by farming; growing millet, yams and taro. Taiwan is not a large island, but it is characterized by a large diversity of microenvironments. Over the centuries, as they adapted to local conditions, the new residents formed into separate communities with distinct linguistic, social and religious identities. These communities were constantly interacting and evolving as they competed with each other for access to hunting grounds and arable fields.

Contact with the outside world through trade was common, but the population of the island remained almost exclusively Austronesian until the Dutch East India Company established a fort near present-day Tainan in 1624. The Dutch understood the strategic importance of Taiwan, then known as Formosa, as a hub for trade with the Chinese Ming empire, and with Japan. In order to provide a stable economic basis for their colony, they encouraged Chinese farmers to migrate there. They also tried to subdue local Indigenous communities and bring them under their control. This was the beginning of the long and complex process whereby Indigenous peoples were gradually, but steadily displaced or assimilated by settlers and colonial powers.

Large-scale migrations of ethnic Chinese (often referred to as Han) began in the seventeenth century, and continued into the twentieth century. Those migrations overwhelmed Indigenous peoples, along with their cultural and economic structures. Indigenous communities were deprived of most of their land, and they were forced to the margins of the newly formed settler society. For example, the Bunun people, who are the main protagonists in *The Soul of Jade Mountain*, had originally inhabited the plains areas of west-central Taiwan. Under pressure from Chinese migration, they moved to resettle in the southern regions of the Central Mountain Range where they eventually occupied an area second only in extent to the more northerly Atayal people.

In their dispersed, clan-centric communities, the Bunun were constantly vying for resources with other high mountain peoples. They were to became known for their prowess as hunters and warriors, and their villages often featured displays of the bones of game, and of the skulls of slain enemies. After the Japanese colonial regime (1895-1945) brought the Chinese population of the agrarian plains under control, they were anxious to exploit the rich resources Taiwan's mountain areas. This required the subjugation of the Austronesian peoples who had established themselves there hundreds of years earlier. It was a much more challenging project than the pacification of the plains. They encountered stiff opposition in rugged alpine terrain where their modern military apparatus was often ineffective. The Bunun, as well as the Atayal, resisted fiercely, engaging in guerrilla-style raids on Japanese outposts that resulted in the loss of many Japanese lives. Ultimately, however, the modern technology and organizational methods of the Japanese won out. Most Indigenous communities, including the Bunun villages, were forcefully relocated from the high mountains to areas closer to the plains that were more easily accessed and controlled. Traditional hunting practices and slash-and-burn millet farming were replaced by wet-field rice cultivation, and this in turn meant the end to many of the millet cultivation rituals that so characterized Bunun culture.

Like all other European colonizers during the so-called "Age of Discovery," the Dutch had been assisted by missionaries who sought to convert local populations to Christianity and make them more culturally receptive to their new rulers. In Taiwan, the Indigenous population proved more open to the foreign religion than did the Han, and today the majority of Indigenous people are Christians, mostly Presbyterians and Roman Catholics. The spread of Christianity to the mountain areas was slower. It wasn't until the 1940s that missionaries began teaching in Bunun villages. While Christianity offered a buffer against Chinese and Japanese incursions, it also severely undermined traditional religious and social structures.

The assimilative policies administered by Chiang Kai-shek's Chinese Nationalist government after 1945 and continuing into the 1990s further eroded Bunun culture and language. The Nationalists took over the 'civilizing' project of the Japanese by educating Bunun children in the history and culture of China, rather than allowing the traditional knowledge to be passed down by the elders. By the time Husluman Vava (1958–2007), the author of *The Soul of Jade Mountain*, began to write his stories about Bunun life in the high mountains, most of the customs and beliefs that characterized that life had disappeared.

In comparison to other Indigenous groups in Taiwan, the Bunun people in traditional times were known for the number and variety of their religious and social rituals. As we see in the pages of *The Soul of Jade Mountain*, their lives were lived within a cycle of rituals, many of which were related to the cultivation of millet, the staple of Bunun life. Others, like the famous "ear-shooting ritual" described in Part I, Chapter 10, were coming-of-age rites. Underlying all Bunun rituals was a belief in the pervasive presence of spirit entities, both benign and malign. All things, animate and inanimate, were intimately connected and life was only possible if people constantly aware of their reliance on the spirit world.

With the possible exception of their traditional head-hunting practices, Taiwan's Indigenous people are best known in the Western world for their singing. This is primarily because a recording of two Amis singers was sampled by the Romanian-German musical group, Enigma in their song, "Return to Innocence" (1994). Indigenous people are known for their outstanding musical talent, with some of the nation's most famous performers being Indigenous. However, the Bunun people are unique in having developed a style of singing in multipart harmony. The melodies produced by this form of song are eerie, enchanting and exceptionally beautiful. As Vava describes in the novel, whether in celebration of a solemn religious rite, or as part of joyous social gatherings, the Bunun people gave voice to their emotions in polyphonic song.

In so many ways, the historical experience of Taiwan's Indigenous peoples over the past four hundred years runs closely parallel to that of the native peoples of North and South America. And sadly, the consequences of that history are similar as well. Today in Taiwan, Indigenous peoples, like their counterparts in the United States, Canada, Mexico, and all over the world, are working to escape the oppressive conditions that have been imposed upon them by the national governments that now control the lands in which they have lived for thousands of years. They strive to reassert their cultural, economic, and political sovereignty. In their own communities, they endeavor to promote ethnic pride and to reinvigorate cultural traditions, endowing them with contemporary meaning. They also reach out to the mainstream population, making use of the open media environment to educate and to seek allies in their struggle.

Cultural production, including literature, creative performance, and the visual arts, is a central part of any movement that seeks to validate and redefine a traditional way of life and its inherent values. In Taiwan since the 1980s, Indigenous writers have led the way in revealing the inequitable situation of their people within the structures of the modern nation of Taiwan. They have also acted as historians and ethnographers in documenting ways of life that existed in Taiwan before the arrival of Han settlers. Husluman Vava was one of a pioneering group of artists and cultural workers who answered the call of the Indigenous Rights Movement for cultural content in support of the movement's political and social work. Along with a small number of very dedicated men and women, Vava participated in the rise of an important new form of literary expression in Taiwan. As with the works of early Native American authors, such as N. Scott Momaday and Leslie Marmon Silko, who have made an indelible impression on the progress of English literature, the novels and short stories of Indigenous writers like Husluman Vava now occupy a position of undeniable importance in the development of Chinese-language literature in Taiwan.

Husluman Vava was trained as a teacher and taught for a number of years at an elementary school in a village populated largely by people of his own Bunun nation. Although his teaching position afforded him many opportunities to become involved in the cultural life of the village, Vava soon felt the need to expand his horizons and become a part of the larger movement to assert the presence of Indigenous people in the life of the Taiwanese nation. In 1995, his first composition, "My Life Under the Crotch of a Giant Woman's Trousers," was published in the *Taiwan Times* newspaper. The following year, he retired from his teaching career and threw himself wholeheartedly into the rising tide of Indigenous cultural production. 1997 saw the publication of more writings in newspapers and journals, as well as a trilogy of books depicting the many facets of Bunun life. In 1998, his story, "The Hunter," which examines the ethos of Bunun hunting culture, was awarded the prestigious Wu Cho-liu Prize for Literature. A number of his other books and stories have received literary prizes from a variety of organizations, and several stories have been included in school textbooks in Taiwan. However, the most significant recognition of Vava's status as a writer came in 2007, just one year before his untimely death, when his magnum opus, *The Soul of Jade Mountain*, was awarded the Taiwan Prize for Literature, the highest literary award in Taiwan.

In many respects, *The Soul of Jade Mountain* is a summation of Husluman Vava's creative project. It is an ethnographic novel in which the cultural traditions and foundational values of the Bunun people are woven into a coming of age narrative set in premodern times. Vava evokes the hard realities of life in the high alpine regions long before mechanization. As in many of his other works, the reader is made acutely aware of the interconnectedness of the continuum of being from inanimate life forms, through animals and humans, and extending to the gods and ancestral spirits. The annual rhythm of life in the village is regulated by a cycle of rituals that appeal to the divinities of nature for protection and guidance. The abundance of the millet harvest, just as the success of the hunt, depends not only on the correct performance of ancient ceremonies but also on the fastidious maintenance of a complex set of taboos passed down by the ancestors. Certain behaviors offend the benevolent spirits, while others encourage the forces of malevolence to draw near and to bring their curses of disease and famine down on the people. More than anything else, it is the unforgiving rigors of life in the mountain forests and the awareness of their vulnerability that impress community members with the importance of close observation of the ancestral teachings. Examples of the dire consequences of violating the taboos have been burned into the collective memory of the village.

The central protagonist in the story is Umas, the son of a brave hunter and the grandson of the venerated village elder who led a small group of intrepid families in quest of a new village site when their original community had reached the limits of its ability to support a growing population. From an early age, Umas' curiosity leads him to seek an understanding not only of the customs and life technologies of his people but also of the rationale and the values that underlie traditional life. It is through the eyes of this boy, a boy destined to take up his father's and his grandfather's mantle of leadership, that we are educated in the manner of being a true "human," a Bunun. Umas is constantly being instructed about the importance of following the teachings of the ancestors who worked out the rules for living in the mountain forests over many centuries of bitter struggle. As the boy's mother reasons when she suspects him of disrespecting the powers of the village shaman, "...humans are far from the strongest animals in the mountains. They have to rely upon the life experience of the ancestors in order to survive in a world full of things they find unfathomable" (Part I, Chapter 6, p. 122). The wisdom of the ancestors can never be questioned. It is Umas' duty to learn to live according to that wisdom. Without it, survival is impossible.

The teachings of the ancestors are not arbitrary. They are based on empirical experience over the millennia. These teachings are also based on unchanging values. People must learn respect for all things in nature, for all life, animate and inanimate, is sacred and mutually supportive. Humans may think that they stand above or apart from animals and trees and the mountains they reside upon, but they are, in fact, only one small part of the all-embracing fabric of existence. Failing to understand this reality can have profound consequences. For example, hunters must adopt an attitude of respect towards the game that they kill. For if the animals feel that they and their sacrifice has not been respected, "[they]will never again reward the people's hunting efforts. [People] will never again capture any game" (Part II, Chapter Two, p. 245). Life in the mountains is precarious. People must maintain an attitude of reverence for the lifeforms upon which they rely for their own lives, otherwise, no matter how skilled or clever they may be, nature will turn its immense powers against them, and there will be no way for them to resist. This is perhaps the most fundamental truth passed down by the ancestors.

Yet, however hazardous and uncertain life in the mountain forests may be, the author constantly reminds us of the incomparable beauty of this environment. Though often a challenge to render faithfully into English, Vava's depictions of the everchanging interactions of wind and sky, clouds and mountainside are exquisite and moving. As the seasons pass, we feel the changes that move through the mountains and valleys, the trees and flowers, and the animals that make their homes in their midst. We also see the manner in which the village responds to the cycle of the seasons, whether it be the hard drudgery required in the cultivation or millet, or the courage, patience, and stamina needed in the hunt. In all cases, the natural environment is the stage where the action unfolds. People are ever conscious of the unpredictability of that environment and the dangers that lie within it, but their lives are also infused with the sheer, dynamic beauty that surrounds them.

The central narrative of this novel concerns the life of a Bunun boy as he progresses from childhood to manhood and fatherhood. Here we see the workings of the larger cycle of human life unfold. As Umas matures and graduates through the stages of life, which are often marked by ritual initiation, we become aware of the ways in which members of the village community relate to each other, and the bonds that run through extended families, making them the core unit of social organization. Umas observes the many ways in which community solidarity is established and maintained. Resources and labor are shared. Women work together to weave clothing, cook food, ferment millet wine, and raise children.

Men share a special sense of fraternity as they coordinate their hunting parties upon which the entire village depends. In the final chapter of the novel, Umas is a young husband and new father preparing to accept his responsibilities as an adult in the community. At the same time, his highly respected grandfather, having lived to see the birth of his great-grandson, seems to be on the verge of passing on to the eternal home of the ancestors. Nature's cycle is moving, and the creatures of the mountain forest join the villagers to dance and sing the praises of the host gods who protect them and ensure the orderly progression of that cycle.

The Soul of Jade Mountain is a paean to a vanishing way of life, but it is not accusatory or polemical. Despite his personal involvement in the Indigenous rights movement, Husluman Vava has no interest in shaping his story into a victimization narrative. Rather, he relies on personal experience and oral history passed down in the villages to create a vision of traditional Bunun life that is realistic yet infused with hope and pride —hope for the future and pride in the past. In the process, he educates us and offers an alternative paradigm for the relationship between humans and the natural world. In the lives of Bunun villagers who live in the shadow of Jade Mountain, we see a vision of an ecosphere where the things of nature and the things of humans exist on an equal footing. The Bunun are not the masters of the mountain. In their struggle to survive they must develop and intimate awareness of the natural environment and demonstrate deep respect for its power. But nature also provides; and through ingenuity, cooperation, and hard work, the Bunun thrive on the diverse resources that nature makes available to them. Thus, from the perspective of a modern world threatened by ecological collapse, the traditions of Husluman Vava's ancestors appear not only enlightened but worthy of emulation. For that reason alone, the publication of this English translation of *The Soul of Jade Mountain* is timely and a valuable contribution to contemporary discourse on the environment. The fact that this novel is also an outstanding example of the seldom-heard but much-needed literary voice of Indigenous peoples in Taiwan makes its presentation here all the more essential.

Among contemporary Indigenous writers in Taiwan, Husluman Vava is revered as a fearless pioneer who devoted himself tirelessly to the cause of Indigenous cultural revival. For a translator with an abiding interest in Taiwanese literature, especially Indigenous literature, the work of rendering Vava's text into English was both rewarding and revelatory, but also frustrating in some respects. The text of *The Soul of Jade Mountain* is not simply a record of a people whose very identity is now being crushed under the wheels of the modern global economy, it is a literary experiment in which the semantic conventions of standard Mandarin Chinese are challenged and subverted. Rather than seek to emulate the masters of Chinese prose, Vava moulds Chinese phasing to the forms of his native Bunun language. His intention is to project his people's linguistic logic, as well as their unique creativity, through the unavoidably distorting lens of the colonizer's tongue. The result is a text that is not easily located within the spectrum of Chinese language literature, yet it is a text replete with literary artistry. For example, the depictions of the foreboding mountainscapes which serve as a stage for the unfolding tale of the Bunun are composed with imagery that a Chinese speaking writer would eschew as inappropriate or even awkward. The opening paragraph of Part I, Chapter Five, demonstrates this well:

> The weather had turned extremely hot and humid. The mountain wind was like an old man breathing his final breath after a long illness. It didn't have the strength even to blow away the frivolous mountain mists, leaving them to linger at mid-slope. Then, as if something had suddenly come into its head, the wind started careening around, bringing a dramatic, foreboding look to the sky until finally it allowed the rain that the people had longed for to fall. (p. 95)

While this personification of the landscape seems not especially remarkable to the English language reader, it strikes the Chinese language reader as unconventional to say the least. Yet, Vava's aim is not so much to discomfit the Chinese language reader as to assert the cultural and aesthetic differences between his people and the Han mainstream.

Unfortunately, the translator has few tools with which to convey this writerly strategy directly, and this is where frustrations arise. At the same time, the beauty of Vava's expression does not lie in his contested relationship with the Chinese language, but rather in skill with which he is able to evoke the vitality of the Bunun people and their organic vision of the world of mountain forests in which they make their home.

The situation of Indigenous people in Asia is very poorly understood in the Western world. The idea that there are Indigenous people in Asia at all is surprising to many. However, in Taiwan the question of Indigeneity, and the marginalization of Indigenous peoples and their culture has figured prominently in the ongoing discourse over national identity that began in earnest even before the implementation of democracy began in 1987. As Indigenous peoples seek to add their voices to that discourse, cultural expression, including literature, has played an important role. The writings of authors like Husluman Vava have served to redefine what it means to be Indigenous and forced the Han population to begin thinking of Taiwan as a multi-ethnic nation in which the early Austronesian inhabitants occupy a central position.

The Soul of Jade Mountain is a record of a people who have seemingly been swept aside by the tide of modern technology and economic development. Yet, it demonstrates the ways in which those people, the Bunun of central Taiwan, learned to live in harmony with each other, and with the forces of nature by holding true to a set of values passed down by their ancestors. As we, as a global community, confront the bleak realities of human conflict and environmental collapse, this unpretentious story of a boy growing to maturity in a village that draws a precarious livelihood from the high mountains inspires us to rethink our assumptions about the human condition. It is thus timely that we are able to offer this translation of *The Soul of Jade Mountain*. Voices from Taiwan are often drowned out by the aggressive roar of her much larger neighbor to the west. This novel is especially important because it speaks of and for Indigenous peoples in Taiwan who, until recently, have received little notice even in their own country. It is our hope that rendering these voices into English will help them to join with other Indigenous voices around the globe in articulating their unique vision of life in harmony with nature, a vision now so urgently sought by all humankind.

THE SOUL OF
JADE MOUNTAIN

Memories of a Change of Key

It was so that the children could feel closer to their own people, including the present situation in the villages, our language and everyday life. Every year during summer vacation we used to go to visit a different Bunun village for a day, sometimes two. We would pick a time when there were no official holidays and there would not be too many people and cars around. Sometimes we would stay in a guesthouse run by villagers, other times it would be the parsonage of the local pastor. In the more remote areas, we would just pitch a tent and camp. Those were times when we were closest as a family. They were the happiest of times. One year we decided on Lidao Village in Taidong County. Aside for giving us the chance to enjoy the scenery of the Southern Cross-Island highway, the main reason for our choice was that all the villages to the south of the highway in Taoyuan Prefecture were places where Bunun people lived. For our purposes it was a real treasure trove. The scenery in the majestic mountains surrounding Lidao Village is nothing short of entrancing. We were filled with envy for our ancestors who once lived there. On our second day there, the sun shone brightly. As we drove, we had a perfect view of the forest on a beautiful day. But as we followed the twisting highway higher and higher into the mountains the air grew noticeably cooler. After we passed the highest point—the Yakou Tunnel—and started to descend we couldn't get used to the rapid decrease in elevation and the quickly changing highway conditions. Everyone complained about their ears constantly popping. So, I decided to stop the car beside a mountain lake for a rest. There was a Highways Department building there and I guessed that there would be rest stop facilities and we could all stretch our stiff, aching joints.

In front of the two-story building was a wide parking lot where bus passengers traveling in one direction from Kaohsiung, and in the other from Taidong, could change buses and have a rest. That day the bus from Kaohsiung had arrived a little bit early but the bus from Taidong was probably still on the way, so travellers in twos and threes were sitting or walking around in the parking lot. I spotted an older man with greying hair squatting on the edge of the lot with his arms across his chest and his hands in his armpits. He was gazing off to the endless line of mountains extending into the distance. His very Bunun facial features gave me a sense of familiarity, and I was moved by how lonely he looked. "Tama, are you crossing the mountains to Taidong?" Our people always use the respectful term, "Tama" (father's generation), to address older people. That is our custom.

"Yeah, our elder daughter who married a guy in Taidong is sick and she wants to see me. Where are you from?" When the old man heard the only language that he understood he sized me up happily. In no time we were chatting like long lost friends. I told him which social group I belonged to and my parent's clan, making a point to tell him the Bunun name I was given when I was born in the village. A lot of older people don't really understand the more recent use of Chinese names. For his part, the old man openly talked about his children's recent affairs, how many daughter-in-law's he had, and how cute and special his grandchildren were. He also gave me an animated account of what had happened in their village lately. But most of all, like all older Bunun men, it was stirring tales of the hunt that he talked about most. While recalling hunting adventures from the past his dejected expression was transformed as if blow on the wind to the deepest of the deep mountain valleys.

"When I was young, I often came here to hunt with the elders." The old man suddenly gave me a wide-eyed look.

"Here, you mean this parking lot?" The old man turned and painstakingly sketched out a rough map of the hunting ground. "Once I shot a mountain deer in this hunting ground. It was probably right about here! There used to be a huge old stone over there. The deer was clever enough to circle the rock to throw off my line of sight, but before he could get away I ran forward and took aim. My first shot hit him behind the foreleg in that area about three fingers wide where his heart is. That deer was one of the biggest that our village had ever seen." The gleam of deserved pride still hung on his face as he lifted his right hand and pointed to the icy cold building.

"What? Right in the building?" Surprised, I looked where he was pointing.

"That's right! But believe it or not, people who don't understand the forest and don't understand hunting built that big building right in the middle of a path that the mountain deer used. So many people used to catch so many animals here. Those were the best of times. Ah! There are more and more things that don't belong here in the forest. Sometimes when I pass by I even wonder if those years and months ever really existed. Seeing the changes, it seems like the things that I did here in my youth, and all my memories, are nothing but a series of dreams dreamed in the darkest of dark nights; now they've paled and lost their color." The old man was tired. He returned to squat on the edge of the parking lot to gaze forlornly at the distant line of mountains. As I stood behind him and looked at his shrunken, squatting figure, I too was overcome by feelings of dejection. I took his hand and shook it reverently, wishing him a safe journey and good health. He patted my children on the head and told them to be good, respectful children.

After we returned home, I spent the whole night tossing and turning as I wrestled with the thought of how unbearable it must be to live a life that makes you doubt your own memories. What pernicious force could make people wonder if the lives of their forbearers were really as glorious as they once believed? What kind of nation could force a people to alter the very stuff of their memories? It was a long time afterwards that I saw something written in a book that shook me from that night's desolation and brought me to a sudden realization. It also gave me the motivation to finish this novel:

"If you have come with the intention of helping me or teaching me, please go back. But if you will take my experience as a part of your own life, then perhaps we can work together."

June 25, 2006
in the mountain forest of the Bunun people

PART I

CHAPTER ONE

AT THE BEGINNING

At the beginning of Heaven and Earth, the Earth was empty and dejected. It needed a special kind of lifeform to come and fill it up. So, the ancestors of the Bunun[1] people with their naturally satisfied, humble spirit came forth to dwell there. After that the Earth was like a *cina,*[2] full of love and acceptance. It carefully protected these good, simple people day and night.

Any time the sun or the moon shone, people saw a toiling figure hurrying back and forth under the sun or moonlight. It was as if she felt that there was some very important matter that still awaited completion.

During the day she stood on the mountain peak at the junction of Heaven and Earth discussing things with Dihanin.[3] As for what they were talking about, nobody knew. And since these were affairs of the gods, none of the Bunun people dared to ask them. Nonetheless, from their serious expressions it was clear that they must be discussing matters of the gravest import. When the opinions of the two were completely harmonious, a happy atmosphere prevailed, and this brought a beautiful new glow to everything all around. The sound of the laughter from all creation filled the world as if the Earth was singing one ecstatic song after another. However, when they could not agree on something, the irascible spirits of Heaven would immediately bellow from the black clouds and bring forth thunder and lightning. Not the least bit intimidated, the stubborn Earth responded with a dark scowl of displeasure. In an instant, Heaven and Earth turned dark and foreboding, and all the creatures cried in distress. The people were also frightened and hid away in the darkest corners that they could find, like a herd of timid *sakut*.[4] They had no idea what to do so they quietly begged the two most intelligent elders to figure out what the most appropriate way of settling the dispute might be.

When night followed, taking the place of day, the exhausted people all collapsed on a great sleeping platform made of *batakan*.[5] The children smiled as they slumbered. In their dreams they were continuing their games with their daytime playmates. *Cina* didn't dare rest or slack off. She spelled off the people to keep watch over the crops in the fields. To disperse the heat of the day she lightly fanned the fields until the trees on her body swayed with the mountain winds making whispering "sha, sha, sha" sounds. From time to time, with her *mamaghan*[6] hands, she stroked the seeds in the soil with her hand, just as you might stroke the hair of a little girl; lightly, softly, ever so carefully. Under her doting care the crops in the fields quickly sprouted luxuriant green leaves and formed beautiful fat fruit. This way the people could peacefully make it through the cold months of winter.

Cina presented quite distinct appearances to people living on different mountains. Some people lived near a towering waterfall. When the wind and rain came to visit, the changing shape and sound of the waterfall made them very afraid. People living on another mountain just laughed at them and said, "You're living between Cina's thighs, so you're always going to see Cina peeing." Other people lived in a mountain hollow where the wind liked to roam. The clothing and food that they laid out in their courtyards to dry was often stolen by the greedy mountain winds. This made them extremely angry. Some people believed that the hollow was Cina's mouth, and when she talked to the Heavenly spirits or any kind of *Hanido*[7] the powerful sound of her voice created the wind. As for villages near mountain walls which were prone to landslides, everyone believed that the walls were the soles of Cina's feet. So it was only natural that when she was scurrying around, hard at work, there would be great earthquakes and dust filling the sky.

One extremely self-confident Bunun man said that they were the most fortunate of people because, aside from the fact that they lived on Dunqul-Savi[8] that was relatively close to the sky, there was nothing that could stop their eyes from going where ever they wanted to go. They could easily see all the people who lived hidden in the deepest mountain forests. For example, they could see the mountain deer and mountain goats who live as far from humans as possible, as well as the muntjacs who frolic at the foot of the mountains, the squirrels who use their paws to wash their faces, and the pairs of eagles who help each other preen. For the Bunun, the mountain ranges arrayed beneath their eyes were like verdant waves on the sea that constantly surged forward bringing endless surprises. They went so far as to raise their eyebrows and proudly declaim, "The place where we live has two worlds. One is the world that is the same as everyone else's. The other is a beautiful world that belongs to us and nobody else can see it."

But deep in their hearts there were many people who did not believe this. That's because everyone lives on Cina's body. They all share in the warmth of Vali's[9] feelings and the gentleness of Buwan.[10] The great Heavenly spirit could never let only one village enjoy all the good fortune. But there was one thing that everyone did believe. The Bunun were an extremely fortunate people because they all lived in a place that had been blessed by the multitude of divinities.

From its peaks to its base, the majestic mountain range traced out a beguiling silhouette. A young man sat on the grassy slope. The jet-black pupils of his bright eyes were as deep as the deepest gorge, while the ridge of his nose running between those eyes was like the tall, proud cols in the distance. The prominent line of his mouth traced around his glossy red lips, and when those lips parted they revealed sturdy, even rows of teeth, like the white rocks washed clean by a rushing stream. All fierce, virile animals possess such teeth. His sleek dark skin had the hue of fertile soil.

The young man leaned back with his arms supporting him and his legs casually crossed. He looked perfectly contented as he surveyed his surroundings with keen smiling eyes. The *tusisidi*[11] bushes grew lushly around him, their light purple blossoms giving off the scent of sheep's urine. Probably his people had given them that name because of their smell! That day, the reek of sheep's urine wafted through the air making the young man furrow his eyebrows and wrinkle up his nose trying to resist the vexing aroma.

Over his right shoulder, the slopes were overwhelmed by the dense trichodesma plants and shell ginger. Bunun people collect shell ginger then they peal the stems, dry them, and carefully sort them so that they can weave all kinds of mats, baskets and other useful things that catch their fancy. Stalks of *pusaksak*[12] grew opportunely in the spaces between the trichodesma plants, extending their gorgeous blossoms, contributing several different seductive colors to the scene. Moving further afield the acacias, Lagerstroemias, Zelkovas, Formosa gums and a profusion of other trees created an everchanging, uniquely variegated forest vista. Crowned by their small star-like white blossoms, the mountain gardenias wove their way through the scene with complete ease and abandon. And as if refusing to be left out, a dense thicket of knotweed spewed fringes of their light green flowers that looked like green mist rising from the woods.

A clear, cool alpine breeze floated like a butterfly now here, now there, as all Nature's creation rose to dance, swirling right, then left with fluid, elegant steps. The young man smoothed his windblown hair as he abandoned himself to the pleasures of the luxuriant mountain scenery.

The layered peaks of the mountain range over his left shoulder were like mounds of emerald, rising steeply to pierce the deep blue sky. Some of the cols seemed to have struck through the mountains' breast to show their gleaming rock faces. Countless stones, big and small hung suspended from their walls. An eagle soared on the wind following the contours of the cliffs, its movements light and unhurried as if unburdening his lonely soul to the cliffs. Beneath the cliffs lay piles of huge fallen boulders like cast off goods; some stood stock straight, others leaned together, still others lay broken into several pieces on the ground, their tops covered with thick moss that obscured their expressions. Towering dark trees reached out from the cliffs, the sun penetrating their densely clustered leaves making them look like translucent green forest spirits dancing nimbly on the wind.

"Oh mountain forest! Mountain forest, you are Nature's most magnificent spirit." The youth proclaimed respectfully from the depths of his soul.

The mountain forest has powers that far exceed what ordinary people imagine. At any moment it can transform its appearance any way it pleases. When the mountain winds are lazy, the nearer ranges wear the deepest green as they display their stunning silhouettes in the sky. At such times, the silence is broken only by the gurgling of running waters and the happy songs of the birds. The forests compose Nature's music and the mountain wind sweeps it across the rivers. The mountain wind blows constantly, like a besotted poet who chants his heart's joy, anger, and sadness over and over. When the dusk approaches, a few playful mountain peaks wear the sun-filled evening mists on their heads like hunters from the village who tie red ribbons around their heads as emblems of their great courage. When the mountain wind is agitated, huge balls of greyish-white cloud roll in to cover the entire alpine domain. At such times, Heaven and Earth grow close and intimate. The sense of treachery in the air disturbs the people and sets them running off in all directions. When the fat, engorged rain clouds dance through the mountain vales, guided hurriedly on by the powerful winds, they are bound to collide with the sharp rocks piled high on the summits, splitting open their bellies and releasing their load of rain.

The mountain peaks are closest to the sky, so it is they who know best the sky's temperament. The cleverest of our people often observed the changing face of the mountains in order to ascertain changes in the weather. Their observations were never wrong, so now, before they venture outside, all people gaze reverently towards the sacred summits that rise steeply into the sky.

The youth concentrated on the appearance of the mountains as he sought the mysterious relationship between the mountains and the weather. He could see a long deep gorge running between a line of cols and into the distance. It was as if the mountains had been cut apart from base to peak by a great sharp knife. An ancient river rushed on as it passed through the winding course of the gorge. In many places the river water crashed angrily over the enormous rocks that stood in its way in the narrow riverbed, white froth exploding into the air with furious deep booming sounds. At its most placid, the river was like a bashful girl trailing ribbons of silk as it silently and proudly made its progress towards the farthest land. The profound cavern formed by the mountain walls made peoples' legs feel weak. On some of the cliff faces grew not a single blade of grass. They looked like a giant's powerful bare breast.

The escarpment a little distance to his right was split open from the side by a rather small gorge from which sprang a limpid rivulet like a strand of silk. Because of its gentle demeanor it often attracted herds of mountain deer, mountain sheep and muntjacs who liked to drink from it and roam at their ease. Eventually the rivulet glided into the great valley like a beautiful, gleaming lizard. There was a secluded, mysterious fairy glade just where the rivulet entered the valley. Where the high valley walls sank away into murky shadows, a radiant expanse of emerald sunlight shone above the glade. Everywhere huge virile ferns of all description grew lushly under trees of every shape and kind with their perfectly formed leaves. Wild fruits of all hues and shades dotted their branches looking just as if the trees had been hung with multicolored garlands. It dazzled the eyes, besotting all that looked upon it. But no people lived in this magnificent place because everyone believed that it was the most pure and unsullied place in all of Nature. It was also the sacred place where all the Masial-Hanido,[13] dwelt.

The youth's wisdom did not yet allow him to understand the relationship between the mountain slopes and the weather, so he decided he
may as well close his eyes to give them a rest. Then an inspiration like
a lightning bolt made him cast his eyes upon the great winding valley
again. He raised his right hand solemnly and moved it left and right in
a slithering motion following the shape of the valley.

"Is the valley really the scar left behind by a giant snake after its defeat
in battle?" He recalled the *palihansiap*[14] of the battle between the great
crab and the giant snake that his *hudas*[15] had told him a few days before.

Whenever the dark night took control of the mountain forests, Bunun
people liked to gather around the *banin*[16] to warm themselves and chat.
It was a custom that had been passed down for thousands of years. That
kind of custom was like an old root that had grown so deeply into the
earth that no one dared try to change it now. The firelight spilled over
the ground like a crowd of playful red spirits, sparkling and leaping in all
directions. Not only did it liven up the whole house, it allowed everyone
to see where the others were.

With his head of white hair and face scarred by the passage of the
years, Talum held a long, odd-looking *kakaunan*[17] in his teeth. From
time to time he used his hand to tamp down the tobacco embers then
sucked deeply on the pipe. He exhaled puffs of white smoke with a look
of contented satisfaction. The smoke hovered in the air in front of him
revealing, now and then, a blurred image of his old face. Taking the
long pipe from his mouth, Talum drew in his cheeks and hawked a glob
of thick yellow phlegm into the fire. When it landed on the glowing
red embers the phlegm immediately shrivelled into a scorched black
stain. The children were all amazed by this. They gazed wide-eyed, as
if transfixed by how the phlegm was consumed by the flames. Some of
the children even arched their bare feet and lightly used their toes to
push pieces of wood that lay on the ground into the fire. This quickly
made the flames rise even higher and more vigorously. Other children
watched intently at the way the old man gathered phlegm in his mouth,

and when saliva leaking from the corners of his mouth began to glisten, they craned their necks as far as they could, like chicks waiting excitedly as the mother bird brings a worm back to the nest. They were especially quiet because they hoped for a clear view of the thrilling scene of flames consuming the yellow phlegm.

"Hudas, tell us a story about the ancestors, okay?" When one clever child noticed Hudas place his pipe in the *kulin*[18] on his chest he knew that the battle of the phlegm and the fire was over, and he wanted to get something even more entertaining going.

Talum knew that the night had not yet reached its darkest point and he wasn't ready to retire, like some forgotten black stone, to his chilly bamboo bed just yet.

"Luhi,[19] bring your eyes and ears over this way and give your mouths a rest. I'm going to tell you a story passed down by the ancestors. When you are old and white-haired like me you, in turn, will tell this story to your children."

"Okay, okay." "For sure, for sure." Because they were all anxious to be taken into the enchanting world of legends, the children, big and small all promised, nodding their heads gravely as they did so.

Talum cast his benevolent look over the faces of all the children and slowly began to recount a story of things that had taken place in ancient times:

> At the very beginning, the world was an enormous plain the stretched without end. There were only a few hemispherical mountains that stood on the plains like eggs randomly laid by a huge beast. We Bunun people lived on the plains. The rich fertile soil made the crops grow fat and luxuriant. An abundance of water allowed the animals in the wilds to grow up quickly, and the Bunun people lived a life of ease and satisfaction.
>
> But a life of good fortune and happiness always leads people to forget the things that are truly important. It also makes people lose

their humility and sense of gratitude. The sacred rites of worship in honor of the gods had gradually fallen into abeyance, and in the once resplendent and sacred village assembly hall, weeds had begun to grow, making it look thoroughly desolate. People in the village started to behave arrogantly, and imagined that they possessed the power to control their own lives and futures. This kind of behavior made the heavenly spirits very angry, and they decided to punish the egotistical, self-important Bunun people.

On one accursed day, the anger of the spirits transformed into the biggest, most destructive storm in memory. The rain poured down so hard it was as if the spirits were trampling the earth with a deafening roar, 'Hua! Hua! Hua!' The drops of rain were like arrows angrily shooting downwards from the cracks in the black clouds into the forest. It was accompanied by sharp, powerful peels of thunder that drowned out all the sounds of daytime.

The deluge then produced flooding that rose like the black Makuan-Hanido,[20] destroying all the crops that stood in the fields. The wild gales went about the forest like madmen, ripping up enormous trees by their roots. The slate houses in the village all shook so violently in the gusts that they almost collapsed. It was terrifying.

But to make things even worse, a huge *i-vut*[21] blocked the flood waters as they tried to retreat. With nowhere to go, the waters filled the heavens with their howls and struck out in all directions. In the end, they surged in the direction of the Bunun village with the strength of a thousand black bears."

Hudas's tone of voice was extremely urgent, like the village facing the flood waters. It set all the timid children on edge.

"That snake....was it this big?" Some of the youngest children who were just learning to speak innocently spread their short, chubby arms as wide as they could.

"It was big! Enormous. Lying there on the ground, the snake looked like a mountain range. The flood waters with all their strength could neither push through it, nor cross over it. They had no choice but to stop in their tracks, seething with anger." Talum reached and pointed as high as he could. The children followed his finger upwards.

> The suddenness of the arrival of flood water had shocked the villagers out of their wits. They could only take the simplest of life necessities and, with the men leading the women, and the big leading the small, flee panic-stricken to the nearby mountains— Asan-banud.[22] Their lovely lands and the animals they had raised through so much hard work had all been completely washed away by the raging floodwater. It was as if those things had never existed.
>
> Fortunately, the people who managed to flee the disaster were able to huddle together in the cold mountains of Takbanuaz. Some lay under the trees, others crowded into dark caves. They were all frightened and exhausted.
>
> "If we continue like this, we'll all die in this strange land." Hugging her small infant to her breast, a terrified woman cried in distress.
>
> "It's true. The *Madadaingath*[23] once told us that all hardship begins when your feet stray from home. If we don't go back to our familiar land right away, we will surely die of starvation." Even the elders, with all their experience of hardship had begun to be afraid.
>
> "When will the flood waters leave our village?" "Who can think of a solution? Who can save us?" One after the other, the people complained. In face of this great disaster, aside from being terrified to their core, they had not the slightest idea of how to respond.
>
> "My people! The spirits of flood waters will hear the sound of your squabbling and follow you here to attack you. They will do everything they can to charge up the mountain peaks and wrest away what little good luck we have left," an elder appealed to the people as they continued to quarrel. "Be quiet and listen to me. The flood waters remain in our village and show no sign of leaving. That's because the giant snake has blocked the water's path, keeping it from returning to where it belongs."

"The ancestors once taught us that you can block any road, but never block the water's course. If only the giant snake will unblock the flood water's road home, then our land will naturally be returned to us. But how can we make the snake leave?"

"Makavas![24] For the sake of the people's safety and to protect our homeland, we must go to war with the giant snake. The snake must die!" A warrior who had always enjoyed the respect of the people declared, clutching his bow and arrows.

"Right! We are a peace-loving people. We have always hoped that we could abide harmoniously with all other living things on this earth, but now that our very way of life is being threatened, we will not retreat. We will strike back fearlessly so that even the gods will not be able to stop us. It is because our name is Bunun!" The warriors all pledged an oath to fight to the death for their survival.

"That giant snake has the most evil, strongest powers in the world. Can we defeat it?"

"From their many years of experience in the mountains, the warriors are already heroic hunters. They have the ability to 'hit whatever they aim at.' Besides, we already have experience in going to war with other people. All we need to do is cast our fear into the darkest of dark places and gather the sublime strength of every man together. That way we can surely make the giant snake feel the great power of our exceptional nation. It will feel fear as never before and hide away someplace where our eyes cannot see. Look! Our arrows are so sharp, they can pierce the *haputon*[25] of the most malicious spirits, so there is no doubt that we can easily send that giant snake off to the valley of death." The warrior took an arrow from his quiver. Its head shone with an icy gleam.

At dawn on the second day, after having made ceremonial prayers to the spirits for protection, and having received the blessings of old, young, women and children, thirty warriors set off, fervently determined to preserve life and honor. Without a moment's hesitation they leapt into the flood water and swam with all their might towards the place where the giant snake lay. They were prepared to drive the snake away and reclaim all that was theirs before.

Seeing the furious warriors descending on it, the giant snake didn't think that it had anything to fear from such short, small foes. So, it just continued to lie there enjoying all the carefree pleasures that the cool flood waters had to offer.

Once the warriors had swum to a place within range of their bows, the *lavian*[26] ordered them to form a single rank, take out their arrows, aim at the giant snake and begin shooting. "Swoosh, swoosh, swoosh!" One sharp arrow after another took flight for the vast body of the giant snake like vicious boars charging through the forest. Then something strange happened. When the arrows struck the sleek, slippery skin of the snake it was as if they had struck a hard stone wall. Some arrows ricocheted off the snake and flew into the distance. Others broke with a snap and fell on the water's surface then floated away on the waves, dispersing in all directions. The arrows had completely lost their deadly power. The leader immediately ordered everyone to concentrate on shooting at the snake's eyes. The eyes are the weakest part of the body, but the cunning snake just calmly closed its hard, thick eyelids and the arrows made no impression at all. By that point, the attacks of the warriors were starting to annoy the snake. It angrily opened its ferocious mouth to swallow up the enemy attacking it. The snake's counterattack frightened the warriors stiff, and the leader knew the situation was dire, so he called out to his comrades saying, "This must be a malicious spirit that has transformed its appearance. We are as weak and puny as ants before it. There is no way we can gain a victory here, so we must quickly retreat back to the mountains of Takbanuaz!"

The warriors fled as fast as they could through the churning waves of the flood waters back to the mountain top. Those who lacked strength or who had bad luck were eaten alive by the giant snake. Others drowned after being bitten and seriously wounded. In that first battle between men and the snake, it was the people who suffered heavy losses, ending up in a sorry state.

After their defeat in battle, a sense of insecurity and fear again enveloped the entire community in the Takbanuaz Mountains and there was nothing anyone could do about it. Just as everyone was sobbing and sighing in anticipation of the arrival of the God of Death, they suddenly heard a voice like muffled thunder saying to them, "Friends, please allow me to try to ease your suffering."

The people all swung the heads on their necks back and forth looking for the source of the voice. They eventually saw *Kakalan*,[27] the giant crab, standing beside a stony cliff waving his claws in the air. When they saw the great crab, their hopeful expressions slipped away and their faces froze into looks of icy suspicion. That was because in the minds of the people, the great crab was an extremely benevolent creature. In more normal times, playful children liked to swing back and forth on its huge protruding eyes. The crab not only did not get angry, it would use its giant pincers to pick up children who fell off the swing. The pure, simple character of the crab and the innocence of the children both seemed to flow from the same spirit.

"Doing battle with that malevolent giant snake is like dealing with the God of Death. Do you know what I mean?" A well-intentioned elder tried to explain the seriousness of the situation to the crab.

"I know. I know this in my heart...however, in normal times you all took good care of me and the time to repay you has come." The crab's voice was still very deep. When the people heard this, they responded with joy. They were extremely moved that this good friend had come to stand up for them in their time of need.

"Is there any way that we can help you?" Thinking about this enormous task, some of the elders were still had their doubts.

"My pincers are hard and sharp. The strength of my body can overwhelm ten great bears, but my back is extremely fragile. I'm afraid that if the snake attacks me with its two huge fangs, I might be vulnerable. This is what most worries me." The big crab knew its own weak points, but its concerns only made the people feel helpless and they could offer no advice.

There was a woman who was cooking some food. Since it was dirty and crowded where they had taken refuge, the woman accidentally knocked over the *kama*[28] next to her. As it fell to the ground, the clay pot first started spinning in place, then gradually fell downwards. As it fell, the spinning pot smashed into several other things, breaking them to bits, but when it stopped spinning, the pot itself sat quietly in the corner where it fell still miraculously in one piece. After watching the apparently ordinary pot whirling around like that, and seeing that it appeared to have magical powers, the people were absolutely astonished. One of the wise elders suddenly had an inspiration and excitedly told everyone, "It's a miracle! The power of the ancestors has manifested itself before our eyes. Since all things have life, all we need to do is awaken their inner spirits and the great power that has languished in them unused for millennia will be released." The elder walked over to the big crab and continued explaining, "If we work through the night, we can fire a huge, sturdy clay pot. We can then mount it on your soft back, and that way you will be able to ward off the giant snake's poisonous fangs."

Once things had been decided, the people started to work the clear water and mud to fashion a pot as huge as the crab's body. After a few days they finally fired a pot that fit over the crab's body. The great pot had been burnished red by the intense flames and as the elder gazed at it he said, "We'll wait until the pot is a little cooler then we'll put it straight on the crab's back, that way our brave friend will be ready for battle with the giant snake."

Being attacked by the warriors had put the giant snake in a very foul mood. It continually swung its great body back and forth in the water stirring up row upon row of huge waves that rolled toward the Takbanuaz mountains like malevolent spirits. Under siege by those waves, the mountains began to collapse, inch by inch, into the water. The situation was growing ever more urgent, but the freshly made pot was still giving off sheets of transparent heat waves.

The big crab said to the people, "There isn't much time. Put the pot on my back now so that I can go off into the water to do battle right away." The people were powerless to refuse the crab's demand, so a few dozen of them took the pot and raised it onto the great crab's back. The crab's back gave off a "Phssss!" hissing sound and the scalding heat of the pot made the crab froth at the mouth. But as soon as the boiling hot pottery armor was placed on his back, the crab slid into the water and swam off in the direction of the giant snake. The people all watched the white steam rise from the crab and prayed for the assistance of the ancestors in releasing them from this predicament.

The snake was startled by the sound of splashing water. When it saw the giant crab descending quickly towards it, the snake opened its cavernous mouth without giving it a second thought and made ready to strike its enemy dead. The clever crab quickly submerged itself and began attacking the belly of the snake with its sharp pincers. Refusing to be outdone, the snake bit ferociously at the crab's back from the surface of the water. But because of the pot, the snake's attacks didn't cause any serious injury, and only left rows of even bite marks on the pot's surface. Locked in mortal combat, the two enormous creatures roiled up the waters, sending froth and foam flying in all directions, until the sky was completely obscured and darkness fell on the land. With their colossal strength the struggles of the great crab and the giant snake made the dark earth shake uncontrollably. It seemed as though the world and all its beauty might be coming to an end.

Eventually the great crab managed to cut several holes in giant snake's belly. Unable to endure the pain in its belly, the snake writhed and twisted as it fled in the direction of the ocean. As it slithered away, all the places that it passed through were scarred by the deep imprint of its gigantic body. The flood water, stained red with blood, began to drain away following the path of the snake toward the sea. After a time, dry land, so long absent, began to reappear before peoples' eyes. The earth was gradually restored to its former likeness.

"Children, have you ever seen a snake's belly?" Talum looked over his rapt audience of children.

"Nowadays a snake's belly is marked with scars across it. Those are the scars that the crab made with its pincers. Even today, all snakes move by slithering back and forth. That's because snakes are afraid that it will hurt if they touch their old wounds."

"I know. I've caught a snake. That's how they move." One of the older children swung his hand back and forth imitating the movement of a snake.

"When the giant snake fled, the deep winding grooves that it made became the deep, deep mountain gorges. The clever water makes use of those gorges to find its way to the sea. After that great battle, the crab got the habit of spitting out foam, and the uneven patterns on its back are where the giant snake bit it. You all know that when you burn a crab's shell it turns red. That's because the crab's shell is the glowing red pot that we put on its back." It was getting late and Talum's voice was sounding a little tired.

"I know. I've felt a crab's back. You can easily tell where the giant snake's bite marks are. I've also roasted a crab, and its shell really does turn slowly red in the fire. It's beautiful." One of the children said, feeling pleased with himself.

"Bahan! Bahan!"[29] The other children shouted curses at the boy and made striking motions with their hands. They couldn't believe how anyone could put a good friend into the fire and burn them to death.

Notes

1. The Indigenous Bunun people of Taiwan.
2. Mother.
3. One of the Bunun gods. A heavenly god.
4. Muntjacs.
5. Cassia bamboo.
6. Divine power of the gods.
7. Earth spirits.
8. The highest peak recognized by the Bunun people, Jade Mountain.
9. The sun.
10. The moon.
11. A plant with a fetid smell.
12. Wild peony.
13. The benevolent spirits.
14. Popular village legend.
15. Grandfather.
16. A cooking stove formed by three rocks.
17. A traditional bamboo pipe used for smoking tobacco.
18. Chest pouch, a traditional accessory for Bunun people.
19. Puppies that have not been weaned. A familiar name for children.
20. Evil spirits with malevolent powers.
21. Snake.
22. A large mountain near Takbanuaz (Luanshe) in Qingjing prefecture, Nantou County.
23. The ancestors or forerunners.
24. Go to war!
25. Heart.
26. Military leader.
27. Crab.
28. A cooking pot made of clay.
29. A curse word referring to the buttocks.

Chapter Two

A Place Called Lumah

"Umas....Umas....where have you run off to now?" A woman's voice cut through the air.[1]

"Cina, I'm here." The boy stood up in the grassy field, brushing off the bits of dried grass and leaves that covered his hands.

"What were you doing over there? Don't be like the *hathan*[2] flitting about the mountain forests. Can you come home and give me a hand with something?" Her long hair falling over her shoulders, and her hands covered with white wood ash, the pressure of all the work had pressed her face into a rigid slab of stone.

"Umas, keep your hands busy and be a man people will be proud of, all right? Don't waste the food that your elders have cooked for you."

"I was just admiring the beautiful mountains." Umas pointed to the forest, then swept his hands left and right indicating the mountain valleys.

"What's the matter, Cina?"

"Tama[3] is fixing up the *pagilasan*.[4] Get over there and help him."

"All right. And also, Cina, I'm not a mountain bird, I'm your son." Umas then bounded into the thatched house like a spirited little muntjac, leaving that stony face behind in the wind.

The thatched houses in the village were almost all the same. Toddlers just learning to walk and adults who were drunk sometimes couldn't tell which house belonged to whom. When it came right down to it, the only difference was that some were slightly larger than others. The people all built their houses on the slopes midway up the mountain. They first dug out the rocks on the relatively higher ground and then piled them up on the lower part, thus creating a small manmade platform. The houses looked out on the wide vista of the canyon below, while their rears butted tightly against the earthen wall that had been dug out of the slope.

Having a house that "looked down from above" made Umas very happy. That way he could see any person or animal that was approaching the house, including both friends and relatives visiting from the village, and ill-meaning poisonous snakes or ferocious animals. Thatched houses were generally constructed using local materials. The four outer walls were made from flat pieces of slate which were skillfully piled on top of each other. The roofs were made by spreading out large bunches of sogon grass, while the pillars and beams were fashioned from appropriately sized lengths of local timber.

Umas entered the family's rectangular house. Sturdy, carefully made bamboo walls divided the space into three, with the two side rooms serving as bedrooms. Those bedrooms were used by his parents and by the adult couples because they could protect the other members of the family from harm with their martial skills and the strength of their *Hanido*.[5] The middle room was a level living space which served as a common room used by the whole family. Long narrow hallways extended right and left. At the end of each of these were traditional cooking stoves. The one on the left was used for cooking the family's food, while the one on the right was for cooking food for the livestock. It was taboo to mix the use of the two. The stove on the left burned constantly all year.

If it were extinguished, that would be a transgression against the *samo*[6] laws and would bring down curses from the evil spirits. It could lead to serious damage to life and property. To the rear, closest to the other wall was the storage room for food. A low platform was also constructed over the ground for the temporary use of visitors from afar and friends.

He couldn't remember how old he was, but while he was living with relatives who live in the direction of the sun's return (west), they had broken a taboo. As a result, they were unable to harvest the crops in their fields, nor could they bring so much as a turd back from the hunting grounds. The entire family were in danger of falling apart. So, for the sake of all in the family, young and old, they came seeking help, their heads bowed low.

When Talum saw how pallid the children looked, and how their bellies were so distended they looked like pregnant women, he was deeply moved and immediately offered to let them stay and use the sleeping platform below the storage room. He also invited them to join his family in working the fields and hunting with the hunting party. They came out of a fear of disaster, but their arrival brought a joyous air to the village simply because it meant more people and more activity. In fact, Umas really enjoyed those lively, bustling times.

Banitul held his mouth tightly shut as he concentrated on repairing the bamboo fencing around the grain storage room. Accumulated damage over many years had left the fence crooked and broken. He was hopeful that he could help the fence regain its former abilities so that the millet could live securely in the storage room and not spill out onto the ground. Those who do not respect food not only are cursed by the gods, the food itself feels unappreciated and will leave the house.

As he toiled, Banitul's sleek dark bare back arched like a fully drawn black bow. Several small insects had alighted on his back, but you couldn't see them. Only when he made some sudden move were the insects startled into flight. Then they circled around once before dropping down to blend in with the color of his back once again.

"Tama, can I help you with something?" Umas squatted beside Banitul. His small hand carelessly touched Banitul's bare back and found it covered in sweat.

"What's Cina busy with?" Tama's was a master at weaving bamboo fences. His hands moved with the ease of flowing water, setting every muscle in his body into graceful motion.

"She's in the courtyard using wood ash to make the family's clothing beautiful again."

Cina was a clever, vigorous woman, all her life she had followed her man's family as they moved constantly from one mountain to another. Long ago, Cina had learned the skills necessary to survive in the mountain forest. In order that her family would have clean, comfortable clothing to wear she often carried loads of *tulpus*[7] down from the mountain. This she would burn, carefully gathering the ashes. By adding beech ash to the clean spring water clothing could be washed so that it looked clean and fresh again, like the colors on a butterfly's wings.

Tama and Cina were just like the *haluwa*[8] on the ground, running about all day long, constantly busy with work. By the time the sun had opened its unsteady eyes on the mountain forest, they would already have fixed their sharp eyes on the work for the day and beads of sweat would be rolling down their foreheads. When moon took over command of the forest from the sun, the work of the day would already have disappeared beautifully into the dark night, guided by the industrious hands of mother and father. They shared a mysterious power between them that other people had no way of comprehending. Driven by that mysterious power, all tasks repetitive and sundry would be delegated out and completed in a natural and orderly manner. The elders in the village all said that letting a man and a woman live together was called *mapadangi*.[9] Perhaps when a man and a woman live together, they always combine some secret things together, or just by being together a kind of mutually supportive strength is generated. This is what Umas imagined.

In the past, during those countless deep nights, everyone lay together on the sleeping platform seeking their own dreamscapes. At times, Umas noticed that his mother and father, lying at the end of the platform, often became very agitated and couldn't sleep. Perhaps they were tired from working, or worried about the days to come. Aside from feeling respect and gratitude for them, an unbearable sense of concern for them would enter his mind. However, today when he thought about the word *mapadangi*, a different thought flashed into his mind making his whole body feel hot.

"Banitul, when you finish your work take Umas to the stream to draw some water, okay? The sun is already lying exhausted on the mountains and I want to make dinner for everyone." Malas strode in hurriedly.

"I'll be done in a blink of an eye. Umas, go to the storeroom and get the *muusulan*[10] for carrying water." Banitul instructed Umas as he shook the bamboo fencing to test how sturdy it was.

"Malas, where is our younger son, Subali? Why can't I hear his bawling?" Wiping away his sweat, Banitul showed concern as he spoke to his wife.

"He's sleeping on the bed. Go get the water and I'll take care of Subali." Malas turned to leave the grain storeroom, her steps as quick as always.

Umas stood at the edge of the storeroom. He put eight bamboo flasks into two *palangans*[11] The flasks for drawing water had to be carved out of thick *batakan*,[12] leaving the lowest segment in place. They made simple, practical, tubular water vessels.

Umas followed his Tama's footsteps as they entered the small path into the dark mountain forest. Trees grew densely on the slopes beside them. Some of the trees proudly spread out enormous, towering branches. Fragments of deep blue sky appeared through the gaps between the leaves. From the mountain walls hung countless small rivulets, their clear, clean waters burbling as they fell. Their voices rang through the valleys, sometimes taking turns, other times singing in harmony. The harmonies were like the *pasibutbut*.[13]

"The bamboo flasks are really heavy when they're full. How many can you carry?" Banitul had chosen a stream where the water was clean and the flow generous. He used a thick taro leaf to guide water into the flasks.

"Tama, I can carry as many as you can." Umas was very confident of his own strength.

As Banitul looked across at his young son, an unconscious sense of distain crossed his mind, but this distain lacked any trace of malice. An odd smile came to his lips and he gave his head a gentle shake. Umas was apparently not the least bit interested in his Tama's expression as he climbed down to stand on a large rock beside the stream. With nothing particular in mind, his eyes wandered in all directions. The surrounding forest was dense and dark. The lush growth of emerald trees meant that the ground was cool and damp all year around. Tama knew that such a lovely place drew big flocks of mountain birds to sing in the trees, and animals frolicked and chased each other over the slopes. Clouds of fluttering butterflies were tossed wildly in the air currents that formed over the rushing stream, and crowds of brightly colored forest sprites ran riot in the glades. On the surrounding slopes masses of wildflowers that his people had not even named yet were competing with each other to paint every corner of nature's land with hues uniquely their own.

"Jia! Jia! Jia!" The crisp resonant call of a bird rang from a deep corner of the woods. Umas looked in the direction of the call and discovered that under a moon peach bush was a collared bush robin with its bright red bib. It hopped around a pile of moss-covered rocks with its breast puffed out making urgent cries, seemingly irate about the presence of humans in its territory. It was accompanied by small birds flitting in and out of the clumps of small trees chirping in fright. From the tops of the tallest trees they could also hear the deep drumming sound of large mountain birds beating their wings as they took flight. The once hushed forest had been thrown into turmoil by the bush robin's rage.

"Umas, go and find some big leaves to plug the flasks with. Let's go home." Banitul could see that the bush robin was still hopping around nearby, getting closer with every hop. It looked like a fierce warrior chasing away an enemy.

"Does that little bird think it's master of the forest, treating us as though we were stealing its water?" Umas walked over to a clump of mountain taro and deliberately tore off a huge thick taro leaf with all his might. The violent motion startled the bush robin into flight. It fluttered around before disappearing into the forest darkness.

"Let's go, Umas. Do you want me to help you put your back-sack on?" There were three flasks full of water in his back-sack. Banitul was concerned that this would be too heavy for the boy. Members of the older generation all held at least one thing in common. They all had their suspicions about the life skills of the younger generation. Many young people were discouraged by this attitude, and Umas was one of them.

"No need. I can carry it all the way home without stopping. Tama, you can even give one of your water flasks to me." Umas pointed to Banitul's back-sack as if to protest. The sack bulged with five long water flasks.

The sun now lay exhausted in the hollows of the mountains. Great flocks of unnamed birds flew along the rays of evening light making it impossible for anyone to tell what route they took back to their nests. The soft evening sunlight used the last of its strength to caress each mountain with a golden glow. Heaven and earth looked unreal in this golden aura. This made people feel as if they had fallen into some illusionary world.

"Umas, has your Hudas come back yet? Ask him to come into the living room to eat." Malas carried a pottery bowl heaped high with millet towards the living room. Her face was twisted into a ball because of the heat of the bowl in her hands. Banitul spread out a round *tanpu*[14] in an open space. It was shaped so that the round bottom of the bowl would sit in it securely.

Aside from the millet, Umas saw that his mother had laid out a pot of soup full of *sanlav-hudu*,[15] *samah*,[16] *duduk*[17] and *hulidan*.[18] On the wooden plank to the other side were blanched arrow bamboo shoots covered with thick *hasbitath*[19] to give them a saltier taste. Except on festival days for the worship of the gods, Bunun people seldom go in for elaborate cooking. They still follow a frugal lifestyle developed over thousands of years. But from the point of view of the children in the village, the luckiest of days were any day that some adult stumbled upon a honeybee hive, or sugar cane, or some juicy, sweet fruit.

"If you can hear my call, come to the living room to eat." This was Malas's habitual way of calling people to mealtime.

Banitul's younger brother, Husung, and his wife, Hanagu, and their three children all marched into the living room like a file of ants. The last to arrive was Talum leading Subali who, having just learned to walk, rolled in on unsteady legs. With all the people crowded in, the living room that usually seemed so large now felt small. Malas pulled her smallest son to her side so that the older people could eat in peace. The whole family sat surrounding the pottery bowl waiting for the elders to take the first bites so that all the others could dig in with their *taku*[20] and begin filling their own stomachs.

"Millet is greater than the Heavens." This is a saying that has long been passed down among Bunun people. The force of this proverb was to remind people that they must bring an attitude of respect and gratitude to every meal.

The ancestors have passed down many proverbs and legends. With their sharp memories and evocative storytelling skills, the older generation recite them all for the next generation, instructing them to abide by them religiously. So, although the people have never devoted any form of religious ritual, or erected any totems to them, the moral notions contained in the proverbs and legends have attained a status equal to that of the many gods. They are important guides in the lives of the people.

So it is that the ancestors used proverbs and historical legends as the basis for many taboos to instill in later generations of children an attitude of gratitude and respect toward the food that sustains the lives of the people. Those taboos are in force whenever people sit down to enjoy a meal of millet. For example, when eating millet people are not allowed to speak in loud voices or to bang on the bowl with their wooden spoons. That might make it seem as though people are celebrating the suffering of the millet that was boiled in the flames. That would make the millet feel very upset. It is also prohibited for people to strike their spoons against the spoons of other people. That would have given the appearance of greediness. Besides, the unique sound of wooden spoons could give rise to the curses of evil spirits. All kinds of frivolous, silly behavior also make the adults angry. In some cases, they even use their spoons to hit those who offended against the taboos. That is because such behavior will prevent the millet from being cooked properly. And if people do not respect their food, the gods will not protect the fields, allowing the evil spirits and harmful birds to damage the crops and prevent them from growing to maturity. If that happens then the children will cry out from hunger day and night, and the adults will be so weakened from starvation that the disease demons can easily attack them.

Little Subali gazed around curiously as her mother fed him. Because he kept moving around, lots of grains of millet spilled out and stuck to the corners of his mouth. When Malas saw this, she immediately swept the millet into her son's mouth, and those that wouldn't go in, she swept into her own mouth. She was very afraid of the millet falling to the ground and raising the ire of the elders. When Subali looked around, the hunting dogs who crouched around the periphery of the group took the opportunity to lick the grains of millet from his mouth with their big tongues. Umas immediately pushed away his favorite dog fearing that one of the adults might hurt it. But there was no need for concern. When the adults saw what the dogs were doing they just raised their eyebrows and kept on eating as though nothing had happened. Or perhaps the adults just thought that the hunting dogs had to eat as well. And they did prevent the child from violating a taboo by stopping the millet from falling from his face to the ground.

The village hunting dogs lived a happy life. Umas had seldom seen any of them beaten or scolded for no reason. Everyone thought of them as beloved relatives, so the dogs lived with great dignity. The people all believed the ancient legend about what had once taken place in a Bunun village:

In a strange and distant land, the daughter of the chief of the people became ill with an unusual disease. Her skin grew inflamed and swollen until she moaned in pain day and night. In order to relieve his daughter's suffering the chief issued a decree: whatever man could cure this strange disease would marry is daughter. When a certain male dog heard this news, he claimed that he could cure this kind of illness. Since he was utterly desperate, the chief had no choice but to let the dog have a try. The dog licked all over the affected areas with his big tongue until the daughter's disease was miraculously cured. But since the chief felt that the dog was not a human he began to regret his decree. He fabricated all kinds of bizarre reasons for why the marriage should not proceed, and in the end he did not give his permission for his daughter to marry the dog. But the dog changed into human form and took the princess across the ocean to a beautiful island. There they settled down, began to farm and procreated. Afterwards, their children called themselves the "Bunun" people.

Because of that legend the Bunun people especially respect and protect their dogs. If a dog dies, they bury it with a formal ceremony, as if it were one of their family. Hunting dogs like to lick the cuts and sores on peoples' hands and feet. Perhaps this is because they are aware that they have abilities that humans do not.

Talum painstakingly scooped a spoonful of millet from the bowl, placing his other hand underneath the spoon to guard against any grain falling to the floor. At the same time, he kept an eye on other family members as they ate, and when appropriate, he pushed some vegetables in the direction of the slower eaters to ensure that everyone ate their fill.

Talum was an elder who commanded great respect. Life in the mountain forests is not as easy as you might imagine. You are constantly running into difficulties that can't be solved, and this creates great hardship for people. But Talum always seemed to have a way of overcoming difficulties, no matter how complex or how severe. Add to that his naturally intelligent, kind-hearted nature, and you can see why all the people placed their trust in him.

At the beginning, in the earliest days, the Take-Banuao[21] who occupied the Luanda mountains were growing ever greater in number. The cultivated fields and hunting grounds were no longer able to sustain such a large population, so the community leaders gave permission for the strongest of the warriors to take their families and go in search of new homelands.

It could be said that the young Talum was the leader of the Husluman sub-clan of the Luanda community. When this new opportunity presented itself, several dozen people in the clan close in age to Talum gathered excitedly to discuss all sorts of plans for moving away and establishing a new homeland. After making up their minds, they symbolically broke the stone pillars in front of the slate slab houses to show that they were giving their ancestral homes over to their predecessors who were buried under them.[22] Before setting out, aside from receiving the blessing of the people in the community, Talum and the clan members who were about to depart slaughtered a fine, healthy rooster as a sacrifice to the omnipresent ancestral spirits. They believed that this way they would obtain the strength of the spirits and have a safe journey. Finally, a file of people from the clan carrying the simplest necessities of life on their backs and leading their family members followed Talum out of the village towards a distant land where their fate could not be foretold.

Talum and his group had no fixed route. They allowed the all-powerful heavenly spirits to determine their destination for them. Talum believed that human life was insignificant and weak. Human beings are so lowly that they have no way of standing alone on the earth. The only way for them to make their dreams come true is to rely on the guidance and mercy of the gods in Heaven.

On their journey, when the group stopped to rest in unknown territory, Talum always urged people not to forget their dreams. All dreams are bestowed upon people by the heavenly spirits. By observing their dreams people could know the intentions of the gods and estimate how much longer they must wander in search of their new home. This was an extremely important kind of ritual for these people. Without the permission of the gods they might end up wasting the prime of their lives in this quest. Their dreams might all come to nothing, their days would hold no promise for the future until the day they finally went to reside with the spirits of death.

When they arrived at the next unfamiliar place, they decided to pass the night there in order to restore their spirits and prepare for the next day of their journey. That evening, as Talum looked out over the land before his eyes, it looked as though it was cloaked in a soft, transparent red cloth. The woods, mountains, rocks, and rivers; indeed, the entire scene laid out before him seemed to glow with a magical red light. This uncanny sight startled him, and he dashed in all directions, but to no avail. No matter where he went, the red glow was already there, waiting for him. He shouted out angrily: "What on earth is going on? Why are you treating me this way?" But the mountain forest was silent. It was as though the world had been colored red for thousands of years. What was this place? Talum grew even more furious and showed not the slightest sign of fear. After a long silence, a voice suddenly issued from the depths of his soul saying: "This is Madanhasan![23] Everything is just as you see it before your eyes."

On the second day, Talum recounted this strange dream to the others. They all started excitedly sharing their opinions. Some thought that the red color indicated that this was a demonic place "where blood flowed."

It was not the place intended by the heavenly spirits and they should leave as quickly as possible. Others felt that it must be a "place of the brave," since only brave warriors were permitted to wear red cloth in their headdresses.

Talum frowned and regarded the exhausted people in silence. He thought about the arduous journey of the past few days and considered how their supplies of millet and dried vegetables were almost completely gone. It was true that with the help of the spirits they had been fortunate to catch a few monkeys and muntjacs, but it was not enough to replace the energy that they had expended on their long trek. The soles of some of the women's feet were swollen and deformed. Bulging veins crept up their thin legs like ancient rattan vines. The children with their empty, flat stomachs all had a slack, dispirited looks in their eyes. Their bodies all exuded the foul odor of unbearable fatigue. Taking all these things into consideration, Talum did not hesitate. He told the people: This is the land of the brave. The mountain forests before our eyes are the new home that the gods in Heaven have bestowed upon us. He instructed the people to cut down the dense trees to create a clearing on the mountain slope. This was the beginning of their new homeland. It wasn't until the people all stood excitedly in the courtyards of their newly constructed houses that Talum knew for certain that in total seven families had made the journey with him, and their new community had fifty-seven members old and young.

Their new home was situated on a warm, sunny mountain slope where the blue-green of the high mountains blended with the lush green of the village surroundings. The elders in the group looked at the unique conditions of the area and named the new village, I-pahu, which means a place "nestled on the mountain slope."

There were an amazing number of maple trees in the area. Maple trees of all sizes grew everywhere, as if this was the place where they had originated from. In the seasons when they changed colors, the maples on the mountain slopes combined under the rays of the evening sun to give life to countless brightly hued forest sprites. The sprites frolicked in the spaces between the thatched houses, leaping from one house to another. People couldn't tell if these leaping sprites were the red maple leaves, or the red of the evening sun. People from other villages were astonished by these sights and called the place "the land of red."

When they first arrived at I-pahu, Talum and his wife Tanivu used their experience and their memories to teach the people how to cultivate their crops and raise their children and livestock. In order that they might continue to live in the unfamiliar new land, they never stinted in their cooperation with others, even taking the lead in doing the heaviest tasks. Talum was the most just and wise of leaders. When he allocated the lots for people to build their houses he ensured that the rafters of each house would enjoy an equal amount of the sun's warming rays and the mountain's cooling breezes. Even the amount of time and effort that each family needed to go to draw water from the stream was more of less equal.

Before Tanivu returned to Maiasan,[24] she was the most skillful and hardworking woman. The love that she shared with Talum was sustained by the purest of affection. This made their marriage as stable, self-assured, and eternal as the great mountain ranges. Tanivu usually went out with Talum to labor in the fields. Her strength and capacity for work made people think that there was no difference between men and women. Her entire life she was filled with the spirit great courage. She never shrank from any task, approaching everything with complete fearlessness. When confronted with the most difficult situations she liked to quell her inner uncertainty with song. The melodious strains of her singing made the people think that she was everywhere. From dawn to dusk, she wore clothing that she had woven from *liv*[25] herself. Her long skirt of stiff ramie made a faint "sha, sha" sound wherever she might be laboring. The sound of that long skirt was especially clear and urgent when everyone was working hardest.

When Tanivu returned to the eternal home of the ancestral spirits, Talum's heart for being leader to his people disappeared overnight. In its place came endless silence. Talum changed from being a fastidious man full of life into an old dotard. His spirit was broken, his clothing dishevelled, his appearance bedraggled. The concern and attention of his family members had no effect on him. Perhaps in his heart he felt as though he had already departed from the new homeland with his wife. The people who had followed him there were perturbed. They thought that if Talum's powers had reached their end and he no longer had the ability to control the multitude of spirits at the new homeland, he must have been sacrificed by a curse from the evil spirits. Some people even advocated returning to the Luanda mountains.

As Umas recalled, that most unforgettable evening of his entire life took place during the season when the sun was at its strongest and hottest, after he had celebrated his sixth millet harvest festival. Talum was sitting beside the window as usual, lost in thought. From outside the house, sloping rays of sunlight shone on his grizzled, hardened face, illuminating a profoundly melancholy image. To the people in his family it looked as though he had fallen into a world without any sun.

It was like that one day when Talum saw a child in a sun-filled courtyard. The child was bawling its heart out and embracing its bloodied knee. This sight shocked him to his soul and made him think about his own childhood. It stirred all of his old memories back to life. A young woman hurried up to the child. She was wearing a skirt similar to the one his wife wore, and as she ran the skirt made a "sha, sha, sha, sha" sound. She held the child and wept with it. At that moment Talum finally became aware that his own family had been living by his side all along. As the child lay weeping in its mother's arms a firm resolution was ignited in his heart: for the remaining days of his life, he would do everything in his power to protect his family and this new homeland that lay before his eyes. He concentrated hard, trying to take in every detail of that courtyard. At the same time, all the joyful times that he had spent together with his wife streamed across his mind. The two of them had lived happily through endless months and years. Through those times, the sun rose every day full of hope and set behind the mountains with a beaming smile. And...And...there were so many, many...In the end his eyes clouded, and he had to use the back of his hand to wipe away the tears. With a sense of submission to Heaven's decree he heaved a long sigh before getting up and walking into the sunshine.

Talum's eldest son, Banitul already had two children of his own. He was able to work his fields by himself and lead the village hunting party into the forest to hunt. His face was square, and he was body strong and tall. Over many generations the ancestors had passed down to him a character able to endure great hardship. Talum's second son, Husung, had brought up four children. He was a more gentle, taciturn type, but he had an unquenchable enthusiasm for work. Originally, Talum had also two adorable daughters, but sadly, they had died, one after the other, in the hands the disease demons, this despite the fact that Talum had done all in his power to fight the ravages of the environment and the inconstancy of fate.

As the forest entered nighttime, it lay absolutely still. There was utter silence as all things entered deep, tranquil slumber. Umas had trouble believing that nature could really be so quiet. The pristine beams of moonlight spread like a *pusut*[26] over the cold, cold woods, making the land shimmer with clean, silver radiance.

The mountain winds arrived belatedly, swirling around the outlines of the mountain range, playfully blowing bits of moonlight over to the sides of the opposite slopes. Under the shelter of the enormous trees, countless fragments of light danced along, following the wind in all directions. It seemed as though the fireflies were celebrating their own ritual.

The moonbeams slipped through the spaces between the houses. Umas lay on his bed holding his hands in the strands of their light. The patterns made by the moonlight remained still as they reflected on the black outline of his hands.

"Tomorrow will be a day that belongs to the sunlight." Umas lay on his bed with his tired eyes open, straining to gaze at the little patch of sky outside his window.

NOTES

1. *Lumah*, in the title of the chapter, means "the place where one lives" or "the place where one was born."
2. Mountain birds.
3. Father.
4. Grain storeroom.
5. Life spirit.
6. Taboo.
7. Taiwan beech wood.
8. Ants.
9. Marriage.
10. Bamboo water jug.
11. A string back-sack used for transporting things.
12. Cassia bamboo.
13. Ritual songs that Bunun people chant at the millet ritual. The Bunun people are unique among Taiwanese Indigenous peoples in their use of multi-part harmony in their traditional songs.
14. Stand made from rattan.
15. A kind of leafy vegetable.
16. Goose grass.
17. Fresh ginger.
18. Hyacinth beans.
19. Chinese sumac.
20. Wooden spoons.
21. One of the six communities of the Bunun nation.
22. The Bunun people traditionally bury the deceased inside their houses.
23. The red land.
24. The eternal resting place of the ancestors.
25. Taiwan ramie.
26. Ramie sleeping quilt.

CHAPTER THREE

FESTIVAL TO OPEN NEW LAND

The crimson hot evening sun passed over the woods beside the courtyard, beating down on the ground inside it. The shadows of a few trees followed, running over the dirt floor, dancing excitedly in all directions on the evening wind. The dirt in the courtyard was moist, clean and slick. Its soft and cool surface soothed the tired soles of your feet.

A flock of hens were gathered in the hollow beside the stone wall. They scratched up dirt with their claws to spray over themselves, then puffed up their feathers and gave themselves a hard shake. The rooster beside them was digging into the soil with his thick sharp claws, croaking to call the hens over and to eat whenever he found grubs or insects, his resonant voice laced with pride.

Umas carried Subali in a *tavuk*[1] on his back so that they could enjoy the spacious courtyard along with the chickens. Subali, sunk deeply in daydreaming, drooled from the corner of his mouth.

Umas never showed impatience when he had to take care of his little brother or sister. As with other Bunun children, as soon as he was strong enough, his parents made him help with chores around the house and take part in production activities in the village. During their years of *uvath*,[2] with their parent's supervision, children did cleanup work, as well as simple tasks like lighting the cooking fire and taking care of younger siblings. When they reached *mintlmindu*,[3] aside from continuing to do those chores, they also became responsible for more varied tasks such as feeding the pigs and chickens and pounding the grain. However, Umas had not yet passed enough years to become a *tamaidu*,[4] so while he worked and developed his life skills, he wasn't yet allowed the vanity of tying his hair into a ponytail.

"Umas, is Subali sleeping? Put him down and I'll put him in bed." Malas walked over to Umas, undid the slipknot on the carrying sling and took Subali in her arms. "Wah! Wah! Wah!" Having been shaken from sleep, Subali bawled out. Groggy from sleep he was as limp as wiggly worm. He collapsed into Cina's arms and resumed breathing in the sweetness of deep slumber.

"Hooo..." Umas roared like a mountain sheep that had just slipped its bonds as he charged out onto the sunlit courtyard to bound back and forth. Some of the more easily frightened hens were startled into jumping up onto a low wall, clucking angrily as they went.

"My child, don't make a ruckus, okay? When you act that way, it makes us nervous." Talum squatted beside a shiny black stone sharpening an iron tool with a curved stem. The striations on the concave stone were very even, indicating that this stone was specifically used for sharpening iron tools.

"Hudas, what are you doing?" Umas ran over, fascinated by the sheen reflecting from the shiny iron tool.

"This is called a *navu*,[5] and it's extremely sharp. Never touch it with your bare hand."

"Oh?" Umas squatted down beside Talum, his mouth hanging open and his eyes fixed on the gleaming blade.

"This blade is so strong that it can pass through the skin and steal the blood in your body. It will hurt so much that you'll cry." Talum lightly ran his thumb in the direction of the edge of the blade then quickly drew his hand back in a motion indicating that the blade was now extremely sharp.

"Give it to me, give it to me, I want to see."

"Umas, be careful, you'll hurt yourself." Banitul was afraid that his son would cut himself on the blade.

"Umas, don't upset your elders. Come over here and help me.

"Tama, what are you going to do with these nice wooden poles?" Umas saw that Tama was using a *haili*[6] to trim a wooden pole that reached to his shoulder.

"Umas, pull some hair off the mountain boar *sapa*[7] and then stick the individual hairs onto these pieces of wood." Banitul pointed to the boar skin and the hand-size square pieces of wood that he had cut. There was a thick, sticky layer of pine tar on the pieces of wood.

"How should I stick it on?"

"Stick the boar hairs in a row around the edge of the wood. Start with the thickest hairs."

"That's a lot of trouble. What is it for?" Umas complained, but he started plucking out the thickest strands of boar hair.

"In a few days I'm going to *pahal*[8] this year's new field with Hudas, so we need markers.

"So, these are the markers signs that you're going to put on the new field. Why do we need to stick this ugly black boar's hair on them? Can't we use other animal hair? Some rooster plumes would look a lot better." Umas looked over at the rooster who was busy courting the hens.

"Mountain boar hair is thick and stiff and really strong. When we use it for our markers signs it means that we hope that the millet that we plant there will grow strong and won't be bothered by pests. That way the golden ears of millet will hang from their stalks all over the field like strings of pearls."

"Has the land that we used last year been spoiled? Or is it because that piece of land can't produce fat, beautiful millet anymore?" Umas stood there with a handful of boar hair, looking thoroughly confused.

"The spirits of the land are too strong. Humans spirits don't have the power to control them completely, not to mention take possession of the land as our own. So, before we sow our crops every year we have to ask the gods in heaven to lend us land that is suitable for us. It's only after gaining their permission that we can start to use the new land. The ceremony of putting marker signs on our new land isn't just a way of asking the gods to grant us the use of the land, it's also to let other people know that the gods may let us use the land and that they should look for land somewhere else. That way conflict can be avoided." Banitul looked up at the bottomless blue sky.

"Tama, will the gods let us use a piece of land in the forest?" Umas knew how important the land was to the livelihood of the family.

"In the next few days we're going to have the Mabilao.[9] From now, everyone in the family has to be very respectful and carry out the ceremonial rites strictly. Each day we have to observe the taboos established by the ancestors. We absolutely must not violate them. Only then will our virtue be as clear, clean and stainless as spring water. That is the only way that we will receive the blessings of the gods in ensuring that all things that we undertake will result in good outcomes." Banitul took a wooden pole from the ground and cut a notch into it just big enough to fit one of the pieces of wood trimmed with boar hair.

"Take me with you, okay?" Umas loved the broad expanses of the forest. It was much more fun than being cooped up in the courtyard all the time.

"No, a child's spiritual power isn't strong enough to resist being led astray by the evil mountain spirits. They would make you violate the ceremonial taboos." Banitul slipped his knife back into the sheath at his waist.

"I'm already grown up. I may not be old enough to go hunting with you, but I always help you carrying water, taro and wood...and I carry Subali around as well." Umas drew himself up straight so that his elder could observe how his body had grown more and more like that of an adult.

"Ha, ha. It's true you really have grown, but when you carry water, you only use the thin sweet bamboo containers, and when you carry taro and other things from the fields you use a small backpack. So even though it looks full, there's no comparison with the amount that we carry." Banitul burst out laughing, as if he had heard a really funny story.

"What kind of taboos are they? Why couldn't I respect them?" Umas was well aware that certain kinds of behavior were not permitted during certain rituals. It was just like when the moon had to hide its glow during the daylight hours, and at night the sun had to do the same. It was as if there were an invisible road that ran through the universe and all of creation, including the people, had to move forward along that road. If they deviated from that road, the world would be thrown into chaos and descend into hardship from which there was no return.

"Children can't control their farts and their sneezes. That violates the taboos and prevents the adults from continuing the work at hand. It also wastes the warm regard that the sun bestows on all things."

"You can't help it if you fart or sneeze." The body is a very strange thing. We like to think that we can control everything, but it isn't like that. Sometimes the body acts like an evil stranger that makes you do all sorts of things that you don't like or find repulsive, things that make you feel so much shame.

"Farting and sneezing are both bad behaviors. Farts smell really bad and make everyone close by unhappy. Didn't the ancestors say, 'The bodies of those who are unfilial will be eaten by dung worms.' That is a warning to us. Being respectful of the elders is the pathway to the gods. Besides, if your body is eaten by dung worms you can't go to the eternal resting place of the ancestral spirits and you can't obtain the great power needed to protect your descendants. Sneezing calls forth the evil spirits. The evil spirits have the power to prevent the gunpower in the hunters' guns from going off and then they can't take down even the weakest and smallest game. They also have the power to make the crops in the fields wither and turn black. Then insect pests and harmful birds will come to occupy the fields that we worked so hard to open up. They will steal our food before we can harvest it. Then our people will have no control over their lives just like dandelion fluff blown around in the sky." Talum patiently explained all of this to Umas. He hoped that his own descendants would understand the divine power that underlies life and avoid unnecessary curses. Life in the mountain forests is just like a pathway that winds along the top of a steep cliff. If you don't stay on the path, any kind of deviation or deliberate transgressions can mean that you fall into the gorge and perish.

"When we set up the marker signs, we must always arrive at the land we have selected before the rooster crows to awaken the land. Umas, do you think that you could get up while the world still lies sleeping and go into the mountains with us in the frigid morning air?" Was it because the elders wanted to frighten the younger generation, or because they wanted them to develop the ability to work and figure things out for themselves? It is foolish to go into the mountains if you don't know that limits of your own ability. Only reckless animals rush into the hunters' traps.

"Before the rooster crows everywhere is pitch black and you can't see anything, so what can you do? After the rooster crows the sky sends down its rays of light and your eyes become nimbler. It is a lot easier to do just about anything then." Umas thought that the adult way of doing things wasn't the wisest.

"Going to set up the markers before daybreak we avoid running into snakes and rats. That would be taboo and the work of setting up the markers would have to stop immediately. We wouldn't be able to continue until we have done three days of penance. The penance will delay us so that we can't carry out our sowing in time." When speaking of the traditional rules of life the elders always looked especially stern.

"What happens if you meet snakes or rats every time?"

"Anytime we run into snakes, rats or other taboo animals we always have to go home and rest. If that happens five times in a row, then we have to give up on the piece of land that we had set our hearts on and look for another piece of land. It means that the gods did not give us permission to use that land. In other words, it means that we have to be even more diligent than the rooster in order to win the pleasure of the gods. Lazy behavior will never gain their blessing." Banitul joined in the instruction, letting Umas know that getting a new piece of land was a complex, difficult and sacred endeavor.

"Are snakes and rats really that bad?" Umas had seen and caught both of these animals before and he couldn't understand what powers they had that made them so frightening.

"According to an old myth the rat was originally a lazy, greedy old woman who changed her form. In order to compensate for the wrongs that the woman had committed, the rat spends its entire life eating millet. It eats and eats until there is no more millet left. The snake is a strange animal. Its skin is especially slippery so it can't hold onto anything. Even tiny grains of millet slip from its grasp. So, if you think about it, if we're about to start sowing the millet and we meet with lazy, greedy animals that can't hold onto millet, isn't that a bad omen? It means that their spirits will damage or eat up all the millet we're going to grow, leaving us with nothing. That isn't the result we want." Talum rung his hands as if those hateful snakes and rats were right before his eyes showing off their malicious powers.

"Ah, so rats changed from a woman?" Umas was amazed and curious. He was like a boy who discovers a bird's nest in a tree for the first time.

"In past, our people led a very easy life. No matter how many people were in the family, all they needed was one grain of millet and they could cook a pot of food big enough to fill everyone's stomachs. Afterwards, there was a lazy woman who wanted to cook enough for three meals all at once. That way she would have more time to sleep and rest. So she put a lot of grains of millet in the pot. She didn't realize that the millet would just keep expanding and expanding until it filled the entire room. She tried to hide by squeezing herself into a little hole in the wall, but in the end the millet squeezed her until she changed into a rat. Because of what she did thousands of years ago, our people lost the ability to make a whole meal from a single grain of millet. Ever since that time, in order to atone for the terrible crime that she committed, the rat gets excited and starts gorging itself anytime it finds any millet. That's because it thinks it has to eat a whole room filled with millet. Even today we think that women can change into rats."

The sound of men and women singing *tusaus*[10] carried through the still air. The men's voices were deep and rounded like the majestic mountains. The women's voices were clear and crisp, just like the water that flows in a brook. Our people have always expressed their feelings of joy, anger, sadness and joy by singing. For that reason, we all have excellent singing voices. We sing with reverence, and our unique voices create stunning melodies. With the power of our souls we can express our deepest, most sincere feelings so that the gods will know the hardship, pain and love that we experience in our lives.

"It's Tama, Subali and Cina Tanivu singing." Umas looked over at the thatched house next door.

"It's such a blessing that a husband and wife can share that kind of affection! The love between a husband and wife can chase away all the troubles that life may bring. Ah, the songs sung from love are enchanting." Talum tilted his head as if he were thinking back to the times when he and his wife sang together. Everyone fell into silent reverie.

That night, the family were all huddled around the fire trying to get warm. In the mountains this is the only activity possible before going to bed. It is the time when people discuss the work that needs to be done the next day.

"It's been really chilly in the forest these last few days. A lot of trees are still silently waiting for the growing season to start." Talum spoke of the changing weather as he stirred the campfire. He was thinking about what work should be done.

"A few days ago when I went up the mountain to check the *ahu-dun*,[11] I noticed that many of the weaker trees were no longer able to support their own leaves. There were layers upon layers of leaves lying on the ground with the look of death. It made the mountain slopes look like poor people with no clothing to wear." As he spoke, Banitul grasped at the warm air rising from the flames.

"The weeds on the slopes have all died, so it will save us some work when we start working the fields. We have to get those markers out on the land we want as soon as possible, before the gods forget this family of ours." Like the other women, Malas, was always thinking of the details.

"I'm also worried that we won't be able to do the sowing in time." Since he was the leader of the family, the wrinkles of concern on Talum's face always appeared especially deep.

"Banitul, make sure you get up before the rooster tomorrow morning. We'll go to the slopes at Pat-valian[12] to put up the marker signs. The soil over there is the most fertile and the water in the nearby stream sounds abundant and sweet. I'm very satisfied with that piece of land."

"Of course! Of course! I'll be up before the rooster and I'll get you up on my way. Look! I've already made the markers." Banitul pointed to the brand-new markers in the corner, their wooden plaques all radiating boar hair. They looked like little suns bringing warmth to everything around them.

"That would be best. Remember that year when you overslept and made us run into a snake that had just woken up? We had to give up on that fertile piece of land. Even now when I think about it it seems such a shame. You! Even the snakes get up earlier than you!" When Talum recalled this unfortunate event Banitul's whole face flushed red. He looked like a child who wanted to keep playing but was reprimanded by his parents. Umas found a special pleasure in seeing his Tama being scolded by his Hudas.

The gods had granted Talum and Banitul their blessings because of their devotion and diligence. They had an uneventful trip and were able to reach the fields that they had planned to select without any difficulty. There they set up their marker signs that looked just like little suns. Talum made a symbolic slash in the most prominent tree on the land and then prayed to heaven:

"Hu! May the gods in heaven protect us and allow us to take possession of this land easily. May this land be a great benefactor who will nourish the lives of our family. Gods in Heaven! Please allow the crops that we plant on this land to grow healthy and fine. May the crops be plentiful and may the evil spirits that harm the crops not enter where we have cultivated. That way the food that grows here will be so abundant that my family will not be able to eat it all."

After the ritual of placing the markers was complete, Talum poured all the millet wine that he had brought with him around the tree as an offering for the enjoyment of the local good spirits. He hoped that those local spirits would bless the work that they later did in the fields and protect the millet that they planted as it matured, grew strong and produced healthy ears of grain.

As soon as he got home, Talum summoned all the heads of the other households to discuss preparations for the land opening ceremony. Aside from asking all the families about the land that they had chosen, he fixed the times for them to break ground, and how they could support one another. He hoped that with the cooperation of all the families and the blessing of the gods, the work of opening the fields would proceed smoothly. After all, when it came to that most important matter of the people's lives, no detail could be overlooked and there could be no mistakes. The assembled family elders were filled with enthusiasm. They crowded into the living room shoulder to shoulder making it very uncomfortable. Even the air that they breathed was hot enough to make a bystander sweat.

Today the village of the "red place" has undergone big changes. Whether it was those who followed Talum themselves, or the tales of the many hunters who passed by told of its fertile soil, abundant water, and the ingenious way that the village is protected by the dense cover of trees, what began as a cramped cluster of huts is now a village bustling with people and abundant livestock. It is exactly like the village in the Luanda mountains that they departed from so long ago.

Although Talum was getting on in years, his accumulated life experience and his wisdom gained him the respect of everyone. He was also respected by the newly arrived. From the selection of the site for the construct their house to the many problems faced in everyday life, they first discussed everything with him. Everyone was always completely confident of the solutions that Talum came up with. For that reason, all of the other family heads hoped that Talum would continue as that year's *Liskadan Lusan*[13] and lead them as they carried out the field opening festival.

Before the meeting wrapped up Talum said that all members of all the families would make note of their dreams every night. If anyone had an auspicious dream it meant that the gods had given their permission for the villagers to commence their work of opening up the new fields. It also meant that the work in the fields would go smoothly and that people would be very satisfied with the harvest. If anyone had a nightmare, then they would have to continue waiting for the permission of the gods to start work. This was a tradition passed down by the ancestors for thousands of years and no one could alter it. Just like the path that the sun follows on its journey across the sky, it had not changed since the beginning of time.

On a night blessed by the host of gods, Malas dreamed that the *ithuk*[14] that she had planted had already blossomed and begun to fruit. There were so many pomelos that the tree was bent over by their weight. This implied that they could now begin humbly worshipping the gods.

When Talum heard the story of the dream he gleefully spread the word:

"This dream is extremely auspicious. There is no need for anyone to give up the new land that they have chosen, the gods have granted us that land. We just have to cultivate it according to the traditional rules with devoted effort, and the millet will grow free of pests and not suffer any natural disasters. The millet won't allow our sweat to be shed in vain. It won't stand by in winter as our faces turn as white as frost with the cold, nor will it permit our souls to cry out in the night from hunger. This year we will surely have an abundant harvest. As early as possible tomorrow morning we will go to the new land and start breaking the ground!"

From the last frost of this year until the first frost of the next year only one crop of millet can be sown. Everyone in the village understood that they were about to take part in the most solemn and sacred land breaking ceremony. This opening of the land and sowing would determine whether or not the lives of the people were to continue flowing like the endless water from a wellspring.

The solemn air of the land opening ceremony instilled a sense of self-restraint in all of the people. Even when they walked around, they bowed their heads and tread lightly like squirrels moving about in the trees. If children were naughty or boisterous the adults immediately reprimanded them sternly:

"Don't make a fuss! You'll upset the millet and it won't want to come to visit our house."

People approached all things as if they were taking aim at some prey. If they had to push aside some leaves obstructing their aim, they did it very gently, as if they were deathly afraid of the leaves swinging back noisily and scaring off the prey. Even babies crying to be nursed seemed more cautious and restrained.

The people all believed that neither the gods nor the millet liked those who were noisy and rowdy.

At dawn on the next day when even the most diligent of roosters were still sound asleep, Talum hurried out to the new land carrying the ceremonial millet wine, some yams, his hoe and sickle. All of his family members followed behind as did the villagers who came along to help them. Umas carried Subali on his back as they advanced down the narrow, dark mountain trail.

When they arrived at the new land Umas was a little bit disappointed. The land that was to be their new fields turned out to be nothing more than a waste land overgrown with trees and brush. Since it was also the season when the leaves fall from the trees, it looked all the more desolate. But when he smelled the moldy scent of dead branches and fallen leaves caught in the air, he immediately understood why the adults liked this piece of land.

A dozen or so adults followed Talum to the center of the field and started hacking away at the weeds and bushes there. Soon the middle of the field was looking clear and tidy. Right away, Talum ordered everyone to plant the yams in hopes that the crops that they eventually planted on that land would grow as hardy and prolific as the yams. Once the yams were planted, Talum walked over beside one of the marker signs that he had previously placed there. He undid the wine-filled gourd that he carried at his waist and sprinkled the wine over the ground while he intoned in a loud voice:

"Hu! From today we begin cultivating this piece of land. Please do not allow the people to be harmed by their tools as they work. When we cut down trees, do not let people be crushed. Oh, ye gods! Please chase away the snakes and rats from their burrows. We have been granted permission to work this land so they must depart. I am going to begin breaking the land. We pray that you allow this field to produce abundant crops, and that all the millet, yams, taro, and squash that we plant will grow healthy and safe and produce a fine yield. We will farm industriously, and we pray that like the sun and the moon, you will continuously shine down upon this new land. Hu! Hu! Hu!"

The people from the village watched from a distance as Talum carried out the land opening ceremony. The windless forest seemed to stand beside them, silently observing the solemn rites.

The next day, Banitul led those who were to help him out to the field to continue clearing the land. When the sun shrank everyone's shadow to a small patch around their feet, he said to his wife Malas:

"You and the children go back. We are going to have a ceremony at dusk so you should prepare the things that we need for it. When the sun returns home, we'll carry back the alder trees that we cut from the field. Then we can pray to the ancestors to grant us an abundant harvest season."

With his mother's guidance, Umas was able to prepare the things for the ritual very quickly. He then went to rest under the camphor tree by their house. Umas liked to go there to meet with the cool clear mountain breeze.

At dusk, the sun lay down exhausted in the mountain hollows. The pale red glow of evening changed all of nature into a resplendent world of gold. The people who had been working in the field returned home in single file along the winding trail carrying the alder trees with them. After they entered the courtyard, they gently beat the alder branches on the roof of the house. With the sound of beating, the dust on the roof fell to the ground. With this ritual the people prayed that the millet that they planted would receive plenty of the sun's rays and grow up cleanly.

Banitul showed everyone how to cut the tree trunks into equal lengths which they then piled in front of the main gate. The alder was piled higher and higher until it almost reached above the house.

The people then gathered before the pile of equal length logs. Thinking about how the alders had grown tall, they discussed who had carried back the thickest trunk. Talum appeared from inside the house carrying the skull of a recently killed mountain boar. He placed it before the highest point in the pile of logs. As he sprinkled wine on the logs he reverently chanted a prayer:

"Hu! Great Spirits of our Ancestors! We pray that the crops that we plant this year will produce a plentiful harvest, and that the piles of millet will rise higher than the pile of logs now before our eyes, even higher than the gate of our house. Allow our people always to have plenty to eat so that they will grow as strong as black bears. May all malicious illnesses be blocked from approaching our bodies. Hu! Hu! Hu!"

After the ceremony was over everyone started drinking the millet wine that the owner of the new field had prepared for them. Many of the elders got carried away and drank too much wine. They were found wandering unsteadily around the area. Umas stood in the distance thinking that those drunken elders would have trouble getting up the next morning.

In the days that followed, whether the sky produced sunshine, or fog or rain, everyone gathered to work in Talum's new field. With the efforts of the many villagers what had been weed covered wasteland gradually became a field of fertile black soil. The more you looked at it the more familiar it seemed, as if long, long ago you had known this land. Carrying Subali on his back, Umas observed the changes in the field from a distance. As the patch of black soil grew larger and larger, his younger brother seemed to grow heavier and heavier.

"Umas, take Subali over to the tree and have a rest. Otherwise the sun is going to change him into a *sisiwn*[15] who doesn't dare go home." Malas was afraid that the vicious heat of the sun would harm the baby.

Umas carried Subali toward the edge of the field. There was a pomelo tree that the villagers had deliberately left standing. The tree's branches and leaves grew lush and dense, so the villagers had brought over stones of various sizes and piled them up neatly around the trunk of the tree. That way the tree had a nice, sturdy home.

Near that pile of stones, Umas spied a bit of tail that a lizard had shed. It looked like a pretty twig except that it moved.

"Can a baby really turn into a lizard?" He poked at the squirming tail curiously. As he poked at it, ancient legends that the elders had told him about lizards flooded into his mind.

In one cursed time, for no known reason, two suns appeared in the sky. When one of them sank into the mountains to the west, the other would rise from behind the mountains in the east. Because two suns constantly shone, there was no chance for the earth to sleep at night.

A husband and wife were out working in their field. Because they didn't want their baby to suffer sun stroke in the torrid heat, they placed the baby in the shade of a stone wall. They also placed thick *bunbun*[16] leaves over the child to keep it cool. But the banana leaves were no match for the fierce sun's rays and they quickly dried out. The baby's Cina saw this and was very worried, so she immediately covered the baby again with *asik*[17] which are more resistant to the sun. But even the palm leaves couldn't stand up against the force of the sun's rays and this left the baby to the mercy of the powerful sun. In the end, the sun baked the baby into a lizard that hid shyly in the gaps between the rocks to stay cool.

The baby's Tama was extremely angry. He made a firm vow to get revenge and then pricked his finger to let the blood sprinkle on the ground. The Tama took up his bow and arrow, and with firm resolve strode out on the long hard road to revenge. In the time that it takes a small tree to grow into a large one he finally walked to the place where the sun rises. There he saw his sworn enemy. The rage in his heart transformed into overwhelming strength. In a flash he drew his bow and with a "swoosh," let fly a sharp arrow carrying all of the hatred of revenge. The arrow struck the sun square in the eye. Little specks of fresh red blood splattered over the sky creating a pale red glow. Now blind in one eye, the sun lost its dazzling glare and humans could clearly see her round, bulging body. From that time onwards the sun with its wounded eye became as shy as the lizard. She dared climb stealthily into the sky to play only when the people were asleep. Although the father had got his revenge, his child remained a lizard hiding in the rocks. It seemed like there was no way it could change back into its original form. The only way that it could let its parents know that it was still hiding from the strong sun's rays in the gaps between the rocks was furtively to leave a piece of its tail behind. It never dared show its lizard form or reunite with its family.

"That baby was really strange. It didn't even want its own tail. It's a good thing I don't have younger brothers or sisters like that." He took Subali from his back, set him down and rubbed the baby's head:

"Don't change into a lizard, okay. There's no way we could shoot the sun in the eye and create all the stars in the sky like that baby's Tama."

"Come on everybody, don't stop! We've got to push this big rock over to the side of the field. Quickly now, push!" Umas could hear people shouting in the field.

There was a big rock standing in the middle of the field and the villagers were racking their brains trying to think of some way to push it over to one side. That would free up more space to plant food. But the rock wasn't just big, it was sunk deep in the ground. After wrestling with it for a while everyone could only stare hopelessly at the immovable stone as they gasped for breath. One villager, his face covered with dirt, raised his eyebrows and he clutched his bloody finger:

"This old rock has grown roots. There's no way we're going to move it. I say we just leave it. Let it serve as a marker post."

Banitul was wiping the sweat from his forehead. With distain tinged with pleasure he replied:

"Chisbangath![18] We're a proud people. If this rock puts us to shame, other people are going to make fun of us. They'll say that the men in the Husluman clan have only got one dick left between the lot of them.

A flock of mountain birds swooped overhead just as Banitul came up with a way of moving the rock. He told the villagers;

"We can use the power of fire to break up the rock. When it has been broken into smaller pieces, we can move it more easily."

He began giving directions:

"Some of you go and collect dried reeds and bamboo, the rest go to the stream and draw some water. Let's do this quickly so that we can combine the fire with the power of the sunlight. By combining their strength, we should be able to break the rock into smaller pieces as quickly as a hunter divides up the game he brings back."

It wasn't long before the rock was covered with reeds and bamboo making it look like a hastily constructed thatched hut. As the flames began to engulf the dry reeds they were assisted by the wind. It looked as though the huge rock had sprouted flaming wings. Even its face was stained fiery red. The rock responded by making muffled popping sounds.

One of the younger villagers who was watching said excitedly:

"Ha, ha! Are you crying in pain? We tried to push you, but you didn't let us, so we need to use the fire to make you do what we want."

The people standing around stared at him and said:

"Don't make things worse. The spirits of rocks all have ears and if they get angry, they'll make it so we never finish our work. Don't forget, the clear sounds of the planting season already fill our ears and we don't want our behavior to offend any of the mountain spirits."

Maybe the spirit of the great rock really resented being mocked by humans because suddenly a *saufsauvath*[19] slithered out from beneath it. Some of the people were caught off guard and fled in all directions, but Salivan, who was tall and powerfully built quickly stepped on the snake's tail. He then grabbed it, swung it around a few times then placed it back on the ground. The snake was so dizzy it squirmed around on its back flashing its white belly. It looked so comical that people bent over with laugher.

Salivan picked up a long leaf, wrapped it around the snake's head, then turned to shout in the direction of the pomelo tree:

"Umas, let this snake come over and play with you."

With a "whap!" the brocade snake landed right in front of Umas like a bird landing on a tree branch. The snake squirmed, trying to shake the leaf off its head. It had lost its sense of direction and had no idea which way to go. Umas took a firm hold of the snake's head and removed the leaf. The little snake wrapped itself around Umas' hand, all the while flicking its long thin forked tongue. Umas found this quite threatening. He gave the snake a rap on the head and told it:

"I've caught *kaviath*[20] with their poisonous fangs. Do you think I'm afraid of a toothless brocade snake like you?"

Umas thought about relations between his people and snakes. This brought him a twinge of regret. Originally, they had been good friends, but now they harbored a lot of suspicion and hostility to each other. In the conversations of the adults Umas frequently heard tales of the intimate relations between the Bunun people and snakes...

In the time when humans and animals spoke the same language, the Bunun people and hundred pace vipers lived quite close to each other. That made for extremely close feelings between the two groups. The Bunun even called the vipers, *kaviath*, which means "friend." The snakes, for their part, came and went from the Bunun villages freely, while the

Bunun often went to visit the vipers in their homes. Intimate feelings and friendly interactions between the two sides were the norm.

One time a Bunun woman went over to a viper's house for a chat. She happened to notice that the regular triangular pattern on the snake's back was very beautiful. It looked like exquisite rows of mountains running off in long curving lines, creating a sense of boundless vitality. The more the woman looked at the pattern, the more she liked it. She thought to herself, if only I could weave patterned borders with that pattern, my husband and children could have the most beautiful robes, and the other villagers might praise me.

The woman told the snake what she was thinking. She asked the snake if it would be willing to accompany her home so that she could more easily copy the snake's patterns on her weaving machine. The female snake replied straightforwardly, "Of course! But I've got a lot of things to do and I can't get away right now. How about this, I'll lend my child to you. The patterns on her back are exactly the same as on mine. There shouldn't be any difference."

The woman took a look at the snake child and found that its patterns were just as appealing, it's just that they were a little smaller. When she got home, she took out her loom right away and started weaving the patterns on the body of the snake child. The work went very smoothly except that the snake child had no patience. She looked left or rolled right making the patterns shift around chaotically. The woman felt like she was trying to watch a butterfly in the wind and just couldn't get the shape and direction of the patterns right. She then thought up an ingenious way of preventing the child from wiggling around. She tied the child to the top of a wide chair. That way she could check the patterns on the little snake's body and copy it in her weaving without any problem.

After a time, she managed to weave a cloth border with a pattern exactly like that on the hundred pace viper. She was so happy that she took the cloth and dashed out to show it to the other women. When they saw the unique and beautiful totem design the women of the village immediately sighed in amazement. At first, they all praised the skill of the woman's handiwork. Then someone asked about the actual technique that she used in the weaving. In the end, everyone begged the woman to teach them her weaving technique. The woman was gratified and accepted the invitation. For a time, she was very busy instructing one family after another in her method of weaving. After a day and a night had passed, the woman finally remembered that she hadn't untied the snake child. In a panic she ran back home to check on it. The snake child was still tied to the top of the chair but the vibrant colors on its body had faded. It was now the pallid hue of death. The woman was so alarmed that her legs felt like rubber. She tried every way she could think of to try to revive the snake child, but the child just lay there on top of the chair like a cold, dried out piece of rattan.

When the mother snake saw her child lying there as cold as ice, she persuaded her whole clan to go and attack the Bunun village. Their poisonous bites killed everyone in the village with the exception of one child who fled to a nearby village to seek help.

After a sincere apology from the people, the two groups agreed upon a treaty that they both promised to respect: If a member of the Bunun people killed a hundred pace viper, the vipers could come and demand a life in return. The reverse would hold true as well. But if one of the people wounded a hundred pace viper by accident and in return was bitten by one of the snakes, the snake would have to cut off a piece of its tail and give it to the person as the price of neutralizing the poison. Although the treaty received support from both sides, since that time people and snakes have not had anything to do with each. Just like that, a friendship that had lasted for thousands of years turned to nothing virtually overnight. All that remained was deep, irrational suspicion.

Umas looked into the innocent eyes of the brocade snake and thought about the treaty between humans and snakes, then he said to the snake,

"I'm going to let you go back, but you have to tell the adult snakes that the Bunun people did not harm you. Nor should you attack my people for no reason." Then he put the snake on the ground and watched it disappear into a clump of grass.

"Now quickly pour the water over the top of the rock. You have to get the whole rock wet. Quickly now!" Once the rock had been completely consumed by the flames Banitul calculated that the time had come, and he ordered the people to start pouring water over it.

As streams of water splashed over the scalding rock, it began making sharp hissing sounds as clouds of white steam billowed from it. The steam made some of the people cough uncontrollably. In a few moments the steam gradually dissipated into the air. The crowd of people gazed at the great, silent rock waiting for a result that they could control or predict. Suddenly there was a series of cracking noises and the big rock was set in motion, splitting into several pieces of different sizes. Fragments that came from the upper part of the rock rained down on the ground raising curtains of dust that settled over the dark faces of the surrounding crowd. After a moment, a joyous roar such as only heard after an abundant harvest filled the mountain vales. Banitul stood tall and erect beside the shattered rock pursing his fire-singed lips with a look of immense satisfaction.

With the protection of the gods and the unstinting labor of the clan members, the field had taken on an entirely different appearance. The vigorous weeds and bushes now lay around the field like defeated soldiers. Banitul then took a torch and burned their corpses so that nothing but a thick layer of ash covered the ground. But there was still no rest for the people of the clan. They all set to work pulling the roots of the trees and weeds out of the ground. The field was now as clear and flat as the courtyard in front of a house. In fact, it was as if the end goal of all the hard and diligent labor was to build a sturdy, comfortable house for the millet.

The next day, Talum led everyone except the pregnant women out to the new field to carry out the *Isikaliban.*[21] The purpose of the stone-casting ritual was to throw all of the exposed stones from the field out past the edge of the land. At the same time, people threw *tamol*[22] at each other. With the dregs stuck all over their faces, the villagers looked comical. Startled shouts and raucous laughter rang out as the heavy drudgery of the past few days was replaced with joy and merriment.

To help Umas understand the meaning of the stone-casting ritual Banitul explained to him:

"The ancestors performed the stone-casting ritual because they wanted to chase the evil spirits from the fields and prevent them from harming the millet that was to grow there. In past, the people would divide themselves into two or three teams and stand around the edge of the field. They used the stones that they picked up from the field to throw at each other. Everyone ended up bleeding, but they continued to counterattack bravely until there weren't any stones left on the field. The people were fierce and courageous, so lots of them ended up wounded. That made it impossible from them to go to work the next day. Eventually, a very wise elder decided that with future stone-casting rituals, when they got to the part where they threw stones, they should replace the stones with wine dregs. The stones were thrown outside the border of the field. The further the stones were thrown, the more they received the blessings of the ancestral spirits."

After the stone-casting ritual, the stoneless field looked flat and fertile. Umas really admired the bravery of the ancestors who had been willing to suffer serious injuries in order to establish their fields and chase away the evil spirits.

Once the ritual was completed, Talum began tentatively planting the new millet seed. While he was at it, he announced to the gods in heaven and to the host of local spirits that the villagers were going to begin sowing that piece of land. A few of the strong, heavily built men cut down stalks of mature, emerald green *badan*[23] These they stuck into the ground around a small piece of the field that had been set aside like an altar. The people called this *pinulakoan*.[24] The millet that grew on this plot of land was reserved for the gods to eat. It was a special kind of millet called *lokaival*.[25] Then they suspended some *dahodaho*[26] fruit from the reeds. Talum took some *lokaival* seeds from a gourd container and sprinkled them on the ceremonial plot. He pressed the seeds into the soil with his hands. Taking a mouthful of wine from another gourd he sprayed the wine over the reeds. Raising the *somsom*[27] in the air he shook it in a circular motion over the ceremonial plot and intoned loudly:

> Oh, Ye great ancestral spirits!
> Everything that we possess is a gift from you.
> You prevent us from walking in the darkest of dark directions,
> Please lead the millet in resisting the calls of the evil spirits!
> Oh, Ye great ancestral spirits!
> Use your power to lead us into times of plenty,
> So that from today onwards,
> All of our descendants will have more than enough to eat.

After they returned to the village, Talum called everyone to gather outside. Then he asked twelve men who had been successful in the hunt to form a tight circle with everyone placing their arms around the waists of the men beside them. The men were told to look upwards toward the sacred place where the heavenly spirits dwell. Following Talum's lead they began to sing a *pasibutbut*.[28] The rest of the villagers all joined in according to the special qualities of their own voices, closely following the men in eight-part harmony. The men in the circle then began moving from left to right in even steps. At the beginning, the voices of the adults were low and gentle, like the warm mountain breezes floating in the deep, tranquil mountain valleys. Soon the song began to rise along the mountain slopes and roam between the trees. It soared over the cliffs and mountain peaks until the resonant, spirited harmonies suddenly swept skyward to surge into the deepest recesses of the sky. The multiple levels of harmony created a sound that was understated yet profound. It was as if a vast swarm of bees were buzzing overhead as they flew towards new, richer fields. It was like the sound of a waterfall that cascaded over an uneven bed of slate. The melodious sounds were crisp and powerful, yet also hummed softly like nimble drops of water, that splash over the leaves, rainbows reflecting from their backs.

These ritual songs needed no musical instrument to accompany them, nor did they require lyrics to explain them. With reverent spirits and unique vocal intonation, the people were able to create the most surpassingly beautiful melodies. The key was that everyone knew the strengths and weaknesses of their own spirits, and through that self-awareness and humility they determined the vocal register most suited to them. When they joined to sing together, they could express every possible emotion in the entire universe.

This song-and-dance routine was filled with the soulful force of the mountain winds. It was like a blazing fire. The people were intoxicated by the sound of the intricate, passionate melodies. Even the host of spirits was profoundly moved by the harmonious, ravishing sounds that went on and on.

For thousands of years the people had always believed that this ritual that imitated the spinning of a *huvias*[29] would make the millet that they sowed grow then flow into the grain storehouses as swiftly and smoothly as a spinning top. From there it would nourish the bodies and souls of the people. The circular movement from left to right represents the hope that during the sowing season the evil spirits that reside in the left shoulder of people will move to the right shoulder and become good spirits. With the protection of the good spirits the millet can grow without problem and come to fruition in abundance.

Once the opening of the fields had been completed, the people eagerly awaited the arrival of the time for sowing. Everyone rested in their houses. They were prohibited from going hunting or going out to call on friends. With only pure thoughts in their hearts, they waited for an auspicious dream that would indicate that the gods had given permission to begin sowing. Each of the villagers hoped that the lucky dream would be granted to them. That was the most propitious of events. It meant that the other villagers would praise and respect them. For that reason, as soon as the adults rose from their beds in the morning the first thing they did was ask each other about their dreams. Talum then interpreted whether the dreams were favorable or unfavorable, and that would serve as their guide in deciding when to start sowing.

Umas and the other children secretly hoped that the adults' dreams were all inauspicious. When the adults were resting at home there were always lots of fun and interesting things going on. The women all brought out the cloth and decorative borders that they were working on and gathered in the courtyard of someone's house to exchange ideas about weaving and sewing clothing. They also sang popular songs with multiple part harmony. Nearby you could often see the men using long lengths of string made from ramie to spin the tops that they had painstakingly fashioned. A dozen or more tops all spinning in unison sounded like the voices of the adults singing "Prayers for a Good Millet Harvest." It made you feel the same sense of respect.

However, there were other things that made the children angry. One was the monotonous diet. Before the millet had been sown, it was strictly forbidden to eat anything but steamed millet and *sanlavhudo*[30] soup. That was because any food that was salty, sweet or spicy would violate the taboos. This meant that a lot of people lost their appetites. The dogs, on the other hand, were all in good spirits since they had lots of leftovers to eat.

Talum often told the clan members:

"If we lead a luxurious, wasteful life before the harvest is in, will the gods still take pity on us? Will they grant us a prosperous future? If we haven't shed enough sweat to irrigate the fields, are we justified in asking the land to give us an abundant harvest? Will the millet grow quickly and vigorously in the fields?"

The old man's words made Umas think of a number of different things. For example, in the evenings, little Subali had the habit of crying disconsolately in front of his parents. So, every night his parents let him lie in their arms, warm and comfortable. There was also a saying that the adults all believed: if sweat from someone's body dripped onto fertile soil it would soon change into a something made of gold. Therefore, when the adults were out in the fields working and sweating, they never complained of being too tired.

"When I grow up, I'm going to work really hard so I sweat lots and lots. That way there will be things made of golden things all over the place." Umas thought about the strange, distant future.

One cold, dark night, the earth was very still, and all the creatures seemed to be held motionless and silent in the air. "Hoo! Hoo! Hoo!" An owl hooted outside their house. Malas turned to her husband lying beside her and whispered:

"The owl has come to visit our village. Somebody must be pregnant. The hoots are low and rough, so it must be a boy child. I wonder which woman it is."

"Banitul was in no hurry to reply and put his left hand on his wife's belly. Malas rolled over to face the other way then said quietly:

"The owl wasn't hooting in our courtyard."

Umas was sleeping on her other side. Unaware of his parents' subtle movements he interjected:

"It's a really scary sound, something dangerous must be going to happen."

"Did the owl's cries scare you, or are you and the owl both trying to scare us?" Banitul withdrew his left hand. He sounded especially disappointed.

He had just finished speaking when a painful, startled cry suddenly came from Husung's room:

"Anana-kai![31] Something bit me. It hurts like hell. Tama, come quickly! Anana-kai!"

Hearing the child's cries, Tama Husung and Cina Hanagu quickly picked up a chip of pine wood and set it alight. The room suddenly brightened. Everyone scrambled from their beds and ran over to see what had happened. When they lifted up the covers, they could see that Tama Husung's eldest son, Asulan, had a red swelling on his calf. It was as if a piece of raw venison were stuck there. Beside him, a big shiny black *hasipa*[32] was darting around in all directions, desperately searching for some dark place to flee to. Tama Husung angrily raised his hand and smashed the bug over and over until it lay in a crumpled mess.

Talum, naked from the waist up rushed over and asked:

"What's wrong with the child?"

"He's been bitten by a brute of a centipede." Cina Hanagu was distraught and only wanted to have a good cry.

"Take him over to see Hudas[33] Bisazu. He's a powerful *isamiminan*[34] and he can root out any kind of ailment from the deepest parts of our soul and then cast them on the ground for us to see."

Before Talum had even finished speaking, Husung carried his son out of the room. Holding a piece of burning pinewood, his wife followed close behind as they hurried off with swift, if unsteady steps.

When he heard he child crying, Hudas Bisazu got out of bed. He seemed as clear and sharp as if he had never been asleep. He lit lots and lots of pinewood chips so that the living room was as bright as daylight.

He took Asulan into his arms and spoke to him in a kind voice:

"Don't be afraid, we're all here to protect you. When you cry it makes the evil spirits really happy because that's exactly what they want. Be brave. We don't want to let the evil spirits feel proud of themselves, okay?"

The old man looked at the wound and said to his son beside him:

"Go fetch the *muchiu*[35] then grind them into power and have Asulan eat it. The pain will be gone by the morning. When the sunlight fills the land, the child will have forgotten all about this."

Gall stones taken from the intestines of animals and then specially prepared were one of Hudas Bisazu's treasures. If one of the villagers or a hunting dog was bitten by an animal and the wound was festering, he always ground the stones into a powder and applied it to the wound or had the patient eat it. He had successfully cured many people that way and this made everyone believe that he was a shaman with powerful skills.

Umas liked to ask Hudas Bisazu to tell him stories about the spirits and the gods in heaven. Shamans always speak with the gods about matters pertaining to the Bunun people.

It was still not light, but the roosters outside in the yard were already following the ancient custom of singing to each other and arguing. According to an unwritten agreement, the hardworking heads of each family had assembled at Talum's house and were huddled around the eternal flame in his stove. As they tried to get warm, they discussed their dreams from the night just passed. Talum looked very serious. He was afraid that if the gods didn't allow the sowing to begin soon, it might be too late and the millet would not have time to produce grain. Then it would end up no different than ordinary weeds.

After the other villagers told their dreams that had nothing at all to do with sowing, all they could do was look aimlessly into the flames. The light of the fire swirled around, dancing freely over their sullen, silent faces.

Suddenly, Cina Hanagu spoke up cautiously;

"Last night I dreamed that my eldest son, Asulan, had already grown up to be a strong, healthy youth. He was in the forest trying to catch a *dumath*[36] with a bee on its paw. The startled bear ran off as fast as it could, but Asulan seemed to have uncanny powers and immediately dragged the bear to the ground then tied it up with no difficulty. When I looked closely, I could see that my child had grown as many legs as a centipede. I was worried that the centipede that bit him left behind a curse that couldn't be broken."

When Talum heard this, his eyes brightened and he said gleefully:

"The gods in heaven have finally given us their permission to begin sowing. Our ancestors learned the method of cultivating millet from the black bears. To show their gratitude to the bears, the ancestors made a rule that only three bears could be killed in a year. This year's millet harvest will walk into our grain bins with as many legs as a centipede. Good! Everyone should now do all the things that they need to do before beginning the sowing. Make sure that you do those things with extra care. We don't want this year's millet to be cursed by the evil spirits. We might be left with no means to survive the winter just because of the laziness of one person. When the weather is good, I will lead everyone out to the fields to start the sowing."

Everyone heaved a sigh of relief. It had been a difficult time, but now, finally they could sow their millet. With it they sowed all their hope and expectations for that year. The adults all talked about how the fact that the centipede bit Asulan might have been a sign given by the gods. For his part, Umas thought that the now dead bug could not have been more stupid for having the nerve to bite a member of the Bunun nation. That's what he was thinking as he walked over to Asulan who was lying in bed groaning in pain from the wound on his leg.

Notes

1. A length of cloth used for carrying an infant.
2. Six to ten years old.
3. Ten to fifteen years old.
4. Fifteen years old until marriage.
5. A sickle.
6. A long, machete-like knife.
7. Dried animal skin.
8. Stake out ownership on a piece of land.
9. Festival for Opening New Land.
10. Traditional Bunun folk songs.
11. Animal snares made of cord.
12. A place name meaning, "the slope where the sun shines first."
13. Master of ceremonies.
14. Pomelo tree.
15. Lizard.
16. Banana.
17. Palm leaves.
18. Useless man! A Bunun curse.
19. A non-poisonous brocade snake.
20. A hundred pace viper.
21. The stone-casting ritual.
22. Dregs from the millet wine.
23. Reeds.
24. Ceremonial plot.
25. An ancient variety of the grain that was taboo for human consumption.
26. Soap wood or sweet locust.
27. Ceremonial wand made from boar skulls.
28. A song in eight part harmony praying for a good millet harvest.
29. A top.
30. Black nightshade.
31. A cry of pain.
32. A centipede.
33. Hudas is a form of address for people of one's grandfather's generation. It must be used before the name of the individual. Aside from expressing

respect, it indicates the generation that the person belongs to is the same as one's grandfather.

34. Shaman.
35. Gall stones from animals.
36. Taiwan black bear.

CHAPTER FOUR

THE SOWING CEREMONY

Talum formally announced the performance of the Lusan-mapinang[1] ceremony. In order to ensure that the work of sowing the millet proceeds smoothly, the people of the village have to finish many tasks associated with daily life before the ceremony begins. Everyone is concerned that if they are unclean in their everyday activities, it will bring ill fortune on the millet crop or cause it to be cursed. So, this is always a time of intense activity in the village.

"Umas, get up! You need to scoop out the ashes in the stove and dump them outside. Remember! Don't let the flame in the right-side stove go out." Banitul pinched the boy's thigh which stuck out from under the covers.

Umas jumped out of bed in pain. He looked outside the window and, seeing that it wasn't yet daylight, he grumbled, "Let me sleep a little more. Subali is getting bigger every day and carrying him is like carrying a big rock around. My shoulders really hurt, and I've got a long black mark from the sling."

Banitul didn't like that his own son was getting into the bad habit of talking back. His expression changed and he blurted out,

"The whole family is busy with all the things that need doing and there's no one else to take care of the ashes, do you want this year's millet to end up dirty and black like the ashes? Would you still want to eat it then?"

Umas knew that the ashes had to be taken from the stove before the sowing of the millet could begin. The ashes have the power to harm the growth of the millet and turn the ears of grain the color of ash. But why did people put ashes on their wounds to help them heal. Why was it that when a hunting dog came down with *wankalavan*[2] ash was used to cleanse and treat the sores? He also remembered clearly how the curious Subali once walked off into the woods by himself and shoved all sorts of flowers into his mouth until he was spitting up foam and starting to lose consciousness. When the adults found out what had happened, they forced the child to drink a lot of ash dissolved in water. That made him vomit up all the multicolored petals. In the end, Subali was left with a mouth full of ash but he was able to open his tear-filled eyes.

"Wood ashes are the same as people, they possess both good and evil spirits, so it depends which powers people want to use. If we can harness the power of the good spirit of the ashes it will bring good fortune. Otherwise, the evil spirit will cause some disaster that leaves the people moaning and weeping." Umas still had a vague, throbbing pain in his thigh. Filled with resentment he thought, Tama is the same, sometimes he's good, other times he's bad.

Malas organized a number of women to start brewing the millet wine required in the ceremony. Before they started, the women carefully reviewed whether their methods were the same as those of the ancestors. The fact was that, aside from ceremonial occasions, there were almost no opportunities to make wine, and for some women it was their first time taking part in the work.

"My lovely ladies, as you sit there under the bright rays of sunshine can you tell me if there are those among you who, since the last millet harvest, have done anything to bring shame upon your souls?" Hudas Halusin asked the assembled women. She was now old, her cheeks sunken.

"Oh?" The question made some of the women uncomfortable, as if a swarm of ants was crawling all over their bodies. Others looked confused, not really sure what was going on.

"What I mean is, in the last while have any of you allowed a man other than your husbands to touch your bodies?" She spoke more directly this time because, for Hudas Halusin, this was a very serious question and it had to be asked clearly.

Brewing wine is a sacred activity. If someone does not have a pure soul the wine that they brew will turn out foul smelling, like their virtue. This brought the displeasure of the host of spirits and would spoil the sowing ceremony about to take place.

"Hee, hee." The women blushed as they looked at each other, then started laughing.

"Venerable lady, our feelings for our husbands are as solid as rock and as pure as the mountain springs. We wouldn't be so foolish as to cast our souls into some filthy, defiled corner." Cina Buni, who had extensive experience in brewing wine and had participated in numberless rituals great and small, informed her elder that the women taking part all possessed virtue as pure as moonlight.

"Hudas Halusin, there aren't that many people in our village, and we all share deep bonds of blood. Nobody would do such a thing." Some thought the old woman's thinking came from someplace very distant from their own.

"It's because of those connections of blood that it is even more important that there be no incestuous entanglements. Our ancestors were once extremely careless about relations between men and women. You could get married to or sleep with anyone, even if it was your sister or niece. That kind of behavior made the gods angry and eventually brought down all manner of natural disasters, destroying the entire village." The old woman recounted the ancient legend by way of admonishing the women.

"What kind of disaster could be so frightful that you don't dare look at it?" The legends were captivating. The age-old stories passed down by the ancestors always aroused deep curiosity.

"Some people had incestuous affairs after being deluded by the evil spirits. Some of them turned into mountain deer, others turned into mountain boars. Many parents lost their sons and daughters and ended up living in silence with only their tears for company. Even worse, in some cases, entire families were set upon by plague demons. Heaven and earth forgot them, and they disappeared from the mountain forests without a trace. Even the strongest magic cannot release people from the curses brought down by incestuous behavior." Hudas Halusin's wrinkled mouth was agitated as she continued to speak:

"Remember, even though it takes the best millet and much experience to produce the sweetest wine, the most important thing is to be pure in your behavior and your mind. The best wine is brewed by those with souls as pure and clean as moonlight."

Usually, when the women heard something new and unusual, they liked to exchange glances and smile, but in this case everyone looked absolutely serious.

"All right. Everyone, first pound the millet using a *nusun*[3] and *husau*[4]. If you've done it before you can do a little more. If you haven't done it before you should use this opportunity to learn." Malas wanted everyone to begin work and get the task out of the way. All adults knew that whatever you start, you can't let it carry over into the next day. That's because unfinished business always finds a way of punishing the lazy with even more work.

"Dong, dong, dong!" The pleasing rhythm of the millet pounding rang. The women busied themselves placing the golden kernels of husked millet in water to soak. Then they put it a *haungu*[5] and boiled it over a large fire. Then they took the cooked millet and laid it in a cool, shady place to dry naturally in the wind. Some of the slightly older women ground *tamul*[6] berries into a powder to use as yeast. Finally, they poured the powder and the wind-dried cooked millet evenly into fermentation pots filled with warm water. If they found that there wasn't enough yeast to make the millet ferment, the women would chew the cooked millet and add it to the large iron pot in order to accelerate the fermentation process. A number of women went to the banks of the stream and brought back thick, heavy mountain taro leaves with which to cover and seal the fermentation pots. The pots looked like big green mother hens quietly sitting on their nests incubating their eggs.

By the middle of the night the air, no longer able to hold the warmth of the sun, roams around bringing a chill in its wake. Every so often Malas got out of bed and went over to check around the fermentation pots. She bent over to sniff the contents of the pots or rub their outsides. After hesitating for a moment, she got a pile of firewood and built a fire around the pots. She wanted to raise the temperature in the pots and speed up the fermentation.

"After two or three days the golden kernels of millet will become sweet-smelling millet wine." Like the scarlet flames, Malas's face glowed with contentment.

The women were the busiest. Not only did they get all the girls who were old enough to work and have them wash all the family's clothing before the ceremony, any clothing that they were weaving had to be finished before the sowing ceremony began. It was taboo to wash clothing during the time of the sowing ceremony. It would mean that, just like washing clothes, the rain would wash all the millet sprouts from the soil, killing them. Any ramie thread in the house that hadn't been woven into cloth would run off to the millet fields and start growing wild, taking over all the space where the millet grew. The ramie would also block the sun's heat from the newly sprouted grain, making it wither and die in its cold shadows.

"Boom, boom, boom!" The sound of something being pounded came from the courtyard. But it wasn't the sound of millet being pounded, it was something thick and hard. Umas followed his curiosity to the courtyard. Subali toddled closely behind on his short, fat little legs. The effort made him pant, blowing big transparent bubbles of mucus from his nose.

"Hudas, are you going to make wine, too?" Umas thought that making wine should be women's work. How could a man be doing that kind of thing?

"Take Subali a little further away. The pestle might hurt him." Talum put down the wooden pestle.

Umas pushed Subali away with his hand then fearlessly poked his head into the wooden mortar for a look. What he saw was a ball of animal skin that had been pounded out of shape.

"Hudas, why did you pound the *sidi to sapa*[7] like that?"

"I am making Subali a man's *sapa*[8]. Of all the men in our family only he doesn't have a fur coat. It is a source of shame for us adults. I have to get it done before the sowing ceremony so that Subali will look strong and impressive in his fur coat at all future ceremonies and rituals." Talum turned the skin in the mortar over, then raised the pestle to continue pounding.

"How did the peanuts get in there?" Umas noticed that there were bits of peanut covering the animal skin.

"The oil in the peanuts softens the tough dried goat skin. That way it's easier to work with and much more comfortable to wear....Millet dregs have a similarly power." Talum pulled the softened mountain goat skin from the mortar and placed it on a *siam*[9] on the ground. Then he started treading it with his feet.

"Hudas, why don't you just keep pounding it with the pestle? Isn't it much harder using your feet?" The purple veins on his feet bulged as Talum worked the skin hard. That made Umas feel badly and he suggested an easier method.

"When the peanut oil softens the skin enough it makes it easy for the heavy pestle to damage it. If you make holes in the skin, you can't use if for clothing, just like a tree trunk that a woodpecker has pecked holes in is no good for making the posts and beams of a house. Do you want Subali to wear a fur coat with holes in it? Would you be happy if others laughed at him? My child, you must always remember one thing, the black cloud of shame covers more than one person, it covers the whole clan. If you want to establish a clan that others respect, every member must take great care to make sure that everything they do is perfect."

"Where did Tama go? I haven't seen his face all day." After listening to the old man, Umas became quite excited. He immediately thought of his Tama and how he could establish a respected clan.

"He took some men with him to go into the mountains to catch rats."

"What? To catch rats?" The tone of his voice rose at this surprising thought. Umas was a little disappointed. His Tama, who usually garnered a lot of respect, was off catching little animals that children catch.

"The wine that the women are making is already giving off its nice aroma. The time for the sowing ceremony is almost here. We have to prepare a banquet of fine food and wine to show our gratitude to the people who came to help us. We know what makes people happy. It's the way that you treat friends and it's also what makes the gods happy. In the future it should bring us plenty good fortune."

"It's not hard to catch rats. I've caught lots of rats using a *hatup*.[10] You once told me that even the strongest and smartest rats could never escape my rat traps. You also said that I was sure to become an outstanding Bunun hunter."

Umas would always remember that evening. It was an evening when he was closest to the host of spirits. He had spent an entire day alone in the forest surrounding the village. The ancient mountain range rolled towards him in waves from some distant world, just like green breakers on an ocean that came to rest just by the village; an ocean of rocky cliffs and dense forest. Umas was exhilarated by the scenery, as if he had discovered some secret that he had searched after for many years. Anyone who understands the forest knows that any territory full of boulders and rock is where rats most like to live. Tiny, narrow *dan-aluwath*[11] worn hard and shiny, often appear under the boulders. Umas could tell which trails were old, disused ones, and which were newly established.

Umas set up his slate slab traps close to a number of well-used rat trails. These traps would crush a rat to death. He used a large "Y" shaped tree branch, and a few small pieces of wood to hold up a flat slab of slate. Then he used a piece of yam for bait. After completing the trap he carefully covered his own footprints with dirt or dried leaves that he found nearby. That way the clever prey would not be frightened away because they would not discover that a human had entered their territory. By the end of the day, Umas had set up almost twenty slate slab rat traps.

On the evening of the third day, he ran as fast as he could back to the area of rocks and boulders to check on the traps. With the blessing of the gods he found that twelve of the traps had captured prey. He strung the big fat rats together in a string with tough *valu,*[12] then ran back to the village feeling excited and proud.

In the forest after dark it is as if the heavenly gods have issued an order for all things of creation to don a cloak of black. Even familiar paths can't be distinguished in the darkness. Feeling disquieted, Umas walked along the small trail shaded by trees. Disturbed by the sound of his footsteps many unseen birds called out, bringing the entire mountainside to life. Occasionally a crisp, gentle bird call made Umas look in the direction of the sound in curiosity. Other sounds, deep and mysterious, startled him and made him quicken his steps until he was hurtling along. Sometimes one foot would brush the other, almost making him trip.

When he finally ran through the front door of his house, his exaggerated puffing and panting drew his family members into a circle around him. They thought that something must have happened and were just wondering how serious it was.

"Umas, what happened?" "Did you do something wrong?" Banitul and Malas spoke as if with the same mouth.

"I went up the mountain to check on the rat traps that I made, and I caught twelve rats." Umas raised the rats strung together with kudzu vine, but the weight of the prey made him lower his hand quickly.

"They're really big, they're really big!" Subali cried out haltingly as he ran forward.

The rats in the rocky area are relatively large members of the *aluwath-tuhlas* family.[13] The fact that it was the season when all kinds of fruits were ripening, meant that those rats were especially big and fat.

"To kill such big rats, you'd have to use really large slabs of slate. Only an adult has the strength to could handle slate that size. Umas, you must already have the strength of an adult." As he looked at his son's prize, Banitul made exaggerated gestures in the air to show how big the slabs must have been. He looked as pleased is when he first shot a mountain boar by himself.

"Banitul, our child has grown up." Malas turned happily to look at her husband. If a family member has special survival skills, it means that life is that much more secure. That is the law of life in the mountains.

"You like going into the mountains, that's a great habit to have because being able to move around the mountain forests by yourself is how you start to become a Bunun hunter. By becoming intimate with the mountain forests, you unconsciously gain a sense of the forms and locations of the mountain peaks, as well as the size and direction of the streams in the mountain gorges. You will also be able to tell the location and track the movements of all the different kinds of animals just by looking at the forest itself. That is all part of the wisdom and courage that it takes to traverse the vast mountain slopes." Talum spoke earnestly as he took the rats from Umas' hand.

"All I did was set traps to catch rats in the rocky area of the nearby forest." Umas had never gone so deep into the forest before and he didn't know what it was really like. So, he didn't understand what the old man was saying.

"Come, my child. Sit here beside me." The old man gave Umas' small hand genial a tug.

"If you want to become a great hunter you have to approach nature with humility and a spirit of learning. It's just like getting to know your smartest friend. Before you can do battle with your prey you have to first learn how to understand the language of the trees, the voices of the streams and the hints given by the wind. Then you have to take their advice with an open mind. The wisdom that it takes to defeat your prey is held in what they tell you." Talum fixed his eye on Umas, as if he was determined that the boy should understand what he was trying to say.

"Uh-huh!" Umas nodded his head seriously.

"Hunting isn't a game, it's a sacred ritual of survival. If you don't have a reverent mind and the assistance of the gods, the animals will refuse to die for you."

Umas didn't fully understand the point of what Hudas was saying. But he was sure that when he entered the world of adults, with the guidance of his people and with life experience, he would come to understand. More than that, he would follow the laws of nature that his people had placed their trust in for thousands of years. The skills needed to continue living were found deep inside nature.

Umas was clearly very pleased with the praise of the adults. It made him think that not far in the future he would become a great hunter. Having been shown respect by his family and the villagers he grew excited. The fright of the forest trail had long since been cast into the blackest of the black mountain gorges, leaving no impression on him at all.

"Before we start the sowing, we must give a banquet of rat meat. That's why your Tama invited a few other adults to go into the mountains to catch rats. By working together, you can get even the heaviest, most tedious work done quickly." The old man's words brought Umas back to present reality.

"Are we having guests over tomorrow? How many people are you inviting?" In the days before the sowing began the simple, poor food that people prepared out of respect for the traditional taboos meant that the children forfeited much of their accustomed pleasure. Umas assumed that if they were going to have a banquet, it would be a day of good fortune for his tongue and his stomach.

"All of them. So long as they live in the village or know that we are having a feast, they can all come. Since ancient times there has been a mysterious and invisible cord that binds all the people in the village tightly together. For that reason, all things in the village are undertaken as communal activities, whether it be farming, weddings and funerals, hunting or rituals...all are done as a group. For example, when there is farm labor to be done, every family sends one person to take part in a given family's work party. Afterwards, they go to the next family and continue working. That way there is a rotation and circulation until every family has finished their farming work. It's called *Kiuthu*.[14] It is an orderly, efficient work system. It is also the most precious wisdom for survival passed down to us by our ancestors."

"Everyone in the village? That's a lot of people for a banquet." Umas thought of the delicious food, but a sense of regret drifted into his mind.

"The ancestors told us: "Other people all start by being brothers." All people begin from the same ancestors. There are deep ties of blood between all people. That sense of family is eternal. It is the everlasting reality of the world. Umas, having lots of brothers is a good thing. For example, they may decide to first help us plant our millet, then afterwards it will be our turn to help them. With such humble, friendly brothers doesn't it just make sense that we would want to share a delicious meal with them?" Out of habit, Talum rubbed the child's head.

"Umas, you must always remember, there are no outsiders in our village. There are only brothers and sisters." As the adults patted him with their heavy hands, Umas could only keep nodding his head.

At the break of dawn, the first cock's crow broke the tranquility of the valley. In their expansive houses everyone was carefully trying to awaken the sleeping children beside them. Gently and carefully, they helped their children into their most beautiful and warmest traditional clothing under the light of the moon and the flickering glow of pinewood sticks.

Umas could see Subali in the darkness trying to suppress his fear of the dark while Cina turned him first left then right as she dressed him. With practiced skill Umas donned his mountain goat skin clothing. It was the skin of a mountain ram that Tama had personally shot the last time out with the village hunting party.

Adjusting the fur robes to make them more comfortable, Umas walked out of the house to wait for the arrival of daylight. Perhaps Old Father Heaven knew what an important day it was because it seemed as though it was becoming lighter earlier than in the past few days. The outline of the mountains opposite the village was perfectly clear. They had a faint glow following along the line of their summits. Still deep in slumber, the sky was completely empty save for a few lively stars. Then, ever so slowly, as if dyed in the deep pool at the bend of the great river, the sky turned blue; a deep, distant blue.

The first rays of sunlight shone from the distance and fell first upon the mountain peaks closest to the sky. From so far away it looked like a shining spirit. Then suddenly, that ray of sunlight cascaded like a waterfall from the top of the mountains down into the bottom of the valley. On the mountain slopes thousands of drops of morning dew that had been sleeping on the leaves of the trees instantly shot forth dazzling multicolored radiance that blinded Umas.

Talum and Malas scurried around inside and outside of the house cleaning and sweeping. For Umas, this brought endless delight. It was the most beautiful day of all because so long as he could remember, it had always been him standing there in the courtyard with a broom in his hand welcoming the dawn's first ray of sunlight.

Malas was busy in the kitchen knocking the soot from the *tapa*[15] and cleaning the thick ashes from the wall. Banitul had climbed up on the roof to clear away the dust and debris that had accumulated there.

"Umas, gather all the dust and refuse into a pile then take it and dump it on the roots of the big tree near the yard, okay?" Banitul moved carefully around the roof like a monkey. The people all believe that when the millet arrives in the fields its life spirit is completely reliant on the owner of the field, and its fate will follow that of the owner. If the owner lives a clean and orderly life, then the millet will also live in a clean and orderly environment. Because of the owner's unblemished actions, all the weeds, vines and other unclean things will naturally disappear.

"Hu! My people, those of you who are going forth to my field to help with the planting of the millet! With a reverent heart I call to invite you to my humble house. We are going to worship the great spirits together." The resonant sounds of the summons rose from the peaceful village. The calls were loud enough to set the light of dawn now covering the land trembling.

Umas looked urgently into the courtyard and saw Talum in his *tamun-haipi*[16] sewn from mountain goat skin. There was a pair of mountain goat horns standing in the middle of the headdress, giving a it an impressive, martial air. He wore a crisp, pure white *hapan*,[17] and under it a single skirt that revealed his strong, thick legs; legs that belonged to a man who knew how to traverse the mountain peaks and ridges.

The plangent sound of Talum's voice gave all the houses a start. Soon, all the villagers, resplendent in their ritual clothing and looking clean and radiant, were striding gracefully towards Talum's courtyard.

"My friends, you all look wonderful." Holding Subali by the hand, Umas squatted in a corner under the eaves gazing with rapt attention at the ever-increasing throng of villagers. Subali's mouth hung open as he intently followed his brother's line of sight.

What most attracted Umas' eye was the costume of Hudas Bisazu, the shaman who had the ability to cure people's illnesses. His long robe made from mountain deer skin, his *tavi*[18] sewn from mountain goat skin, and his shoes all emanated a rich cream-color that spoke of his advanced years and esteemed position.

"Hudas Bisazu looks like an animal that can walk on two legs." Umas turned and spoke to Subali who shook nervously from side to side thinking that something had happened.

As the master of ceremony for this year's sowing ritual, Talum stood before the assembled crowd. He grabbed a handful of millet kernels from a gourd container and threw it as hard as he could toward the highest point of the roof. Then he pronounced in a loud voice:

"Hupikaunan![19] Today we call all our guests to a feast and to drink the very finest millet wine with us. Please allow the millet that we sow this year to come to life! Please allow our food to increase! Please allow all of our crops to grow a little larger. May the yams, taro and beans that we plant in our field live healthy lives because of the ritual feast that we provide today!"

All those participating in the ceremony came forward in order and took a handful of millet from the master of ceremony's gourd. They then cast the grain towards the roof of the house while repeating invocations praying for the peaceful growth of their crops. As the grain on the rooftop grew deeper and deeper the roof began to look like a huge ear of millet.

After the millet-scattering ritual was completed the people in full costume quietly followed the master of ceremony into a corner of the courtyard. There they gathered into a tight circle which symbolized that they would circle around to protect the fields where the millet was to be planted this year. They pressed together so tightly that they looked like a silent swarm of ants.

A rather plump woman with long thick hair falling over her shoulders raised a wooden bowl filled with *bin-sah*[20] with her left hand. In her right hand she held a *hainis*[21] full of millet wine. As she walked forward with solemn steps three men with red cloth tied around their heads and carrying hoes pushed directly into the center of the circle. They started hoeing the ground, breaking clods into fine, soft soil. Master of Ceremonies, Talum, took the millet seed from the plump woman's hand and sprinkled it over the broken-up soil. Taking two *tahnas* stocks,[22] he stuck them into the center of the patch of earth and then intoned:

"Hupikaunan! Oh, Millet! Please come to live in our fields that you may grow as tall and lush as the red silvergrass!"

The woman poured all the millet wine over the red silvergrass and raised her voice in an excited prayer:

"Hu! Oh, Millet! You are so blessed with good fortune! You come here as the guest of such an honest family. The head of this household will serve you with warm hospitality, just as the head of this household will shed the most sweat to ensure that you grow quickly. Oh, Millet! May your grain grow as firm and abundant as the fruit of the *balishin*.[23] Each and every grain must be as clean and beautiful as spring water. Hu! Hu! Hu!"

All those taking part in the ritual joined in to repeat, "Hu! Hu! Hu!" solemnly in unison. The sound of their voices flew over the undulating mountain slopes and entered the broad mountain forest.

Banitul and Malas each carried large wooden platters filled with pealed taro and roasted mountain rats. After the steaming platters were placed on the edge of the symbolic field, Banitul announced:

"Beloved friends, we thank you for coming to help us. Those who are able to labor in the fields are few in number and we are a lowly family, so we must rely upon all of you. Our taro does not grow as fat and fragrant as other families. When you take out their dry, hard bones, I don't know what will be left to eat of the rats that we have caught. All we can do is offer our warmest gratitude to make up for the shame of such a poor feast."

Everyone took a piece of taro and a roast mountain rat and ate as they stood around the small patch of field. The amount of taro and the number of rats was exactly right for the number of people who were in attendance. That was something that could be traced to Banitul and Malas's diligence in preparing for the feast. It would have been in violation of a very strict taboo if the numbers had not matched. People believe that any excess food belongs to the evil spirits who remain after they eat to join in the ploughing. But these days of "dancing" with the evil spirits always end up very badly. It was even more taboo for the food to be insufficient, because the ancestors abandon those who do not receive food. Even if those people do their utmost to help with the work, the sweat that they shed will not help the millet to grow. It is as if they had never left their footprints on the fields in the first place.

After the food had been evenly distributed, when Talum signalled with a nod of his head, everyone blessed each other:

"May we again enjoy this wonderful food when the next sowing festival comes."

The people also prayed that in the long days of hard work ahead, none of them would be injured or meet with anything that made them weep or grow angry.

Like a mischievous Bunun child, the sun poured its scalding hot rays over the land. The dazzling white sunlight stabbed at the eyes. In the surrounding forest the air was set ablaze, sending out heat waves that made the trees look ragged and unsteady.

Along with some of the other women, Malas formed a line. With their right hands they took handfuls of millet seed from the woven basket at their waists then cast the seed out in a semicircular motion. They weren't showing ritual praise for the gods, but rather trying to ensure that the millet seed fell evenly on every inch of ground. The men followed closely behind turning the soil with their hoes to bury the seed. It was as if there was a competition to see if more beads of sweat or more grains of millet fell on the soil. In the meantime, the children had all taken shelter under the shade of the trees where they watched the adults under the torrid sun appear then disappear behind clouds of dust.

After a few suns, the people were able to complete the year's sowing. With everyone's diligent, quick work, what had been nothing but a wasteland covered with weeds and brush had been transformed into the location of all hope for the future. The level, stately field with its soft, fine soil gave the people an intense feeling of release. They had confronted their anxiety about the future and overcome it. Now they could heave a sigh of relief.

When the sowing was completed, Talum called on the people to assemble around the ritual plot where they earlier had stuck a number of reeds. Lowering their heads, they stood in silence. Talum then used *paiail*[24] to wrap up the *painu*,[25] *sipus*,[26] *bunbun*,[27] *chiau*,[28] *hasila*,[29] and *kakalan*[30] in separate bundles. These he hung on the long-since dried out reeds. Waving his boar bone ritual wand in the air to make a rattling sound, he reverently prayed:

> Oh, Ancestors!
> We respectfully place all our food before you,
> This food is as pure and clean as the deepest heavens.
> We pray that you will bestow the loveliest millet upon us,
> Just as we now offer you this food.
> Oh, Millet! May you grow as dense and healthy as
>   mountain boar hair.

After we have carried you into our granaries, we will kill a boar for you to eat!

Talum led the people in single file around the field that they had just finished planting, leaving behind a hard, smooth path. The people all believed that this path created by the power of their spirits would defend against the evil spirits of snakes, rats, and harmful birds who could damage the millet. The millet could then grow peacefully and rapidly under the protection of the peoples' spirits.

That night, as Umas and his family sat around the earthenware pot eating dinner, Umas noticed that the grains of millet in the wooden spoon appeared to have changed into the beads of sweat that had been shed in the fields by the elders. He quickly cupped his hand under the spoon fearing that the sweat in the spoon would fall to the ground. Then he carefully put the millet in his mouth and quietly savored the sweet flavor filling his mouth.

NOTES

1. The Sowing Ceremony. This rite is primarily intended to announce to the gods that the sowing of crops is about to commence.
2. Skin disease.
3. A *nusun* is a wooden mortar.
4. A *husau* a wooden pestle.
5. A wooden cooking pot.
6. A wild plant.
7. Dried mountain goat skin.
8. Coat made from animal skin.
9. A mat woven from moon peach stalks.
10. A pit trap made from stones.
11. An animal trail, in this case, a rat trail.
12. Kudzu vine.
13. White-bellied mountain rats.
14. Rotating work system.
15. A frame located about the stove for placing food and other miscellaneous items.
16. Battle headdress made of animal skin.
17. Traditional Bunun man's robe.
18. Leggings to protect the calves.
19. A summons calling the gods near.
20. Millet seed.
21. A ladle made from a gourd.
22. Miscanthus or silvergrass, which resembles pampas grass.
23. Chinese honey locust tree.
24. "Grandfather's sister taro" or night-scented lily leaves.
25. Peanuts.
26. Sugar cane.
27. Bananas.
28. Stream fish.
29. Rock salt.
30. Crab.

CHAPTER FIVE

THE BIRD-CHASING SEASON

The weather had turned extremely hot and humid. The mountain wind was like an old man breathing his final breath after a long illness. It didn't even have the strength to blow away the frivolous mountain mists, leaving them to linger at mid-slope. Then, as if something had suddenly come into its head, the wind started careening around, bringing a dramatic, foreboding look to the sky until finally it allowed the rain that the people had longed for to fall.

In all of heaven and earth there is no more amazing spirit than the rain. It brings a feeling of happiness and good fortune. Umas squatted in the hallway watching the changes going on outside. Initially, the majestic cloud formations were not very generous. They brought very little rain. Only thin sheets of drizzle fell from the listless sky. A few remote flashes were the only light in a grey world. But in the end, the layers of cloud could hold back no longer, and the smell of rain mixed with dust blew in from the distance. The unique aroma brushed over the tips of the trees on the mountain wind, absorbing the fragrance of wild plants and turning the forest cool and pleasant.

Umas watched the rain bring the dry courtyard back to life again. Raindrops fell to the ground, whispering a language of drips and splashes. When they poured over the low courtyard walls, they seeped down through the crevices to wash over the plants at the wall's base, bringing a moist emerald sheen to their leaves. Small rivulets appeared all over the courtyard carrying foam on their surface. They seemed to be in high spirits as they bounded and gurgled down familiar channels and out past the walls. From there they entered the depths of the forest, speaking in soft voices. Umas looked into the distance and found that the colors of the mountains were changing. The pallid soil that had once covered them, wind-blown and dried by the sun, was now turning the dark brown hue of mud, and it grew darker with each drop of moisture that fell. After the rain passed, the flowers and trees were greener. It was as if the spirit of the rain had dressed the world in bright new robes.

Umas walked out of the house and stood in the courtyard. He turned his face skywards and let the rain splash over his face. The fine streams of rainwater ran down his neck until his clothing was soaked and stuck to his dry skin, pleasantly chilling him to the bone.

"Umas, why are you bringing the rainwater inside?"

Talum and Banitul were sitting in the living room. Using both hands, they were rolling two or three strands of ramie fibre together on their strong thighs. Once they finished rolling the strands into a length of sturdy cord, they gave it a light pull and let fall slowly onto the steadily growing pile of cord on the ground.

"You want to be and adult, but you still have the heart of a child who likes to play with water. Come here! Arrange the cord that we have rolled." Banitul spat into the palm of his hand as he complained good-naturedly.

After you have rolled ramie cord for a long time, the palms of your hand take on a mottled red texture. The men had very thick knuckles, and their short, hairless fingers looked like they had been cursed and turned into wind-dried tree roots. It was the result of spending years traipsing around the mountain forests trying to eke out a living. Since ancient times, all things that live in the forest must change their forms to adapt to the difficult realities of life there.

"What are you going to do with so much cord?" Umas was searching the big pile of cord for its fiendishly difficult-to-find end.

"The millet has already started to form heads and droop over. Lots of monkeys, squirrels and rats are getting busy in the fields. The worst are the big flocks of *tulpin*.[1] They're the most industrious thieves. They work day and night to steal our millet. They not only drink our sweat dry, they steal our future, it's very annoying. So starting tomorrow we are going to perform the Pusbaihazam[2] ritual. We hope that our mature souls can prevent those diabolical animals from continuing to steal our food." Talum bowed his head and continued rolling the cord.

"How do mature souls let the gods know?" Umas knew that the soul was a highly intimate self that constantly controlled a person's joy, anger, and sadness. But a soul was like the air and had no color or smell. It made no trace or shadow, almost as if it never existed. This kind of thing confused Umas.

"We must maintain the traditional way of life and the teachings of the ancestors! Through the observance of strict taboos and the performance of many rituals the ancestors ensured that the gods were pleased. That is how they lived for many, many happy years. The ancestors have told us that in the time of the bird-chasing ceremony everyone must live more simply and work harder. Eating yams and meat is forbidden because those foods increase our appetites, making us gluttonous. It makes us like the harmful birds who devastate our fields. Being gluttonous leads to the habit of being wasteful with food, and that means that we won't have surplus food to store up." Talum looked wearily at the ramie cord in his hand and, seeing that it was finished, shook his hands from side to side.

Umas knew that when you live in the mountain forest the traditional rituals, great and small, formed a great circle, like two rainbows joined together. He had forgotten how many ritual cycles he had lived through, but the simple, poor food that people ate during festival times had left a deep impression on him. It was a custom that you had to get used to, just like the *dala*[3] that had to respect the changing of the seasons. Sometimes its green leaves turn red, then yellow, then fall to the ground. Only after all that can it begin to renew its greenery and start life again.

"During the bird-chasing festival time men and women cannot be too intimate, especially during the darkness of nighttime. That amounts to saying that husbands and wives are not allowed to be intimate at all. The ancestors have told us that if the harmful birds imitate us and have intimate behavior, their numbers will continually increase, and their ability to damage the millet crop will become as great as a *balivus*[4] which we will have no way of fending off."

When he thought of the intimacy of men and women Umas remembered what the old men of the village said. When a man and a woman live together it is called *mapadangi*.[5] It means adding or placing things together. It seemed that the harmful birds also knew how to place things together in secret. As much as Umas wanted to avoid this issue, he could not.

"For the next few days it is best to keep the main door to the house closed so as not to let friends and neighbors enter." Banitul didn't speak until he had finished the work at hand. Perhaps his cord making skills weren't yet good enough to allow him distractions.

"What if, for some reason, my friends need to see me? Or what if people come to offer their help?" When the main gate is closed, the sun is shut outside and people can get very unhappy sitting inside their pitch black rooms. Besides which, the villagers weren't brave enough to knock on other people's doors uninvited, so Umas was afraid that if his friends saw the door closed, they wouldn't come and ask him out to play. Then his life would be as devoid of activity and fun as stagnant water.

Banitul said, "During the bird-chasing festival, in all things that we do, we have to keep the millet in the fields in mind. If we let outsiders in our front doors whenever they please, all the harmful birds will come and go from our fields whenever they please. If that happens, they'll end up eating all of the millet and we'd have nothing left to harvest. From now on, we have to link our spirits to the spirits of the millet. That is the essence of respectful behavior, and it is only with respectful behavior that all of our heart's desires can be fulfilled."

"What are you going to do with so much cord?" Umas had finally managed to sort out the jumbled cord and wind it into a neat ball.

"Umas, tomorrow you and Tama Husung's son, Asulan, are going to the fields to take part in the bird-chasing ceremony with Hudas. Remember! You have to listen to what Hudas says if you want to defeat the birds. Otherwise they will use their light, nimble wings to humiliate you." Banitul bent down to pick up the bits of cord remaining on the ground.

"You're not going, Tama?"

"I'm going to the top of the mountain with Tama Husung to weed the taro field there. I once heard someone say, 'If bad business grows wings it comes easily and fast.' At the time, I didn't think much of it, but now I know that it's very true. All you can see now is weeds growing as tall and free as they please. They are pushing out the taro that we planted. If we don't go and help the taro out of its difficulties now, we won't have any taro to harvest."

Umas had inherited his family's traditional character. He now had over ten years of life experience, and his strength and ambition had grown. The spirit of industriousness planted deep in his soul had sprouted leaves and flourished. So, when he heard that he was going to the fields to take part in production activities shoulder to shoulder with his family, Umas could hardly wait for the next day to come.

"Hu! Our child got up really early this morning." It was dusk, and when Talum saw the determined expression on Umas's face he smiled with satisfaction.

"Hudas, Tama, Mihumisan!⁶" Full of energy, Umas greeted his elders in the kitchen.

"True men have to keep a distance from their beds." Banitul was squatting on the ground, busily packing the things needed from the bird-chasing ceremony in a *davath*.⁷

"That's right. The day doesn't really start until your feet hit the ground."

"Isn't Asulan going with us?" Umasi looked around as he grew more animated.

"Husung, what's with your son? Is he up yet?" Talum called his second son and asked him about his son.

After a bit of commotion, Asulan walked in stiffly, his black hair looking like a patch of weeds. His long locks hung over his neck and streaks of sleep glinted in the corners of both eyes. A ramie robe that was too big for him hung over his shoulders, swinging back and forth as at will. He was a little younger than Umas and he was a little smaller, but he had an especially large abdomen that bulged out confidently. What most caught people's attention were that small scars that ringed his naked calf. They glowed like stars in the sky. Umas knew that these were the scars left by the centipede.

"Hudas, I'm up." His voice was weak, as if he was speaking from somewhere deep in a dream.

"The bed is a dirty pool of stagnant water. Those who love their sleep are like dead leaves that have fallen there. They rot quickly." Talum looked up at his drowsy grandson. Having been reprimanded, Asulan quickly wiped the sleep from his eyes hoping to wake himself up, but he only managed to wipe the sleep into one big patch.

"The main thing is that you're up. Asulan, you are a hardworking, brave child. Quickly! Jump up and down to get yourself going. In a minute we're going up the mountain." Even though Banitul didn't like laziness, when he saw how hard put upon Asulan looked, his tone quickly softened and he tried to comfort the boy.

It was pitch black outside save for a few energetic stars that sparkled through the breaks in the clouds. Nature was cloaked in heavy slumber. Everything was still. A layer of mist floated in the air and the surrounding wilds look blurred and indistinct. It made them all feel a chill.

Before they began to file up the mountain, the hunting dogs under the eaves grew excited, sensing something was afoot. Some stood up on their hind legs while others jumped and twirled around, expecting to be taken along. But as soon as Talum scolded them they put their tails between their legs and gave him a beseeching look, as if they understood perfectly well what he meant. Some even ran to the edge of the eaves and howled sadly out of disappointment.

Out in the wilds, hunting dogs love to run back and forth. They aren't steady spirits. Although they don't eat the millet, Talum felt that it was best not to have both the harmful birds and the hunting dogs around the fields at the same time. From the point of view of the millet, their combined powers could add up to a major disaster.

The millet field was located in Itasipal. Itasipal refers to the mountains facing opposite. Therefore, after they left the village, Talum, Umas and Asulan had first to enter a dense forest and snake their way down the mountain slope. Once they arrived at the bottom of the gorge that had been scoured out by the stream, they had to start climbing their way up the mountain slope opposite the village.

With a practiced hand, Talum fashioned a torch by binding dozens of reeds together. Led by the blazing light, Umas and Asulan followed the old man's steps along the dark mountain trail.

The light was very faint as they walked along, so none of them could make out the surrounding scenery. They could hear only the sound of their own voices. Asulan didn't like the gloomy darkness of the forest. He had the feeling that he was being forced to walk towards some unknown place by a malicious stranger. The stress made him extremely anxious. The dark dense forest was like a monster that surrounded him and could wrest his life from him at any moment.

As they went further into the depths of the forest, they found the grass on either side of the trail heavily laden with thick dew. The grass was stiff, having lost the softness that grass normally has. They had to keep their calves straight as they forged through the clumps of grass. The chilly drops of dew chased away their sleepiness, but it also soaked their trousers, making them heavier. That meant that it required more and more effort to walk.

The heavy weight bearing down upon their spirits and bodies made the two boys walk more slowly. Their heavy steps echoed chaotically around the mountains, sounding like a multitude of spirits hiding in the darkness and calling to the travellers.

"Hudas! Hudas!" Asulan had fallen behind and he called out.

Talum stopped in his tracks, turned and held the torch to look behind him. This illuminated the trail, giving it a reddish hue. Umas and Asulan took advantage of the rare light to forge ahead more quickly. In Asulan's case, he walked so quickly that he could hardly keep his balance.

"I'm tired." The boys gasped for breath.

"When you get fatigued, you must first check to see if you can still raise your thighs." Talum waited until the children had gained their balance then continued to march on at a slightly slower pace so that Asulan could keep up more comfortably.

The trees started to stand a little further from them and their trunks didn't appear to be as thick and proud as they had. The faint light of dawn had begun to penetrate the leaves, gradually making the trail before them more distinct. As they got closer to the bottom of the gorge many strangely shaped mountain streams hung down from the sheer walls. They tumbled over the rocks making burbling sounds that echoed in all directions, sometimes alternating, at others layering on top of each other.

The mountain wind had begun to stir in the tops of the trees and patches of the bright sky appeared through the spaces between the leaves. Talum thrust the torch into a small pool in the stream. It hissed as the flames were extinguished.

It wasn't until they arrived on the floor of the gorge that Umas realized how broad and majestic the river was. The sounds of water crashing over the rocks coming from the bottom of the river combined with and the rushing water that bubbled like steam in the bottom of a hot pan. This moved Umas in a way that was hard to describe. Ashuli stood dumbly beside the river bed with his mouth hanging open and his belly thrust forward.

"Boys, don't look at it any more. The power of the flowing water will make you dizzy and dazzle your eyes. It will weaken you and then you won't be able to climb the steep road up the mountain slope." Talum was seated on a huge rock that looked like someone had deliberately shaved it flat.

The boys climbed up on the rock with him and let the cool, kindly mountain breeze blow away the sweat that ran down their backs. Talum took some dry, sooty black roast yams from his mesh bag. As Umas and Ashuli munched away they could see the golden rays of sunlight wash over the enchanted mountainscape.

"Hudas, it's the same mountain, so why does it look completely different here than what you can see from the village?" Umas often looked off to the distant mountains from their courtyard, but now, looking up from the riverbed, the mountains he could see were beautiful, yet unfamiliar.

"Although nobody can really understand the true nature of the life spirits of the mountain forests, we can at least start to understand by getting closer to them." Talum looked up at the great summit thrusting into the heart of the sky.

"The mountain forests possess the most benevolent, all-embracing spirits in all of nature. They accept all those who wish to draw near to them. Even more, they willingly share all of their benefits with us. When we enter the forests, we are like infants resting in our Cina's arms, freely and easily drinking the milk of life. You see, the mountain forests are as big-hearted as they are vast." The old man gestured toward the tallest peak that lay before them.

The mountain forests are endowed with mystical powers beyond human wisdom. Talum had once been totally infatuated with that mystical power. From his youth until he grew old he had always made his life there, searching, and pursuing. Yet that power seemed inexhaustible, and ultimately, he could only exchange his infatuation for undying respect.

"The forest really is beautiful! Depending on whether you are close or at a distance, its beauty is never the same. Yet, although the forms of its beauty differ, it always brings your soul great joy and fills your entire body with uncanny strength." Umas jumped to his feet, full of enthusiasm. His tried to contain himself as his eyes swept over their surroundings.

"Not only is the forest beautiful, it is the divine spirit that our ancestors have relied upon for eons. From the beginning of time, the forest generously supplied them with all that they required. Day after day, it never ceased its largess. For countless generations the ancestors were guided by the principles of "sufficiency" and "honesty" as they took what they needed that day and left the remainder for the next day, the day after, and for their fellows. My children! You must constantly be near to the forest in order to understand how important it is. Remember! You must always enter the forest in the spirit of beseeching reverence. You should never enter with the intentions of a thief. This is the attitude with which Bunun people treat their friends."

Talum led the boys towards the upper reaches of the river. When they arrived at the narrowest point of the river they found a few dozen large bamboos bound firmly together with rattan to form a bridge that rose at an angle from a low point on the near bank towards a point on the rocks higher up the opposite bank. Talum leaned forward and bent his knees as he stepped carefully along the bamboo bridge upwards and across the river. Umas and Asulan imitated the old man and climbed onto the bridge, but as soon as it started to sway, they both quickly knelt down and held tightly onto the face of the bridge. They looked like a couple of drunken monkeys precariously climbing out on a branch that reached into empty space.

The trail that led toward the field snaked its way up and down the mountain slopes. Sometimes the trail was cloaked in shade, at other times it was bathed in sunlight. The streams that gradually sank through the fissures in the earth reflected up sparkling ripples of light like rivers of stars falling to earth.

They continued to climb ever forward until suddenly a series of level, newly established fields appeared before their eyes. By then, they were all puffing out billows of white steam in the cold high mountain air. Droplets of dew hung from the bare branches of the low shrubs beside the road and constantly dripped to the ground. The morning sun had slowly grown to a torrid blaze and had melted away the last stubborn traces of night.

The nearby slopes had mostly been formed by loose shale. Below the trail, fragments of fallen shale formed a long scree embankment that fell all the way down to the forest in the river gorge. A few huge boulders were for some unknown reason stuck very prominently in the slope. The twisted trunks of high mountain trees grew upward along the embankments looking as though they were formed by currents of alpine wind. Red-hairy azaleas grew in long rows on the edges of the shale slopes. The rains that year had been abundant, and the azaleas had brushed their patches of red over the hard scree earlier than usual.

The gradient of the mountain trail was no longer as steep as it had been and the wild lilies, now in full bloom, soon flashed into view. Their pristine white mouths seemed to be smiling to welcome the visitors from afar. There were also lovely small wildflowers growing in happy profusion by the path and in the narrow cracks between the stones. Their scent combined with the fragrance of the wild lilies to fill the air to the point of being slightly cloying. It was intoxicating, like the aroma of strong wine.

"We're here! We've arrived at our field." Talum turned and saw that the boys had fallen the length of six mature hundred pace vipers behind.

Umas and Asulan were looking over the golden field with awe. When had the lush, abundant crop of millet filled the once-bare field? It grew as straight as a writing brush. The roots visible above the ground were hard and thick, while the long, fat leaves had sprouted so densely you couldn't see the brown soil below. Under the direction of the mountain wind, the millet stalks happily played a game of slapping back and forth. The full, sturdy ears of grain forced the delicate tips of the stalks to bow at the waist like humble, decorous elders. The adults must have shed a lot of sweat to get the millet to grow this strong and healthy. Umas surveyed the impressive field with contentment.

"Umas, you go over to the work shed for a rest now and let the wind blow away your sweat and fatigue. There are still many things on the field waiting for our attention." Talum always stressed to the younger generation: today's tasks must be completed before darkness falls because otherwise those things will bind our feet like unruly rattan, preventing us from walking towards tomorrow.

The *taluhan*[8] was situated at the very top of the field. In order that maximum light could enter the shed, the front entrance was designed with no door. The roof was made from piles of sogon grass gathered from the local area, while the walls were constructed of reed stalks. Inside, aside from a long sleeping platform on which people could rest, there was only a small open space where simple tools could be kept. The stone cooking stove was located outside so that the thick smoke from the fire would not get into people's eyes. Many people slept over in the work shed during the sowing and harvest seasons so as to speed up the process of sowing and increase the amount of work they got done. But most of the time, this warm, safe shed was home to the nests of mountain birds and small animals.

As it slowly rose in the sky, the sun became like an explosive fireball. Their trousers that had been soaked a sooty black color were now changed back into their original color under the sun's rays. This brought them great relief. Under the intense light of the sun, the field began to swell. The leaves and stalks of the millet drew upright like warriors brimming with courage. Their roots under the ground started to slowly extend outwards, pushing the small stones against each other. The stones gave out popping noises like the sounds of a miniature mountain collapsing. Many seeds still hidden underground showed unimagined strength as they struggled to break through the tough slate shards and join in the morning's frenzied activities with their emerald green bodies. Countless unnamed insects engaged in heated pursuit of smaller insects until the field softly resonated with the desperate tones of slaughter. A great swarm of leopard butterflies, their orange wings covered with black leopard spots and whitish petal shapes on their underwings, danced up and down on the morning wind without a care in the world.

"Dee! Dee! Dee!" A few tiktiks[9] exchanged signals from their hiding places as if they were hatching some kind of plot. Then suddenly a brown-headed prinia, bigger than the palm of your hand, flew into a clump of millet in front of the work shed. It seemed to be looking for insects, its eyes darted about slyly while its tail flicked up and down. Or perhaps it was trying to lure the people in the work shed out to play. Umas was taking it all in, as was Asulan. They could even hear the green cicadas in the depths of the forest singing their praises to nature. The mountains birds exchanged their morning greetings and the wind soughed in a low voice as it danced with the mountain forest.

"The world is awake! Nature is starting to breathe!" Umas exclaimed as he lowered his head.

"My legs can feel the rhythm of Nature's breathing, too." Asulan also lowered his head to listen.

"Tuhas,[10] is our village over there on the opposite mountain? Where does our family live?" It was the first time that Asulan had been this far from home. He felt a little concerned for his family in the village.

"Right. That long shiny line is the waterfall behind the village." Umas pointed behind the village where there was a silver waterfall. It looked like a graceful silk sash lying in the embrace of the mountains. From where they stood it was difficult to imagine the column of water's wild, majestic cascade. The sky was clear and cloudless. The clean, imposing mountain peak behind the waterfall slipped in and out of the mists.

"Hey, how come Hudas hasn't come back yet? Do you think the local evil spirits might had caught him and taken him away?" Asulan looked left and right, clearly feeling ill at ease. He looked a lot like the brown-headed prinia bird they had just seen.

"No way. Hudas is the most respected elder in the village, he's got the wisdom and ability to scare away any evil spirits. Even us, because we've got the same blood as him, the local evil spirits wouldn't dare come near us, either." Seeing the frightened look in Asulan's eyes, Umas used the sensitivity of a hunter to sense the direction of the other boy's feelings. Then he let loose a genial arrow of comfort.

"So, what are we going to do then?" With no adult accompanying them, the boys felt afraid and helpless.

"Don't worry, I'll be here with you until Hudas gets back." Older brothers always assume the role of the adult in times of difficulty, taking up the responsibility of protecting their *nauba*.[11]

"Hudas! Hudas!" Umas looked toward the field below the work shed and shouted. His calls echoed through the air. With the enthusiastic assistance of the mountain gorges the sound of his calls were broadcast far and wide. A flock of white-rumped munia that had been hidden in the nearby clumps of grass flew up with a start and flitted around in the air in unison. Looking at them from a distance they looked like a length of faded black cloth flapping in the wind.

"U------w![12] I'm just below the millet field. When you get your energy back you can come down here and help me." The sound of the reply was even more resonant, so the pale black cloth started flapping again, but this time more quickly and more evenly.

When he heard the voice of an adult, Asulan charged off into the middle of the millet field.

"Walk more slowly! You'll break the millet." Umas called after to slow him down. When he saw that it had no effect, he took off after him.

"Did you see some evil spirits? Is that why you're running so fast?" Talum squatted on the ground looking at the panting boys. Then he tilted his head to look at the trail that they had beaten through the millet.

"Hudas, what are you doing?" Asulan asked resentfully, as if he had lost something precious when the old man was too far away.

"I'm making sure that the nasty creatures that steal our millet will go away and hide someplace that we can't see them." Talum was tying lengths of unevenly sized bamboo tubes onto long, thin wooden poles. The old man said that these were *pahpah*.[13]

"Umas, bring the ramie cord over here." Talum stuck one end of the bamboo noise-makers into the ground, then pointed to the cord at the other end.

When Umas picked up the cord a clattering sound came from the other side of the field startling the whole field into motion. The cord was tied to the noisemakers on the opposite side and when someone pulled it, the noisemakers made a piercing racket.

Talum had distributed about ten of the noisemakers around the millet field. When the cord was given a yank, all of the noisemakers were set in motion, making a racket that frightening the birds away.

"Take the end of cord back to the work shed."

When the boys got to the shed, Asulan was curious and pulled on the cord with all his might. All of the bamboo noisemakers immediately began to shake. Clattering noises rang out from every corner of the field. It was a crisp, resonant, deafening sound that shot in all directions like sharp arrows. It was very disquieting. Not only did it scare away the squirrels and munia birds, but the praying mantises, locusts and colorful beetles also scattered in all directions. For the animals, this manmade noise was even more frightening than nature's rolling thunder, and more intimidating than the screeches of an eagle.

"Asulan, give me the cord. Taking care of our food is sacred work. You're not allowed to make it into a game." Talum sounded severe as he took the cord and stored it away.

"You aren't allowed to pull the noisemaker cord when there aren't any birds eating the millet because it will frighten the innocent animals in the area. They never did anything wrong, so we can't disturb them." Talum was very agitated and spoke with exaggerated gestures. It made Asulan stop what he was doing and stare dumbly at the old man. He didn't even have the nerve to blink.

"Boys, stand off to one side." Hearing the old man's command, Umas immediately pulled Asulan off into the furthest corner.

"Hu! You evil spirits who keep company with the dead. In the name of our family I command the monkeys, squirrels, munia birds and all animals that may harm the millet to leave our millet field immediately. Our family is in possession of strong powers and we can easily defeat you. We have sacrificed to the gods on this piece of land and we have been granted their protection. You must leave this millet field so that we may never see you again. Hu! Chis! Chis! Chis! Hu! Chis! Chis! Chis!"

As Talum pronounced the invocation, he pulled on the ramie cord. The clattering noise provided accompaniment for his solemn prayers that streamed off in all directions while the powerful tremors rendered the millet field a sacred space that could not be violated.

"Hudas, two munia birds just flew into the field to steal millet." Asulan pointed to where the trees and the millet field converged. Under the light of the sun, the millet appeared especially golden and radiant and a lot of things that did not belong in the field could be easily distinguished.

"Hu! You thieving couple, beat it out of our field. We absolutely forbid you from stealing the millet that we have nourished with our sweat. Hu! Chis! Chis! Chis!" For a time, the sound of the curses and the sound of the bamboo noisemakers bounced off each other and threw the entire forest into turmoil until not a single harmful bird remained in the millet field.

"White-rumped munias wear an ugly black and dark brown coat." Many of the small mountain birds are born with brightly colored plumage that make people mistake them for playful flowers when they flit around. But the munia bird wears a coat of strange blackish brown, and when they show up on the millet fields they dart around slyly, as if their intention is make as much mischief as they can.

"That's because they were made from animal flesh and when they were roasted over a roaring fire, they naturally turned black and brown." Talum spoke very naturally, as if he were describing something right before his eyes.

"What? The munia birds are roasted meat? Then how can they still fly?" Umas wrinkled up his nose as if to sniff the aroma of roast meat.

"It's all because they are such gluttons. Once there was a man who always took something good to eat with him no matter what he was doing. In his mind, enjoying good food was always more important than exerting himself at work. During the season when the crops were ripening, like everyone else in the village he had to go to the fields to check on things. But his carrying bag was always full of tasty things to eat, like peanuts, yams and sugar cane....Plus he always had big chunks of mountain goat or muntjac meat, so it looked more like he was trying to serve his gluttonous habits rather than preparing for work in the fields." Talum stopped for a moment and gave the cords in his hand a jerk. He didn't want to neglect the work of chasing the birds just because he was talking.

"Maybe the host of gods didn't like the extravagance of enjoying good food before the harvest was in. In any case, once while he was busy cutting up big pieces of meat to roast in the fire the blackish brown pieces of roasted meat magically flew out of his house and changed into flocks of striped birds. From then on, those striped birds spent day and night stealing millet from the fields. This meant that the villagers often suffered the curse of famine. You can't transgress against the gods. Their punishments always result in disaster. That's why when we do the bird chasing rites everyone has to live even more simply and work harder than usual. In this way we follow the instructions of the gods to please them and receive their blessings. This is also the reason why we don't eat yams or meat during the bird-chasing festival."

At noon, the sun hung high in the center of the heavens making its rays even more dazzling to the eyes. Muggy, hot air poured down from the sky causing the steaming breath of the soil to rise from the fields and from the wilds. In the insufferable heat and with the piercing rattle of the bamboo noisemakers, the harmful birds were in no mood to do their dirty work. Aside from the occasional faint sound of explosions caused by things expanding in the high temperature, the mountains were still and quiet.

"Umas, you take over the job of chasing the birds. Remember, don't pull the cord unless you see birds flying into the field. You don't want to stir up the forest around here. This is a tranquil world and shouldn't be disturbed." Talum gave the cord to Umas and then, as if talking to himself, he said:

"I'm going for a walk around the forest for a looksee. I'm not sure what kind of animals might be around at this time of year."

Umas was especially fascinated by the wisdom and abilities that hunters possess that allow them to tramp around the vast forests. How was it that they could so easily ascertain the shape of the mountain peaks, the location of the mountain streams as well as the direction and volume of their flow? How could they sense the distribution of all kinds of animals and track the movements of game? After watching the old man, Umas finally understood that it was all really just the reward that a hunter reaped from years of solitary trudging through the forests and becoming intimate with the high mountain peaks and ridges. A hunter has to face nature's challenges with an attitude of diligence and concentration, and from his experience he must learn the wisdom of living in harmony with nature. Through such interaction the mountains will embrace the hunter, and the hunter's unique knowledge of the mountains will be achieved. Umas watched the shadow of the old man blend with the shade of the forest and then slowly disappear.

"Umas, give me the cord. I want a turn chasing the munia birds." Asulan was spellbound by the power of the cord to cause a racket.

"Hu! All you harmful birds who keep company with the dead, in the name of our family I command you all to depart from our millet field....Hu! Chis! Chis! Chis!" Asulan clumsily pulled the cord back and forth.

The clattering noise of the bird chasers sounded as urgent as he was, as if he had to fight off thousands of pieces of blackened roast meat all by himself.

NOTES

1. White-rumped munia birds.
2. Ritual to chase away harmful birds.
3. Taiwan maple.
4. Typhoon.
5. Being married.
6. A greeting of blessing.
7. A woven string carrying bag.
8. A work shed.
9. The plain prinia or plain wren-warbler.
10. An older brother or sister.
11. Younger siblings.
12. A call to let others know your location.
13. Noise-making devise to frighten away harmful birds.

CHAPTER SIX

TARO SKIN IN THE WIND

"Children are spirits of happiness that you can see." This old saying is absolutely true. In the world of adults, life is a mad rush from one thing to another. But children may be even busier playing and chasing each other around on the level ground by the river gorge near the village.

Children will always be the lords of the river gorge. They divide up and distribute the gravel, the wild plants, and everything else they lay their eyes on. In their play, they also accumulate wisdom about how to share their joy with the earth.

Just like the system in the village, the older children lead and direct all activities. Like monkeys, the first thing they do is hunt around the riverbanks for fruit that they like to eat. That gives them more energy for their games. What they like best are the bright red clusters of *mulasmulas*,[1] salty *hasbital* berries,[2] purplish-black *danhasath* berries,[3] and strikingly crimson Christmas berries.[4] Of course, the children love the *liah*[5] with its roots full of sweet juice, and *lapat*[6] when its seeds all turn red even more. Sometimes mischievous children point at a wild pomegranate tree and say, "One time I took a shit here and now look what grew out of it. Aiya! Come and look at how much fruit it has on it. Come! Come! Come!

Everyone come and enjoy." Then they all lie down under the tree rolling with laughter. Yet the elders in the village often pick the old leaves of the wild pomegranate and mix them with black nightshade from the bush to make a soup. When it cools, you can drink it like water. These herbal mixtures help the elders in the village stay healthy and good-natured.

After they finish eating, the little girls make playhouses in the groves of trees using *hunun*[7] branches for the roofs. Then, while they sit chatting like the women in the village, they weave all kinds of wildflowers into wreathes to wear on their heads. As for the boys, they play fight or wrestle on the sandy banks of the river. Yet, the game that everyone likes the best is imitating the adults in their hunting activities. Someone with a *paginku*[8] goes to the end of river valley and hides in a sheltered position along the flight lines of the small birds. There they wait. Those without bows form an even line to serve as beaters. Then, as the dust raised by the beaters swirls over the river bank, shouts ring out to make the birds take flight.

The most ancient game that the children play is called "dancing with the sand." When they find a place far enough from the water, everyone pulls out their immature genitals and pees as much as they can. This makes the sand sticky so that they can sculpt the things in their imaginations; things like their future houses, their future wives, and all kinds of game from the forests...But in the end, what remains behind on the ground are usually the faces of their tamas and cinas. These images lie quietly on the riverbank, assaulted and covered over by the wind-blown sand until the land returns to its original form.

It was an evening in late fall. The sky looked as though it was balancing a deep pool of water high on its head. Its distant, deep blue was as cool and indifferent as the water in a stream. The cold air was clear, fresh and absolutely still. Smoke as white as pealed bamboo shoots grew from the roofs of all the thatched houses. The mountain peaks, high and low, stretched into the distance presenting an exquisite undulating line in the sky. That evening, the mountains silently exuded a beauty as pure as spring water.

In the broad woods that extended from below the village there were a number of trees that were not robust enough to stand up to the cold winds of autumn. So, fearing the worst, they shed all their lush green, leaving only dried yellow leaves swinging from the ends of their branches. It looked so desolate.

"What power has overwhelmed those strong trees?" Umas was sitting on the stone wall in the courtyard with his legs dangling down.

The mountain range grew thinner by the day, like an old man with a serious illness. The more he looked at it, the sadder Umas felt. Yet he took some comfort in brave trees like the zelkova, the camphor, and the pines that stubbornly maintained their green foliage. Noting this, Umas felt relieved and closed his eyes a little. He was sure that, starting with this bit of greenery, the entire mountain forest could eventually summon the power of warmth to return again to the earth.

"Umas.....where are you? Are you sitting on top of the wall daydreaming?" Malas walked out of the house and saw Umas on the stone wall.

"Huh?" Umas was startled. He jumped down and walked toward his mother.

"Cina, why do the trees have to drop their leaves in the cold weather?" The cold stones jabbed painfully at the soles of his feet, so Umas bent his knees and walked gingerly.

"The fallen leaves are to fertilize the ground."

"Why does Talabal[9] have to leave this part of the mountains?"

"It leaves so that we understand how important it is. It makes us treasure the days of sunshine."

"What does Hamisan[10] come here for? I really hate it." Umas rubbed his hands together hoping that by heating up the palms of his hands he could warm his whole body.

"Winter wants us to learn how to cope with its cold. It's also a chance to kill off the old green leaves." Malas stood there looking at the puzzled expression on her son's face.

"Cina, what are you talking about?" Umas thought his mother's answer was as odd as the winter itself.

"It's going to get dark soon. Aren't you afraid that you'll bring out the evil spirits with all your talk? That's it. Don't ask again. Tonight Tama is going to take Subali over to Hudas Bisazu's house for the night. Tama has worked himself into a lather getting everything ready for the ceremony. You go and help him. Don't make your elders unhappy."

"Why do they have to stay at Hudas Bisazu's house?" Umas knew that Hudas Bisazu was a respected shaman as well as the master of rites for certain ceremonies. But home was the only place where people rested and slept. It was also the only place where their souls felt at peace. He didn't understand why his father had to leave his own home, let alone take little Subali with him.

"Tama Bisazu has decided that tomorrow we must carry out the Mukailev[11] for male children born this year. Last year we didn't have the "Infant Festival," so we're having it this year. This year Subali also learned how to walk on the earth, so he has been invited to take part in the ceremony tomorrow." Malas was feeling happy. She told him, "Tomorrow's Infant Festival is the first ritual of Subali's life, so it's an extremely important day for him."

Several days previous, Hudas Bisazu had employed the wisdom that he had gained from studying nature, and the magic power passed down by the ancestors to determine that the mountain taro in the fields was ripe. He thus decided that the Infant Festival should be performed for all male children born that year before the taro was harvested. Since then there had been an especially large number of things that made people excited and amazed. The laughter of all the tamas had also increased. You could hear it everywhere you went in the village. Even when they called the hunting dogs, their voices betrayed a faint tinge of laughter.

"When do Tama and Subali go to stay there?"

"Before nightfall."

"Why?"

"Because the evil spirits enter our village wearing the black robes of nighttime to harm infants whose strength is weak. Hudas Bisazu's magical powers will protect all the infants."

"What kind of magical power does he have?" The power of his curiosity made Umas bound in front of his cina, eyes wide.

"Tama Bisazu's admirable feats in battle and his pure behavior have made the ancestral spirits wish to draw near to him. For that reason, he has the ability to summon the power of the ancestral spirits and make them return to our village from the most distant, primordial past. They then help us defeat all manner of disaster and curses and give us the strength and courage to continue living even in our moments of greatest desperation and hopelessness."

"Who are the ancestral spirits?" Umas asked quietly, as if feeling a little discouraged by his own lack of knowledge.

"The ancestral spirits are just those ancestors who have departed us.

"Where did they go?"

"They are everywhere. Where there is sunlight, they are there. Where there is moonlight, they are there. Where the air moves back and forth there are ancestral spirits. In the deepest places in the mountain forests there are ancestral spirits. They are in the emerald green meadows and in the rivers that reach to the boundary of heavens. Any place where the soul can perceive them, the ancestral spirits are there."

"Do the dead ancestors really return to the village when the shaman summons them?"

"Since the beginning of the world, the ancestors of the Bunun people have never died. They have only moved to live in the eternal domain of the ancestral spirits. After undertaking the ritual of death, the ancestral spirits attain even greater strength with which to protect their descendants." Cina patted her son lightly on the shoulder, comforting him just like the ancestral spirits comfort the souls of their descendants.

"So....where is the eternal domain of the ancestors?"

"In a place that you can go to in your mind."

"When Subali takes part in the Infant Festival can I do anything to help?" When Umas learned how important the ritual was as a stage in a young child's life he was concerned.

"Those who take part in the Infant Festival must bring along the food needed for the ceremony. You can go inside and pound the millet or cut up the game meat."

"Dong, dong, dong!" The powerful, resonant sound of millet being pounded shook the whole house.

"Tama!" After greeting her husband, Malas immediately knelt down and grasped the wooden mortar to keep it from shifting about too much under the powerful pestle strokes. When Tama raised the pestle she deftly swept the kernels of millet that had overflowed onto the rim of the mortar back into its cavity. Aside from wanting to shake off the beads of sweat that were too cold to fall from his face on their own, for some reason Tama seemed to be angry at the kernels of millet for being so hard.

After Tama said a few words to Cina, he took a length of cloth and placed Umas' younger brother on his own back. Then, following the custom established in ancient times, he took the millet, game meat and other food items and went off to stay in Hudas Bisazu's house.

The crowing of a cock rang through the early morning air, but because it came from a considerable distance, the sound was rather faint. Umas got up and sat on the edge of his wooden bed. Since he knew how cold the dirt floor would be, he first cautiously tested it with his bare feet a few times. When he walked outside, the light of daybreak was growing stronger, allowing the world to show its familiar face under the pale white glow. One of their old hunting dogs had already climbed on top of the stone wall and lay perfectly motionless, as if climbing up there to await the sun was the most important work that he had to do that day. A few small plants beside the wall labored under the weight of a thin frost that the night air had deposited on them.

The mountains in front of the village had for some time been covered in the golden cloak woven for them by the sunlight. The valley below looked like a long thin crack that extended outwards from the narrowest point between the mountains. The stream that flowed eternally through it glinted coldly like the dagger of a hunter in close combat with some wild beast. By then, the intense pressure of the sun was forcing the last remnants of nighttime that crouched in the morning shadows back into the valley below. Gradually, the reflections of golden light from the mountain slopes revealed the birds soaring in the sky, the slumbering village, and the sombre forest before Umas' eyes.

Like a mountain stream, Umas constantly moved around inside and outside of the house. The power of this stream carried all the grime and dust from inside the house and left behind only that which was clean and bright.

"Umas, why are you standing in the courtyard like a stone? The sun is coming out. Aren't you going over to Hudas Bisazu's house to watch your brother's ceremony?" But Umas continued meandering around as before.

"Has the ceremony really started? Why is the sky still so quiet?" Umas looked up into the deep, clear sky.

"What? What did you say?"

"An old man once told me that an invisible line runs between the village and the sky. If the people in the village are busying themselves with the ceremony, then the banks of clouds in the sky should also have been set in motion. They may even shout loud curses when they bump into each other." Umas felt very pleased with himself, like a clever person who gives an answer that nobody else would ever have thought of.

"That only happens when the heavenly spirits are going to pour down their water of life." Like the other women in the village, Malas had established an unshakeable relationship with the gods based on reverence and awe. When her son spoke of the gods in such a flippant manner, she became so anxious that the tone of her voice rose:

"Umas, rituals are sacred times. If you speak carelessly it will make the gods unhappy, and that will produce bad results for the ritual."

"I wasn't speaking carelessly. That was what a white-haired old man told me. It was Hudas Bukun who lives at the top of the village." Umas pointed in the direction of the old man's residence.

When Malas heard this her anger receded. The elders provided explanations for many things in the village. Right and wrong, good and evil were all determined according to their wise standards. Nobody would doubt those things, and besides, it was a shameful thing to second guess the elders.

"Off you go, quickly! Go see what's happening with Tama and Subali. While you're at it you should learn how adults behave at ceremonies." Cina hoped that her son could use his eyes to learn the wisdom passed down by the ancestors. After all, humans were far from the strongest animals in the mountains. They had to rely upon the life experience of the ancestors in order to survive in a world full of things they found unfathomable. So it was that the adults took advantage of every opportunity to convey the wisdom that they had gained from nature clearly and seriously to the younger generation. They hoped that their children and grandchildren would thus be able to dance with the mountains for all eternity.

"Does Tama have the ability to lead little brother through all the tests of the ritual? Will Subali be granted the blessing of the gods?"

"Yes. He is one of the best hunters in the village. More importantly he is a man who wants to protect his family." When she thought of her husband, a veil of morning light seemed to drift over Malas's face.

"When I grow up, I'll be as capable as Tama." Umas spoke with a tone of respect.

"That's fine then, but don't let your mouth get more exercise than your hands and feet. That's how you end up keeping company with the evil spirits. Now get going!"

Hudas Bisazu was an elder who resided close to the ancestral spirits. His long history of coursing around the mountain forests was attested to by his thick, muscular calves and by the prominent veins traced over the backs of his hands. A lifetime of honest behavior had left him with a voice as fine as the moonlight which broadcast to all Bunun villages along with the sound of cicadas. Although the years and months allow the clever spiders to weave dense layers of their webs on the faces of the elders, Hudas Bisazu's genial smile had the power to shine through from under those webs.

This was only the second or third time that Hudas Bisazu had presided over the Infant Festival. Previously, it had been Hudas Itun who acted as the master of ceremonies. But the vagaries of fate resulted in him being no longer able to protect the lives and property of the people. It was true that Hudas Itun had carefully led the people in the performance of the age-old rites in accordance with the changes of nature, but now the gods were no longer satisfied with his manner of carrying out those ceremonies. Many of the children who had taken part in the Infant Festival under his direction had grown up skinny and had sallow complexions. Some had even disappeared before their parents' eyes under attack from the disease demons. This left many people to weep in the silent darkness of the night. As a group, the villagers were distressed by these tragic results. They thought that Hudas Itun himself may have been cursed by the evil spirits and was no longer the person closest to the ancestral spirits. Nor was he able to receive the magical powers bestowed by the gods. Therefore, after some discussion, the villagers decided that Hudasu Bisazu should replace Hudas Itun in leading them towards a peaceful future.

The people held one unchanging belief in their hearts: whoever had the most abundant harvest and whoever most often gave the people game to eat, that person was best able to lead them in the rituals relating to their lives and their farming. But gods would never bestow their glory and honor on only one person. Just like the sun, the honor never remains in only one spot. The people believe even more firmly that all are born equal. Do not the gods give all newborn babies the same cry? Therefore, power and honor in the village was like clear water, it would always flow toward those who had the most powerful spirit.

The paths through the village were icy cold that morning. As he made his way to Bisazu's house, Umas had no choice but to bend forward and run over the muddy ground on tiptoe.

"The season of cracked skin and bleeding feet is here." Umas looked at all the scars on his feet as he ran along.

The courtyard of Hudas Bisazu's house had filled with people some time ago. They were all there to take part in the Infant Festival. Some of the portly attendees rested their ample bellies against the courtyard's stone wall. Those who were thinner climbed up on the wall to watch. Everyone was staring wide-eyed at all the action taking place in the courtyard. They were like hunters pouring all of their energy into watching for prey to come along a trail, afraid that if they weren't very careful, the prey might slip away. The atmosphere surrounding the ceremony was very solemn, and everyone watched with bated breath.

Master of ceremonies, Hudas Bisazu, walked out of the front door. He turned in the direction of the sunrise and proclaimed in full voice: "Hu! In the name of the gods I call on this year's most fortunate people to gather and bring your children forward. With reverent, clear spirit we appeal to the gods to ensure that our children will grow peacefully and in good health under the light of the sun."

Seven or eight adults carrying male babies on their backs followed the old man closely. They formed in a neat line behind him. A buzz ran through the crowd. Their tense, excited breathing filled the air with the smell of vegetables, meat, chilli pepper and garlic. More and more people wanted to squeeze up onto the stone wall. Umas, who had been standing on the wall, couldn't hold off the pressure of the crowd and fell to the ground with a yelp. After he brushed the dust off himself, he took the opportunity to express his dissatisfaction by slapping the dust off the behinds of the people still kneeling on the wall. But there were so many people on the wall it was hard to say who had pushed him, and whose behinds he was now slapping. Umas couldn't figure it out, and besides, everyone was much too concerned about their relatives in the courtyard.

"Everyone must be quiet. The gods will not dare enter our village if you are so noisy and unruly." An old man caught in the middle of the crowd reprimanded the people with his hoarse voice. But the people were excited almost beyond the point where they could control themselves.

Happy to hear this reproach, Umas searched for the old man's location with admiring eyes. He wanted to show his support for this sage view. At the same time, he took advantage of the quiet in the crowd to push over towards the best vantage point.

"Any children who have never killed a game animal must move further from the wall. There is no telling if you might sneeze or fart, and then we will have to cancel the whole ceremony." Another old man scolded.

After a number of elders gave instructions, the people watching the ritual immediately formed into several concentric circles, like the growth lines of a tree trunk. Those who had killed game animals stood closest to the courtyard. Younger men who had gone up the mountain with hunting parties but who had never themselves killed an animal stood behind them. The youngest, like Umas, who could do a little cleanup and could take care of their younger brothers and sisters, or do light work in the fields, were pushed out to the outermost circle. From there, Umas could only strain his neck and stand on tiptoes to see what was happening at the front.

"Hu....My people who have been favored with the birth of a male child. You have been graced by the host of gods. Today I am going to lead you out to the taro fields because the power of the gods may be found there. The strong taro stalks and thick taro leaves will prove my words. There you will pray that the life spirits of your children will grow like the taro leaves, lush and deep green; that their bodies will grow as strong and tall as the taro stalks; and that after they have grown up they will possess abilities so numerous that, just like the taro bulbs hidden under the ground, there will be no way of knowing their full extent,." Hudas Bisazu used his powerful words to move the ritual along smoothly.

When Hudas Bisazu led the men carrying their baby boys on their backs out of the courtyard, the crowd reacted like waves rising before the wind on a deep pond, pushing slowly out towards the further shore, opening up a broad passageway.

Hudas Bisazu led the ritual procession quickly and quietly down the trail toward the taro field. The rest of the crowd followed closely behind. In accordance with unspoken rules, if they got too close, they slowed down to create some space. From a distance it looked like the migration of two swarms of bees.

The taro field was on Hudas Bisazu's land. The mountain taro stalks grew taller than the clumps of weeds around the outside of the field, making them look like a tall, emerald green plateau. When they set eyes on it, the people all believed that it was indeed a sacred space blessed by the gods. After they arrived at the field, Hudas Bisazu took a gourd full of millet wine from his waist and poured some wine into his cupped right hand. Then he faced the taro field and prayed as he sprinkled the wine:

"Hupikaunan! Ye gods who are omnipresent, we bring the most fragrant millet wine to worship you. We beg that you open your eyes and look upon your children. May you open your ears and listen to our prayers. With souls as clear as moonlight our people pray that this ritual will bring excellent results. Hu! Hu! Hu!" The master of ceremonies continued to sprinkle out the wine until it was all used up. The words of his prayer rose gradually higher until they echoed around the mountain slopes.

The master of ceremonies then took up the bow and arrows that had hung across his shoulder. He drew the bow and released an arrow into the air above the field. The arrow left the bow and followed a rainbow shaped trajectory through the sky. It then plunged into the taro field like an eagle descending on its prey. The crisp sound of leaves being sheared apart could be heard as it hit home. Hudas Bisazu immediately raised his voice in loud prayer:

"Hupikaunan! Children who are taking part in today's Infant Festival! Under the watchful eyes of the gods and your parents may you grow up in peace and in health. After today's ritual is over, no matter where they may be, our children will have the power to kill their enemies as easily as if they were shooting at taro leaves. After they have completed this ceremony, no matter what enemies or what vicious wild animals they face, may our children hit their mark with their first arrow. Whether it be fierce wild animals like black bears, mountain boars, or mountain deer, may they have the ability to bring them down with the ease, strength, and accuracy of an eagle snatching up a snake."

After the master of ceremonies had completed his prayer, all the adults carrying children jumped into the taro field as fast as their legs would carry them. They then stood before the taro plant that they liked the best. Their expressions were solemn and their breathing deep; evidence of the pressure that they felt. This was because the next part of the ritual involved the tamas pulling out a taro for their sons. This they had to do with one pull. If they failed to do so it symbolized that their sons would not receive the blessings and protection of the gods, and that the future of these infants would be ruled by evil spirits and illness demons.

Like all the others in attendance, Umas watched his own father fixedly, not even daring to blink. In his heart he prayed that his father would be able to pull the taro out in one pull. After all, a mountain taro stalk isn't as hard as a tree trunk. They are very easily broken. Some mischievous taros also dug their hairy roots very deep into the muddy soil.

"Tama is smart and he surely won't pick one of the mischievous taros." Umas looked with some unease at the taro in front of his Tama.

Adults who have spent many long years working in the fields are very aware of the characteristics of all the different plants. They are aware of the hidden strengths of each kind of mountain taro. Because of this, with the prayers of the master of ceremonies, and the blessings of the people, each of the fathers were able to pull out their taros in one motion, thus ensuring a peaceful and glorious future for their sons. The ceremony had proceeded extremely smoothly. The adults in the field all congratulated each other, and those watching wore satisfied smiles. Flocks of birds hopped about or flew freely around the nearby trees. The spirits of the silent forest also rose, and the dry, yellowed leaves slowly began to sing in the wind. In this most exhausting of seasons, the spirits of the entire world seemed to be offering their warmest blessings to these tiny beings.

While the adults were congratulating each other for pulling out their taros, Hudas Bisazu was returning to the village by himself. On the way back he chopped down several *bakaun*[12] plants about as thick as his wrist, as well as several rattan vines. Not far from the entrance to the village he bound the mulberry stalks with the rattan to make an arched barrier about waist high. The people call this a *tidankulanm*.[13]

When he had finished setting it up, Hudas Bisazu stroked the top of the barrier and pronounced solemnly:

"Hu....after our children return to the village each will have become a courageous, accomplished warrior. The power of the host of gods will enter to reside in our village. From this time forward, killing our enemies will be as easy as pulling out a mountain taro. Even if the enemies are legion, our children will still be able to break through their encirclement and eradicate them with ease. After today's ceremony has been completed my people will continue to give birth to male children as innumerable as the raindrops that the heavens sprinkle over the earth or the beautiful stars that fill the heavens at night. Every boy will be as strong as a black bear and their movements will be as nimble as an eagle in flight. The bravery passed down from the ancestral spirits will allow them fearlessly to enter an enemy village by themselves."

The adults who later returned to the village had to cross the arched gate of the barrier set up by the master of ceremonies with their children on their backs. They could not knock the barrier down in the process, otherwise the lives of the children would fall and disappear like the archway. The adults, being excellent hunters, employed the same raw strength that allowed them to leap mountain gullies on the hunting grounds to do what was necessary to cross the barrier. Umas watched as his tama with Subali on his back and a relaxed smile on his face crossed the barrier like an agile muntjac.

The adults returned to the house of the master of ceremonies and placed the mountain taro in a pile in the middle of his courtyard. At this point the nervous cinas were finally allowed to approach their baby boys. They stepped quickly forward to receive the babies, then turned them left and right to examine them. Their expressions were a mixture of smiles and tears unique to those who are cinas.

As soon as they set down their babies, the men immediately chipped pieces of slate from the eaves of the house and arranged them in a circle around the taros. Under the direction of the master of ceremonies they then chopped off the taro bulbs at the point where the bulb joins with the stalk. They had to cut the bulb off cleanly with one motion. That symbolized the idea that when hunting or killing enemies, the boys would be as deft and fierce as if they were cutting taros. But before the men began chopping, the tamas prayed to the heavenly spirits on behalf of their sons:

"Hupikaunan! Now I cut the mountain taros with great ease. From this time forward, no matter how powerful the enemy, they will not be able to defeat me. I will kill them as easily as I cut the taro. In future, when we go to war, we will never kill our own people in error because my knife and arrows will avoid my own people and fly straight into the hearts of my enemies. After this ritual, with the guidance of the host of spirits I will grow in peace and in health. The evil spirits and illness demons will not be able to violate my body and I will forever stand on this earth as tall as the towering mountains. Hu! Hu! Hu!"

Once the taro cutting ritual was over, the taros were all moved inside the house while the stalks were left in the courtyard to dry. Then the master of ceremonies again addressed the taros with a prayer:

"Hupikaunan! May the heavenly spirits protect these children. Make their movements as nimble as the birds in flight. When they grow up may their behavior be as bright and clear as the moonlight, may their reputations be as lofty as Savah,[14] and may their bodies be as hard as stone. May their healthy, strong bodies never be afflicted with illness and may they surpass their fellow villagers. May all the evil spirits be frightened by ritual that we have performed today so that they do not dare come to our village. Hu! Hu! Hu!"

After the master of ceremonies had finished his prayer several agile women placed the taros in a pot to cook. The cooked taros were only given to the adults who had taken part in the Infant Festival. When they pealed the taros, they had to be careful to leave the skins in one piece and then take the whole skin back to their own houses. They then hung them neatly from the eaves of their houses to serve as the most sacred decorations; decorations that would accompany their children as they walked slowly into the future.

That day when the dark clouds were chased away by the sun, Banitul was sitting under the eaves with Subali in his arms enjoying the view of the mountain forest. Umas playfully pinched Subali's young, soft cheeks making the boy twist and turn in discomfort. Fearing that the boy would fall from his arms, Banitul lightly pushed Umas away with his elbow so that there was a little distance between them. Umas' playful nature made him resist the push, but his father was just too strong and there was no way that he could be budged. After a few attempts, Umas settled down and turned his eyes toward the distant mountains and to an appreciation of the ever-changing world.

"Tama, do the taro skins all have to be hung under the eaves." Umas observed the taro skins under the eaves dancing in the wind.

"Of course. They represent the promises made to our children by the gods. We have to keep them well. Those promises will become the most important power for the children when they are confronted with setbacks." Banitul narrowed his eyes and stared towards the distant point where the heavens and earth meet. Then in a voice filled with warmth he said:

"This Infant Festival was very pleasing to the gods. It means that when our children grow up they will possess robust vitality. They will be able to hunt much game and turn back marauding enemies. These taro skins symbolize the fangs of the animals and the heads of enemies that Subali will capture."

"A lot of respected hunters in the village have many animal fangs hanging behind their houses. Do you think that when Subali grows up he will be able to hunt down that much game?"

"Of course. That's the main reason that we adults hold the Infant Festival. It is also the only blessing that we can bestow upon our descendants.

"Tama, are there taro skins that belong to me hanging under the eaves?"

"Of course, there are. The love that adults have for their children is always the same. Look! The row of taro skins over here belongs to you."

Umas could see that there was another long, neat line of taro skins dancing even more beautifully in the wind. This made him realize that the blessings that he had received were even more numerous and grander. He pressed his face happily against his father's tree trunk of an arm. As he smiled, he could see himself chasing around the hunting grounds with firm, strong strides. His bold footprints filled all the mountain forests that belonged to the Bunun people...

Notes

1. Aralia-leaf raspberries.
2. Rhus chinensis.
3. Perforate fleeceflower.
4. Ardisia cenata.
5. Sogon grass.
6. Wild pomegranate.
7. Absinth or *artemisia capellaris,*
8. A bow.
9. Summer.
10. Winter.
11. A ritual for male infants which also concerns mountain taro.
12. Mulberry.
13. A special structure made during the Infant Festival that must be crossed over.
14. Jade Mountain, the highest mountain in the minds of the people.

Chapter Seven

The Stars that Never Fall from the Sky

After a cold night of tossing and turning, the morning sun is a gift that villagers long for. As if prearranged, everyone steps out into their courtyards at the same time to enjoy the sun-filled ground. They stretch their arms and legs to get their joints moving, yawning as if the night's sleep did them no good at all.

In the cold season, there is nothing to do in the fields, nor any hunting. Aside from organizing their few farming tools and repairing damage to their houses and animal pens, the people spend most of their time gathered around talking about the news of the day. Some complain that there is nothing but hardship and suffering in their lives and their fates seem to be hanging from a steep cliff. Mischievous individuals make people laugh by giving exaggerated descriptions of the misadventures of others. Tales that people tell of their strange experiences remind the listeners of the many mysterious faces of the mountain forest. Stories of how some people violated taboos and have been abandoned by the gods elicit sighs of sympathy because inevitably the health and livelihoods of these people will fall into a deep pit of trouble. Occasionally, those who have travelled or gone to visit relatives bring back reports of distant villages. Not only do these reports serve to expand the awareness of the people, they are the stuff of fantasy. Like the adults, some of the more robust children gather to play together. Sometimes they chase each other around on the stony village paths, oblivious to the cuts and scrapes on their feet.

Apart from that, the frosty ground thaws soft and wet under rays of the sun. The chickens come out to scratch the same holes they were working on the day before, while the high-spirited hunting dogs practiced their fighting skills in the empty lots. Their puppies roam about freely. When they come across a flock of hens eagerly scratching in the mud, they start scratching themselves. But after a time, the pups shake the mud out of their hair and look in confusion at the noisy hens, as if to ask, "And after you dig the hole, what then?"

"Come on over, we've got roast peanuts. What about the children? Have they all run off?" Vava, the slightly rotund host, had a regular face. He walked out of the house carrying a *tukban*[1] laden with roasted peanuts whose thick aroma immediately filled the courtyard. Looking in the direction of the sounds of the playing children, he could see they were off in the farthest part of the village.

"Vava, your peanuts are really big. Look! Three peanuts per shell." Everyone expressed their thanks to the host, amazed at the broad winnow filled with peanuts.

Vava was Talum's wife, Tanivu's, youngest brother. When Tanivu married Talum, Vava was still no more than a playful child. Perhaps it was because their homes were too close together, but though Tanivu had married into another family, Vava still ran over to Talum's house looking for his sister as before. As time went on, Vava basically became one of Talum's children.

There was nothing unusual about this sort of thing because the older generation had a saying: When a woman gets married, her family is always afraid that she will be mistreated, so they send a younger brother or sister along so that the groom's family will know that their new "daughter from afar"[2] isn't alone, and will treat her reasonably.

When Talum led his clan off in search of new land, he never asked Vava his opinion. That was because he assumed that his wife's opinion would be Vava's, too, as if he were no more than a child who follows its mother's footsteps no matter where she goes. Even Vava's own wife, Palahu, had been Talum's choice. That intimate connection led many to believe that Vava and Talum were like brothers. For his part, Umas looked upon Vava as an elder of the same generation as Talum.

"That's what I told my *mavala*.[3] I said that we live on the most powerful land. Only the most powerful land can produce such big, fat peanuts." Taupas' thick beard covered his entire mouth. If it weren't for his habit of talking out of the side of his mouth and showing some of his teeth, nobody would know that he was talking at all.

"Who's talking?" Someone asked in a loud, disdainful voice. Everyone turned and saw the swarthy Salivan sitting there like a great black bear excited to have discovered a problem.

Salivan had long, thick black hair which he usually tied back with a red band around his forehead. He never took the band off, even when he slept. It was as if he was born with it on. Sturdy, sleek muscles showed prominently on his broad chest. When in action, rows of well-defined brawn, hard as rock, formed on his abdomen. From his movements you could tell that he was enormously strong. Every time that he unleashed that strength it was as though an earthquake was coming on. Salivan was also well aware of his own abilities. Most of the time he went around with his hands on his hips, speaking in a voice louder and clearer than anyone else. Perhaps he hoped that his arrogant voice would be testimony to his impressive physical strength. He always appeared as though he was ready to lift the heaviest objects with one hand at any time, just to amaze and intimidate people.

"That was me talking." It was Taupas' habit to respond this way to dispel the doubts of others. Even when he was with his family, he used this phrase to explain the origin of his voice. If there was one thing of which he was firmly convinced, it was that that anyone who grew an annoying beard should never allow others to laugh at their crooked mouth.

"A few days ago, I took my wife back to stay with her family for a few days." Taupas' beard moved left and right with his lips looking like a dried leaf swinging back and forth in the wind.

"Is your family Takis-Taulan.[4] Ha ha...why do they have that name? Doesn't Taulan mean 'fool'?" Salivan's laughter was exaggerated and insincere, indicating that his main purpose was to make fun of the family who chose 'fool' for their name.

"Salivan, must you use your *lihulihu*[5] mouth to make fun of other families? The neighbors of the white-haired old man were evil spirits." Even though Taupas' own family lived several mountains removed, the humiliation that accompanied this kind of ridicule could easily have led to bloodshed in the future. Insults and mockery are like seeds buried in the mud. They may appear dead, but they can suddenly come back to life after a heavy rainstorm. Then, even the most stubborn rocks won't be able to block their rush toward the sunlight. This was a principle that Vava well understood.

"I didn't mean to make fun, but think about it. We are a people who love honor. We would even give our lives to protect our honor. Why would a family deliberately bring shame on themselves? This....it's really strange." Salivan maintained his position.

He had the most stubborn blood flowing in his veins, an ancient blood that came from stone. Once he got an idea in his head, there was no way anyone was going to change it. You could offer revelations from the gods, but he would still reject them without a second thought. From his point of view, the ideas of others were like pebbles thrown against a rock wall; they all just bounced back.

"It isn't only our name. Lots of families have really unique names." Taupas gave a weak smile, as if he secretly scorned the other man's ignorance.

"Taupas, you've forded the most rivers and crossed the most mountains and heard the calls of birds that we have never heard. You've also heard the stories of many different villages. Tell us, which names are the strangest?" Childlike curiosity lies hidden in the depths of all men's minds.

"Really, every family name has its own story. Just like the things that appear before our eyes, they all have their basic principles. Even if some things may leave us baffled, that's only because we don't have the wisdom of the gods." Vava hurried to reply. As an elder he shouldn't have been in such a rush, but he didn't want Taupas to be caught in an awkward situation, and he felt he had no choice.

When he was younger, Taupas had trekked over a lot of mountains with his clan elders, and in the process, he had visited many villages. When he got older, he developed a sense of mission about the future wellbeing of his family and so returned to follow in the footsteps of his forerunners to travel around the mountains. That experience left him much the wiser and opened his mind immeasurably. But his way of talking through the side of his mouth meant that he was subjected to a great deal of bullying. For a long time, he felt discouraged and had difficulty laughing. According to his own account, and that of his clan members, he was forced to stop over in an unfriendly village during the season of muggy heat. He and his family dealt honestly with the local people, but for some reason they were subjected to a curse in return. The locals secretly placed a malicious fire in his body, leaving him to suffer fever for several weeks. When he finally recovered, he had lost control of his mouth. Taupas could only resign himself and be comforted by the fact that he had travelled many trails and survived many disasters and illnesses, and he was still alive. The evil spirits followed him everywhere, constantly hounding him as if born for that very purpose. He came to feel that his whole reason for being was to serve as eternal prey for the evil spirits. But those spirits apparently weren't interested in killing him right away. After Taupas spoke frankly about these secrets, everyone lost interest in making fun of his appearance.

"Right. What Vava says is absolutely true. There was a reason that my family chose the name Takis-Taulan. Originally, several ancestors, without knowing they had been cursed, became deaf. Other clan members thought this strange and were disturbed by it. So, they gave those clan members the unusual name. In fact, 'Taulan' comes from 'Taula". It means 'deaf' and extremely 'foolish'." Taupas bowed his head to think, then, stroking his long beard said:

"But there is another explanation."

"How's that?" It might have been out of sarcasm, but Salivan was unexpectedly polite.

"It's to do with the hunting season. As in previous years, the Takis-Taulan clan had gathered all the able-bodied men in the village to form a hunting party. They went into the forest hunting ground and did *mapuasu*[6] for ten days or more. Back in the village the women and children had reason to expect that the hunt would produce satisfying results. The appointed time for the men's return arrived, but there was still no sign of the them on the craggy surface of the mountain facing the village. The women and children grew anxious. Their thoughts were filled with images of death, and the dark clouds seemed to envelope their spirits." Taupas stopped short. This allowed everyone to become as anxious as the women and children in the story. Even their breathing became as cautious.

"There was among them one child who particularly liked to follow his Tama around. Even when the father went to the latrine, the child followed right behind. Other people called the child, 'Tama's tail," in gest. Perhaps it was because the child missed his father, or because they had been separated too long, in any case, the child stood in the doorway facing in the direction of the hunting ground every day, watching in silence. But the dense forest blocked the child's line of sight. Because he really wanted to see his Tama, he came up with a plan. He climbed up on the roof so that his eyes could fly off to places further away and higher. What he forgot was that, before the hunting party returned home, they shot arrows from the nearest hill straight for the roofs of their houses to convey the news that they had returned safely."

"Others say that when the hunting was over the hunters shot an arrow from a great distance in the direction of the village and because the arrow was as clever as a *kukuav*,[7] it flew all the way back to the hunter's roof." A hoarse voice gave another version of the arrow finding its way home.

"That was a time when the gods were much closer to us, so the hunters used the power of the gods to change their arrows into eagles. Then what?" Vava didn't want his story to break off there.

"Just like in the past, the members of the hunting party gathered together and shot arrows in the direction of the village. Every one of the arrows landed on the hunter's own roof, bringing news of their safety. But while all the families were shouting for joy, they heard the child's anguished cries. They frantically searched for him everywhere to see what had happened. Finally, they saw the boy lying on the roof of his house with an arrow in his chest. Because, 'children are the greatest riches,' when they saw the dead child their faces turned pallid from shock and they forgot about everything else. The hunting party returned with abundant game, but they brought back no joy. The adults felt an inexpressible sense of guilt because they had not been able to ensure the safety of the child. The incident disconcerted people in other villages as well. When a hunting party as about to return home, even sparrows don't dare go up on the rooves, so how could a child had climbed up there? It seemed that the family were more 'taula' than little birds. Afterwards, when anyone spoke of that family, they always remembered how the child had died so tragically on the rooftop. And while they felt pity, they couldn't help saying, "fools." In time, it became everyone's habit to call them, Takis-Taulan. But did they mean that the adults were fools, or that the child was a fool? That is what I heard in a village three suns and moons away from here. And I don't know if these events really took place or not." Taupas took a deep breath as if he had escaped from a desolate forest.

"My wife comes from Havis Village. It was established by the Palalavi clan. All the children know that Palalavi means 'to follow.' That is to say, when anyone does something, they copy them, as if they were shadows with no initiative of their own. Does anyone think that is a strange name?" Pima had reached an age where he garnered everyone's respect. He had a strong, healthy body. He had a graceful air when he walked to and from work past the courtyard.

"It's a bit obtuse just copying what other people do, but it's still better than lying around the house all day like a corpse waiting to be buried."

"There's a story behind why they are called Palalavi, and it's not what you might think." Pima waved his hand to indicate that the other's ideas were all wrong.

"Why"

"I heard the elders say that those people lived on a mesa at mid-mountain. The ground fell off steeply into a gorge on both sides, which meant that anyone entering more deeply into the forest had to go past their village. I don't know if it was because they lacked good hunting skills, or if they didn't have a leader for their hunting parties. It could be that they just didn't know how to establish their own hunting ground, in any case, every time a party from another village passed by, some of the adults would quietly pick up their weapons and set off behind them. They didn't care if others tried to stop them, or cursed them, they kept following to the bitter end. When they got to the other group's hunting ground, they followed the directions of the leader of the hunting party. When he said to do something, they did it, even if it was the most menial work. But when it came to sharing the spoils of the hunt, they didn't hold back and were forthright in making a case for themselves. This habit of using the hunting grounds of others made a lot of people angry, but they couldn't do much about it. So other families disdainfully called them the clan that liked to 'follow' others to the hunt."

"So, their clan name came from the idea that they took advantage of others. Naturally, nobody respects that kind of behavior." After listening to Pima's explanation, everyone pursed their lips and shook their heads. The only thing they didn't do was sigh.

"Why is the pronunciation of Taulan and Palalavi different from what it would normally be?" One of the younger people didn't understand the obscure changes in language.

"So many new things are always happening in our lives and our knowledge never seems to be able to keep up. So, in order to understand and distinguish the principles behind those things, we often explain the principle of new things by changing the principle of things that have been around for a long time. That's especially true with the language that we use to express our feelings. If we didn't, then it would be very easy for unnecessary misunderstandings and conflicts to arise." People really respected Taupas' thinking on this matter.

"In the case of family names, if common words are altered slightly, aside from being less offensive, you still can understand the meaning of the name from the sound."

"Do all family names come from corrupt behavior and shameful reasons?" Everyone was huddled together, so it was difficult to tell who had spoken.

"Not necessarily. The history of every family is different, so their names are different as well. Our elder, Vava, understands much, so much that you'd have to ask the ants for help if you wanted to move all that he knows. You should ask him." Taupas humbly looked to the old man.

"Hudas Vava, if it would be convenient, please tell us! Let us pass our morning in the company of our ancestors." The young man could hardly restrain himself. When the children playing nearby heard that someone was going to tell a story their curiosity rose to the level of disbelief and they all scrambled to form a second ring of the audience.

"Only children like to listen to stories." Vava looked at all the curious little faces.

"When it comes to listening to stories, the interest of both elders and children is as thick as clouds full of rainwater. That's because the stories that come down from the ancestors are like the rain itself, they make people feel cool and invigorated."

"All right then. Let me just fill my pipe." Vava said as he began to light his pipe. The story began as the first puff of smoke slowly wafted from his mouth.

"All family names have a story behind them. The vast majority have to do with place names, plant names, utensil names, animal names, the names of buildings, or special historical events. The Taki-Hunan clan from Takbanuaz got their name because their ancestors lived for many years in a place called Hunan in the Luanda mountains. The name of the Maisonguan clan from Takbanuaz comes from the word 'Songuan'. It means 'mountain peak' or 'lofty place,' so the meaning of the name is found at the end. This clan got their name from when their ancestors lived at the very back of Luanda village. In Kashe there is a clan called Madolaian. 'Laian' means 'green bean.' Maybe it was because their land was best suited to growing green beans. There is also a Takis-Vanuan clan in Kashe. 'Vanu' refers to honeybees. Their ancestors had a special way of gathering honey. Then there is the Islitoan clan from Isbukun. They had the custom of building perimeter walls around their houses, so everyone called them the 'perimeter wall clan'."

"That's really interesting. Hudas, are there any clans that get their names from the heroic deeds of their ancestors?" Children always view things through their own innocent way of thinking.

"There are. Taupas is a descendent of the Ismahasan clan. Matahas originally means 'red cloth.' Because Taupas' ancestors were brave and skilled in warfare, they managed to dispatch the most enemy warriors every time they went into battle. So the members of their clan were permitted to wear bands of red cloth symbolizing bravery on their heads." Vava knocked his pipe on the ground, scattering bits of glowing tobacco. Everyone took this opportunity to shoot a glance in the direction of Taupas. That made him feel as though insects were swarming over every part of his body, but at the same time, his mouth was drawn into a crooked, self-satisfied smile.

"Among the six main branches of the Bunun people, the Taki-Todou[8] took the name of a heroic ancestor for their name." Hudas Talum spoke as he swallowed the last bits of peanut in his mouth. It was only when they heard his voice that everyone suddenly realized that the man recognized as the living ancestor of the village was in their midst. Nobody had noticed or paid attention to the old man, which made him feel like a lonely spectre. But when they discovered his presence, everyone's spirits were raised as high as a rooster's when he is about to crow. The most famous, most stirring stories all issue from the mouths of those who have lived the longest.

"When the Taki-Todou group first split from Takbanuaz they moved northward to settle near Kavalan[9] where they found themselves opposite the Atayal people in the distance. Because of their traditionally hardworking and thrifty nature, they established a very stable life for themselves and their population quickly grew. Their leader at the time was called Chian-Tolu. He was an illustrious leader, the kind of leader who appears only once in thousands of years.

"According to legend, when Chian-Tolu left his mother's body and fell to the ground, the biggest *tungulan*[10] in memory occurred. Everyone thought that the infant had been sent by black bears because only bears would have the strength to shake the earth like that. His entire life he led his people in fighting against the Atayal to the north and the Lailuwan[11] to the south. Because of his bravery and skill in warfare, as well as his exceptional leadership skills, the Atayal were prevented from moving southward to expand their power. It was due to his talent and strength that the northern boundary of the Bunun people was secured.

"At Kapun,[12] where the territories of the Bunun and Atayal meet there is a broad, productive natural hunting ground that both peoples wanted to occupy as their own. It was the Atayal who first discovered this hunting ground and they opened a trail to access it. They often formed impressive hunting parties to go there to hunt. In order to wrest control of this hunting ground and secure the livelihood of his people, Chian-Tolu led a party of over twenty hunters along the Atayal trail and into the area. On the way, they encountered an Atayal hunting party of eight men. Because both sides wanted control over that hunting ground they got into a heated conflict on the spot. With complete self-confidence, Chian-Tolu cleverly pulled out a banana leaf that he had previously hidden inside his jacket and threw it on the ground. He pointed to the leaf and said, "Let me make it very clear to you that before you found this hunting ground our footprints were already here. During the last full moon, we came here to hunt. Look! This millet cake wrapped in banana leaf is proof." The Atayal had no doubt that their opponents were deliberately provoking them, but because they were far outnumbered, they had no choice but to hold their anger and leave.

"After a period of time, Chian-Tolu again led a party of about ten hunters to that hunting ground. They ran into a group of over thirty Atayal hunters who had been there for some time. At first, the two groups hunted separately without disturbing the other. But when Chian-Tolu's party shot a mountain deer the chief of the Atayal couldn't hold back any longer. He ran over and said to Chian-Tolu, 'The first voices to be heard over this hunting ground were the cries of Atayal men in pursuit of game. This land belongs to us. It makes no difference who shot this mountain deer today, I have decided to return home with it!' Chian-Tolu burst into laughter so loud it would frighten away a ferocious beast. He sternly refused to agree to his opponent's demand. As feelings between the two became more and more agitated, one of the Atayal hunters took advantage of all the commotion and stole into a hidden position. He then raised his bow and was about to kill Chian-Tolu. But the sharped-eyed Bunun hunters discovered him and responded with speed faster than the eyes can follow. Before the sniper could get off his shot, they shot and killed him. With the protection of the heavenly gods, after the sniper died his body remained in the position he had taken for his ambush. This made the Atayal chief, who was a proud warrior, ashamed. There was nothing he could do but lead his party from the hunting ground.

"There was once when Chian-Tolu led his own hunting party into a different hunting ground that belonged to them. An Atayal shaman was able to divine their direction and where they were headed. The Atayal chief thought that their chance for revenge had finally arrived. He ordered warriors from the village to go and wait in ambush along the trail that Chian-Tolu would take back to his village. As they approached the ambush point, Chian-Tolu shrewdly sensed that the cicadas in the forest were unusually quiet and that the little birds were flying around chaotically in the silent forest without their usual grace. The abnormal situation in the forest made him think that there was something dangerous afoot. He ordered his hunters to spread out and encircle the area where the birds were flying about. In no time, the Atayal who were hidden in the forest grove were themselves surrounded by the Bunun hunting party. It was as if they had become prey in a pen. A battle broke out. Arrows flew back and forth between the tree trunks like bolts of lightning. The Atayal had no path of retreat. Many of them were shot dead and lay with two or three Bunun arrows buried in their bodies.

"After that battle the two sides remained silent for a period of time. Then, one time Chian-Tolu led a group of villagers into their own hunting ground to fire-hunt for the meat needed for a festival. The weather suddenly cleared up and not a cloud could be seen for thousands of miles. With the sky so clear, the dense smoke from the fire-hunting rose straight

into the heavens. It could be seen clearly from more than ten *li* away.[13]
When they saw the smoke, the Atayal knew that it was an opportunity
that they couldn't miss. They assembled all the warriors in their village
and went to attack the women and children left behind in the Bunun
village. In their attack they were able to kill six women and take their
severed heads back to their village. When the hunting party returned to
the village and saw the dead and wounded women and children, Chian-
Tolu was furious. Right there and then he said to his people, 'If we don't
avenge our dead in equal number, the Atayal will grow accustomed to
attacking our village and we will live in constant fear!' The hunting party
had no time to rest. They immediately formed into a war party. The
original plan was to attack the Atayal village directly, but along the way
Chian-Tolu noticed the footprints of an Atayal hunting party heading
out to the hunting grounds. He decided that it would save a lot of energy
if they simply lay in ambush for them to return. They had to wait three
days before the Atayal hunting party returned, dragging their exhausted
feet. The Bunun swarmed them and killed over ten of them. The lucky
among the Atayal scurried away in all directions like frightened mice. But
under Chian-Tolu's direction, the unremitting Bunun warriors chased
them all the way to the outer boundary of the enemy village. They then
shot more about ten arrows randomly into the Atayal village, determined
to achieve their vengeance: 'a tooth for a tooth, a life for a life.'

On one occasion, Chian-Tolu led a group of over fifty men out hunting.
On the trail they saw a group made up of Atayal. The Atayal spit at
Chian-Tolu and glared at him. Chian-Tolu refused to put up with this
kind of insult and decided to wait in ambush for them. In fact, the Atayal
were on their way to make a surprise attack on the Bunun village of
Taki-Vatan on the other side of the mountain. But they ended up being
beaten back by the Takivatan people. When the retreating Atayal met
with Chian-Tolu's ambush they took even heavier losses and only a few
of them made it back to their village. After that battle the strength of
the Atayal village was severely reduced, and they sent someone to seek
a truce with Chian-Tolu. Chian-Tolu was aware that carnage had been

suffered by both sides. Faced with the dead and wounded among his people it seemed that victory or defeat was no longer the most important thing, so he agreed to the Atayal proposal. He told the Atayal: 'From now on, when my people build fires by their fields or while hunting, don't take it as a signal to come over and harass us. We will also not enter your fields or your hunting grounds without cause.' For a period of time after this, the two sides were able to honestly respect the agreed-upon conditions. They lived for a long time without incident." Hudas Talum's tone of voice was as gentle as a water bird gliding over the surface of the water.

"No wonder our always build a fire first when they go to work in the fields." Everyone sighed in amazement. They finally understood that the work that they did on a daily basis held within it the traces of their ancestors' brave deeds. It was like walking alone a trail that you have traveled thousands of times and suddenly noticing, off to one side, a beautiful little flower has been blooming there for a long, long time.

"It wasn't only the Atayal. Chian-Tolu also waged war over territory with the Tsou people." The resonance of the voice told people that it was Salivan who was speaking.

"Salivan, do you know his life story, too?" Salivan was such a stubborn, boorish man. How could he have known about the exploits of the Mamangan?[14] It made everyone feel as though he had torn up the ancestors, swallowed them, digested them, and then very quickly passed them out his anus.

"My ancestor was related to Chian-Tolu through marriage, so strictly speaking, I have some of his blood flowing in my veins. In certain rituals his clan and my clan shared meat for the sacrifice.

"Once Chian-Tolu heard from someone who had traveled from a great distance that there is a mysterious place deep in the mountains; a primeval forest that no humans had ever entered. This news excited Chian-Tolu. He even dreamed about roaming freely in that mysterious place, as though he had been there for thousands of years. When he was wide awake Chian-Tolu was well aware that behind any mystery there is always unanticipated danger, danger that might cost you your life. But his curiosity eventually overwhelmed his apprehension. After all, he had lived his entire life in the midst of constant danger. Just like a butterfly in a strong wind, the spirit of death threatened his life day and night. But the gods protected him! In the end, he was always able to extricate himself from the danger and walk homeward in peace. He thus had faith that his unbending willpower would assist him in realizing his fondest dreams. After several suns of consideration and preparation, Chian-Tolu called together a group of about ten brave, experienced men to form a hunting party. First, they were to sojourn in Takbanuaz village, then they would head toward the mysterious forest spoken of by the traveller.

"Chian-Tolu found that the mysterious forest was very different from any forest that he had ever seen. The streams were especially numerous, and their sources were teeming and stable. He scanned the surrounding scenery then exclaimed, 'This is the paradise that I have quested for all my life!' Chian-Tolu well deserved his reputation as a hunter of vast experience. He could determine every single move that his prey might make. With his leadership and management, all the hunters that accompanied him had an easy time killing game of all descriptions. It was as easy as picking the heads off millet in a field. They killed more game than anyone expected. But there was a problem. How were they going to get so much game back to the village? Everyone was much distressed. Even if each hunter was responsible for carrying two animals, there would still be a lot of game left lying on the ground. And then there were the large game like mountain boars and mountain deer. How many men would it take to carry two of those? In the end, Chian-Tolu thought of a solution. He ordered everyone in the hunting party to start cutting the game into pieces. They then used a heavy boulder to squeeze all the blood out of the meat, turning it into *haipis*.[15] The dried meat was much lighter and more evenly shaped, so they were able to gather up all that they had killed and take it back to the village without wasting anything.

It takes some time to press game meat, and the hunting party could only wait and rest. When the black night embraces the mountain forests animals that understand the night leave their hidden lairs. At the same time, animals that fear the blackness drag their full bellies back to their own nests. When they noticed all the animals, several of the younger hunters automatically took up their bows and hid behind a big tree to lie in wait for the kill. "Whoa! Whoa! Whoa!" Chian-Tolu called out sharply from where he was resting. As soon as they heard the noise, the animals all disappeared back into the forest in a flash, taking their shadows with them.

"You frightened all the animals away." The young hunters protested. Chian-Tolu told them that they had enough game for this hunting expedition and that to continue killing was greedy behavior. Not only would it bring no glory, the next time they went out hunting they would not be granted the blessings of the gods. He also invoked a proverb from their forerunners: "If your hands are empty, your home is where you stand. If your hands are full, your home is deep in the mountains." His hope was that when in the mountain forests, his people would abide by the principles of "sufficient heart" and "honest hands" and take only what they needed. Leaving something for tomorrow is the most intelligent course of action.

The moment that they stopped seeing game as their enemies the hunters were able for the first time to observe calmly the many different appearances of all the animals. They discovered that the animals were graceful and worthy of appreciation.

Chian-Tolu was very satisfied with the abundant and varied game in the mysterious forest. So, according to tradition he cut a notch in the trunk of a large tree as a sign that formally claimed this precious tract of forest as a Bunun hunting ground.

After several waxings and wanings of the moon, Chian-Tolu again led seven hunters to the new grounds to hunt and enforce his mastery over that territory. But when they arrived at the hunting ground, they saw a party of about ten Tsou hunters already hunting there. They had clearly not given any heed to the sign that Chian-Tolu had left in the tree trunk. Chian-Tolu's face flushed scarlet with anger at the shame of not being respected. He unsheathed his knife, pointed at the Tsou chief and said, "This hunting ground belongs to the Bunun people. My footprints were long ago stamped all over this forest territory. I can take you and show you the sign that I cut into the trunk of a tree! Leave this place right now, or else as masters of this place, we will expel you in the Bunun way." Not wanting to appear weak, the Tsou chief raised his bow and aimed an arrow at his rival. Then he replied, "This hunting ground belongs to us Tsou people! I can also take you and show you the mark that we cut in the trunk of a tree!" But the cut that Chian-Tolu had made was already dry, whereas the mark cut by the Tsou was still wet. One look confirmed who the real master was. But the Tsou weren't willing to give in. The two sides pursued each other around the forest in battle for a day and a night. Of the seven Bunun, five had wounds of varying seriousness. But only five of the Tsou were still alive and they fled the hunting ground. On their return, Chian-Tolu was utterly exhausted and stopped to rest in Takbanuaz village for a night. He also left the wounded in the care of the people of Takbanuaz village.

After a time, because Chian-Tolu refused to let the matter rest, he led a hunting party of about twenty men into the hunting ground determined to protect his own territory. Once again, they ran into a Tsou hunting group. The two sides dispensed with arguments and curses and got straight down to combat. Soon, the whistles of attack, the shouts of pursuit and the sorrowful sounds of death replaced the scur of cicadas, and the songs of birds in the forest wind. The battle raged until nightfall.

With the help of the ancestral spirits, the killing and shouting could be heard by the people of Takbanuaz several mountains removed. The village then dispatched men to support Chian-Tolu. In the end, the Tsou fled in utter defeat. From that time forward that area became the traditional battle ground of the Bunun and Tsou peoples. Whoever entered there to hunt had to be prepared to defend against the attacks of the other side and even to pay with their lives.

To express their gratitude to Chian-Tolu for bravery and favor in protecting the honor, lives and property of the people with his own life, the people gave his name to their younger generations. They also changed the sound from Tolu to Todo in order to show their respect.

"Okay, that's it. I learned half of that from the descendants of Taki-Todou. The other half is what the elders taught me." In recounting Chian-Tolu's heroism, Salivan's resonant voice seemed to have become much gentler.

After he had eaten his evening meal, Umas walked through the indolent night and home to his courtyard. He sat down on a small rock that served as a chair. In the clear, bright sky, not a cloud could be seen for thousands of miles. A halo of light penetrated the darkness and illuminated the thin, low clouds. The beams of light sparkled ever more brightly until the moon rose slowly from the forest. The moonlight shone over the ground allowing Umas to discern the face of the earth again. As the night emerged, he could feel it pulse through his heart until the waves of moonlight flooded the mountain forests like breakers on the ocean.

Neat rows of stars filled the lonely vastness of the sky, radiating their fragile, distant light over the eternal blackness of the broad wilderness, so clear, so cold. A few stars of similar size clustered near the unbounded horizon emitting their sparkling light. Then they slowly rose, making the earth look tiny and black. Nearby, the brightest star was suspended from the sky, lonely yet resplendent like a hunter resolutely standing watch. The light of the moon and stars turned the earth pallid white. Unnoticed, the mountain range had also changed into a half silvery, half dusky monster. The houses were frozen rigid in the hazy evening light, their proud shadows joined the stars taking in the obscure mysteries of the heavens.

It wasn't long before he began to hear the whistling of flying nighttime creatures ringing through the forest. In the distance, flocks of unknown birds harangued each other in their weird voices, creating a unique cacophony heard only at night. The night was pitch black, but the sky was aglow. A frost would form over the earth before the sun appeared again. Umas raised his head and contemplated.

"Umas, aren't you cold?" Talum's steps made a shuffling sound in the damp courtyard.

"Hudas, there are so many stars tonight, and they are extra bright. Has the sky made lots of new little stars?"

"The sky makes little stars? Ha ha." The old man laughed and sat down beside Umas.

"Right. Otherwise, how could there be more stars now than before? If you could walk around the sky, there wouldn't be any space to move around in." Umas looked at the old man hoping to understand this paradox.

"Our forerunners have told us that the stars are drops of blood that came from the sun when our ancestors shot an arrow into its eye. But there are others who believe that the stars are the eyes of our ancestral spirits. They look down from the sky keeping watch over their children and grandchildren, observing their behavior so as to dispense blessings and curses. So, even if you are all alone, you must always behave according to your conscience. That's because the eyes of the ancestors are always watching everything you do from Heaven."

"Is Chian-Tolu also watching us from Heaven?" Umas had endless idealistic imaginings about the heroes of the past.

"Yes. All of the ancestral spirits use their superior powers to protect us. That's why when we are faced with hardship and fear we should confront it squarely and never flee. We aren't alone. The ancestors are always by our side."

"Cina told me that the eternal home of the ancestral spirits is in a place that we can feel in our spirits. Is the sky like that, too?"

"That's right. The sky is our most familiar, intimate friend. It is also the place our spirits most enjoy." The old man and the boy both looked skyward as if their spirits were wandering freely in the wordless, starry sky.

"Let's go. The air is getting colder. We should go inside and sleep." Talum took the boy's hand.

"Hudas, which stars are Chian-Tolu's eyes?" Umas pointed to the sky overhead.

"I never saw him in person, but I'm sure that Chian-Tolu is up there protecting his descendants with his strong powers, just like the stars are always shining down on us from the blackness of the night sky. They will never ever fall down."

As he entered the house, Umas looked back at the stars clustered in the sky. He noticed one solitary, bright star and thought to himself, that star must be one of Chian-Tolu's eyes because no one could ever forget his illustrious life.

"Masiala,[16] all you great ancestral spirits." Umas sent his solumn blessings to the stars filling the sky.

NOTES

1. A flat winnow woven from yellow rattan used as a platter most of the time.
2. The term used by Bunun people for a bride.
3. A person's own family.
4. A family name. One of the clans in the region.
5. Literally, "a white-haired old man." According to legend, an old man once used a disdainful tone of voice to refuse the help of his family.
6. Encirclement hunting. The Bunun people practice three kinds of hunting, encirclement, ambush hunting, and fire hunting.
7. An eagle.
8. From Taki-Todou.
9. An area of the Atayal people.
10. Great earthquake.
11. The Tsou people.
12. A small foothill area of the middle of the Central Mountain Range.
13. A *li* is a traditional Chinese measure of distance approximately 500 meters long.
14. Heroes, or the most skillful hunters.
15. Dried, pressed meat.
16. A blessing meaning, "live well." Here it simply means, "Good night."

CHAPTER EIGHT

OH MILLET!
WE WELCOME YOU
TO OUR HOMES

In nature, all life forms rely upon their wisdom to develop a lifestyle that is theirs alone. Lifestyles vary, in some cases they are strange and uncanny. But they allow life, that precious gift, to take countless rich, diverse forms and to advance towards more perfect states, carrying the mysteries of the seasonal changes with them.

Fireflies flitted about in the enclosing, black shadows, flashing their disquieting glow over the slopes. Amid the murky shadows of the camphor forest they sprinkled their fragments of light which then shot brilliantly in all directions. As the swarm of fireflies hovered over the misty mountain wastes, their pulsing rhythm diffused in all directions, then in an instant the swarm dispersed, splashing their mysterious, untrammelled colors all over the earth. Sometimes thousands of fireflies gather to display their incredible power, flashing and trembling with precision. They are like an enormous fire dancing out their own mysterious story on the forest stage.

For the last several days Talum had sensed that the earth was in the process of change. He made some mental calculations on behalf of the people, trying to ascertain when the big event might occur. He didn't say anything because if he talked about it, it might not happen after all. According to the legends of the ancients, when people are presented with good fortune they have to look upon it as they would look at an animal they are stalking. Before releasing the arrow they have to be as silent as possible.

At dawn one day, Talum stood in the courtyard waiting for the sun at appear. Just at the point where the sun would rise, he saw a brilliant flash of astral light from the mountain ridge. It turned out to be the solitary radiance of Bintuhan.[1] He inspected the broad azure horizons and pondered the situation. The star could not have been any more brilliant, he thought. Probably it was time to begin the harvest. Bunun people have a special affection for this star. They will even lie in their courtyards all night waiting for it to send down its color and lustre.

After Talum received the news concealed in the star's light he excitedly strode back into his house. There he found everyone, old and young, shelling peanuts in the living room. His two sons and their own daughter were sitting together. Husung and Hanagu whispered to each other, occasionally exchanging playful punches. Observing this intimate scene, Banitul and Malas could only demonstrate their indifference by returning to shell their peanuts in greater earnest. Asulan was avidly teaching Subali how to squash the peanut shells on the ground. The crisp crunching sounds got faster and louder the harder they stepped.

"Malas, this year's millet has been growing for a long time now, and it won't just keep growing forever. So...have you finished weaving the clothes that you were working on?" Talum sat down and joined the work party.

In a plain, natural tone of voice that showed concern for the progress of the work, the old man revealed that immensely important even had arrived. It was time for people to enjoy the new grain. But everyone also seemed to understand the idea that you must not jinx things. They all kept their heads down and continued working, although their hands moved more quickly now because of their excitement.

"Tama, I completed the work just a few days ago. When the face of the moon changed to *minitikokoto*,[2] Banitul and I went to pick the ramie, sort it and boil it. Then we personally dyed it, dried it and rolled it out. For the last few days I've been busy weaving the new clothing. I'm really ashamed that I haven't been able to attend to a lot of household chores, so everyone has had to put up with being dirty." Malas spoke with her head still bowed.

"You are a woman whose hands are more active than her mouth and everyone in the family loves and respects you. Which fortunate person did you weave clothing for this time?"

"Umas. I've noticed lately that he is shooting up like a little tree that's reaching for the sky and his old clothes are like meat on a fire, shrinking smaller and smaller. So I wove him something slightly larger. I hope that he will feel proud to show off his beautiful new clothes."

"Ah, that's great. Your eldest son is truly standing at the gateway to the adult world. Umas, you can give the clothes you can't wear any more to your *nauba*."[3] Talum looked at the boy standing before him, his skinny body wrapped in a white cloth robe looking plain, but spirited. The old man thought to himself, if it keeps him warm that's all that matters. That is what clothing is for.

Talum had heard it said that those who live outside the mountains like to wear all the colors of the *halivalval*[4] to attract other people's attention, but they frighten off the animals. People living outside the mountains don't know how to hunt. A hunter's clothing should be plain and simple so that it's more difficult for the game animals to perceive their movements. He thought to himself and smiled the smile of someone who sees a four-legged snake (lizard), ordinarily an excellent climber, fall to the ground for no reason.

"Hanagu, today you have to concentrate on pounding millet and brewing wine. We have to do the Tinsan[5] ritual and we need the wine as an offering to the gods." Talum looked at his second daughter-in-law.

"I'll do it with Husung." Hanagu nodded.

"Everyday something new comes up. As a family we all have to keep our eyes peeled for problems. We don't want problems to get out of hand. The stronger people should take care of the heavy tasks. Those who are not so strong should do things they feel capable of." Talum wanted to divide things up fairly and in the spirit of harmony according to the size of people's shoulders.

"Tama, have you decided when to do the harvest initiation ceremony?" When Banitul saw the old man allocating the work of preparing for the harvest ceremony and openly discussing the blessed events, he had to suppress a feeling of joy that was like a butterfly breaking free of its cocoon and bravely taking flight. But he kept his voice under control so as not to damage his wings.

"When the wine for the ceremony is ready, we'll start to reap the millet." Talum's voice was filled with delight at the prospect of the harvest. He turned to his second son and said;

"This time you can be the *kasimutu*[6] for the clan."

"Tama, all my life I have done things correctly as you have done. My footsteps have never exceeded yours. I haven't even dared raise the dust with my steps. That is because I know that I still do not have the strength to lead our family toward a good future." Husung was like a *mansisit*[7] faced with danger. He straightened himself up, his face tensed up and he shot glances in all directions.

"Your spiritual power comes from my *huzumui*,[8] so I believe that you are a lot like me. What's more, recently you have not been eating very much which shows that your soul embraces a spirit of thrift and appreciation for food. For the purposes of the up-coming harvest season that's an excellent sign because it means that you are about to have more than you can eat, and that we will have a surplus of millet in our storeroom. It is an auspicious indication for the harvest. If the sacred ritual gives you any difficulty you can ask your older brother. He understands how to satisfy the host of spirits." Talum spoke with great firmness. It seemed that the gods had already made their decision.

"The harvest initiation ritual is really important. You have to appear upright and clean, and you can't let the millet see any dirty clothing. New millet will never reside in a messy, dirty household."

Husung was aware that he was like a withered leaf caught in the whirlpool of the old man's strong will. There was no way he could make it to shore. There was nothing for it but to give in, furrow his brow and wonder how he lost his enthusiasm for food. That was why he ended up being yoked with this heavy family responsibility.

The next few days, brothers Husung and Banitul spent more time together than usual. It was almost like when they were children. But now he wasn't begging his elder brother to teach him new games, he was trying to establish the order and details of the harvest initiation ritual so that he could let the gods know that his family were about to begin harvesting their millet. He hoped to secure good fortune and the blessings of the gods when his people brought in the harvest.

As he recalled it, before the sky had reawakened and after they had eaten breakfast, the master of the harvest initiation rite had to lead three virginal males in full regalia out to the fields. Then, with a reverent mind and a serious attitude he had first to gather the new grain growing on the "ritual field." The night before, those leading the harvest initiation ritual absolutely could not allow nightmares to enter their souls. If they did, then either the ritual had to be postponed, or the master of ceremonies who had been defiled by the nightmare had to be replaced. On the way to the fields, the ritual party were strictly prohibited from sneezing or falling down. Such behavior would influence the size and quality of the harvest.

"That's right. All of those things you mentioned are essential to the performance of the ritual. And there's something else, after they enter the millet field the participants must not drink water, not even a drop."

"They can't drink water?"

"Right. If we drink water before harvesting the millet, when we put the grain in our storerooms it will easily get damp and rot." Banitul as adamant.

"What about the children?"

"It's taboo behavior! It doesn't matter if their throats are cracked from thirst, you have to rely on your high mountain toughness to resist temptation. It is the only way to protect the millet."

The gods are temperamental friends. If your spirit and virtuous behavior makes them happy and satisfied, they immediately become guardians of your life. If your soul is under pressure, they will comfort you and embrace you. When your body is violated, they won't hesitate to protect you, not even for a moment. They will even use their great powers to wash away your shame. However, if your soul or behavior arouse their anger, the gods immediately change and will plunder of your life, your property and your dreams. So, if you want to make them happy and content, your behavior must be guided by wisdom and patience.

After a few days of work, Umas' new clothes were altered several times until they fit him with snug perfection, like a second skin. The millet wine that Hanigu was brewing filled the entire house with a thick fragrant aroma. It also stopped most of the mosquitoes and other hateful insects from entering because they were afraid of becoming drunk in the cloying vapors.

On the evening before the harvest initiation ceremony, Banitul took the ritual staff from the *haungu*[9] in the storeroom. The staff was made from *lapohan*,[10] *vahvah*,[11] and *sikis*.[12] The power of this staff could bring together human souls and the gods in heaven. It was the family's most important possession. The ritual staff was normally kept in a box in the storeroom. Women and children were never allowed to touch it. Because the power of the staff could enter the realm of the gods, it was a sacred object. Banitul carefully wiped the accumulated dust from the staff then placed it in Husung's hands, saying:

"Tomorrow you will use this to summon the gods. This is a supremely sacred object for our cultivation rituals. You must treat it as if you are in the presence of the gods themselves."

The ritual staff made a low clattering sound when it moved, like solemn music. It was a sound that no human could produce. It was heavily weighed down with the aspirations of the family, so its tone was especially deep. Husung took it firmly in his grip as though he feared it might disappear at any moment.

"Who do you want for the ritual party tomorrow?" Banitul was concerned.

"Aside from your son, Umas, there is my son, Asulan, and Tama Vava's son, Itun."

"Will those boys be all right?" Because he couldn't personally take part in this important ceremony, Banitul's sense of regret had transformed into uneasy imaginings.

"Those boys are all almost adults. They should be able to control their spiritual power and they won't violate any ritual taboos."

The next morning, the earth lay in silence as if the gods had forgotten to create any wind. In the nearby forest, not a single branch or a single leaf was disturbed, nor was there so much as a breath of wind in the clumps of grass. The glow of dawn still seemed far away as the pale blue of dawn floated through the cold sky.

Talum stood at the front door watching in silence as his family's ritual party prepared to enter the mountains. It was as if he was asking if the party had made all its preparations, and also giving them his blessing that all might proceed without incident.

"Husung, were your dreams last night auspicious? Did the heavenly gods give you any signs?" Talum's voice broke the morning silence.

"No. I didn't have any dreams last night at all. Before I went to sleep, I was busy replacing some of the old cord on the ritual staff. As soon as I lay down, I don't remember anything happening." Husung looked helpless. He could only wait upon the old man's pronouncement.

"That's good. If you had no dreams, that's very good. We just don't want to let the evil spirits take possession of our souls." Talum declared.

"Boys, starting now, in everything, in every action, you have to listen to Tama Husung. Don't let the mischievous spirits misguide your steps. Don't let the stones on the trail trip you, and especially make sure you don't sneeze. Off you go! Pray that our great ancestral spirits lead you by the hand along the path of peace and ease."

Husung led the young party into the deep, somber mountain forest. From time to time he turned to remind those behind him not to be like the *halum*[13] that sticks to the ground. They had to step carefully so that they didn't trip and violate the taboo. The young boys didn't understand, so Husung smiled and told them:

"From now on we are the millet in the field. If the millet falls to the ground its grain will rot, won't it?"

All the way there, the boys concentrated on raising their feet high to avoid tripping over the big rocks that had been so deviously placed on the trail. The grass beside the trail was bent over, heads bowed low as if it couldn't support the load of morning dew. The blush of dawn now became apparent in the pale blue sky and grew ever brighter. The party stopped on the top of the ridge and gazed down. Resting in the embrace of the mountain slope the village was still and silent. It made one wonder what kind of noise it would take to wake the place up. After a little while, all the households lit their cooking fires and smoke rose like milky white strips of cloth in the sky. They dispersed under the morning light and danced in the breeze as if wishing each other good morning, or perhaps they were telling romantic tales about the night just past.

The entire forest was at peace. It was as if all the creatures were awaiting some sound which they would begin to imitate it. As the sun climbed higher, the sky turned a clearer blue and the heavy morning dew evaporated to form mist that gathered at mid-slope. The mountain wind began to blow, eliciting soft whispers from inside the forest. It sounded like the first sighs of an earth preparing to awake. It wasn't long before the myriad life forms of the mountain vastness were calling out and their unique voices were wafting about the woods.

"Today will belong to the sun." Husung looked over the gorgeously illuminated earth.

The millet stalks in the fields hung their heads as if protecting their full ears of grain. They looked drowsy, as though they hadn't slept all night. Close by the field, the residents of the mountain forest unfolded their life forces in the chill of the morning. The sound of a woodpecker intermittently pecking at a tree trunk rang in the distance carrying along with it the moans of the trees. Hidden not far from the work shed, little quails made resolute cooing sounds as if they were struggling out from under a huge rock that had fallen on them thousands of years ago.[14] Dark brown birds swooped back and forth over the millet field and through the forest looking for insects. The sound of their wings sweeping past the branches of the trees broke through the air. At the same time, a flock of about ten munias darted stealthily about, sweeping low over the field, hoping to find opportunities to steal millet.

When they arrived at the work shed by the field, Husung pulled the ritual staff and a *siaku*[15] filled with millet wine from his string bag. He faced the broad field and raised the gourd. He then sprayed the millet along a horizontal line over the millet and pronounced in a stately voice:

"Hupikaunan! Oh, ye great gods, we stand in awe of your powers. We have entered the field that you granted to us without incident. The stalks of the millet have grown as straight and stiff as mountain boar hair and the ears of golden millet hang down like strings of pearls. Oh great gods, prevent us from encountering rats and snakes and other vile creatures that harm the millet. Do not let us sneeze so that the evil spirits and their curses will remain in deep slumber. Under your care and guidance our work here today will surely be completed smoothly. Hu! Hu! Hu!"

"Itun, take Asulan into the gorge over there and gather *buhul*.[16] Make sure the leaves are long and thick." As soon as Husung had completed the invocation he delegated various tasks to the ritual party.

"How much do you need?"

"As much as your two hands can hold." Husung spread his arms then brought them back together forcefully to indicate a tight squeeze. Then he continued;

"Umas, you stay here. We don't have to reap much new grain today so we don't need too much *buhul*."

"Uh-huh." Umas shrugged his shoulders passively.

There was a lizard quietly enjoying the warm sunshine on the pile of rocks in front of the work shed. When it heard unfamiliar voices it suddenly flipped up its tail and arched its skinny body with a ferocious hiss.

"Gis!"[17] Husung cursed and waved in the air. The lizard dove into the millet field and disappeared like a bolt of lightning.

"When they're frightened, lizards always run off in the direction that the sun rises. Hunters use this habit of theirs to find their directions. That's why hunters never get lost. The lizards are chasing the spirit of the sun." Husung watched the fleeing lizard then looked up at the rising sun.

"Tama Husung, are we going to start cutting the new grain?" Umas was industrious by nature, and full of energy.

"Today's ritual is mostly to gather the *lunkaival*[18] planted in the ritual field." Husung pointed to the ritual plot located in the middle of the field. "That is grain for the gods to eat. We first have to offer the fruits of our labor to the gods to make them feel satisfied."

"Tama Husung, did our people plant the grain that the gods eat?" Umas was pleased to know that the food of the gods actually came from their village.

"*Lunkaival* is the most ancient kind of millet. Only the gods may enjoy it."

"So, what kind of millet do we eat?"

"The gods take special care of our people. From the time of our ancestors we have grown eight kinds of millet. Some can be used for making wine, some is good for making cakes, and other kinds are best eaten steamed."

"Are there that many kinds?" Although he had eaten millet for many years, he had no idea that there were so many varieties. Umas looked completely at a loss.

"Of course, but even our respected elders have to concentrate if they want to distinguish the varieties of millet based only on appearance, so let me tell you about them! The kind that has really hard husks on the seeds and leaves covered with spikes is called *kaivun*. The kind with kernels that look white but have no tails on their heads are called *kaluvungal*. The kind with taller than usual stalks and leaves and whose kernels look red on the outside but white inside is called *lepunot*. It tastes the best. *Mantteiong* heads are the shortest of all the varieties of millet. *Mitsilan* kernels are a pale red color, while *tokulatasal* kernels are the purest white. The kind with fuzz covering the husks and with greenish kernels is *toual*. *Tsinkaval* kernels are also greenish, but their leaves are bigger than *toual*." As Husung explained he used his hands to demonstrate the rough appearance of each kind of millet.

"What kind of millet did we plant this year?"

"We planted delicious *lepunot.*"

"Ok. Boy, I hope we don't have to wait too long to eat the new grain."
Umas happily surveyed the field before him. Under the bright sunshine the
millet reflected back a golden hue, illuminating the surrounding scenery.

"Tama, is this the kind you meant? Will it be enough?" Itun and Asulan
appeared out of the bushes with their arms full of thick green leaves.

"Yes. Those are the kind of leaves that we use to bind the millet leaves
into *tapath.*"[19] Husung bent down and took a closer look. There are other
plants in the forest that look similar, but their use and characteristics are
very different. If you aren't careful, you can make a big mistake.

He tilted his head as if he had just thought of something then scratched
his messy head of hair and told the boys that while the millet is still in
the fields it is called *madoh.* When you bind it into sheaves it is called
tapath, and when you pound it to remove the husks it's called *tilas.* The
tilas can be boiled and eaten.

"Let's go into the ritual field and gather the new grain." As Husung
walked out of the work shed the ritual staff in his hand made clattering
noises that seemed to be summoning to the spirits of the young people.

Umas carefully observed the millet in the ritual field. It really did look
different from the grain growing in the main field, but the full heads
of grain were very pleasing.

Husung inspected the entire ritual field and located a stalk of grain
that had a large, ample head and broad leaves that had not been damaged
by insects or disease. He grasped the stalk firmly in his right hand while
holding the head in his left hand. Closing his eyes, he slowly pulled the
whole lovely plant from the ground. He then turned to Umas standing
beside him and said:

"When the roots and leaves of the millet remain completely intact
that's called *ailamuaan.*[20] You have to take hold of it carefully so as not
to damage its body."

Husung pulled up six intact plants then bound them up with a thick green *buhul.* He told the boys:

"Each one of you must go with reverent and joyful heart and pull out six perfect stalks of the new grain as I have done. Then you must bind them up carefully. The millet in the field is about to enter our home. We must be extremely hospitable in our attitude and manners. Do everything possible to avoid being too rough, otherwise they will refuse to become our guests."

Following Husung's lead the youngsters carefully uprooted the millet as if they were picking up a beehive full of honey. When they got back to the work shed, they laid the perfect sheaves of new grain neatly on the ground. Husung held the ritual staff in both hands and knocked up and down above the grain making the staff rattle. Then he solemnly declared to the grain:

"Oh millet, who is going to be our guest this year? You have grown healthy and full. Our family will welcome you with joyous hearts. Here I pray to the gods in heaven that the millet that we harvest this year will be as inexhaustible as the water in the mountain gorges. May it fill our storerooms so full that not an inch of space remains. When we eat this year's millet may our bodies be even stronger and heathier than last year so that we can hunt down the biggest, fattest game. Now I worship you with boar shoulder bone, jaw and trotter. May you return home with us with happiness in your hearts!"

The afternoon wind cooled the entire mountain forest. The mature millet with its coat of yellowish brown bobbed in the wind like endless, exuberant golden waves.

"Let's go! We have to hurry back to the village before the sun turns red. Everyone is waiting to see what the new grain looks like." Husung looked at the sun inclining towards the mountains and realized that the afternoon was already half over.

When Husung and his troop arrived back at the village they noticed that lots of people had already gathered in Talum's courtyard. Among them were men of Hudas' generation, and also Tama's generation, along with women who carried their infants in their arms. Judging by the fact that that babies were sound asleep it was apparent that they had been waiting for a long time. When faced with important events like this people were in the habit of gathering together. Talum had long been the source of wisdom and life support for the entire village.

At the beginning when they left the old village, Talum had led the people with his extraordinary bravery. Under his leadership they had survived many challenges as they escaped hardship and moved toward a more peaceful future. For many years everyone had felt that it was essential that such an elder live in the village, just like every forest must have one giant tree for it to possess deep spiritual influence and an imposing bearing.

"Hu! We welcome this year's new grain to our village. Your healthy appearance and full heads bring us great joy. We hope that every year the grain that we grow will be as beautiful as you." After Talum received the back sack he continued to pronounce prayers and blessings.

With great deference and care, Talum took each of the sheaves of new grain into the storeroom in his house. There he hung them on the wooden posts to the left and right of the entrance to the storeroom then waved the ritual staff to express gratitude to the ancestors and gods for their beneficence:

"Hupikaunan! We are about to commence our harvest. May this year's millet be so abundant that it fills our storerooms and overflows out the doors so that we won't be able to finish eating it for three or even five years! We will kill a boar to show our gratitude. May this year's millet be piled higher than our roofs, and after we have eaten it may our families be healthy and strong so that we may we defeat any enemies who come to attack us and bring down the most ferocious of wild animals. Hu! Hu! Hu!"

As this was taking place, Banitul and several other men had gone out with a thick ramie rope to capture a black boar for the sacrifice. It took them several all-out attempts before they finally brought a boar to ground. The squeals of the beast as it tried to resist death reverberated through the whole village.

When he saw this Umas had a strange feeling. His childhood memories seemed to be filled with the black boar. Whenever his mind was idle or he couldn't find anything interesting to do, he would see the kindly image of the boar. When the drizzly rain was being blown about making people miserable, he could always hear the dignified guttural calls of the boar. When he felt secret shame that could not be expressed to others, only the black boar would pretend to listen to him. The boar was everywhere, and always remained in his heart. Now everyone had grown up. He had begun to sprout black whiskers and his voice had become deep and coarse. The black boar had grown fat with a drooping belly which made it look awkward and stupid.

After it squealed for a time the boar calmed down out of exhaustion. People saw Talum walk before the boar with a sharp bamboo knife in his hand. Facing in the direction of the sun's rise he made a gesture of welcoming an important guest then raised his voice in prayer:

"Hupikaunan! We are about to kill a boar as an offering to the great ancestors and the beautiful millet. Oh millet! Please come to join us quickly. We welcome you to our homes. Ye gods and millet! We have more boar meat than you can possibly eat. We beseech you to bring us the millet of other villages so that it also can enjoy the savory boar meat and increase our store of millet. Come! Call all the millet in the entire mountain forest to come forth to enjoy our boar meat. Hu!"

Thereupon Talum plunged the knife into a space between the boar's ribs. The boar's squeals turned into mournful howls that combined with the sound of its *bak*,[21] *haputun*,[22] and *hadath*[23] being rent apart. Amid the blood curdling cries the people in the surrounding crowd first became excited, then almost crazed.

There is an absolute correlation between the size of the harvest and the killing of the boar. The people firmly believe this. When the dying boar shrieks in pain it attracts the millet from all directions to come and partake of the fresh, succulent boar meat. After they have eaten their fill, the millet will happily remain in the storeroom of the host to increase the size of his supply of grain. So, when the cries of the boar began to weaken, Talum deliberately twisted the bamboo knife inside its body so that the squeals of the nearly dead beast rose again and were carried to the farthest corners. The woods on the mountain slope were shaken by the agonized cries of the boar, as if set in motion by all the millet that had heard the cries and now rushed towards the village.

The black boar looked coldly around at its surroundings with regret, and at the same time complaint. Umas felt a great pain in his heart. It was as if he had been stabbed in the back with a pin, but his arms were too short to pull it out, so he had to endure the pain. He was overwhelmed by a sense of helplessness. This was life. It is like tomorrow's weather; no matter whether you like it or not, or if you have any plans, you have to walk out into that weather. You have no way of refusing it. That is life. That is the mountain forest.

By the time all the millet had been summoned the boar no longer had the strength to cry out. It just lay there in a cold pool of its own blood. Bisazu, the shaman, led people in singing the *maunboknakanunun*.[24] The men selected the tone and volume according to their own abilities and standing in the village. The multi-part music had a definite order and arrangement so that nobody's voice interfered with or superseded anyone else's. But when you listened, it harmoniously blended with the sounds of nature, making people forget the agonized squeals of the black boar.

With their practiced hands, the women then took over and began preparing to cook the boar meat. They would invite everyone present to the feast. Before the feasting began, Talum gave two *makau*[25] fruits to every family, whispering a prayer each time:

"I hope that this year's millet will give every family an abundant harvest. During the harvest season may no family be subject to punishment from the gods and may all the people reverently and diligently harvest millet until their storerooms are filled."

Since he had witnessed all manner of human tragedy and fortune, Talum never forgot to remind people that during the harvest ceremony they must respect all taboos. He had said this so many times that he had lost track, yet he still reminded people over and again: "When you first eat the new grain you cannot use a *taku*,[26] you can only use your finger to scoop out the grain. If this ritual is observed, nobody will suffer from an upset stomach after eating the new millet. After eating the first new grain you must not walk outside your house because the spirits will send a mountain wind to blow your mouth askew as punishment." He also told people that these taboos established by the ancestors are all for the purpose of allowing people to experience personally the importance of millet in their lives. People had to be humble in face of the kindness of the millet and never boast or show off. These are all the rules of life for Bunun people, and it is what they believe in their hearts.

Talum was well aware that each individual's fate is like the shape of trees; each is different. Some families may work more assiduously than the sun, but the crops that they plant wither and die for no reason so that they have nothing to harvest. That is what happens when you are cursed by the evil spirits. Talum always told families stricken with bad luck that before they harvest the millet, they must carry out the Palutsanun[27] in order to avoid the entanglements of ill fortune. For this ritual they need to find an upstanding virginal male in their clan who has never stolen anything or told a lie. At harvest time that individual must enter the family storeroom alone and undertake the so-called Linun.[28] The genitals of the person who serves as the "scapegoat" must be large because the belief is that there is a mysterious relationship between the genitals of the "scapegoat" and the millet in the fields. If the genitals are large, then it will make the millet grow especially large. If the genitals are small, then the millet will also be small.

When the "scapegoat" is shut in the storeroom he must be supplied with good boar and chicken meat as well as other foods. These foods must be prepared by a healthy, attractive virginal girl. This demonstrates the hope that the millet in the fields will grow to be as healthy and beautiful as the girl. The "scapegoat" must not sleep during the day, otherwise the millet will also lie down in the fields. Aside from the girl who prepares the food, no other people may enter the storeroom. If they do, the bad luck from this year will continue to dog them into the future.

All Talum's ideas were as unimpeachable as his reputation. No one had ever cast doubt on them. Many believed that when the people first moved to this 'unique mountain slope,' the local spirits were unwilling to share the delightful place with them. At the time, Talum was not only persistent and sincere in his negotiations with the benevolent spirits, he never rested in his struggle against the harmful evil spirits. The ultimate result was the very gratifying reality that they could now see before their eyes. When some of the elders spoke, they sometimes carelessly mentioned Talum's mysterious experiences. For example, one evening after a rain the earth was especially cool. Even butterflies whose wings had been damaged by the rain flitted and danced about happily over the bushes. The weather made the heavenly gods decide to invite Talum to their home. The trail up to the gods' residence was stunning. It was a joy to walk upon because it looked as though it had been lined with layer upon layer of rainbows. From that time forward, everyone privately called Talum "the man who has walked on a rainbow."

"My people! Everyone gather around. Before we begin to reap the millet, we must make an offering to the gods by slaughtering a boar. In this way we let them know that we are about to start the sacred labor of harvesting the millet. We request that the gods protect us in our time of labor so that our bodies will not be harmed. We hope that everything will proceed without incident and that we will have a plentiful yield." Talum cleared his throat then announced in a loud voice: "This year we must give thanks to you. The *kiuthu*[29] always begins with us so that our efforts in the fields are completed first. In future, it need not be this way. Whoever first needs help, we will assist them first. My people, bring your children and share with us in this feast of fresh boar meat and other dishes."

With the help of many, the courtyard was lined with wooden plates piled high with boar meat, millet cakes, pigeon peas with pork chops, black nightshade, roast bamboo shoots, and barrels of millet wine. The long prohibition against eating fine food was finally lifted. As people contemplated the arrival of the harvest season, they were seduced by all the delicious food and abandoned themselves to indulgence.

Carrying a medium-sized clay cooking pot, Talum intoned a blessing as he distributed pieces of meat equally to all the children kneeling on the ground:

"My children! May you eat this and grow quickly to become as imposing as the great mountains. May your movements be as nimble as the birds in flight that even the fiercest enemies will never be able to defeat you. May your very existence prevent outsiders from daring to violate your relatives and your land."

The children could hardly wait to stuff the meat into their mouths. Some of the smallest among them filled their mouths so full that their cheeks ached. All that could be heard was the sound of chewing as everyone quietly savored the wonderful sensation of fat meat washing around in their mouths.

It was not long before the power of the millet wine began to excite the people attending the feast so that their laughter and conversation got louder. It was as if the entire village was filled with joy at the approach of the harvest. A mountain wind elicited a low, forceful soughing from the forest. The leaves on the trees swayed back and forth as though they were as drunk as the villagers. Countless mountain birds hopped and flew about the trunks of the trees as is they were going to their own banquet.

Dark shadows of dusk filled the sky like a black river slowly flooding in from the furthest distance. As the daylight collapsed from exhaustion and sank into the recesses of the deep mountain gorges, dusk turned the whole forest black. The power of darkest night now took control of the mountains, and the spirits of the night began to scurry about in the bosom of the earth. A shaft of bright starlight drifted over from the mountain ridge, solitary and dazzling. Everyone reminded each other to gaze up at this large star, that great star that had brought the news of the harvest.

NOTES

1. Probably the double star Sirius in the Canis Major constellation.
2. The waning moon.
3. Younger brothers and sisters.
4. Rainbow.
5. Ritual to initiate the harvest of the millet.
6. Master of ceremonies.
7. "Eye snake" or cobra.
8. Testicles.
9. A grain storage container.
10. Boar shoulder blade.
11. Boar jaw bone.
12. Boar hoof.
13. Scaly ant-eater or pangolin.
14. According to legend, people were once moving rocks, making low grunting sounds resembling the calls of quails. In the end a rock fell on top of them, crushing them and turning them into quails.
15. Gourd container.
16. A plant used to bind the sheaves of millet.
17. A sound to chase something away.
18. The heritage millet used to worship the gods.
19. Large sheaves of millet.
20. Meaning "perfect" or "flawless."
21. Lungs.
22. Heart.
23. Liver.
24. A traditional harvest song which is different from songs praying for abundant harvest.
25. An inedible forest fruit.
26. A small wooden spoon.
27. A traditional rite to exorcize evil.
28. Meaning "to take the place of evil." In other words, to be a scapegoat.
29. The rotating labor system.

CHAPTER NINE

THE ROAD TO MATURITY

Dense, drizzly rain floated in the sky, but neither the busy adults nor the children at play were particularly concerned about it, thinking that it was just another of those thick fogs that often bothered them. They all just kept their heads down and continued with the work to hand, or with their games.

From his house, Umas watched the rain falling to the ground in gentle, elegant strands. It was completely silent, yet somehow mysterious. Beams of light shone through the layered clouds making the raindrops sparkle like billions falling stars, leaving the myriad creatures to wander about in their midst. The raindrops themselves were a flock of playful sprites bring moisture to the dry twigs and leaves that covered the ground, giving the forest a fresh, yet fetid scent. They chattered about everything under the sun as they scampered past moss-covered stone walls and undulating rocky gorges. Umas thought that he heard a familiar sound. It was the forest quietly sighing its approval after receiving the nourishment of the rain.

Time passed, and Banitul noticed that the entire mountain forest had fallen still. All that remained was the coarse sound of his own breathing.

Looking outside he saw that threads of fine rain still dripped from the sky, but things had brightened up a little. In any case, he didn't care. He felt very lazy. Having shed its layer of dust, the mountain range with its graceful curves now shone clearly in the sky. Wizened slips of cloud drifted slowly westward to pile up in the hollows like feathers. Now and again, muffled thunder like the belching of children carried through the air. Mountain birds hidden deep in the forest sprang into action. Some chased nimble insects around in the shrubbery, others stretched their muscles in the sky. The long silent earth was now animated by every imaginable bird call.

"Ana-na! Ana-na!" Deep, stentorian shouts of pain came from outside the house.

"Is that Asulan? What's the matter?" Umas bounded out of his house like a frightened grasshopper.

"Just hold on! It's almost over. I'm only making a small hole. Are you a man or what?" Tama Husung was trying to pierce his son's earlobe with a fine, sharp bamboo needle. But Asulan kept dodging him, making it impossible to do the piercing cleanly. All that Husung managed were a few swollen, bloody scratches.

"When we Bunun men enter *mintalmaidu*,[1] we have to have our ears pierced." Umas shot an arrow of reality towards Asulan to encouraged him.

"When Umas had his ears pierced he didn't make a fuss. He was brave. His eyebrows didn't move, and his eyes just enjoyed the distant scenery." As he spoke, Husung tightened his grip. He grabbed and pinched as though he was trying to get a little muntjac out of a pitfall.

Umas had been through this ritual just when his childhood was at an end. He had long ago forgotten the pain, although the suspense of waiting to be stabbed was not so easy to put out of his mind. It was like being shaken from sleep by a nightmare. He only had to think about the process for every little detail to flood into his mind, as if it had happened yesterday.

He had his Tama's encouragement to thank for his resoluteness in face of the ear-piercing test. His Tama told him that people have their ears pierced so that they can wear animal bone earrings. If they don't, then when they die malicious ghosts will pull them to the eternal resting place of the ancestors by their earlobes as punishment. What's more, the malicious ghosts will deliberately choose a trail covered with thorns and prickles so that the deceased with unpierced ears will end up covered with so many cuts and scrapes that they will want to die again.

"If you don't have your ears pierced now, after you die the malicious ghosts will pierce a really big hole in your earlobe and give you a wooden pestle for an earring. The pestles are so heavy that people can't walk straight. My boy, if you want to avoid this kind of punishment you have to go through with the ear-piercing ritual now. If you don't, even the most powerful shaman won't be able to remove the curse." Tama Husung's expression was very focussed, as if he were dissecting a game animal and didn't dare make any mistakes.

"Ana-na! Ana-na!" "Ana-na! Ana-na!" Everyone is afraid of the punishments of the malicious ghosts. Asulan's face contorted into a ball as he endured the pain of the bamboo needle. His cries of pain seemed stuck inside his body unable to find the exit on his face.

"Ai-yo! It hurts like hell." When Tama Husung pushed a stalk of grass into the bloody hole tears flooded from the corners of Asulan's eyes.

"It's done, you little man with no balls." Tama Husung lightly knocked the boy on the head, but he had a friendly, mocking smile. "Once the hole has healed, I'll put in a few more grass stalks to make it a bit bigger. After that you'll be a real Bunun man; one that can race through the mountain forests; a hunter whose footprints will cover the hunting grounds."

"Oh?" It was still a long way away, but when he thought of the second round of adversity, Asulan's face turned ashen and he felt like he had something hard caught in his throat. In the end, he couldn't hold back the tears and they streamed down his cheeks.

By the time Tama Husung had disappeared inside the house Asulan had already let his gaze shift towards the mountain scenery floating in the wind. His expression changed with the dancing mountain forest. For some unknown reason a great flock of birds had flown up to welcome the mountain wind. Although constantly jostled by the wind, except for the movement of their wings, they remained miraculously stationary in the sky. The longer Asulan watched this marvelous scene, the happier he became. Like a lively whirlpool, his youthful vitality swirled back to his lips to become a calm, happy smile. As for the blood on his ear and the pain of the grass stalks, these had become very distant concerns.

Asulan's childhood was not yet over. Umas gently smiled.

As they had done for a million years, a few puffy white clouds wiped the heavens clean like a washcloth. Umas looked up at the cold, blue sky. He piously considered how only the dwelling place of the gods could be so beautiful and pristine.

Subali chased the chickens around the courtyard looking serious and determined. Like all of his people, he had the heart of a hunter hidden deep in his chest. That heart was aroused as soon as he began to walk, and in the long future ahead his actions would be guided by the most primal nature of the ancestors.

When the agile mother hen leapt up onto the stone wall to get out of harm's way Subali turned to chase the flock of chicks on the ground. Astonished at the treachery of humans, the hen paced uneasily along the top of the wall clucking out warnings to her chicks.

One of the spirited young hunting dogs tried to help its young master to round up the tender prey. An older hound quickly ascertained that this was just one of the human's games and not the life and death struggle of the hunt. There being no blood to tempt it, it closed its eyes, lay back down and continued to snooze. Flies covered its eyes, but it didn't even shake its head. Its chin hit the ground with a clunk, but the old dog wasn't bothered. Like an old man lying in bed with a chronic disease, it slept as though nothing had happened.

The frightened chicks darted around on their short legs, dodging left then scampering right. With the clumsy assistance of the young hunting dog, Subali actually managed to catch one of the chicks. At that, the mother hen finally jumped down from the wall and started circling Subali, madly squawking and hopping about. She beat her wings and extended her sharp claws menacingly, as if channelling the brutal power of the death spirits.

"Gis!"[2] Umas was afraid that the hen was going to peck Subali, so he stood up and shooed it away.

"*Tolkuk*,[3] *tolkuk*." Clutching the chick tightly, Subali proudly showed off his booty, unaware that by arousing the hen's maternal rage he had placed himself in grave danger.

"Put it down. All cinas turn into scary monsters when they have to protect their young." Umas took the chick from Subali's hand and placed it on the ground so that it could run back to its mother's side. The hen clucked and comforted the chick as she anxiously inspected it for any harm.

"It ran away, the *tolkuk* ran away." Subali watched in disappointment as the hen herded the chick away.

"That isn't called *tolkuk*, it's called *suswauth*.[4] In our people's language there are always special names for newly born creatures. They never have the same name as mature animals. For example, a newly born child is called *wuvath*, rather than *Bunun*. A recently hatched chick is called *suswauth* rather than *tolkuk*. A new puppy is called *luhih* and not *asu*, and a lamb is called *haniin*, not *hanian*....

Umas once asked why this was so. The adults said that each new little creature represents the way for living things to continue their kind.

They are the future hope of all living things. That's why they must be protected. We all have a responsibility to defend baby creatures from harm. Giving them separate names reminds us that we have to protect them and never allow them to come to harm.

The Bunun language uses words in a novel, powerful way! Every sentence, every word is like the scar left on a giant tree by a lightning strike. No matter how you try, you can't erase it. There is a source of power deeply rooted in the language of Bunun villages. It is replete with creative spirit, uniqueness and heavenly endowment. This takes form as an insightful, original language that is extremely effective. Many believe that it was the first language ever heard over this land. No other language can compare with Bunun language when it comes to being concise and vivid. It is ingenious and deft. It comes from the deepest realms of the soul, making the senses boil over until people tremble to their core.

"*Susuwauth! Susuwauth!*" Umas hadn't noticed that Subali was again chasing around in the courtyard playing the hunter.

As he watched Subali pursue the chicks with determined, steady steps, Umas thought back to the black boar that had been slaughtered a few days ago. Images of the beguiling beast drifted into his mind. Perhaps all people need such a beguiling animal to accompany them as they grow up. He lowered his head and pondered this idea.

Over the next few days, Umas sensed that everything around him had changed. It was as if some unfriendly power was transforming the world before his eyes. Every time an adult looked at him, it seemed as if they were harboring some mysterious plot against him. It was as if everyone knew what was about to take place and only he couldn't see what it was. The suspicion in his mind quickly changed to stress. Usually, instructions from the adults about his behavior, or what was required of him, were like the buzzing of bees swarming in his head; there was too much to take in. But now, overnight, this had all disappeared without a trace, like a rat that crawled into a deep hole in the ground. Elders no longer told him casual stories that made him blush. When he met them on the paths, the adults even moved out of his way. He felt like the most important person in the village, or the most hated, and this made him confused and anxious. He was afraid that he had committed some grave error without knowing it. Maybe he had messed up something important in the village, but the adults had silently forgiven him. Or had he already been purged from the group and cast into solitude? Or maybe...or maybe...the problem was that he really didn't know what had happened. A large stone weighed upon him all day long, slowing his steps to a snail's pace. It was distressing for him.

He tried to shake off that unidentified weight by pulling back the carefree days of his past. Umas decided to ask Hudas for help. The elders were the protectors of life, and they were also proof that the gods live among mankind.

"Hudas, are you there?" Umas stretched his neck and called in the direction of the old man's house.

"Umas, come, come over. I'll get a chair for you." Talum looked up at the young man then searched in the shade for a dark-colored chair.

"I can get it myself. The chair is here." The old man's courteous words and attitude made the look in Umas' eyes even sharper.

Despite having no wife to help with the housework, Talum's room was clean and orderly. All the furniture and utensils were arranged in the most appropriate places, and the air from the forest circulated freely about the wide interior spaces. Where the bed met the wall in a right angle there was a shiny wooden shelf neatly piled with women's skirts and ornaments made of ramie. Late at night when all was still, Talum liked to rearrange all the clothing on the shelf. The skirts always made a rustling sound that made him feel as though his wife had never left him, and that she was still hard at work around the house, always watching over him.

On that summer day filled with sunlight after that boy holding his bloody leg and bawling appeared in Talum's courtyard, he had always maintained his vow to do his utmost to protect his family and their new home. He assumed his wife's responsibility for watching diligently over his family and his own future.

"Hudas, what are you doing?"

"Nothing, nothing." Talum put down the short club he had been holding.

"That's a nice-looking club." Umas reached out curiously to stroke the milky white wooden club. It was so shiny and smooth that he couldn't resist caressing it a few times.

"This is made from beechwood, it's a very hard wood." Talum picked up the club and inspected it closely, as if he thought it the most perfect tool ever made.

"What is it for?"

"It's for pulling out front teeth."

"Has someone's tooth been cursed by the evil spirits?" The unremitting pain of a toothache could make a person feel as though the world had completely changed its complexion.

"My son, with the compassionate nurture of the earth and the blessing of the gods you have safely matured into an adult. Lately I have noticed the strong aura of the *tumathz*[5] surrounding your body. From your behavior I perceive that your life spirit already has the strength to begin racing through the mountain forests. The village and our family need this strength in order to continue standing tall on the face of the earth. For that reason, in the name of the family, I must pull out your front teeth. You must bravely pass through this painful test in order to maintain the most beautiful, fierce and tenacious life spirit. Only then will you be a true Bunun man who can lead his clan and the village toward the unknowable future.

"Oh?" A clap of thunder exploded in Umas' ears. The image of his broad incisors being pulled from his soft, sensitive mouth brought a sense of terror in his mind.

"The removal of the front teeth is an extremely important ritual in a person's life, it is the most difficult test and challenge. A man who has not had his incisors removed has no way to access the strong, resolute willpower that issues from the high mountains. When he goes to war with his enemies, he will lack courage and will not dare confront them. You should know that those who turn their backs on their enemies always end up being pursued and killed. When hunting in the mountains you will be despised by the game and they will not allow you to capture any of them. Women who do not undergo the pulling of teeth ritual will lack the patience to complete the long, complex process of weaving cloth." Talum looked at the boy's terrified face and told him in a serious, forceful tone, "Umas, you must face the teeth-pulling ritual steadfastly. The pain makes a weak body strong, and only perseverance produces that lightning fast, explosive strength in your life spirit. It is the second trial on the path to becoming a brave warrior in our village."

Upon once hearing the hoot of an owl and determining that Asulan was about to face some dangerous ill luck, Umas began to think that his own soul must have some unique power. That power allowed him to foresee events of the coming years and months with clarity. Perhaps his soul could return from the future to foretell the potential results of all events.

He believed that all major events were preceded by distinct portents. It was just like when a hunting party enters the mountains and the *hathan*[6] always fly from the right to the left of the hunters it is an omen of ill fortune. In such cases a capable hunting party leader will call off the hunt. If someone sneezes as you are about to leave the house adults automatically take off their entire outfit and rest for a moment in order to dispel the impending misfortune. These actions have persisted unchanged for thousands of years, so the elder who first perceived the mysterious connections and established the responses must have been a person of exceptional ability.

Since watching the unhappy episode of Asulan's ear piercing and noting the strange looks that the villagers were giving him, Umas had a vague sense that some secret plan to place a wrinkle in his fate had been laid out. As for what kind of secret plan it might be, he was at a loss. His ability to foresee the future was always unpredictable, as if carried on a mysterious wind. It brought absolute confidence but there was no way of controlling the direction that it took. Sometimes it came like the air itself, natural and unexceptional. It wasn't until after the premonition came true that he made the startled realization, as if being suddenly awakened from a dream. In some circumstances he thought that he just had an unreliable imagination. When he heard from the old man that he was to undergo the trial of the tooth pulling ritual, Umas once again experienced the relationship between the power of foresight and himself.

"Umas, before someone undergoes the tooth pulling ritual, or if they are an *ovath*[7] who does not understand things, our people are not overly demanding of his behavior. They may even habitually forgive you. But once you have undergone the ritual, you will be an adult. As an adult, people will trust and respect every one of your words and actions. Therefore, you must abandon your childish temperament and begin to demonstrate the attitude and bearing proper for a mature man. You must be more careful in your words and deeds in order that your character become as solid as the mountains and your virtue as clean as the moonlight." Talum looked sympathetically at Umas with eyes filled with the confidence of having lived long in the mountains.

"Hudas, do I really have to have them pulled?" Umas was still a child and he had to do what adults told him. Besides that, the belief that 'the body of a disobedient child will be riddled by dung worms after death' stood out clearly in his mind.

"For those who fell to the earth in the village at the same time as you, it is time to pull out the front teeth." The old man said.

Umas thought of the familiar names and faces of boys like Biung, Alang, Laung, Tiang and Piling. Outside of his family, his closest relationships were with these boys. They were like the skin on his body, almost all the stories of his life had been acted out with them. Every day of his childhood was filled with their shadows and their smiles. Even the scars on their bodies had been received at the same time and resulted from the same mischievousness, so their scars were like brothers as well.

In his memory, so many special things were tied up with Biung, Alang, Laung, Tiang and Pizing. Their lives were inextricably woven together like rattan vines. Together, under the guidance and encouragement of the adults, they had received training in physical strength, courage, and hunting technique, as if they were a little team. In normal times, elders with respected hunting skills summoned the *mintaimaindu*[8] together. They led them out to the nearby mountain slopes with their little bows and arrows to practice bow-pulling and shooting. The elders pushed boulders from the top of the slopes while the boys shot arrows at them. The boulders followed the contours of the slopes, bounding up and down, feinting left and right, just like mountain muntjacs. Hitting one of the boulders required highly developed skills and the power of calm concentration. Those skills took a long, long time to refine.

When the time for the ritual arrived, the adults summoned all the young boys to gather in the courtyard of the leader. There they organized one-on-one wrestling matches. Umas had long forgotten how often he had won or lost or been injured. The only thing that he remembered was something the elders told them: "After the contest is over everyone has to stand up and brush the dust from their opponent." It didn't matter if one won or lost, the final action was to "brush away the dust." The brushing of the dust had no relation at all to winning or losing. This principle allowed the participants to learn humility and acceptance. They would be left with no thought of revenge or complaint.

Sometimes the boys had to wrestle men in their prime who had been on head-hunting expeditions. The men didn't hold back at all so the boys were like mountain fawns in the paws of a black bear, just an offering for slaughter. Yet, for the sake of their honor, the fawns threw themselves into the fight and never gave up. Dust flew and the arena convulsed with pitched battles. The boys were young and fragile, so they often suffered sprained arms and legs at the hands of the men; broken ribs were not uncommon. Even worse, two helpers from the winner's corner took the losers by one arm and one leg and carried them in front of the village leader where they threw them heavily on the ground as punishment. Fortunately, the leader personally helping them to their feet and offered comfort to those who had suffered injury to their bodies and their pride. Then, as the village leader, he prayed that they be given more spiritual strength. For the boys whose morale had fallen into the deepest abyss this helped them find the self-confidence to climb back out and then ascend the mountain peaks.

In the many wrestling contests that he had entered, Umas hadn't always been defeated amid the mocking laughter of the onlookers. He had also been a victor. He remembered this clearly and could call the event to mind in great detail.

It was when he and his own Tama ended up facing each other in the wrestling ring. It wasn't uncommon for father and son to wrestle each other, and Umas thought about the intimate relationship that he shared with his opponent it made him feel relaxed and comfortable. Long ago he had worked out a strategy for how to defeat his Tama. It was an idea almost worthy of the ancestral spirits, and it had been inspired by his Tama.

It was during the time that the chinaberry trees on the slopes were unfolding their violet petals. The violet hue of the blossoms made each new day in the mountains more romantic than the last. When the weather is good, good things usually happened. A relative of Salivan who lived at some distance had brought over a fat boar to perform the Mankaun[9] ritual. As the strongest man in the village, and one coming from a tradition of heroic natures, Salivan entertained his visiting relative with near feverish enthusiasm. He invited all the important people in the village to come and share the succulent boar meat. Curious children scampered around outside of the banquet venue. Some stared shamelessly at the guest from afar, hoping that on his face might be discovered stories never heard in their village. While the adults were occupied with their conversations other children quietly squeezed into the venue to savor the lively atmosphere. But it didn't take long for the sharp-eyed adults to chase them off to some distant corner.

Salivan had a rugged, powerful body, and has he moved constantly about the crowd people were forced to make way, resulting in uncoordinated, grudging movement. No wonder he made people think that he was like a human earthquake.

"When the wine smells this good even the rocks grow noses." As the effects of the alcohol set in Salivan looked like he wanted to pick up heavy objects with one hand. This alarmed and frightened everyone. Then the alcohol began speaking to him in a clearer voice; he should find someone to wrestle with to demonstrate his bear-like strength in front of his family. He found this suggestion much in harmony with his own thoughts. It was like his left eye speaking to his right eye. So, he stood up in the center of the gathering, raised his hands and demanded that someone defend the honor of their clan by going hand to hand with him. Nobody liked this insulting challenge, but when Salivan spread his arms to expose the sleek muscles on his chest and the rows of hard flesh on his belly, the crowd fell noticeably silent. It was as if unwanted trouble would be called down upon them by the slightest movement of their hands.

"Hu! Let me have a go!" The resonant voice was like the gushing of clear water to the ears of the thirsty. People felt that they had been thrown a lifeline in their time of peril.

When he saw that his tama had responded to the challenge, Umas was struck dumb. Hadn't his tama once told him that a tree that stands out is often the one struck by lightning? Didn't he know how terrifying Salivan's strength was? One thing certain was that people would be talking about the match for a long time to come. For now, Umas could only crowd into the courtyard with the other children. He was extremely anxious and dismayed by the turn of events. His feelings darted in every direction like ants around a bonfire, not knowing where to turn next.

In the center of the courtyard two strong men grasped each other by the shoulders and tried to push the other to the ground. It didn't take much effort for Banitul to prevent his opponent from advancing. This unexpected discovery boosted his self-confidence since he hadn't initially held out much hope for himself. Salivan's movements then became less exaggerated and more cautious. His brow furrowed until his confused face began to hurt. He could feel the ground slipping backwards under his feet.

People aren't really capable of doing barbaric, atrocious things, or of making others think that they are capable of barbaric, atrocious things. All of the people waved their hands in the air to cheer Banitul on. They looked like the wind-blown bushes on the slopes, all moving in unison with the gusts. The pressure of his opponent's imposing manner made Salivan's steps more and more chaotic. His upper body swayed with the force of the other's thrusts. Banitul concentrated on the way that his opponent moved his feet. When Salivan's left foot left the ground because his upper body was being pushed right, Banitul quickly let go of his shoulders, grabbed his left foot and pulled it to his own chest. Bracing his own feet on the ground, he lifted his waist and hands, raising Salivan's left foot to head-height. Unable to resist the combined force of Banitul's thrust and his own body weight Salivan hit the ground with a resounding thud. A thick cloud of dust was thrown into the air then came to rest on his sleek, thick muscles.

Once winner and loser had been declared, the excitement of the wrestling resided like dust falling to the ground. Aside from the partic-ipants now brushing the dust from each other's bodies, it was as if everyone had already forgotten the dramatic scene. Only Umas ran home as fast as his feet would carry him so that he could quietly share the glory with his family.

After that wrestling incident, the way in which his tama had defeated his opponent was clearly imprinted in Umas' mind. Using a big tree as his opponent, he practiced lifting up the thick tree trunk over and over again.

When Umas was matched against his tama, he didn't hesitate to make use of that technique. Banitul wasn't able to adapt to the concerted attack on his lower body and his upper body keeled over backwards. Umas was beside himself with excitement at this miraculous victory. Along with a few of the other boys he proudly carried the loser before the leader and threw him heavily to the ground. Because of Banitul's tree trunk-like legs and boulder-like body, the boys who had to carry him got more tired than they did in the actual wrestling matches. What had actually happened in that match? Umas pondered the question but couldn't come up with an answer that made him proud.

"Hudas, are Biung, Alang, Laung, Tiang and Pizing really going to have their teeth pulled when I do?" Umas thought that having his friends there would reduce the pain and bring special pleasure.

On the morning of the second day, the moon had already set behind the mountains leaving a whitish aura on the top of the ridge. Led by their parents, Biung, Alang, Laung, Tiang and Pizing walked into Talum's courtyard.

The old man wore an immaculate traditional *patwaowan*[10] embroidered around the edges with a hundred pace viper pattern. A square *kulin*[11] hung obliquely around his neck. Ordinarily the bag held a few items like *ginpatus*,[12] tobacco, a pipe etc. When going into battle or for hunting, a dagger could be kept there for self-defence in close combat with an enemy or an animal of prey. He wore a single layered apron around his waist under which a square *tapis*[13] was bound from left to right.

Madadaingath,[14] my child is going to enter the world of adults. I have especially brought him here before you in hopes that he will receive your blessing. You are an elder with great spiritual power. Your blessing will allow him to live a good life in the months and years of the future." Biung's tama's expression was sincere as he held both of Talum's hands.

"Children are the greatest good fortune. The tooth-pulling ritual to introduce these boys into the adult world is also an important event for the village. No person may avoid it. In future, the village will depend upon their leadership." Talum took a firm grip on the hemp cord that was tied to both ends of the tooth-pulling club.

"Pulling out the front teeth is the most painful test of the body. It must be approached with utmost fortitude. While the ritual is taking place, you must be brave and cannot cry. Life in the mountain forests is not as easy as you may imagine. Only those with fortitude and endurance can make their living there."

Talum gazed to where the sun was rising over the mountain peaks. The ridge was growing brighter. He sensed that the morning had arrived in the surrounding areas. Soon the mountain forest would cast off the black gloom of night and radiate the earth's natural self-confidence. The old man pulled the ramie cord on the wooden baton until he was satisfied with its stiffness. Then he said to the boys:

"Children! Follow me. Umas, you go first. Kneel down here under the eaves then open your mouth as wide as you can."

As Umas held his mouth open the muscles in his cheeks began to twitch. It was as if some unseen power was trying with all its might to prevent him from opening his mouth. The old man used his hand to force his mouth wider. Then he took some ground-up chicken droppings from the bag on his chest and rubbed it on the boy's front teeth to prevent the damaged muscles from becoming infected. After that he wrapped the thick hemp cord tightly around the front teeth twice.

"Hu! Hu! Hu! Ye gods in heaven, we are about to pull out the front teeth of our children. After the teeth have been pulled, they will become the most handsome Bunun men who will captivate the hearts of all the young women, just as the healthiest flowers attract all the butterflies. The pain of the tooth pulling will make their weak bodies strong and they will become the bravest, fiercest warriors capable of protecting our lands, women and children. Hu! Ye gods in heaven, please protect our children. After their teeth have been pulled the evil spirits will not leave decay and

Tama's expression was serious, as if he was thinking about something, but Cina's eyes were like a hatchling who was looking at the world outside for the first time. She regarded the boy in front of her with amazement, worry and hesitation. It made Umas feel uncomfortable to be looked at this way. He looked down and said:

"Cina, don't you recognize me? I am your eldest son."

Cina's lips trembled as she said quietly, "My son has truly grown up."

Without making a sound, Tama took out at shiny, sharp *haili*.[16] He placed it before Umas and said:

"For years this knife has served to help me cut away much shame and anger. With its power I have established a name for heroism. Today, I give it to you. A hunting knife is a Bunun warrior's guardian spirit. You must cherish it. When you go hunting or into battle and have no choice but to enter into combat, you can use it to cut the throat of the animal or the enemy and save your own life. This knife has tasted the blood of many enemies and animals of prey. It can access the power of the ancestral spirits to protect you."

Umas took the knife from his tama's hands then nodded his head gravely as a promise. All the while, the cold blade glinted across his father's face.

NOTES

1. The period of male adolescence.
2. Sound for shooing something away.
3. A mature hen.
4. A recently hatched chick.
5. The Taiwan black bear.
6. Eurasian wren.
7. Child under 12 years of age.
8. Boys from thirteen to seventeen or eighteen years old.
9. A ritual to show gratitude to the mother's elder brother by slaughtering a pig.
10. A sleeveless, split Bunun garment that reaches to the knees.
11. A bag carried on the chest.
12. Flints for fire-starting.
13. A cloth to cover the private parts.
14. Venerable elder.
15. Training to develop life skills such as martial arts and hunting.
16. A traditional Bunun knife.

CHAPTER TEN

THE EAR-SHOOTING FESTIVAL

Suddenly the adults picked up their pace. Even Savi, who had a congenital problem with his right leg, scurried busily back and forth along the village paths.

Some people become very impatient when they are excited. Tama Aziman was honing his knife, checking the edge with his finger, when he accidentally cut himself. He wiped his finger on his trousers with such violence it seemed like he was trying to throw his hand away. Then, with exaggerated force, he spat a mouthful of phlegm at the low, moss-covered stone wall. That seemed the best way to chase away the bad luck besetting him.

Everyone had their heads down, working away quietly. Nobody mentioned any nightmares that they had the previous night. Nor did anyone speak of any misfortunes from the previous day. The women especially avoided talking about anything that their husbands may have said to them after the children went to sleep. Yet they all wore an irrepressible look of excitement. It was an excitement that they had not felt for a very, very long time. They were trying to keep their emotions under control in anticipation of the long-awaited Malahdagian.[1]

Like everyone else, Umas was anxiously awaiting the ear-shooting festival. During the time of the festival the men could study archery technique together, exchange their hunting experiences, and enjoy game meat. As a group they would worship the decapitated heads of their enemies, animal bones and hunting weapons. The ear-shooting festival was also a very important time for the shamans. The shamans from each village would gather to teach each other new magic techniques. Sometimes they would draw upon the spiritual force of other shamans to increase their own powers. During the festival, those who were seriously ill, or had chronic conditions, could request that a shaman perform an exorcism. In the festival's spirit of forgiveness, those who had in past been exiled for breaking village rules, or for violating taboos, could return to the village and join their families, their humanity restored to them.

Umas had experienced many ear-shooting festivals. Some of his memories were vague, others were vivid. During the days of the festival he had seen heroic individuals whose reputations were so lofty they carried to the tops of the mountains. But these heroes seldom had anything to say, and their expressions remained severe the entire time. They weren't brilliant and charismatic like the heroes of legend.

All the elders who carried the title, "Hudas," had gathered in the front courtyard of Banitul's house to smoke and discuss matters related to the ritual. Through the clouds of smoke their earnest, stern faces appeared indistinct and deformed. They were concerned that young people should take care of every aspect of the ritual. Nothing could be neglected. Not only would violating taboos bring ill fortune down upon the entire village, they would be ridiculed by the outsiders who came to take part, and that would be a source of eternal shame for the village.

Banitul was charged with being Liskadan Lusan[2] for this ear-shooting festival. The villagers were unanimous nominating him. In the past year, Banitul had brought back the largest amount of game, and he had grown the most millet. Everyone felt that only a man of his ability could lead the ceremonies successfully and ensure the pleasure of the gods. Umas was in very high spirits because his father was to be so honored. It was like the time when his tama had defeated Salivan at wrestling. Over the past few days, Umas had noticed that his tama was the busiest of all the villagers. Sometimes, ritual staff in one hand and Subali in the other, he rushed off to attend to some matter that only the master of ceremonies could deal with.

Seeing his tama so busy, Umas thought: Bunun people spend almost their lives submerged in a sea of traditional religion. They have to observe all kinds of taboos every day. Then, during festival periods, they have to follow even stricter rules. This is because the welfare of every family and every group, as well as the success of the hunt and the cultivation of crops, all depend upon each individual's single-minded devotion to traditional religion. Through every stage of a Bunun person's life, from pregnancy, to birth, their naming, their infancy, their growing up, their illnesses, their possession by demons, their study, the establishing of their position in society, their quest for social relationships, their marriage, bringing up their children, even unto their death, all of these things are accompanied by a long string of "life observances."

To ensure the success of their farming work, the people follow the changes in nature and the rotation of the four seasons and carry out "rituals of the seasons." From the rite of opening the fields, to the stone throwing festival, the sowing ritual, the end of sowing ritual, the sweet potato festival, the weeding ritual, the bird chasing ritual, the harvest festival, the granting of the hoe ritual, the entering the storeroom rite, until the New Year festival, the succession of the rituals tightly bind a person's life like a long rattan vine.

Umas looked up into the deepest part of the sky. He wanted to ask a question but didn't know how to put it.

The moon, now without a mouth, had just dropped onto the back of the mountains, but the world was still held in the pitch-black embrace of early dawn. Although he couldn't see them, he could hear the adults in each household prodding their children to get out of bed. He could also here the protests of the children. The whole village was slowly coming to life in the darkness.

"Hu! My people! We are now going to begin the ear-shooting ritual. Those taking part should bring their ritual instruments and quickly gather in my courtyard." Banitul's voice, carried on the morning air, entered the doorways of every house in the village.

Participation in the ear-shooting ritual is limited to males, so lots of men dressed in full traditional regalia began arriving. In one hand they held their bows, sacrificial meat and *buhda*.[3] With their other hand they led their boy children who could already walk. The men hoped that their boys could enter village life as soon as possible. That way, if they ever encountered difficulties later in their lives, they could rely on the help of all their people. By taking part in the rituals they could also gain familiarity with the wisdom and skills necessary from life and hunting.

Banitul led the people through the blackness along the path covered with weeds. The chill of countless icy pearls of dew on the plants chased away everyone's drowsiness. As the contour of the land before them grew ever steeper, the men's spirits rose ever higher. Unfortunately, the same could not be said for the little children whose heads were still heavy with sleep. Once they had passed through a towering stand of trees everyone could see a level clearing before them. This was where the ear-shooting rite would take place.

The space was extremely broad. To the left was a *daluhan*[4] constructed of bamboo. Row upon row of animal bones hung from the eaves. To the right, stones had been piled up to create a large wall. On top of it the severed heads of enemies were arrayed in the *patpaisan*.[5] A thick aura of death hung over it so that nobody wanted to get any closer.

In the ancient trench in front of the ancestral spirit's home Banitul arranged pieces of four kinds of wood: *halup, bunuth, haspit,* and *kanpatus,*[6] then set them alight. People believe that peach and plum wood can bring a good harvest in the coming year. When rhus javanica burns it makes a popping sound like thunder which frightens away evil spirits. When in the mountains, hunters burn pine wood to keep them warm and defend themselves against unstable weather.

Once the pile of wood had been lit, the men gathered around it to watch the dance of the flames and silently recite wishes known only to themselves. The rhus javanica popped explosively and everyone looked solemn and dignified in the fire's glow.

In the light of the fire, Banitul arranged six stalks of bamboo in three rows on either side of the blaze. The ears of six game animals were wedged into the tops of the bamboo. The first row had two mountain deer ears, the second row had two muntjac ears, and the third row had one mountain goat ear and one mountain boar ear.

"Hu! My people! We now begin the ear-shooting ritual. Whatever you do, you must remember, keep careful watch over your children. Don't let them violate the taboos established by the ancestors. Guide the restless hands of your children as they shoot at the ears of the quarry that belong to them."

In the ear-shooting ritual the youngest child shoots at the ear of the quarry first. Each child can only take one shot and they must hit the target. If they disobey the rules of the ceremony the children may die young. Because they wish to protect the lives of their children, family members choose men with the most extensive hunting experience to hold their child so that they can shoot from as close to the target as possible. The children can only shoot at the mountain deer or the muntjac ears. They must not shoot at the ears of the other animals. If they make a mistake and shoot the mountain boar ear, they will grow up weak and useless. When they meet with mountain boar while hunting, they will inexplicably become frightened and be unable to do battle with them. If they mistakenly shoot the mountain goat ear, it will bring down a curse and the child will become mischievous and impetuous. When they grow up and enter the mountains to hunt, they will try to climb the steep cliff faces like the mountain goats and easily fall to their deaths in the valleys below.

Subali was still fast asleep as Talum took him down from his back and pulled him towards the shooting range. Since he was still in dreamland, Subali walked unsteadily, like a boneless worm. Umas was a little concerned as he watched him. It would not be good if the child provoked the curses of the evil spirits and created misfortune for himself by shooting the wrong ear. But the clever elder held the child so that his arrowhead was practically touching the ear of the deer. As he held Subali's hand and drew the bow, he prayed on the child's behalf:

"Hu! You mountain deer! You must be lonely here in our village by yourself. You should bring your mother and father, you brothers and sisters, all of your friends and relatives to the village to live together with you. We Bunun people have great power, and you mountain deer have no way of resisting our summons. Children of the village! After this shooting ritual is complete your bodies will become as hard as stone and you will be as strong as the tall mountains. Under the protection of the gods our children will never fall ill and will be able to climb Pinunkavan.[7] Throughout their lives our children will shine over the earth and their people like the light of Buwan[8] and Binduhan.[9] My children! From now on you will be as strong as the eagles that soar through the sky above us."

"Swish!" after the children hit their targets their parents blessed them: My child! You have shot the ear of a deer. After this you will be a hunter who hits every target that he aims at. When hunting in the mountain forests you will be able to hunt down any quarry you desire, including black bears, mountain deer, mountain boar, mountain goats, muntjacs....

Talum took a piece of roast meat from the pile of stones beneath the ear of the deer and pushed it into Subali's mouth. This symbolized that Subali had shot the game himself and should reward himself. At this, Subali's eyes suddenly grew as wide as a greed owl's making Umas feel uncomfortable.

After the children had all finished shooting, the men lined up with their powerful *busul-kavi*[10] to shoot from a distance of twenty paces. There was no restriction on how many people shot and sometimes two or three shot at the same time. Other times five or six shot at once. There were also no restrictions on which animal ear was targeted, and how many shots were taken. If they missed it didn't break any taboo or bring any misfortune. Apart from practicing their archery skills, the men always made sure to brag about how excellent their skills were. They also traded bows with the other hunters in the hope that their hunting weapons would be praised.

The master of ceremonies was the last to shoot. Everyone held their breath and focussed on Banitul's shooting form. The result of the leader's archery would determine whether or not that year's work in the fields would be a success. If he could hit a target with his first shot it meant that the people would have success with all the crops that year and the harvest that would bring the people joy. Banitul raised his bow and took aim with accomplished skill. With a "swish" the arrow took flight like an eagle in a high-speed dive. In an instant it had pierced the dainty ear of the mountain deer. The sharp sound of the men's cheers resounded through the sleeping forest. Everyone was overjoyed and relieved that they would welcome an abundant harvest in the months to come.

The sun quietly rose, turning the sky clear blue. It was as if the gods had instructed that the sun should take charge of the sky on this special ceremonial day.

Once the shooting ritual was completed Banitul led the men over to the home of the ancestral spirits. Before he opened the door, he prayed to the omnipresent, omnipotent ancestors:

"Oh, ancestral spirits! We are about to walk into your world and speak to you with deepest reverence. Please guide us as we walk along the paths that you favor. Give us wisdom and strength in our lives and do not allow us to become ill or die in your presence."

They moved the bonfire into the house while everyone entered carrying the sacrificial meat that they had brought. Then they all gathered, shoulder to shoulder, in a large circle around the fire. Banitul was first to swing his sacrificial meat over the fire to commence the Paka-apavunsapudm[11] rite. After that he told everyone to place their sacrificial meat in separate piles according to type; boar, deer, muntjac, goat, etc., making sure that there was no mixing of types. They then roast the meat one type at a time. Before they ate the roast meat Banitul placed *chipul*[12] kernels into his gourd dipper and distribute one kernel to each person present. People clutched the kernels tightly, not wanting to drop them accidentally. That was because if the corn fell to the ground it signified that you would disappear from the ranks of your people. It was a taboo that could not be violated! Everyone was well aware that human lives were far from the strongest things in the forest. They could be compared to withered leaves on a tree, all it took was a light gust of wind and they would be blown to the ground.

After Banitul poured the extra corn kernels out he collected the kernels from the people again. As he took the kernels he prayed:

"With the protection of the ancestral spirits, no matter what danger you encounter, your life will be like the kernels of corn that return safely to the village."

Having collected all the kernels, the master of ceremonies carefully counted how many were in the dipper, "one, two, three, four, five...." Then he cut the roast meat into the same number of pieces as there were kernels of corn. This process took concentration and care. It was forbidden to cut either too many or too few pieces. Evil spirits would eat the extra pieces, then they would take away the life of one of the villagers. If there were too few pieces and someone didn't receive his share of roast meat, that person would be cast out by the ancestral spirits and either would become weak and sickly, or simply go to live with the dead.

Before the adults ate the meat, they gave the children what remained after it was divided around the ritual circle. Then they asked the children to leave the house. Once they exited the house, the ear-shooting ritual was completed for them.

"My people, because of everyone's generosity and solidarity, you can all have one piece of roast meat. We will now eat the meat together." Banitul raised the roast meat in his hand as he spoke.

"I hope that at the ear-shooting ritual next year we will again eat roast meat together in the home of the ancestral spirits." Everyone blessed one another to chase way the anxiety and feelings of helplessness that they had about the future.

As they chatted and ate their meat the atmosphere changed from solemn and dignified to relaxed and happy. Once in a while there were even peals of cheerful laughter.

"The meat prepared for the ceremony must not be taken from the home of the ancestral spirits, and it absolutely must not be given to women or hunting dogs." As he chewed his roast meat, Banitul reminded people that they must pay attention to the taboos.

"That's right. If they eat meat from the home of the ancestral spirits, their guts will start to rot and they will continue to rot until they spit blood and die."

"Any leftover bones must be buried. Otherwise the hunting dogs will get them and end up the same as the women."

"Umas, gather up everyone's bows and arrows and place them in the center of the home." Banitul ordered his son, hoping that he might learn something from the ritual.

The people neatly arranged the bows and arrows in the middle of the home. Banitul told everyone to take a handful of millet wine dregs, then he led them in the performance of the Pis-lai[13] ritual. The intention of this ritual was that the people's weapons should be endowed with the power of the ancestral spirits and thus be able to bring down any game that they wished while hunting.

When the ritual began, the men sprinkled the dregs over the bows and arrows. Banitul began to sing:

"What will come before my gun barrel?"

"Deer, boar, goats, and muntjacs from the mountain forest all will come before my gun barrel!" The men in attendance all joined in the song with multi-part harmony to express their sincerest wishes.

"What will come before my gun barrel?" The master of ceremonies again led off.

"All wild animals will come before my gun barrel!" The group continued to reply in multi-part harmony.

The master of ceremonies and the celebrants sang the pre-scripted ritual song back and forth. It was melodious and elegant, making it seem as though the entire ritual had entered the realm of the gods. The leader's restrained, deep lead song was like a *vanu*[14] that buzzes overhead as it leads the queen bee to a new home. The sound was robust and perfect. The multi-part responses of the group were like a *dasdas*[15] that plunges to the valley floor and sprays in all directions over the rocks high and low producing a clear, powerful sound as though all of nature was singing. The song brought the ancestral spirits great satisfaction and they nodded off into a deep sleep. Banitul and the other men continued their song until all the wine dregs had been used up.

With the conclusion of the weapon ritual, Banitul led the men out of the home of the ancestors and towards the shelves of enemy heads to prepare for the Makavas.[16] He took a smoke-dried head from the shelves and commanded that any man who had not taken part in a head-hunting expedition to leave the ritual circle. Only those who had brought back an enemy's head were allowed to participate in the enemy head ritual. Umas and a few other younger men withdrew to stand as some distance from the others.

Holding his gourd ladle full of millet wine, Banitul stood in the center. He dipped his finger into the wine and sprinkled it over the head, saying:

"Hu...! You head who has traveled so far, I will kill your entire family because I possess powerful magic. Even the strongest enemy can never defeat me, so there is no use in resisting." All of the men were required to stand and watch. It was not permitted to sit down because doing so would mean death the next time they entered battle. When the ritual was completed all of the warriors picked up a piece of meat and stuffed it into the mouth of a severed head. As they did so they spoke solemnly;

"Welcome to our village. You are a very important guest. We hope that we will kill everyone in your family and bring them here to keep you company. Otherwise you will be very lonely in your stay here. Although we killed you, we still reverently worship you and comfort you. We will bring much game meat for you to eat and brew much wine for you to drink in hopes that you will not harm us."

After the warriors had worshipped the severed heads, Banitul made them form a large circle around the heads. They then began to sing the traditional "Sacrifice to the Enemy Heads Song."

Resonant and powerful, deep and robust, the multi-part harmony of the song flowed from the throats of the warriors with meticulous precision. The highest notes shot straight into the clouds sounding like the shriek of an eagle before it kills its prey. The low tones were like muffled thunder on the horizon, like a mighty black bear standing on a mountain top. When the bear stands, he shows the 'V' of white fur on his chest that speaks of his ferocity. He displays his great fangs and roars with a fury that makes all that hear him tremble!

"My people, please join together to clean up the ancestral house and the area around it. Put anything that was moved back in its place." All of the rites were finished and Banitul commanded that everything be returned to its original state. They didn't want the ancestral spirits to feel harassed. Then he led everyone back to the village along the trail that they had come on. As they neared the village, they found a campfire already burning on the path. Before they entered the village, everyone had to pick some embers out of the fire and pass it from hand to hand a few times so that the fire could purify any defilements on their bodies. That included all illnesses and ill fortune as well as demons that may have secretly attached themselves to the men's bodies in hopes of stealing into the village.

After they stepped over the fire, the men who had taken part in the ear-shooting ceremony walked straight to the leader's house. Umas saw all the women who had been waiting at home come over and follow the men to his house to join in the festive activities. However, it was necessary to let the old hens go into the house first. That was because the masculine energy of the men who take part in the ear-shooting ceremony is very strong and can crush the spirits of the women, which is not good for their health.

A large vat of millet wine had already been placed in the middle of the living room. Umas joined the adults in kneeling at the edge of the vat. Banitul sampled the wine first then passed the cup around by way of initiating the fast paced *Malusdapan*.[17] This feast gave everyone the opportunity to tell of their brave exploits and superior ability. People gather around to repeat the stories and dance around to show their approval.

Banitul scooped up a ladle-full of wine and walked over to Salivan because he considered Salivan to be a man deserving of respect. Then he raised his resonant, powerful voiced to sing his introit:

> Hu-pikaunan [a forceful exclamation or a call for people's attention]
> Tumananu (I want to speak the truth)
> Sima aupa (Who wants to speak?)
> Savandipan (The one who stands before you)
> Talaidu hai (He is so handsome!)
> Istahuavat (Tell us.)

Nalaihaban (Your experience!)

Salivan took the wine ladle, threw his head back and downed the wine.
Then, without the slightest hesitation he made his reply:

Hu-pikaunan
Ukas bunun (There is no one)
Saikalaku (Who compares to me)
Matamasath (With my massive strength)
Masa maindu (When I was young)
Namalavi (I once followed)
Lavian tanhai (A great leader)
Namakavas (To attack the enemy)
Dusa siahhai (Two water ladles) [a skull and
    a water ladle look outwardly similar]
Samamangan (I possess the abilities of a warrior)
Hu Hu Hu [a forceful exclamation]
Hu Hu Hu

When a hunter finished "boasting of his accomplishments" he scooped
another ladle of wine, passed it to the next person, and asked about their
heroic exploits. If the person had no personal experience of going into
battle or hunting, they still drained the wine in their hand and replied:

Hu-pikaunan
Uninahai (Thank you, everyone)
Sauntauhuwan (I can only raise my cup)
Sinkadaidath (To your friendship)
Tainkanaian (My mother's clan)
Ha husluman (Is the Husluman family)
Hu Hu Hu
Hu Hu Hu

The question and answer dialogues at the "merit-boasting feast" must
be made up of sentences with four syllables or four stresses. The dialogue
must have a very clear order, and the words must clearly disclose the
person's own glorious merit and accomplishments. Since each person's

experience and ability is different the subject matter discussed is extremely diverse and varied. The women who stand at the back also become excited about their husband's bravery and jump around like mountain boars shot with an arrow. The shouts of people proclaiming their prowess in battle were reinforced by chants of approval, filling the house with exuberance and the craving for glory and honor.

It's hard to say if the adults wanted to make fun of the boys who had just joined the ritual circle in the village, or if they were caught up in the spirit of the festival and just wanted to encourage the youths. In any case, a middle-aged man who had just finished recounting his own accomplishments scooped up a ladle of wine and walked over to Umas. In the manner of the merit-boasting feast he called upon the boy to list his own glorious achievements. The room went silent and everyone watched with curiosity to see how the boy would respond. When Umas received the ladle, his mind was a complete blank and he stood there as motionless as a lump of stone.

"Tell us about what you've brought home from the hunt."

"What about the greatness of your family?"

"Just proclaim your parent's clan name, that'll do."

Some of the villagers gave Umas suggestions on how to replay. Umas himself was thoroughly flustered. Aside from catching rats he personally had no experience with the hunt at all. Nor had he ever done anything to bring the respect of the village upon himself.

"Just drink it down, there's lots of people behind you waiting to drink."

"Umas, the people behind you are dying of thirst."

People started suggesting bizarre reasons why Umas should be brave and take care of the cup in his hand so that it could continue to circulate.

Umas couldn't resist everyone's prodding. Feeling utterly dejected he drained the ladle of millet wine in one gulp. The bitter wine made his face contort, bringing howls from everyone who took delight in his discomfort. As Umas passed the ladle back to the man who had invited him to drink he thought to himself that it should be good enough that he had downed the wine. But another elder suddenly came forward and took the wine ladle. He filled the ladle again and walked up to Umas making the boy thoroughly confused. Once again, in the manner of the merit-boasting feast, the elder entreated Umas to speak of any life experiences that would lead people to respect him. This time Umas' eyes opened as wide as possible in astonishment: surely not? What is this about? He had no choice but to receive the heavy ladle, but he had no idea how to deal with the situation.

"Just drink it down. The people behind you are getting angry."

Again, the same kind of indirect coercion. After draining the second cup Umas' belly felt like it was on fire and his ears burned. The alcohol seemed to race directly to his throat, and he had a strong urge to throw up. But none of the other people there appeared to be concerned about his distress. All they were interested in was how he was going to describe his accomplishments.

Umas had only one thought: escape. But the weight of the gourd ladle prevented him from moving his feet.

"The Hudas who gave you the ladle will help you." A woman's voice came from the back of the room. Umas felt as though he had sobered up and he searched for that Hudas. The old man had already returned to stand beside him. He led him over to the vat of wine and once again filled the ladle with wine. Then, in skilled, fluent Bunun he loudly proclaimed Umas' family background, his participation in military training, and his brave deportment during the tooth-pulling ritual. After that he downed the wine effortlessly and passed the ladle on to another man. The merit-boasting feast became boisterous again.

The wine ladle passed smoothly between all of the men at the feast. Each one of them did their utmost to declare their own heroic deeds.

In the formal setting of the feast the men could speak of their abilities without restraint and in doing so hoped to establish a more respected position for themselves in the village. An individual's status in society depends upon gaining the consensus support of the group and the merit-boasting feast was a ritualized occasion for soliciting that support.

"Umas, how about we go out for a stroll?" Talum could see that the boy was on the verge of being defeated by the alcohol.

Umas followed the old man into the courtyard. At the courtyard's edge stood a large banyan tree whose dense foliage provided shade for most of the yard. The old man explained to the boy that people liked to show their approval in mischievous ways and that he shouldn't take it too hard. Umas could only grudgingly nod his head.

There were a lot of young women and women holding their babies standing under the shade of the tree as if they were waiting for something. When they spotted Talum they immediately gathered around him. Talum calmly took a ball of cooked millet from the bag on his chest. He placed pinches of it on the backs of the hands of the infants and young women and then blew into their ears. After that he rubbed their heads and solemnly pronounced a blessing: Mihumisan.[18]

"This ritual is called Mahuhu. Any infant born this year and any new brides all must go through this rite in order to become full-fledged members of the village. Placing millet on the back of the hand is a prayer asking that the babies and brides be well provided for future. Blowing into the ear signifies that the strength of the ancestral spirits will enter into the depths of their souls and become a force in resisting disaster and illness."

The sun's face was flushed red with exhaustion as it slid down between the mountain peaks. In the process it extended the shade of the banyan tree so that it overflowed the courtyard. From inside the house boasts of accomplishments still rang forth along with the vigorous chants of response and peals of laughter from the women. The racket wafted through the entire village as well as the forest, leaving people with a sense that the ear-shooting festival was a blessed time when the ancestral spirits drew nearest to their descendants.

Talum sat on a large rock under the banyan tree watching everything unfolding before him with tired yet satisfied eyes.

"Hudas, is the ear-shooting festival over?" Umas sat down on the other side of the rock.

"No. It's still not over. Tomorrow the shamans will perform the Pistahu."[19]

"What's that?"

"Tomorrow shamans from all of the villages will gather here. They will meet at Bisazu's house because Bisazu's status has been established the longest and his powers are the strongest."

On this point Umas nodded in agreement.

"The ritual for becoming a shaman has three objectives: Firstly, for those who are already shamans, it is an opportunity to strengthen their magical powers and to learn new techniques from other shamans. Secondly, those who wish to become shamans can ask to study with shamans with strong magical power in hopes of one day becoming a respected shaman themselves. Thirdly, those who are healthy can come and receive the blessing of the shamans to gain the protection of the benevolent spirits. Those who are weak or ill can ask the shamans for a cure that will make the sickness demons leave their bodies."

"What do they do in the ritual?" Umas had always been very curious about the mystical powers of the shamans. What would it be like if a lot of shamans gathered together?

"The shamans circle around a large bundle of reeds to do their ritual. Each shaman who is taking part holds the end of one of the reeds while the shaman in charge of the rite chants a spell. Everyone repeats after the leader. The spell is mostly about giving praise and boasting about the greatness of the shamanic arts that they are about to study; how strong it is, how it can cure any illness, and how it can attack any enemy no matter how powerful." Talum stopped for a moment and squinted. It was as if he could see something from the very distant past.

"There was once while I was still living in the old village at the foot of Luanda Mountain when the village performed the ear-shooting ceremony. There were many, many people from other places who came to take part. People were everywhere and it was really lively. More shamans took part in that ceremony than ever before. Because of that, the ritual lasted for a full three days and three nights. All the people and all the creatures on the earth could sense the magnificence of the divine power."

That night, Umas tossed and turned in his bed. He couldn't sleep because his head was filled with thoughts of his forefathers traditional ear-shooting festival; the shouts of joy that shook the mountain valleys, the elegant melodies that brought satisfaction to the multitude of spirits, images of boys holding their bows and arrows, the inspiring merit-boasting feast, the carefree laughter of the women, the shamans with their omnipotent magical powers, and all his people who would be healthy and happy ever after. These delightful scenes danced through his mind, on and on and on and on, never ending.

NOTES

1. The "ear-shooting festival".
2. The master of ceremonies.
3. Dregs left over from the fermentation of millet wine.
4. A small house dedicated to the ancestral spirits.
5. Shelving for displaying enemy skulls.
6. Peach, plum, rhus javanica, and pine with pitch.
7. Jade Mountain, the highest peak in the minds of Bunun people.
8. The moon.
9. The stars.
10. Bows and arrows.
11. Ritual of sharing game meat.
12. Kernels of corn (maize).
13. Celebration of weapons.
14. Swarm of bees.
15. A waterfall with an abundant source.
16. The "enemy head ritual" devoted to the severed heads of enemies.
17. The merit-boasting feast where men declare their accomplishments in battle and tell stories from their family history.
18. A word of blessing.
19. Rite for becoming a shaman.

PART II

CHAPTER 1

THE ONE NEAREST TO THE ANCESTORS

A few scattered stars still sparkled in the grey daybreak sky. Wind blew from beneath the black clouds, driving the mist swirling over the mountain slopes. The thick fog was like an enormous headless snake boring into the heart of the forest. While the indolent sun refused to rise from behind the mountains. streams, pools, the grassy slopes and the woodlands were wrapped in the cool, bewitching glow of early dawn, bathed in dew.

Talum was the first to rise. As he grew older, he had lost his ability to sleep, although he still remembered the sweet pleasure of slumber and hoped that his family could remain blissfully asleep. Thus, he was careful not to wake anyone as he donned his old, yellowed ramie cape and walked out of the house. But, no matter how he tried, he couldn't avoid creating a disturbance in the courtyard. The cock started crowing inside the chicken coop, the hens flapped their wings neurotically, and the carefree herd of black pigs rose from their wallow and started squealing as well. A couple of hunting dogs sprang from their shelter, stretched themselves then darted over to Talum's side. If he hadn't noticed them coming the dogs would have knocked him over, upsetting the basket of feed that he carried in his hand.

The grass outside the courtyard wall shimmered with limpid crystals of dew. He let the chickens out of their coop and dumped the corn from the basket over the ground. Instantly, chickens large and small surrounded the glistening yellow feed and started pecking away, their heads bowed like pious devotees at worship. Not wanting to be left out, the black pigs also came to show their devotion, thrusting their big, sharp snouts left and right, startling the rooster with his bright red comb.

"Beat it! You worthless creatures who don't know your place. You make such a fuss with those four feet of yours. Beat it! Get away!" Talum bent over to pull the pigs' tails, but just as he was about to give them a yank, the tiny, hairless tails slipped away.

The old man kicked at them, but the pigs couldn't resist the temptation of the corn. They gave a few perfunctory grunts then continued as immoveable as big black stones. Talum could only shake his head and move on to other things. He glanced over and noticed a small black speck at the gate of the chicken coop, trembling and swaying as if wanting to move but not knowing which way to go. He took a closer look and saw that it was a seriously ill chick, its eyes swollen as big as ripe wild loquats. Having lost its sight, it could only wander about nervously on the soft morning ground.

"Poor little thing. Who could be so cruel as to leave you behind?" The old man picked up the diseased chick then looked over to the flock of chicken busily feeding in the courtyard. He would have liked to find the irresponsible mother hen, but he didn't know where to start.

He carried the chick over to the shed where the firewood was piled and picked a big, round *mahav-ah*[1] from the corner. Then he stuck the pepper directly in the chick's mouth and stroked its neck to make sure the pepper made it into its stomach. At the same time, he quietly uttered a blessing:

"Eat this. Let the chilli pepper use its strong spice to kill the disease demons hiding inside you! The little chilli pepper will change into a blazing fire that reaches everywhere and burns the disease demons into the lightest dust. Eat this and your eyes will become even brighter than they were before. Then you will easily catch the bugs under the dry leaves and even under the ground. From now on you will become the healthiest, most beautiful little chick and you will live peacefully and happily with your family."

Chilli peppers are Nature's most precious gift to mankind. They have miraculous and universal powers. When people go into the cold mountain forests, they crush them up and place them in their chest bags. The chilli helps keep people warm as if they carried an invisible fire with them. When thin, weak children cry in the middle of the night because they cannot endure the cold, their parents rub chilli peppers on the soles of their feet. The warmth rises from their feet through their whole bodies, allowing them to sleep until daylight.

A hunting dog with tiger stripe markings walked excitedly up to Talum wagging its bobbed tail. Its eyes were eagerly fixed on the red pepper in the old man's hand. Its tongue hung out shamelessly, dripping foamy saliva.

"Beat it! Your spirit is fierce enough as it is. If you eat chilli pepper you might start biting me and the family." Talum raised his hand holding the chilli pepper high over his head.

Aside from stimulating people's appetites and giving them lots of energy, chilli peppers make hunting dogs braver than any quarry they may meet. People say that it isn't its master's encouragement that gets a hunting dog to stand up to a black bear ten times its size, it's the power of chilli pepper.

"Hudas, what are you doing with Tanputulaz?"[2]

Like people, dogs have their own names. Once while on the hunt, this tiger-striped hunting dog had its tail bitten off by a mountain boar, leaving only a little stump which it wagged constantly. So, out of mocking sympathy, its master changed its name to "Shorty." Umas went up to pet the dog to show his affection, but the dog didn't show the slightest interest. Instead, it just kept jumping around, trying to get at the red nugget in the old man's hand.

"Maybe he doesn't think he's ferocious enough yet and that's why the boar bit his tail off. Or maybe he remembers the humiliation when he first lost his tail, and now he wants to steal the chilli from my hand to help him dispel his doubts about himself. Who knows? Who can know what kind of strange reasoning a hunting dog whose tail has been bitten off by a boar can come up with?"

"He may have seen the power of chilli at work and remembers clearly what it can do. Still, there's no power in the world that can bring his tail back to what it once was."

The old man couldn't hold out against Shorty any longer, so he simply threw the red pepper onto the top of the chicken coop. Shorty looked up at it with despair, still wagging his meaty little stub of a tail. Then, with a low whimper he walked back towards his comrades.

"Umas, after the sun comes to the village catch two chicks and take them over to Bisazu. You can tell the difference between a male and a female chick now, can't you?" The old man looked up at the sky calculating what time of morning it was.

"Tama Bisazu? You mean the village shaman?" It was a misty grey morning and Umas' eyes lit up unexpectedly.

"A few days ago, Bisazu cured Subali's strange headache and we have to show gratitude to those who have helped us."

After the completion of the impressive ear-whooting festival, Subali suddenly lost the energy that he should have had as a child. He always wanted an adult to carry him as they went about their business. When the adults were too busy, he curled up in a sunless corner somewhere with a blank stare on his face like a little old man who had lost his soul. The seeds of some unidentified pain had taken root and sprouted in his body and it was becoming more acute by the day. Then one evening, Subali couldn't stand the pain any longer and started wildly banging his head on the ground. Fortunately, the adults always kept an eye on him and Banitul quickly picked him up and held him tightly. If he hadn't, the child's young, soft skull would have ended up with a few big holes in it.

When Talum saw the child's strange condition he suddenly realized that his family had not been attacked by disease demons, but rather by witchcraft. So, he took the bewitched Subali to see Bisazu hoping that the shaman could perform the Lapaspas[3] to expel the evil spirits from the child's body.

That day, Bisazu was wearing a kind of black hemp gown that only shamans wear, with red cloth tied around his head. He took a long time carefully inspecting Subali's body before he came to his conclusion. He sucked in his breath as if receiving a chill before pronouncing that child's soul had not been ravaged by disease demons but had been harmed by magic herbs or magic stones employed by another shaman. Then he gave his taut, black neck a resounding slap, as if wanting to slap away the doubts in his mind, and announced to those present in his hoarse voice:

"I just can't believe it. Why would another shaman use their magic stones to trouble such a small child?"

"Might it be that we adults violated some taboo, and that led to the hardship for the child?" Cinas always think that it must their fault when their children suffer. Wide-eyed with fright, Malas stared at the child in her arms, kissing and nuzzling him. Her heart was filled with terror and guilt.

"With this sort of thing it's hard to say for certain. Abiding by the traditional taboos is something that affects one's own soul and it's hard for others to be affected. From what I can determine, among the shamans who came from other villages to take part in the shaman ceremony, there was one whose moral character is like stream water after a heavy rain: dirty, turbid and completely undrinkable. With the protection of the ancestral spirits I hope that that person's magic powers of will not overwhelm my own. Otherwise, ...even if you cry your eyes out you won't be able to wash away the grief in your hearts." The shaman was so angry that he stomped his feet when he walked.

There was a good reason for Bisazu's anger. Those who came from other villages to study how to be a shaman, and clansmen of the shaman himself had all gathered in his house. He had personally taught them powerful magic techniques that can defeat any enemy or that can defend against any disease demons. Now it seemed that one of those outsiders had used magic herbs or magic stones to harm one of his fellow villagers. The sense of betrayal made him feel that the world had turned upside down. It was as if the solid ground beneath his feet had suddenly gone soft and the mud covering his feet had defiled him and made him appear ignorant.

"Curses are spirits with wings and they always fly back to the person who made them. I have heard that many who have used the shamanic arts to harm others have in the end been the subject of their own curses. They have watched as their descendants died one after the other, leaving them to shed their tears in solitude. The gods forbid us from using their power to do evil, that's the rule." Talum tried to diffuse the shaman's fury by talking about the ultimate fate of the evil doers. Then, with the greatest good will he added:

"You are our venerated shaman. We believe that you have the ability and the magic power to undo this disaster. Our family needs your help and we ask that you reach out a helping hand to us."

"You know that I am not a proud man. Pride is like a mountain. It divides us from our intimate relationship with the gods. However, I am happy to tell you that Subali's illness is not a serious one and I should be able to deal with it. You keep an eye on the child while I go and get the things that I need for the Kaihoheh."[4]

Bisazu patted the child on the head and strode quickly into the dimly lit bedroom. When the shaman came back, he was holding a bundle of sogon grass bound with brambles that made a swishing sound with each step that he took. The sogon grass swung back and forth as if filled with spiritual energy. It seemed to hold great power. The shaman used the index finger and thumb of his right hand to move the middle finger on his left hand back and forth making a sound like bones breaking. Each time the middle finger made the sound he blew out sharply as if to give a warning of the gods. He kept this up until the middle finger could no longer produce the sound.

"Little Subali, our brave little boy, some unwholesome thing has entered your body and gives you so much pain that you cry and cannot sleep. We will suck it out of your body. Don't be afraid! Just lie there quietly in your cina's arms. I won't hurt you." Bisazu took the bunch of sogon grass in his right hand and walked over to Subali.

Bisazu then lightly swept the grass over the little patient's forehead. With a loud but very controlled voice filled with strength he said:

"Hu! This magic instrument that I have made is unyielding. All demons, no matter how strong, will flee before it. From now on, this instrument that I have made from sogon grass bound with nettles will prevent the invasion of all demons. No demons of any kind will ever enter my village again." As Bisazu was performing the rite he arched his left eyebrow and twitched his nose in an extremely unusual manner. This gesture made people think that he was sniffing at something.

The sogon grass tickled him, so Subali squirmed around, but Bisazu continued to intone his spell, paying the child no heed:

"All demons must get out the village. This is not where you live. Ye spirits in Heaven, if the demons have harmed this child, we seek your help and protection. May Subali quickly recover. Any magic herbs or magic stones in his body, regardless of where they come from, must heed my command and get out! Get out!"

Immediately after this, the shaman bent over and sucked hard on Subali's forehead. Because this was an important ritual, the room was extraordinarily still. Everyone anxiously waited for something to happen. Finally, Bisazu was able to suck out the magic stone inside his patient's body.

The shaman spat the black stone into his hand and then said to Subali:

"You see, I have sucked out the magic stone and Subali's body will soon be healthy again. He will never be so weak as he was before. From this day forward you will joyfully welcome the arrival of every new day."

Bisazu walked quickly from the room and threw the sogon grass and the diseased magic stone into the grass outside of his courtyard wall. Subali, who had originally been so weak, now scratched his head with both hands where the sogon grass had made him itch. He wanted to get out of Malas's arms and walk for himself, but his mother was still uneasy and held onto him tightly. This miraculous incident made people believe firmly that Bisazu's magical powers had driven away the most malicious demons and restored Subali to health.

"You are all good people and you have been granted the protection of the heavenly gods. Subali's skin wasn't swollen or ulcerated. If it had been, I would not have been able to use the sogon grass as my magical instrument." Bisazu walked calmly back into the house emptyhanded.

His stride was powerful. His movements and the keen look in his eyes were full of self-confidence. The people in the village respected him and gave him virtually the same kind of veneration that they gave to the gods.

"How do you deal with that kind of disease? How do you cure it?" Someone couldn't resist asking.

"Only the power of magical stones can protect a sick person's life." Talum narrowed his eyes, hiding the cold light of his pupils under his heavy eyelids. It seemed that he too wanted to play the role of an aged figure with an important position in the realm of magical power.

"That's true. It doesn't matter whether there are unruptured *chjhaih* swellings or ruptured *hanuhnus*, you have to use magic stones in the ritual in order to affect a cure." Bisazu agreed with Talum's view. Then, in his knowledgeable manner he explained:

"However...the power of the magic stones doesn't always heed my directions. You have to employ the spirit of magic stones to determine whether or not the patient's illness can be cured that way."

"Oh?!" Everyone exclaimed in astonishment.

"When you use magical stones to cure an illness you first must carry out a divination ritual. The shaman places the magic stones in his left hand. If he can stand up straight it means that the person's disease can be cured. If not, then even if the family of the invalid were to sacrifice a large pig, there is no way the illness could be cured. Then there is absolutely nothing that can be done apart to wait for the approach of death." Talum butted in with a reply but Bisazu just nodded with satisfaction, as if it had been himself who had spoken.

"Heavenly Gods protect us! May no one get welts that become ulcerated...Do not let our bodies grow welts like a woman's private parts... Ha...Ha..."

The shaman's residence shook with raucous laughter. Still in Malas's arms, little Subali looked up with a slightly foolish expression but couldn't figure out what was going on, so he joined the others in their merriment with a drawn-out laugh.

Umas embraced the two chicks, their feet bound with hemp cord, and walked down the narrow village path. Since it had been established many years ago and people walked over it constantly, the path was now as hard as stone. It ran between the stone walls around the houses which were all covered with highly robust moss. It looked as if the path was bounded by exquisite vertical green fields that ran parallel to each other.

A dark cloud flooded across the back of the mountain, its miserly black wings sprinkling down a few drops of rain as if expecting the villagers to thank it for its generosity. Umas paid no attention to the misty rain swirling above his head as he made his way unhurriedly, chicks in his arms, toward the house of the shaman. He knew that the weather in the mountains was sometimes like a woman with a baby in her belly, you could never predict how its mood would change. You just had to take what came.

Bisazu's house was extremely traditional and extremely expansive. The courtyard was bounded by low stone walls on all sides. The walls of the house itself were made from flat stones that had been piled with consummate skill. Sogon grass cut in equal lengths was elegantly arranged to form the roof. People always gave it a second look when they passed by.

"Tama Bisazu! Tama Bisazu. Is there anyone home? I am Banitul's son. The adults told me to bring over a couple of chicks for you." Umas called politely from outside the door.

"Creak...creak..." The big door opened listlessly. The weather outside made the inside of the room appear even more dark and gloomy.

"Who is it? I'm weaving a *davath*,[5] come in." Umas shot into the room even before Bisazu had finished speaking.

The years and months fall away silently like leaves in the valley. The divinely bestowed time for walking over green grass is extremely limited...In his later years Bisazu had grown fat, his body expanding outwards. His spine was slightly bent but his physique was well-balanced. He body was still firm, and his walk was a lively as a civet cat. Gracefully curved, exquisitely crafted *vanis*[6] hung from his ears, and he had a *haulus*[7] made from animal bones around his neck. His beard and hair remained raven black even in his old age. When he went to work it was always as if his life depended on it. That clearly had the effect of making his once strikingly beautiful wife, Cina Aye, age prematurely. She had also long suffered from a kind of woman's disease and now she was a fat old woman with a spiderweb of wrinkles ringing her face.

"Umas, you've grown so big. When I saw you last you were still a child who spent his whole day at play. Ai..." Cina Aye shuffled over to invite their guest in. She carefully looked him over then quickly turned to look in the other direction. In the village it is considered impolite to stare at someone's face for too long.

"Hudas told me to bring these two chicks over for you." Umas explained the reason for his visit as he placed the chicks in the hostess' hands. But the high-spirited chicks seemed as though they could easily jump out of those chubby, wrinkled hands, so he was reluctant to loosen his grip. For their part, the little chicks were scared stiff at being grasped by four different hands at the same time.

"What are we going to do with chicks? By the time they're big enough to cook these fat old bones of mine will be rotting under the ground." The weary voice seemed overwhelmed by the prospect of the many months that it would take to raise the chicks. At the same time, because of the unexpected arrival of these little creatures, the old woman happily made fun of herself. His hostess' emotions made Umas feel awkward and he didn't know the most appropriate way to respond.

"You're already so old that even the big trees respect your age, but you sound like a child that hasn't got any sense." Tama Bisazu took the goat skin laced with hemp cord in his hand and waved it in the air. What he meant was: Old woman, stop talking nonsense.

"Umas, you really have grown up. You're ready to take over any work that adults do." Tama Bisazu placed the half-finished string bag into a cabinet at the foot of the wall. He walked into the living room with Umas then laughed and said:

"Sit. Sit down and have a rest."

"I...I should really be getting back. Hudas wanted me to thank you in person. It's for your help in curing Subali." Umas didn't sit down right away because he wasn't used to sitting in a chair the same height as his elders. He just stood there, erect as a bamboo on a windless day.

"My powers are there to help people live their lives. There is no need to thank me. Besides which, the stainless virtue of your clan members won the delight of the gods and the respect of the people long ago. Having peerless virtue is in itself a great power. It will enable your family to live peacefully in this sinister mountain forest." Bisazu smiled brightly and looked up at his guest. This made his eyes appear much smaller. Umas really appreciated his sincere manner.

Hearing his entire family praised gave Umas a real sense of satisfaction. The look of delight on his sun-tanned face, pimples dotting its forehead, was the same as when he watched his tama defeat Salivan at wrestling.

Umas took stock of the arrangement of the room. The long hallway on the right was full of the paraphernalia of everyday life; *balagan, sasputan, tukban* and *tsibunguan*,[8] as well as *davad*[9] used for transporting game animals...This were arranged and hung according to the size of the object. But it was the greyish-white stone strung with hemp cord that particularly drew Umas' attention, or perhaps one could say that its uniqueness made it seem especially precious. It was like finding a wildflower in a wasteland. It looked lonely, so it caught his attention, even stirring his appreciation.

"Umas, you seem lost in thought. Find a place to sit down. Here, have a piece of roast meat." The man came over with a large piece of shrivelled, black game meat in his hand.

"Uninan."[10] The thick fragrance of the meat gave Umas the sense that his relationship with Bisazu was very close. This, in turn, gave rise to a wave of realization in his mind. He was stirred from his naturally shy, reserved manner and a desire to talk rose from someplace deep inside him, breaking like bubbles from the surface of water. That desire grew stronger and stronger.

"Tama Bisazu, why is that small stone hung from the wall over there?"

"That is a magic stone that we shamans use to deal with evil powers."

"Magic stone?" Finally, he had seen one. An object that he had always wanted to see had suddenly appeared before his eyes. Umas could only sit there with his mouth open. He was unable to think, as if he were in awe of some powerful demonic force.

"We shamans always have two magic stones: one is kept at home, the other we keep with us." Tama Bisazu took the magic stone from his chest bag. This stone looked blacker and harder.

"Can any stone be used as a magic stone? Or are they the most unique stones in the world?" Umas began to smile attentively exposing his teeth blackened by the roast meat. He couldn't keep still from excitement.

"Right, magic stones are made from a very special kind of stone." Tama Bisazu carefully placed the stone back in his chest bag as he continued to explain;

"The old shaman who taught me the shamanic arts originally chose two stones as large as fists for me; one was *haha*,[11] which is naturally very hard, smooth and shiny. The other was greyish-white *halipusun*.[12] The old shaman struck them together and the small pieces that broke off were the so-called *aminamin*.[13] Those who study shamanism gather the broken fragments and place them in a newly woven winnow. Then they put in a large piece of fat boar meat as a gift which they present to the old shaman."

"You have to give a gift to study shamanism?"

"Shamanism isn't like other powers, so naturally, those who want to study it must first contribute something. It's just like if you want to have food to stay alive you have to labor diligently in the fields. Birds have to make the effort to fly about in the forest if they ever hope to catch fine, plump insects. The relationship between giving and receiving is just like that between our left and right hands. If the hand of giving isn't there, there is no way to make a clapping sound. So, you first have to make the old shaman happy before he will teach you all of his powerful magic." Tama Bisazu spoke with great conviction.

"So in future, can everyone have magic powers?" Umas asked as he turned his lively eyes to cast a meaningful look directly at the shaman.

"Offering a gift is only the beginning. The long and difficult journey to becoming a shaman only starts there." Tama Bisazu took a pipe from his chest bag, filled it deftly with tobacco and lit it.

"The ritual for studying shamanism lasts all day and night for five days. It involves chanting spells so long they could stretch over several mountain ranges with voices so loud that nobody nearby can sleep." Cina Aye mumbled softly as she dragged her frail legs across the room and quietly entered the bedroom. The sound of her deliberately drawn out sigh hung in the air. Then she formed like a pearl of dew on the sleeping platform arranged in the bedroom, silently, without a word...

"The old shaman brings out four sogon grass stalks and holds them erect in the middle of the room with his right hand. The students kneel down in a circle around him and take hold of the tip of one of the blades of grass. Then the old shaman leads everyone in chanting spells." The host spoke in great earnest, apparently unaware of the hostess' complaint.

"What do the spells say?" Umas suddenly became animated because he was curious and excited by the mystery of spells.

"The spells are quite long, and mostly they describe the power of the magic techniques that are about to be taught; how they can overwhelm any enemy, no matter how fierce they may be; how they can cure the most serious of diseases with greatest ease. These spells must be chanted for five suns and five moons. While they chant, the students shake the sogon grass in their hands until the old shaman decides that the ceremony should be concluded." Tama Bisazu's eyebrows furrowed, as though he were reliving those difficult times of study.

"Don't they get to rest? Is everyone who studies shamanism that patient and determined?"

"Everyone wants to learn the powerful magic arts and they make a firm commitment to develop unlimited powers. For the first four days they chant until the cock crows three times, which is just before daybreak. Then the old shaman performs the Maptano aminamin[14] ritual for everyone. He pounds his own magic stone into a powder, adds the best quality *ihimuoin*[15] wine and places it on the palms of the students. The old shaman uses all his strength to ensure that the magic stone powder enters the arms of each student. When the magic power is poured in it inflames your arm and causes great pain. Those whose spiritual power is feeble, or those who cannot stand pain, sometimes just pull their hands back." Tama Bisazu didn't actually smoke his pipe, he just let the fragrant smoke rise freely and float around in the air.

"How could anyone be like that? Do they still get the powers from the old shaman?" Umas waved his hand trying to sweep away the smoke swirling in front of his eyes.

"Those who cannot endure hardship will eventually be abandoned by the ancestral spirits. What's more, both hands have to undergo the rite of pouring in the powers, and that requires superhuman resolve and courage. When the rite is being performed on the left hand the old shaman chants a spell to the effect that the left hand does much harm to people and it can easily deliver enemies to their death in an instant. With the right hand the chant says that the right hand can cure all diseases. That is why when shamans perform black magic, they use their left hands; and when they perform white magic, they use their right hands."

"Do you become a shaman just by having magic stones?"

"It's not that simple. A shaman has many magical instruments." The embers in the pipe had gone out so Tama Bisazu simply tapped the pipe on the ground, sending sparks everywhere.

"Aside from the magic stones there are five magic herbs including *salinda*,[16] *paiial*,[17] *kanhan*,[18] *sahal aval*,[19] and *tuli*.[20] All of these magic herbs must have spells pronounced over them and be subjected to rituals before they possess the power of the gods."

"How strong is the power of the magical instruments really? That is to say, do these plants that you can find in nature produce the power to protect people's lives?"

"Of course. On the fourth day of the ceremony the students must try out the power of their own magical instruments. They first practice on a large, hard stone. When they do their experiment nobody can come too close out of fear that the magic may cause harm to those close by. The students hold their magic stone in their left hand and chant a spell to the large stone: You are a friend of the evil spirits. You are a bad person. I am going to use my magic stone to annihilate you. Then they toss the magic stone at the large stone and tiny fragments of the magic stone bore into the large stone making it split apart. Afterwards, the old shaman orders that they find a way to heal the large stone. The students then use sogon grass to perform an exorcism ritual before the broken stone. They chant that the pieces of magic stone should be drawn out of the large stone. Then they touch the broken surface of the stone with the tips of the sogon grass leaves and suck on the stems of the grass in their hands. This sucks out the magic stone and the large stone is restored to its original form." Tama Bisazu painstakingly described every detail of the test of magical power.

"Do they have to practice with *grandfather's sister's taro leaf* and the *biting dog* herbs as well?"

"The power of all five kinds of herbs must undergo tests before they can be used. They can be tested on wood or clothing. These are left to rot, then they are cured. If the cure is successful, it shows that these ordinary plants have become unique magic instruments."

"After they have completed their study can they all become powerful, respected shamans?"

"Not necessarily. The process of becoming a shaman requires that you complete three ear-shooting festivals and rituals for bringing the millet into the storeroom. The whole procedure is arduous and lengthy. Some people don't have the patience and withdraw. Others don't have a gift to give the old shaman and they unfortunately can't continue their study. And even if they do complete their study, there's no way to guarantee that in the years to come, they will continue to have the status of shamans. That's because sometimes when a shaman performs the Mapinsial[21] they may kill their patient, or not cure them properly. Such a person is forced to relinquish their position as shaman. The old shaman will suck the magic stone from their arms and their magic powers will disappear. Then they will be like ordinary people again."

"Is the process of curing illness very mysterious? Does it take a long time?" Umas leaned toward the old shaman and smiled innocently as he asked.

"When a shaman cures someone's disease they must first do a *patihaul*[22] with the patient. The patient has to tell the shaman all their private affairs from before and after the time they became ill. They can't hold anything back or be deceptive, otherwise the spirits of death will quicken their pace and destroy the patient."

"What kind of private affairs to they have to tell?"

"Before they attempt to cure someone the shaman wants to know if the patient has had any nightmares recently, if they have violated any ancestral taboos, or if they have seen, heard or touched any inauspicious objects. Have they transgressed against any traditional virtues; for example, have they stolen, or been arrogant, told lies or offended their elders? Have they had any disputes with people over property, or used a weapon to injure someone? Do they have evil thoughts in their minds, or have they thought about having illicit relations with a married woman? After investigating, the shaman determines whether it really is the work of evil spirits or disease demons, or if the patient has been acted upon by another shaman's magical herbs or magical stones. In the latter case, the shaman would have to personally work against the magic powers of his opponent in order to protect the life of his patient and himself."

Aside from curing illness, what other powers do shamans possess?" Umas was focussed on the old man.

"A shaman's powers can allow a person's spirit to live in the most beautiful place." The old man scratched the back of his head. A reserved, but irrepressible smile shone from under his sparse whiskers.

"The most beautiful place?" The old man had a mysterious look about him that made Umas feel completely at ease and happy. The shaman had powers beyond his imagining, but he felt no apprehension, only sincere reverence.

"Our people live virtually their entire lives in difficult surroundings. Aside from physical illness and injury, the spiritual misfortune and mistreatment that they feel can be even harder to bear."

"Tama Bisazu, can spiritual injury really have such a huge influence on people?" The lack of life experience can make people ignorant, even ridiculous. This was the case with Umas.

"Without any doubt. Spiritual injury is like the mountain wind. You can't see it, but it can shake the entire forest. The spirit governs a person's joy, anger, sadness, and pleasure, just like *is-an*.[23] Although we can't see what it looks like we have to breathe it every day if we want to continue to live."

Umas thought of the black boar sacrificed in the ritual. This made him feel as though he had been struck a leaden blow. Unconsciously, he clutched at his chest. It felt as though there wasn't a heart in there, just a poison centipede squirming around. It was unbearable.

"I often feel upset about a black boar. It was my childhood companion."

"Things from the past can leave scars in our heart no matter whether they are happy or sad."

"Can a shaman help people forget their past sorrow?"

"No, a shaman has no power to control he past. But he can make people's wishes come true." Bisazu lit his pipe again. After enjoying a few puffs, he spoke calmly;

"A shaman can make everyone feel as though they have entered a delightful, beautiful world."

"How does he do that?" Umas stretched his neck like a rooster that has discovered a fat, juicy worm.

"For single men and women, if one of them is in love, but the other is not aware of it, the one in love can ask the shaman to make an *inaul*.[24] It can make the object of their love submit and give them their love without knowing why. Husbands and wives who have been married for many years can easily let small matters turn into a source of resentment. If their family members can't stand to let the situation deteriorate, they can invite a shaman to make a love potion that will make the husband and wife give in without knowing what is happening. After that, their feelings will return to what they were when they were first married."

"What is a love potion?" Young people are always fascinated by matters of love.

"For a love potion you first wrap up some meat. Then the shaman secretly activates it in the household while at the same time using the power of his magic stone to place the souls of the partners into the potion. After that, he lightly brushes the potion and says to their souls; henceforth you must truly love each other and be friendly to each other. Only your partner will exist in the eye of your soul. The two people cannot know about the love potion otherwise the potion will lose its effect."

Bisazu was in high spirits. It seemed as though he could talk about shamanic matters for several suns and several moons. Next, he went on to describe with childish exuberance the shaman's unique methods of praying for rain, praying for sunshine, banishing ghosts, protecting against plague, summoning departed souls and searching for lost objects.

The technique that made the deepest impression on Umas was one called Mapakauva.[25] The shaman sweeps sogon grass over a woman who cannot give birth to expel the impediments to her becoming pregnant. He prays to heaven for the health of her children then inserts the index finger of his left hand into the place below the woman's navel. If this method will not succeed the shaman will simply steal a child from another woman and place it in the infertile woman's body so that she can give birth without problems.

The *ngingi*[26] in the forest had started chirping energetically. It was as if they were conversing with each other or exchanging signals, but even the wisest of the people could never know what they were saying. All that they could tell from the chirping was that night was about to take control of the earth.

After taking leave of the old shaman, Umas walked along the village pathways now bathed in evening glow. He looked back at the old shaman's house and noticed that sun seemed to be standing on its yellowed rooftop radiating a damp golden lustre. He could see several *balikaun*[27] flying in circles around the house, sweeping up and down with greatest easy. More and more butterflies gathered, sometimes catching the wind to flutter over the rooftop, other times circling around it, wrapping the house in the most exquisite whirlpool.

"The shaman dwells nearest to the ancestral spirits." Umas felt as though he now understood this mystery.

NOTES

1. A native Taiwanese chilli pepper.
2. Meaning short and stubby.
3. An exorcism ritual.
4. Ritual to dispel the magic that others have imposed.
5. A string bag made from hemp cord.
6. Mountain boar tusks.
7. Necklace.
8. Backpacks, woven rattan winnows for filtering wine, rattan sieves, head straps.
9. Tightly woven rattan hunting bags
10. Meaning, "Thank you."
11. Granite
12. Limestone.
13. Magic stones.
14. "Pouring in" power, or teaching magic arts.
15. Wine of the finest quality. It has three different flavors: sweetness, sourness and bitterness. Normally in must be drunk with added water, but in the ceremony no water is added.
16. "Biting dog" or dendrocnide meyeniana. The leaves of this plant cause pain and irritation on contact with the skin.
17. "Grandfather's sister's taro leaf," or alocasia odora, also known as "night-scented lily."
18. A grassy plant that causes skin irritation.
19. Also a grassy plant that causes skin irritation.
20. A grassy plant with prickles.
21. Procedure for curing illness.
22. Discuss the private affairs of the patient.
23. "Air" and "soul" have the same meaning. Therefore, "no heartbeat" is the same as "no air."
24. A love potion.
25. Curing infertility in women.
26. Cicadas.
27. Butterflies.

Chapter 2

An Appointment with Food

A nimble mountain breeze swirled between the houses in the village. All the flowers and grass also rose to dance, and the entire mountain forest now followed in a gentle ballet of life. Then, suddenly, the smell of burning animal fur arrived on the wind, setting Umas' nose on edge.

"The sweet smell of game." Although they couldn't tell what kind of game it might be, when it came to any smell associated with animals, the villagers all had intimate and familiar associations.

Umas sniffed at the air hoping to find the direction that the smell was coming from. He noticed thick smoke billowing from a corner of his own family courtyard winding its way into the sky's embrace.

Four or five men stood around a bonfire roasting game. From the unusual shape of the animal's horns you could tell that it was a mountain goat, probably an older goat that would have had some status in the flock. Unfortunately, the roaring flames were burning it into a big black ball, destroying the graceful lines of animal's body. There were a lot of elders and children standing around, which made the business of roasting the goat into a bit of a party. Some were men who just didn't like being alone, others wanted to relive the excitement of that year's hunt with those who had made the kill. The memories brought smiles to their faces, as if they themselves had captured the goat. Some people just wanted to savor the wonderful flavor of game meat. As everyone knew, if you lay eyes on it, you can enjoy its flavor. That was because people in the village had a tradition of sharing the spoils of the hunt.

"Who was lucky enough to bring down such a big fat mountain goat?" Umas asked Subali and the gang of children sitting around on the ground.

"I don't know. I came out of the house because I smelled roasting game." Subali looked up at his brother. From the bored look on his face it seemed as though he had been squatting there for quite some time.

"Right, I don't know either..." "I just got here and all I could see was the big fire." The children all offered their point of view. The way they opened their mouths made Umas think of a nest full of little birds who see their mother return to the nest.

"Be quiet! Don't make fun of this spirit from the forest that has died for us." A severe sounding voice assailed the children, frightening them into silence.

"Don't make a fuss. Just watch." Umas wrapped his arms around the children as if to protect them, while at the same time reprimanding them in a low voice in an effort to please the elders.

He was well aware that you must adopt an attitude of respect towards game that has been killed. The death of an animal holds profound meaning for the lives of the entire village.

The people believe that all creatures are mystically created from spirit matter. That means that the affairs of life, death and mundane phenomena only affect their physical bodies because spirit matter never perishes. Therefore, people always silently express their commiseration with, and gratitude to, game that has been killed in the hunt. If at any point in the process people make fun, or are rowdy, the game animals will think that their sacrifice has not been respected. In that case, animals will never again reward the people's hunting efforts. They will never again capture any game and even the most accomplished hunters will return empty-handed. That is why when adults see children playing and joking around in the presence of game, they all automatically become furious with an anger intended to ensure their future livelihood.

"Umas, bring a bucket of water." Banitul, who was in charge of slaughtering the animal called to Umas as he wiped the blood from his hands.

"Here it is." A little while later Umas returned swinging a wooden bucket full of water. The water slapped at the sides of the bucket as he walked, splashing over the edge and leaving the trail wet behind him.

"Wash that large pieced of slate." Banitul spoke as he busied himself with the blackened ball. His hands moved swiftly and deftly, like bubbles rising from boiling water. For a man, the feeling of the game meat in his hands is more seductive than a woman's breast.

A large piece of slate lay beside the firepit. Judging by the thick layer of fallen leaves covering it, nobody had used it to butcher game for a very long time.

Several men were working to divide up the carcass of the mountain goat. They had either pulled out the knives carried at their waists or were holding the goat's legs to steady it. Wielded by skillful hands, the sharp knife blades worked over the carcass precisely and safely. In the time that it takes a butterfly to drink nectar from a flower the large goat had been divided into pieces of meat just the right size for cooking in a pot.

"My friends, this mountain goat seems not to be as large and fat as we imagined, so we won't be able to give so many pieces of meat to each household. Everyone present should delegate one person from their household to come and receive the meat." As Banitul wiped the blood and bits of meat from his knife he decided how the meat was going to be apportioned to the people of the village.

"Banitul, some households don't have anyone here."

"It doesn't matter, we don't need to wait. There will be lots of opportunities in future."

Banitul immediately delegated a group of capable, experienced elders to take responsibility for the work of sharing the meat. A hunter cannot personally divide up the game meat that he has brought back so as to avoid being mistaken for being prideful. Banitul dared not abandon this age-old injunction.

"Is the Hudas in your family still healthy?"

"Take this piece of rump meat for the old man! Eating it will make him as strong and stalwart as a pine tree, and he will forever watch over the behavior of the villagers."

"Can your *luhi*[1] walk yet? This meat is fresh and tender. It's for your child. I hope it helps him grow up quickly to become a hunter who brings lots of game from the mountains and one who is willing to share his glory with the people in the village."

When the elders distribute the game meat they always ask after the members of the family, then they apportion the meat according to the age and status of the family members. In this way, the food taboos passed down by the ancestral spirits are respected and people of all ages are able to enjoy the amount and kind of meat appropriate for them.

That night, Banitul was busy cooking the goat's head. This is the singular privilege of the hunter since all other parts of the animal are given away to others. He cut the hard skull into several pieces and added dried *halidan*[2] so as to make the portion larger. The pieces of bone and meat slowly swirled around in the soup while the rather thin nuts floated from the bottom of the pot to the surface of the mixture. The sweet fragrance of meat slowly filled the kitchen, growing ever thicker and richer.

"Tama, did you shoot this goat with a bow and arrow? Or did you trap it in a pitfall?" Umas walked up to the stove and pushed some of the logs further into the fire. The flames became more intense.

Subali followed him in and started playing with the firewood as well. Perhaps it was because he had spent too many years sleeping on Umas' back, but even though he could run around on his own, Subali always seemed to feel that his brother's shadow was especially comfortable and safe. But from Umas' point of view his younger brother was like a *vini*[3] sticking to his skin, or like a little tail that he couldn't shake off no matter how he tried.

"This kind-hearted mountain goat eventually stepped into a trap that we had set. Now we can share a delicious meal with our fellow villagers." Banitul braved the billowing smoke to pull the tender white goat brain from the pot and put it in a wooden bowl. He set the bowl aside in the cool air to allow the scalding white steam to dissipate.

"Tama, Subali's really going to enjoy these tender goat brains." Umas looked at the food in the wooden bowl.

"I want some, I want some." When he heard his own name, Subali started pointing to the steaming bowl.

"Children can't just eat anything they want. Goat brains are for Hudas and old people like him." Banitul raised his voice as if the children had done something naughty right before his eyes, something that made him extremely unhappy.

"Right. There are certain parts of an animal that children cannot eat." Tama Husung's voice rang clear and bright as he walked. He craned his neck like a rooster to see how things were doing in the pot.

"So, what can children eat?" The room filled with the aroma of meat and when Umas looked around at Subali, the child's mouth was obviously watering.

"Bunun people have established a lot of traditional taboos related to food. The tender, fatty parts of an animal, like the head, legs, rump and genitals are mostly given to the elders. Children are forbidden to eat these. After all, the elders are our leaders in the forests, and younger generations should observe these food taboos as a way of developing respect for their dignity." Tama Husung reached into the boiling pot and grabbed a handful of nuts which he stuffed into his mouth, but when he started to chew he realized that his mouth was more sensitive to heat than the thick skin on his hands. He grimaced but didn't want to spit the nuts out.

"Why is it like that?" Experience told Umas that in the world of the village everything had a reason, just like the millions of small streams that flow together to create the great ocean.

"Damned nuts! Hot! Hot! Whew...whew." Tormented by the scalding nuts, Tama Husung was making faces. In the end, he resolved just to swallow them. Then he puckered his lips like a chimney to let the scorching steam pour from his mouth.

"Hu!...Those damned nuts! Okay, I'll tell you about how our food taboos got started." Tama Husung tried to cover his embarrassment by effecting a serious, fawning expression.

"A long, long time ago there was a respected hunter named Bukun who went to visit his relatives in a distant village to take part in the infant ritual there. His relatives received him enthusiastically and he ended up drinking quite a lot of wine. Day and night, he could be seen passed out beside the vat of wine.

"The infant ritual, which went on for several days, finally came to an end. Bukun and the other guests were busy organizing their gifts in preparation to return to their own villages. Bukun was strongly built but the effects of several days of heavy drinking had taken their toll. The power of the wine was still at work in his body as he started out on the road home. Since hiking over steep mountain trails takes a lot of energy, Bukun decided to stop and have a rest by the side of the road. He would strike out again after he recovered his strength. Still drunk, Bukun quickly slipped into dreamland.

"Just then there happened to be a mother bear out looking for food in the forest nearby. She needed to go out every day to find food as quickly as possible for her cubs. As luck would have it, she caught the scent of a human. When she went to have a look, she saw a man deep in slumber. She grabbed him gleefully, all the while congratulating herself because that night her babies would not go hungry.

"The mother bear climbed into her den in a tall camphor tree with Bukun in her mouth. The cubs were excited and ran to greet their mother and the prey that she had returned with. They were curious about the man and groped him all over. Bukun was paralyzed with fright and had no strength to resist.

"The first cub pointed to the man's head and said, "I want to eat his head!"

"The mother bear replied, "There are a lot of evil ideas in there and children shouldn't eat it. Leave it for the adults!"

"The second cub felt the game's hand and said, "This is my share. I'm going to eat the hand!"

"No! Those have done many bad things and children shouldn't eat them."

"Next the cubs suggested that they wanted to eat the man's rump, and his toes, but the mother bear answer no: "Those parts aren't for children. You have to leave them for the adults and the elders!"

"The mother bear patiently taught her cubs the etiquette and rules of eating meat. Then she said: "You be good and wait here. I'm going to get a big rock. Once we divide up the game meat, we can enjoy a fine meal together."

"When Bukun saw the mother bear leaving the den he realized that his chance to escape had come and he had better take advantage of it. He took some clothing out of his *davaz*[4] and used it to distract the cubs. The cubs were really intrigued by the beautiful colors of the clothing and began fighting over it, completely forgetting about Bukun. So, he quickly left the camphor tree and scampered back to his village like a frightened muntjac.

"After he got back to the village, he told all his friends and relatives about his experience of almost dying. An elder filled with wisdom bowed his head to think for a long time, then he solemnly told his people: "Black bears are tall and strong, and they have almost divine powers. There must be some secret principle at work. I think that it's their rules about eating that have allowed them to become such a great tribe. We should learn this wisdom from them.""

"After this there was a major change in the eating habits of the people. The tastiest, fattiest kinds of meat were reserved for the elders and prohibited for children. These food rules seemed to bring pleasure to the gods, and everyone grew stronger and healthier. The amount of game brought back from the hunt and the amount of millet cultivated in the fields gave the people great satisfaction. The curses of the evil spirits also shrank back into the blackest of the black mountain gorges, and from then on, the joyful sound of the people's voices and laughter constantly drifted through the mountain forests. This went on for days on end, and has continued ever since...""

Tama Husung picked something from between his teeth. Some stubborn bit of nut stuck to his fingernail. He looked surprised and gave his finger a flick, sending the bit of nut flying into a dark corner of the room. Then he swept his tongue over all of his teeth. The feeling that his mouth was now fresh and clean made him give his head a little shake before he continued speaking:

"In the village, food taboos are not only directed at children. There are also quite strict rules for women."

"Are there also things that cinas can't eat?" Everyone viewed cinas as virtually divine beings. They shouldn't have had restrictions placed on them.

"Subali, take the goat brain and give it to Hudas. Be careful that you don't trip and fall." Banitul placed the wooden bowl in the child's hands.

"Tama, let me do it." When Umas heard his father a vision of the child tripping and scattering goat brain over the ground flashed into his mind.

"No! Let him take it. True respect towards one's elders is found in action, not in the imagination."

"Hudas, Hudas." Subali lurched off towards the room where the old man slept alone. From the excitement in his voice is was as if this delicacy was for him, but he really just wanted to tell the old man who loved him so dearly about it.

"The food restrictions for women depend on the changes to their bodies." Banitul added a few sticks of firewood to the stove then bent over and blew on the fire until his face was flushed red:

"I'm not sure what's gotten into... these nuts... they've been cooking for so long but they're still not done...ah hei, ah hei, he blew on the flames,...looks like we may have to eat a little later tonight."

"How do women's bodies change?" Umas wasn't especially concerned about the question of dinner, he just wanted to get answers to all of the questions in his mind. It was like a butterfly sucking nectar from a flower; they aren't concerned how big the flower's petals are, or what color.

"Aside from girls who can't weave, women have two special statuses. One is *sinilumah*,[5] the other is pregnant women. After a bride first enters the village, during the performance of the ritual to drive out plague, she is not permitted to eat pig entrails. If she does, then the shaman's power will not be effective in driving away the disease demons and evil spirits that attach themselves to her body. When a married girl returns to her own village, she may not eat meat from the head of a pig that her family has used in ritual sacrifice. That would allow the protective powers of the village ancestors to be carried back to the village of the woman's husband, and her own family's village would lose the ability to live in the mountain forest. In normal times, women are not allowed to eat chicken feet or pig trotters. Those who violate this taboo lose their ability to maintain the hygiene of their family because chicken feet and pig trotters are constantly treading over the filthiest ground." Banitul looked down to arrange the wood in the stove, then he looked into the stoneware pot with a look of frustration. The stubborn food was giving him problems.

"What about women with big bellies?" Umas asked with some urgency.

"There are a lot of things that they can't eat. Husung, you come and explain." Banitul used a *haidasu*[6] to give the pot a stir, trying to get the game meat on top to sink to the bottom so that it would cook a bit faster. The long wooden spoon was simple and plain. It wasn't a fancy utensil, but it made life much easier. People who live in the mountain forests have many different skills. Simply by relying upon the deftness of their own hands they can pass their days in the mountains at ease in harmony with the cycle of the four seasons.

"How's that? You want me to tell your kid?"

"Yeah. You and your wife have three children. You know more about food restrictions for pregnant women than me."

"All right then." Husung thought for a moment. Maybe his procreative abilities were better than his older brother's. He tilted his head with satisfied and said to the youngster;

"During the time she is pregnant a woman can't eat flying squirrel meat. If she does, the child she gives birth to will enjoy coming to steal things during the dead of night. She also can't eat dead chicken or monkey meat. In that case the child would be as skinny and ugly as a monkey. In the first five days after she gives birth no outsiders can share food with her. That would indicate that in future the child's upbringing would be divided up, and that would be a big disadvantage for the child. When she nurses the child, the mother cannot eat taro, sugar cane, glutenous rice or pork. These are all sanctified things that her husband's family use in performing rituals. Eating them would mean that the milk produced from them belongs to the world of spirits and a mortal child will not be able to absorb its nourishment."

"Then what about the food taboos for children?" Umas was aware that in this life there was a place of great beauty. In that place you can find sweet and unique things; things that bring intoxicating pleasure.

"My child, listen to me. In normal circumstances when a chicken is killed at home the children may not eat the head, the belly, eyes, meat from the buttocks, the internal organs or the feet. Eating those taboo things will hinder a child's growth. As far as hunted game, a child cannot eat the head, otherwise he will become very stupid. A child cannot eat meat from the rump because that will make his body grow very strangely, or he may even grow a tail. Children are forbidden from eating meat from the feet because if they do, when they grow up and go into the mountains to hunt their own feet will not have the strength to conquer the steep mountain slopes, or they may meet with an accident in the forest, or they may even die of starvation in the wilderness. If children eat meat from the waist area their bodies will grow very weak and they will not have the energy to combat the cold. It is especially important that children do not eat the ears because that could make them deaf and dumb. Then they will never be loved by the older members of the family, nor will they learn the life skills and wisdom of the elders. Ah hei! ah hei!"

Banitul pulled out the unburnt firewood, leaving only burning embers. The food in the pot continued to simmer. Removed from the flames, the wood immediately billowed thick smoke that filled the whole kitchen. Everyone covered their noses against the fumes.

"Ai-you! This cursed smoke! Heavenly spirits...protect us... Ah hei! ah hei!" Banitul coughed and started to shout from apparent surprise.

"When did this become a family of thick smoke? Can't all you men even keep this thin bit of smoke under control?" Talum waved at the smoke before his eyes as he walked in. His head of white hair immediately blended with the white smoke in the room.

Banitul and Husung felt the sting of the old man's scorn and started trying to extinguish the dense smoke by hitting the firewood, but this just sent the logs rolling all over the place, creating even more smoke. The situation became more and more chaotic. When he saw Husung picking up some of the wood and carrying it out of the house, Umas got the same idea and he also picked up some wood and ran out of the house. The draught that the two of them created carried a lot of the smoke with it. Afterwards, Umas realized that he had acted because he didn't want to be insulted by the smoke, or by the old man's ridicule.

"It's already dark. Was there some problem with the goat head?" The old man stared at the pitch-black pot as if the answer lay there.

"It's done. We should be able to take it out now. *Cough! Cough!*" As the soup boiled the aroma spread in all directions. Banitul coughed a few times then in a low voice that sounded like the gloomy season when the leaves fall, he said, "Umas kept asking about the rules for food taboos and that delayed our work."

When Umas heard this, he knit his eyebrows and his head sank as if he were exhausted. He thought his tama's attitude was like the *lihulihu*[7] during the flood season. In order to avoid responsibility these birds rub power from white rocks on their heads and then claim that they are getting old and can't do it any longer and that they have been misunderstood. Banitul had used Umas' curiosity about traditional life as the white powder that he rubbed on his head to brazenly avoid any personal responsibility.

"Umas, you're really in luck today. You were able to hear about the real wisdom of the ancestors." Talum beckoned to Umas then indicated that he should sit down beside him.

"My child, you must keep the wisdom of the ancestors stored away in the most important corner of you soul. You must also follow in the path of ancestral knowledge to live your life conscientiously and carefully."

"I will. I'll make sure I remember. And it will be my guide in my future life." Umas' agitation was calmed by the old man's earnest tone of voice and he respectfully made this promise on the spot.

"Banitul, did you talk about any other food rules apart from those for children and women?" It wasn't that Talum didn't believe his sons, it's just that he didn't know if their knowledge was thorough. People often gathered in the emerald green woods near the village to beseech the gods to protect their children and to watch over their behavior.

"What other food rules are there?" His future life and the world outside were a huge enigma filled with danger of all kinds. That is why it was necessary for him to preserve the memory of former generations' way of life. Only in that way can people live simply in a safe and secure place.

"You should already know the foods that are prohibited during agricultural festivals like the ear-shooting ritual, the sowing ritual and the harvest ritual. You've taken part in those important events. What I particularly want to tell you about are the food customs that you must observe during the hunting ceremony. When someone in the family goes out hunting—it doesn't matter if it is a simple *mitala*,[8] or if they are taking part in an encirclement *mapuasu*[9]—those remaining at home cannot eat taro. They cannot eat anything that has a strong flavor because the smell will frighten away all the game animals and the hunters will return home empty-handed. At dawn when the hunting party is setting out, none of the hunters can eat or drink. They have to wait patiently until they have shot their first quarry to allow their stomachs to enjoy the sweet taste of food." Once the kitchen had cleared of smoke the air was much fresher and the old man's white hair stood out in its solitary whiteness.

"Hudas, it's empty...Hudas, the bowl is empty." Subali clutched the wooden bowl and ran over to the old man looking as though he was still not satisfied.

Umas could see the milky white morsels sticking to the corners Subali's mouth. The more he looked at him the more those morsels looked like

the most tender, fragrant part of a game animal, the kind of delicacy
that only an old man can eat.

Notes

1. A recently born puppy. Here it refers to a human baby.
2. Nuts.
3. Leech.
4. A backpack made of ramie cord.
5. Brides, also referred to as "women from afar."
6. A wooden spoon.
7. The light-vented bulbul.
8. Ambush hunting.
9. Encirclement hunting which involves the use of hunting dogs.

CHAPTER 3

A GIFT FROM THE GODS

In the season of falling leaves, as soon as the sunlight lets up a little bit a dense fog rises from the mountain forest making the world and all its creatures miraculously disappear. This skyless world is completely still, so still that the cries of any bird carry from one mountain range to the next, echoing back and forth until it is impossible to guess what kind of bird it is. The thick mist that accompanies the falling leaves contains no moisture. It is just a dense, dark vapor. In the chill of dusk, this mist grows thinner, gradually allowing the shapes of the earth and the golden yellow leaves to reappear until, in the end, even the furthest mountain ranges are filled with reflected light and clouds the rosy color of sunset. Yet the pale, thin mist remains to drift about the cold forest, reluctant to depart until it is swallowed up by the fierce, black night.

It was that sort of still, quiet morning when Umas walked out of his house. He immediately felt a layer of thin, almost imperceptible moisture remaining in the air. Perhaps it was because the transparent, hardly discernable moisture lent a lustrous shine to everything before his eyes. The mountains at daybreak were hung with a diaphanous layer of cloud. As the morning sun rose it gave the clouds more definition, making them brighter. But eventually, the sun refused to be obscured by the clouds.

It leapt skyward to hang in the bright blue sky, leaving the gilt-edged clouds to sink onto the backs of the mountains.

Umas stood in the middle of the courtyard as if waiting for something to happen. He watched thick smoke floating from Tama Biung's courtyard two houses away. The heads of several people flashed in and out of sight above the low wall. Of their own accord, his feet started moving in that direction, drawn by curiosity.

A flock of chickens was busily clucking away in the dugout at the foot of the wall. As soon as they saw a stranger approach they started scurrying around in fright. A few hunting dogs were stretched lazily on the ground in all sorts of odd positions, enjoying the warmth that only the morning sun can bring. When they discovered the intrusion of a stranger, they all stood up at once. As if answering the call of duty, they advanced toward Umas aggressively, forcing him to stop in his tracks.

"Chis! Get away! You can't tell the difference between the scent of quarry and the scent of a guest. What kind of dogs are you? Useless beasts! Chis! Beat it!" Biung picked up something and waved it at the hostile dogs. Then he realized that he only had a handful of chaff and dust.

One of the dogs with brindle tiger stripes strode fearlessly over to Umas and started sniffing at his thighs. The other dogs followed and did the same thing. They seemed to smell a familiar scent and gleefully barked to their mates. Then they began bounding around, even pouncing on each other, but it was all good-natured play. The dogs were so happy that they almost started rolling around on the ground. They weren't the least bit concerned about their master's anger. It was almost as if nothing had happened. Maybe they had just grown accustomed to their master's sudden impulses and willfulness.

"Umas, your tama is here. Find yourself a place." As Biung spoke he nodded to Umas, indicating his status as host.

"Mihumisan." Umas bowed slightly to his host and gave a faint smile to the elders gathered there. Then he crowded in beside his father, forcing Banitul to shift over.

"Banitul, your son has grown more and more like a great tree on the mountaintop, tall and strong. I remember..." An elder with a rotund build licked the corners of his mouth with the tip of his tongue, unable to believe that a child could grow so quickly, as quickly as the wind blowing over the mountains without leaving a shadow.

"Children are like tender sprouts in the rain, they grow especially fast. They force us to shed the green leaves of our own youth. Sometimes I even suspect that they secretly steal our youthful energy." Banitul looked at his son with satisfaction tinged with melancholy.

"My friend, that is the way of the world. As one generation grows old and decrepit, another generation grows strong. When this generation dies off, new lives create a new era."

Since ancient times the people have understood that aging and death are nature's wisdom and a basic principle of the world. What's more, they believe that death is only a case of a life spirit moving to another place; it is the process of *is-an*[1] leaving the earth, transforming into *malantangus*[2] and going to *Maiasan*.[3] Through the phenomenon of death a person's life is exalted, it transforms into an omnipotent ancestral spirit that exists everywhere like the wind, following its descendants earnestly and piously, living in nature's embrace.

But has anyone ever had a clear experience of the valley of death? Fear of the strange and unknown makes everyone apprehensive, paralyzing them. Nobody can comprehend what it will really be like when they depart the place where they were born and raised. When they are alive, the people appear so clearly formed and real. All kinds of feelings formed in the village, and the emotions hidden deep in people's hearts can easily be brought to mind anytime that people wish. Even the most inconsequential of things are as if carved on a slab of slate: the stone walls covered by weeds; the clear tangy scent of things rotting in the mud; the gusts of wind blowing through the forest and the thick fragrance of trees; these things all make up the intimate and enchanting ambience of home. Will all of this be destroyed upon death? Will the deepest strata of memories grow vague and fragmentary, leaving only black lumps, or will they simply disappear in the wind? Can all the things that made up a person's life pass through death and begin again? Why was it that people spend their entire lives tossed between endless wandering and interminable suffering? Apart from wandering and suffering, can the living hope for anything else?

Sitting amid the sombre elders, Umas also fell silent, although his glance kept drifting to that brindle striped hunting dog who had sniffed the scent on his body. The dog's courage was admirable, as well as frightening. It seemed uninterested in playing with the black or brown dogs, and just lay listlessly basking in the sunlight. Eventually, it started snoring thunderously in time to the rise and fall of its ribcage. As Umas admired the graceful posture of the sleeping dog he discovered that its head was triangular and its jowls tapered downwards towards its mouth, just like the head of a hundred pace viper. Its belly was drawn inward and raised, while its waist was extremely narrow. This made it look like a perfectly round, hard wooden pole. Its legs were long and thin like a muntjac's. No wonder these dogs can sprint up the steep slopes and sheer canyon walls so effortlessly. The dog's long, thin, moderately hairy tail swept upwards in a semi-circle just like the half-moon in the night sky exuding a simple, but forceful vigor.

"Tama. Tama Biung's dogs are all strong and fine looking." Umas nudged his tama's shoulder and pointed to the hunting dogs with his chin.

"We are a people who love dogs, so they all live good, happy lives."

Umas thought of their own black hunting dog, Tahdoun. When there was no hunting to do, he just slept indolently on the ground. His eyes were always covered with flies, but he was too lazy even to shake his head. His chin could drop on the ground with a thud and he just kept on snoozing. Yet, Tahdoun was the dog that the hunters best liked to take out hunting. They all thought that Tadhoun was the best hunting ground manager. He patiently led the other dogs in pursuit of the quarry until his master was finally able to make the kill. Hunters often brought half of a pig's head for Banitul because Tahdoun had been the first dog to discover the boar and had pursued it tenaciously. According to hunting rules, the first to discover the quarry, and the one who shoots it have the right to share the glory of receiving the quarry's head. That is because pursuing and shooting both require persistence. Tahdoun's natural abilities had won the respect of all of the people, it was a pity that he just slept through it all. Umas couldn't help shaking his head and smirking at him.

What many of the elders say is right; we and dogs belong to the forest. If we lose the forest and lose the ritual of the hunt, we are just like empty *ngingi*[4] hanging on a tree trunk; there is nothing left for us but to wait to rot and disappear.

The mountains that lay opposite to the village were set in motion by the howling of the mountain wind. The entire forest resounded with a deep rumbling sound that was carried in all directions over the surface of the ground. Everyone could sense the subdued trembling of the earth under their feet. It was a message.

For thousands of years our ancestors have been hunters. It is the most important role that we Bunun people play in the mountain forests. It is also the role that we have played for the longest time. That is why our people treat information from the forest with worshipful veneration. Many pricked up their ears and gazed to the mountain forest dancing in the distance. They hoped to discern some mysterious information from the appearance and sounds of the forest; information that would serve as a beacon to lead the souls of the hunters forward.

After a time, the wind grew tired, and slouched down somewhere. The forest quieted down along with it. On the other hand, the courtyard started to liven up. People were stretching and bending, others pulled pipes out of their chest bags, filled them with tobacco and lit up. Every so often they tamped down the tobacco with their fingers as they puffed away sunk in thought.

"Brothers, yesterday we passed by a grove of arrow bamboo on the hunting ground and discovered that there was evidence of mountain boars moving further down the mountains to dig up bamboo shoots. I don't know if this is because it has been especially cold higher up the slopes, or if there are more and more mountain boar, so many that they have to come down the mountain looking for food in places full of the scent of hunters. I think we should pray to the host of gods to allow us to enter the mountains to hunt." Biung spoke quickly out of excitement.

"I have also found that the fruit of the *mumulas*[5] above the mountain streams is plentiful and especially big. It is also really red. The *lito*[6] on the mountain slopes have lots of fruit as well. So much that their branches are all bowed over. Even the flower buds on the *asik*[7] are bigger and fatter than last time. Their golden-yellow blossoms look like millions of honeybees huddled together; completely still and just gorgeous. With so much wild fruit growing over the mountains and valleys it's sure to make all kinds of animals so excited that they lose their wariness. We should take good advantage of this opportunity." The robust Salivan was animated as he described the things he had seen recently in the mountains.

"Perhaps it's because I'm too old and the ancestral spirits pity me for having lived too long on this earth, but I wake up in the middle of the night for no good reason and can't get back to sleep. All I can do is go out into the courtyard to look at the sky and listen to the voices of nature until the sky grows light. Recently the forest has been full of the sounds of activity. I almost get the feeling that all the animals are moving about in the forest. I'm sure that the abundance of food has made them big and fat." Hudas Laung poked at his sparse white whiskers a little awkwardly. His throat moved a few times as though some stubborn words were stuck in there and didn't want to come out. Finally, he pulled himself together, raised his eyes and spoke to Banitul who had his head bowed so that he could listen more carefully;

"Lavin,[8] the work in the fields has been completed and the time of urgency for the crops has passed. You should organize a hunting party and go into the mountain hunting grounds to try your luck. The coldest season will soon take control over the mountain forests and the women and children need the strength that they get from meat to bolster their resistance. Once there is snow on the mountain slopes you will have lost your chance. In that kind of weather hunting parties easily become Nature's prey."

Since the time when memories began, the people had never gone into the mountains to hunt during the winter. That is because the cold has the power to bury everything in the mountains under a layer of snow and ice. Then there is no place for the animals to find food. The only thing that they can do is seek out a warm place to hide and wait peacefully for the season of green to return to the mountain forests. The people also wouldn't go into the mountains to hunt when the sun is at its strongest because that is when they join the glorious sunshine in watching over the crops in their fields.

Hunting is a sacred and prolonged ritual of survival. It is necessary for someone to take responsibility for directing the hunting parties because only then will the hunters be able to defeat the nimble, clever animals. The one who accepts responsibility for leading the hunting party must obtain the permission of the gods and the tacit but sincere approval of the people before he can assume such an illustrious position. The privilege of leading the hunting party doesn't belong to a particular clan or individual, it flows with the mandate of the gods and the endorsement of the people to the person whose life skills are the most accomplished. It has flowed that way for thousands of years.

Banitul was this year's hunting party leader. In the past year he had returned with the most game and his crop of millet was the healthiest and most abundant. For those reasons he had gained the highest regard of the villagers. In their hearts everyone acknowledged that only someone with such abilities could please the host of gods and lead the people towards a prosperous and peaceful future.

"The time should be right. Everyone should prepare their hunting weapons. All we need is for the gods to give their permission for us to enter the mountains and we can begin this year's hunting ritual." Banitul's steady gaze drifted towards the dark, moody mountain range now shrouded in clouds.

"This time we should allow a few young men to take part in the hunt, they will reinforce the village hunting party." With his sparse white hair and slack yellowed skin, Hudas Ulang looked older than he really was. His pipe constantly circulated in his mouth but there was not a single strand of tobacco in it. It seemed as though he used the pipe to draw out the dark yellow mucus that he was always coughing out.

"Which young men?" Banitul immediately raised his eyebrows and asked suspiciously. It was part of the leader's character that he maintained an attitude of skepticism along with his pride. Unless the logic was as clear and forceful as the sun, he questioned everything.

"Those who have grown up with Umas." The skin hanging from Hudas Ulang's face swayed like a taro skin in the wind as he made his point a little too forcefully.

In the village, aged, sagging skin is only a misleading external factor. In fact, what it represents is that a person has overcome all the trials that life presents. Only by skillfully transforming rich life experience into precious wisdom does skin become so heavy and saggy. The fervent strength that it holds within is superior to the obstinate, disdainful flesh of youth. As leader of the hunting party, Banitul understood what the old man had perceived, and he began to consider whether the time to supplement the hunting party had arrived.

The old man's idea had a profound effect on the secret, shy, yet exuberant minds unique to young people. They were finally getting the chance to become acquainted with the true spirit of the mountain forest.

As Umas thought this over excitedly he puffed out his chest in hopes that the adults could see the strength harbored in his body. His genuine anticipation took shape as a benevolent smile.

"Umas and those kids...okay then! On the evening before we go out on the hunt the young men who we have been newly admitted must come and spend the night at my house."

Having been subject to the abuse of time, the thatched houses in the village had lost their original luster, yet they still looked solid and strong like old pine trees, giving people a sense of comfort. Opposite to the village there stood row upon row of towering mountains. Graceful mists slowly moved in and around the embrace of those peaks. Some were so vain as to wrap the rosy hues of the evening sun beguilingly around themselves. The nimble mountain breeze raced between the trees and through the clumps of grass, leading all the flowers and trees in a precise, fluid dance.

"Only the most blessed of people could live in such a beautiful land." When he wasn't busy, Umas liked to run out into the courtyard to view the surrounding scenery. He liked the invisible feeling of unrestrained freedom even more.

A strong smell of burning wafted by on the wind. He wrinkled up his nose and shook his head only to discover that the smell was coming from the kitchen of his own house. He raced back inside right away wondering what new things might be going on today.

"Tama, what are you doing?" Umas leaned against the door frame of the kitchen watching Banitul busily roasting several wooden sticks and long fine pieces of bamboo.

"I'm making hunting weapons." Banitul spoke very quickly as if not wanting to spoil the work to hand by getting caught up in conversation. Our people always carry out solemn, sacred work with an attitude of concentration and silence. It is one of our traditional qualities.

Banitul tempered the wooden sticks by turning them in the flames. Then he quickly took them out to see if they were straight. He firmly bent any curved parts on his knee while the sticks were still hot. The scorching heat and his exertions brought beads of sweat to his forehead. The beads reflected the rosy glow of the flames.

"Why are you roasting *busul-banaul*?"[9] Umas picked a stick up from the ground. From the look of the bark he could tell that it was plum wood.

"Plum trees are companion trees given to us by the gods. Their wood has the strength of stone and the softness of water. It also won't crack or split for a very long time. Holding these sticks in your hands is like holding the power of the gods."

"These bamboos are really fine and beautiful."

"Those are *talum*[10] for shooting. Put them down, I haven't finished them yet."

"What will you do with them?"

"Make them straight. As straight as a taut hemp cord." Banitul continued to work with the wooden sticks in the fire. Umas knelt down and started passing the sticks and bamboo one by one to his Tama, hoping that he could be of some help in this work.

"Ah…my kinsmen, is your work going smoothly?" Talum was holding a bundle of ramie cord used for making bowstrings. The words were hardly out of his mouth when his eyes lit up. Seeing his family working so industriously together made him feel as though someone had spread a layer of sweet honey on his soul.

"Plum wood is a lot of trouble. Bamboo arrows are much easier. But we're almost done and what remains is like a pile of dust; give it a blow and it'll disappear." Banitul took the thin bamboo from the flames and looked up at the old man.

"Did you ask the gods before you started making these things into weapons?" Talum was well aware that humans were far from the most powerful beings in the vast forests and there were a limited number of things that they could do on their own. If they wanted things to proceed as happily as they hoped they had to rely on the assistance of the gods.

"In my dreams last night I vaguely saw an elder who gave me his hunting knife, then...I don't know how, but he left." Banitul squinted at the bamboo shafts in his hand to see if they were straight, then he continued, "That was an auspicious dream about making weapons, so first thing in the morning I went up the mountain to collect plum wood and arrow bamboo."

"What if you hadn't dreamed of that elder? Would that mean you couldn't make weapons?" He knew that dreams were a way of receiving the instructions of the gods, but Umas still asked.

"Auspicious dreams and inauspicious dreams are just like people; they look different, and they make things turn out differently." Talum sat down on a seat cut from a log and told the young man, "If you dream about enjoying a nice sweet yam, or that someone brings good wine to drink with you, or if someone from the village gives you a hunting knife and a ball of prepared ramie, or maybe you have to fight off and kill an enemy who has invaded your home, or a lot of people have come to our house to remember our brave ancestors; these are all auspicious dreams. The materials that we collect to make weapons will be blessed by the gods and this will be a great help during the hunt."

"What kind of dream should we avoid?"

"If you dream that you are wrestling with someone and you lose, or if someone steals something from you, or maybe you just can't find something that has gone missing, or if, for no good reason, your house catches on fire; these are all inauspicious dreams. The weapons that we make won't be any match for our quarry."

The men of our nation are excellent craftsmen. In the time that it takes to cook a pot of millet there were four powerful black bows made of plum wood and ramie leaning against the wall, and stock straight, razor sharp arrows lying coldly to the side.

"Umas, give this a pull." Banitul picked up a black bow. Umas gave it a pull and immediately drew it into the shape of the halfmoon in the night sky.

"Try this one." "And this one." Banitul gave each of the bows to Umas to try.

"My son, that black bow belongs to you." After testing the bows several times, Banitul pointed to the third bow that Umas had tried.

"Why? What about the others?" Umas looked doubtfully at the bow that had been selected, then at the other bows that had been rejected.

"The stiffness and durability of this bow are an excellent match for your strength. Your souls will be as close as brothers. This brother of yours will not only allow you to draw very quickly, it won't be so stiff as to make your arms tremble and spoil your aim. But try it again a few times just to make sure that this bow came to the village especially for you."

Venerable Talum remained seated at a considerable distance from the weapons quietly watching the way in which the young man and the black bow were being united as one. For the longest time the only thing disturbing the silence of the kitchen was the sound of Umas pulling the bow then putting it down again. The embers in the stove slowly went out. The air, now growing chilly, was absolutely still.

"My boy, have you chosen your bow yet?" Talum's voice was deep and firm. He carefully looked Umas over from head to toe as he smiled and rubbed his streaked grey beard.

Umas nodded and handed the bow to the old man. Talum took the bow and then ceremoniously leaned it back against the wall. Then, with his left hand he took a gourd ladle full of millet wine and with two fingers of his right hand began to sprinkle wine over the finely crafted, powerful black bow. As he did this he quietly prayed:

"Hu! This black bow belongs to our respected, populous, fiercely martial and strong people—Takis-Banudum.[11] My descendants will use it and rely upon it forever. I solemnly beseech the gods in heaven to wash away all defeat, filth, shame, and those things belonging to the evil spirits. May those things be carried in the river waters to the most distant ends of the earth. In the months and years to come this bow will surely become a part of Umas' soul. It will follow its master's eyes and shoot straight at anything he aims at! May he hit the racing quarry with every arrow that he shoots. Here I stand and beseech you that no arrow will ever strike one of our own people in error. Henceforth, may the master of this bow occupy a position as lofty as the tallest mountain. Hu! Hu! Hu!"

We Bunun people who live in the high mountains must establish a second life; a *hanup*[12] that has been formed through long and severe training.

If you wish to possess powerful hunting skills you have to submit to long, arduous training. As a youth you must accompany your elders into the mountains to capture game. If you are unlucky and are unable to catch any game, you will be faced with the situation of having nothing to eat or even drink. You will have to suck the dew from the weeds in the early morning, or possibly you will have to eat non-poisonous wild plants and wild fruits to avoid starvation. Under normal conditions the stern elders will order the younger boys to fetch water, cook the food, do the washing, divide up the game and smoke the game meat. This will continue until an image of the boys living freely and ably in the mountain forest forms in the minds of the elders. These traditional customs have persisted for thousands of years and have become the unquestioned responsibility of all men as they study all things related to hunting. These traditions have become the totems that shape Bunun men.

For several days, Umas and his new bow were inseparable, as if they were the closest of brothers. He had owned weapons like this before, but the bows were thinner and the string slack, which meant that they were only good for hunting small birds and squirrels and the like. Besides, that was more like child's play.

Whenever Umas had a little time he would run out into the courtyard and practice drawing his bow. He drew the bow as far as he could then waited in that position until his face turned beet red and his arms began to shake. Sometimes he pretended that the chickens running around in the courtyard were imaginary quarry and tried as hard as he could to keep the prey in his sights. He only stopped when a chick ran and hid in the feathers under its mother's breast.

"Umas, are you killing chickens?" A friend called Biung came over from his cina's. He wasn't very tall, but his nose was bigger than most people of average height. This meant that adults often made fun of him because they thought he was especially suited to play the part of the "scapegoat" who stays alone in the grain storeroom during harvest season.

"Are you killing one for our dinner?" His friend Alang always had messy hair. He was a little cross-eyed, but his eyes were clear and mischievous. Tagging along were Tiang with his protruding forehead and a face like a ripe spiked plum flower,[13] as well as Pizing who had one shoulder higher than the other. This characteristic was exactly like his tama, and the two of them also had the same comical, coarse laugh.

"Alang, the only reason you managed to grow up is because you've always eaten other people's food, right?"

"Umas, your soul must have died, you've gone stupid. Haven't you ever heard that there's nothing that tastes and smells more delicious than somebody else's food?" Pizing walked over with one shoulder up and one down. He was always making jokes.

"Aiya! You *daimangaths*[14] come sneaking over here like a flock of ghosts. What kind of trouble are you trying to make this time?"

"Without you to lead us, how can we make any trouble? You're the trouble-maker-in-chief." Alang drew an exaggerated outline of Umas' body in the air.

"Ai!...Your mouths are as sharp as silvergrass. You're nothing but mouth. The rest of you is good for nothing...eh!" Umas deliberately drew out his words, smiling and looking excited to see his friends.

"Hey! Isn't this bow a bit too stiff? Try and draw it and all you'll get is a string of farts." Tiang burst out in crazed laughter which in turn made everyone else laugh until they were falling all over each other.

"This bow has been ritually blessed and now possesses the power of the gods. Your disrespectful attitudes are going to bring down some curse that you won't be able to shake, and your future hunting trails are just going to lead you out into the wilderness where even the game animals don't go." Umas' youthful face looked serious as he thought of the process which gave birth to the bow.

Alang and the rest of them hummed and looked around awkwardly, not knowing how to respond. They all knew that there is an invisible force in the world that always stands watching from the highest places, constantly judging the actions of people.

The slightly humid mountain wind blew from deep inside the forest, sweeping through all the canyons and gorges and finally drifting into the courtyard as if exhausted. Everyone could tell that after the sun set behind the mountains it was going to be a very chilly night.

"Uvath,[15] come! Huh? Why are we missing one?" Banitul stood in the main doorway, his tall frame erect and his arms crossed in front of his chest. Then he opened his mouth and gave a hardy voiceless laugh.

Tama Banitul, Lao...Laung. It's Laung. He stepped into a hole while he was walking and the *bikni*[16] on his foot swelled up...as big as a *paat*.[17] If he came along with us he'd be like a rock in the mud, he'd always be sinking and wouldn't be able to stand on his foot." Banitul's status as leader of the hunting party made Tiang so nervous he had difficulty breathing and his flushed red forehead looked all the more like a cockscomb.

"Never mind then. If someone can't even walk on a level road, they'll definitely be laughed at by the animals on the hunting ground. Besides, there are small holes all over the hunting ground. Come in! Don't let the local evil spirits see what we are about to do." Banitul turned around with a easy grace and went into the house. The young men quickly scrambled in behind him.

Perhaps it was because he was focused on practicing his archery skills, but Umas only now realized that a lot of things had happened in the last few days. Those things were going to bring about startling changes in the days to come.

That night, Banitul dreamed that there were a lot of pigs and chickens walking around in their courtyard. After a discussion among the members of the hunting party, everyone considered that this was an auspicious dream in which the gods granted their permission to enter the mountains to hunt. For his part, Banitul felt extremely stirred up by the dream. Thereupon he announced that the lengthy ritual of the hunt would commence on the following day.

Talum, who always gave accurate and excellent advice on the basis of his extensive experience, was also delighted and told everyone:

"There are more animals in our mountains than we can ever shoot because our ancestors always tell us when the most suitable time to go hunting is. Now is that time."

In order to receive the forceful protection of the leader of the hunting party and be shielded from injury at the hands of the evil spirits, on the night before they set out, Umas, Biung and the other young men who were joining the hunt for the first time had to go to stay in the house of the leader.

That night, Banitul made a special point of sharing his evening meal with the young men. In the presence of the hunting party leader their hands and feet were very stiff, and you never would have imagined that they were usual so lively and restless.

Before they went to bed, the leader took the young men outside his house and had them look in the direction of the hunting ground. One after the other he pressed his right hand to the foreheads of Umas, Biung and the rest. Then he looked off into the mysterious black sky and prayed:

"Hu! Ye heavenly gods! Our children are about to follow the village hunting party into the mountains to hunt. After this prayer they will be endowed with great strength and daring and will be able to kill the most ferocious of wild animals. Moreover, they will share their catch with all of the people. They are going to be the most courageous of hunters, and more still, they will be the healthiest of hunters. Ye heavenly gods! From this day forward the glory that they achieve from hunting will be as bright as the rays of moonlight that shines in the sky over other villages. During this hunt they will use my power to resist the temptation and harm of the evil spirits and preserve their naturally benevolent spirits and healthy bodies. Aside from the blessings of the gods, there will be no power that can bring harm to the hunt that will begin tomorrow. Hu! You heavenly gods! We beg you to protect all those go out to hunt and may those that they leave at home also enjoy peace and good health."

NOTES

1. The soul or self.
2. The general term for ancestral spirits.
3. The eternal resting place of the ancestral spirits.
4. A cast-off cicada exoskeleton.
5. Taiwan raspberry.
6. Wild loquat.
7. Taiwan sugar palm.
8. The leader of the village hunting party.
9. Plum wood.
10. Arrow shafts.
11. The Takbanuaz (Luanshe) branch of the Bunun nation. There are six branches of the Bunun nation.
12. The ability to hunt.
13. Crown of thorns plant.
14. Fools.
15. An address used by adults towards those of a younger generation.
16. A general term for joints. In this case it refers to the ankle.
17. A pumpkin.

CHAPTER 4

THE HUNT

A familiar morning breeze blew from the mountain forest, but the languid earth had no desire to rise and dance with the wind. This left only the most primeval mystery and tranquility to stroll carefree in its embrace. Leading their children by the hand, the women of the village had gone to stand by the low, dense *butngus*[1] some distance away. They were as silent as the world around them, afraid to engage in idle conversation.

After rising from their beds, the members of the village hunting party could not eat or smoke tobacco. They went directly to gather in the courtyard of the party leader, Banitul. Aside from their bows and arrows, everyone also carried a *davath*[2] on their backs in which they placed millet, a clay cooking pot, flints for fire starting and other necessities. However, they were absolutely forbidden from bringing any kind of meat or strongly flavored food. That is because hunting is a ritual in which the people reach out to the mountain forest to beg for game meat for their family to eat. If they bring lavish food with them the gods will never extend their generosity. Moreover, there is an ancient legend that clearly instructs the people: if you are greedy towards nature, all your meat will change into sparrows that will fly off into the forest, leaving you with nothing.

There was a great bonfire blazing in the center of the courtyard. Sparks crackled and rose on the fresh, clean air, taking the flames with them high into the sky. As leader of the hunting party, Banitul began by waving his bow and arrows over the fire in a circular motion. Then he prayed solemnly:

> Dihanin![3] Dihanin!
> Please make the fat *gigi*[4] gather before our bows,
> And chase away all unclean wild beasts
> So that we may avoid the misfortunes brought by their evil spirits.
> Ye multitude of gods! Ye multitude of gods!
> Please chase away those *andidip*[5] leading their young,
> That is not the objective of our hunt,
> Let our arrows fall to the ground and not fly forward,
> Like them, we have a young generation
> Who are as numerous and beautiful as moon peach flowers.[6]

One after the other, the members of the hunting party repeated the leader's actions while using the power of the flames to convey their personal hopes for the hunt to the heavenly gods.

"You hunters of great skill! Please arrange your bows around the outside of the fire." Banitul shouted. The members of the hunting party placed their weapons around the edge of the fire according to their status, then kneeled in their positions. With the fire at the center, the hunters and their weapons formed two large circles so that all could enjoy the power and warmth of the fire equally. Taking a gourd ladle filled with millet wine, Banitul dipped the fingers of his right hand into the wine and sprinkled it over the weapons. With passion in his eyes he stared deep into the forest and, in a deep, serene voice, began to sing the ancient song of the weapon ceremony:

> "What comes before my bow and arrow?"

The hunters replied as a chorus in their loud, pure voices.

"All the mountain deer will come before my bow and arrow."

The leader sang again:

"What comes before my bow and arrow?"

The group again replied as a chorus.

"All the mountain boar will come before my bow and arrow."

"What..."

"All the..."

"..."

The ritual continued with this repetitive call and response song until the hunters had called out the names of all the animals on the hunting ground. The ceremonial song was firm and resolute, like a dense bank of white cloud floating gracefully into the heart of the heavens. It beseeched the gods to open an invisible gate into the mountain forest to allow the hunters to return again and race through the woods, to embrace it, and, with the compassion of the gods, to enter and suckle at its breast so that they might strengthen and perpetuate the life of their nation.

As if it understood the importance of the day, the sky began radiating warm, clear light. When the hunting dogs realized that the ritual was completely finished, they immediately started barking and scuffling, bringing the whole village to life. They were all wide-eyed, peering off into the distance, or looking down to sniff the scents of the earth. The hair around the necks of several of the more respected dogs stood straight up and their eyes turned slowly. From time to time they raised their shiny, wet, black noses into the air to try to discern what scents were borne through the air. Some charged about excitedly, bounding up and down as though they were in heat. The sight of the bristling hair around the dogs' necks was a sign for Banitul and it made him feel extremely happy. He knew what it meant. In the mountain forest there are signs that people have learned to recognize through experience gathered over thousands of years. There is no mistaking them.

Preparations for entering the mountains: examine all gear, perform the weapon ritual and the hunting ritual, elevate the spirits of men and hunting dogs to a fever pitch. Under the strict supervision of the leader all arrangements were completed very smoothly and without disorder.

After entering the mountains, in order to protect the hunters who were participating for the first time, the party placed Umas, Biung, Laung and the others in the middle of the file. All experienced hunters know that not all of the forest spirits are friendly, there are alluring monsters everywhere. The older hunters have a responsibility to teach the younger men how to avoid the pernicious powers and bolster their courage. It is just one of the ways of maintaining the life of the village.

The hunting party moved through the forest like the wind. But aside from the sound of footsteps trampling fallen leaves, the silence of the mountains was undisturbed. Seemingly accustomed to this kind of expedition, the hunting dogs also raced ahead in silence. Jade green foliage slept proudly in mid-air, apparently unaware that a file of black shadows had passed by under their canopy.

"Look! See the direction the *ngito*[7] are flying." Husung sped up so that he could get closer to his brother in the lead.

"Thanks be to the gods. This hunt will surely bring all the hunters satisfaction." Banitul slowed down and tilted his head to watch a wren fly from his left to his right.

Everyone believes that the left shoulder is where the evil spirits dwell, while the right shoulder is the domain of the benevolent spirits. If the wrens fly from left to right, it means that the evil spirits are walking towards the world of goodness. There they will accept the direction of the benevolent spirits and that will have a very positive effect on the results of the hunt.

Once again, the tiny wrens raised the morale of the hunting party. Banitul had originally planned to let the party rest there to allow them to catch their breath, but seeing that their spirits had been buoyed, and that they no longer showed any signs of fatigue, he didn't hesitate to simply stride onwards, leading their dark shadows straight in the direction of the hunting ground.

After passing over a ridge, the dark path took several turns and the air suddenly became crisp and fresh. It carried the faint scent of countless wildflowers mixed with the fetid smell of rotting branches and leaves from the groves of low trees. It was the fresh yet fetid aroma often encountered in the dense forest. The hunters thought of it as only the healthy bodily odor of the forest, an odor that had not changed for thousands of years.

The mountain slopes rose and fell, the scenery in the woods constantly changed. It was very difficult to keep track of it all. That seemed to be how it went with the luck of the hunters as well. A long, thin red bamboo snake with its coat of pale crimson lay by the trail enjoying the rays of sunlight filtering through the leaves.

"Bahan![8] May the gods forgive us pitiable men! May the gods protect us ill-fated men! Leader, we have seen a snake." A middle-aged hunter announced in a terrified voice. Everyone immediately stopped in their tracks. He was frozen in his tracks looking like a rotting stump, his eyes focused on a clump of grass by the side of the path.

"Salivan, catch it. Don't let it get away." Banitul was almost frantic as he shouted to the person closest to the snake. When they heard that someone had seen a snake, many of the men started to shake uncontrollably. Their faces drained of color as though they had been dropped into deep, frigid water. When he grabbed the thin little bamboo snake, Salivan found it unusually heavy and he broke out in a cold sweat.

"Haisul Duhasi,[9] why do you have to be so sharp-eyed. You...ai." None of the hunters at the front had noticed the red bamboo snake hidden in the clump of grass. When Haisul spotted the snake, it thrust unnecessary bad luck before everyone's eyes. Some felt an inarticulate anger about how sensitive he was when walking through the forest.

"The power of the gods is still with us. Fortunately, we met with a snake and not a rat. Otherwise we would have had to cancel this expedition and go back to the village to wait for the next opportunity to hunt. Beat that evil spirit to death! Here, I'll do it." Looking disconcerted, Banitul knelt down and took some dry grass and tree branches from the surrounding area to make a fire. Then he threw the red snake into the blaze. As it was transformed into a length of dry, black rattan by angry flames the snake gave off the foul stench of the evil spirits.

"Standing in the smoke, Banitul glared at the forest and shouted over and over:

"Vai sang![10] Vai sang! Vai sang! Vai sang!"

Banitul hoped that the game chased off by the snake would respond to his calls and return so that the hunting party didn't go home empty-handed. In order to resist and transform the bad luck before them, the hunters had to start hunting on the spot.

Banitul instructed the first-time hunters to stay behind. He wanted them to make sure that the evil spirit had been completely destroyed by the flames and also to ensure that sparks from the fire didn't spread to the nearby forest. After that he directed the other hunters to go into the forest and employ guerilla tactics to kill any animals that they caught sight of, including wild birds. In no time, the surrounding forest rang with frantic noises. From the tops of the trees they heard large birds beating their heavy wings to take flight. The entire forest was set on edge by the unsettling sounds provoked by the hunters.

"The mumulas[11] here are very large and red, do you want to try them?" Biung wiped his big nose and reached out to pick some mock strawberries growing on the slope. For these young men who were in the mountains to hunt for the first time the curse encountered by the hunting party was no match for the temptation of the lush fruit.

"I've heard old people say that mock strawberries and monkeys are related. If the mock strawberries grow big and juicy, the monkeys will also be big and fat." Alang's mouth was full but he seemed already to have set his slightly crossed eyes hungrily on another patch of wild strawberries.

"Ah!...Damned *hasuth*,[12] what are they doing here? They've blocked the spread of the strawberries, otherwise we'd have more strawberries than we could eat." Tiang gave the large clump of umbrella trees growing above the strawberries a rough push sending dead leaves as well as butterflies and other insects that had been drinking nectar fluttering in all directions.

"Don't break them. Umbrella trees are good friends of our people. Women often pick their tender leaves to use in their cooking, and when they are working in the fields, people put them on their heads to relieve the headaches they get from getting too much sun." Umas had learned the uses of dwarf umbrella trees from the daily lives of his elders.

"I know that, Umas, but you trample *bubukun*[13] all the time. They are our friends, too. If you boil it in millet congee, the taste is so good it makes you forget about everything else. Unfortunately, you squashed all that good food under your bum." Alang waggled his head of messy hair and his mischievous eyes rolled in their deep sockets.

"It's not like that. They like growing all over the fields and although they grow fast, they die even faster, just like rainbows in the sky. People think that they are the power that makes fat, abundant millet crops grow." As he tried to prop up the umbrella tree branches lying on the ground, Umas spoke quietly to himself:

"Bubukun, bubukun, please don't be angry. The next time that we cook you with our millet please don't be stingy with your wonderful taste, you have to let us enjoy it, okay?"

As Umas performed his quasi-ritual everyone held back on making fun of him. On top of that, the sound of footsteps approaching from all directions startled them and made them quiet down.

"Did someone make a kill? Did someone make a kill? What kind of animal?" Banitul asked anxiously as he appeared from a grove of trees brushing sticks and leaves from his body. Even though a red bamboo snake had brought them bad luck, they could make use of the local life forms to dispel that bad luck.

"Hu! This *kukun-bapu*[14] is really heavy." Salivan walked out of a grove of low trees with a limp animal in his hand. He left a trail of trampled grass and broken trees behind him that looked like the work of a rutting black bear.

"Aiya, the blessings of the gods have all fallen upon you. Did you get it with your first shot?" Banitul asked cautiously as he grabbed Salivan to greet him. If you don't hit your target with your first shot it indicates that your weapon has lost its power and can't control the animal's spirit and life. That is not good because it means that the hunt may bring sadness to the entire village.

"Of course, of course I got him with the first shot. This civet had climbed into a *huna*[15] tree looking for food. The fat, juicy fruit made him forget to be vigilant. When I shot him down, he still had berry juice dripping from of his mouth." Salivan looked at everyone standing around empty-handed. He looked at them as if to say, "What's wrong with you?" This made them hang their heads in silent shame.

"There should also be lots of birds in the mulberry tree." The creatures of the forest all liked fruit from the paper mulberry the best.

"Okay, the main thing is that someone has shot some game. Husung, you make another fire. Umas, you cover the evil spirits in the old fire with mud, the thicker the better so that they never see the light of day again." The leader once again took control of the hunting party.

When the first kill is made, no matter how big it is, it is immediately roasted so that everyone can symbolically share in eating it. The internal organs are distributed equally to the dogs. This gives incentive for everyone to work as hard as they can on the things that they are responsible for, because whatever the hunt produces will be shared by the whole hunting party, and the dogs are no exception.

By the time they arrived at *buasuan*[16] it seemed that the sky had grown dark earlier than normal. Layers of cloud obscured the heavens and became darker as they pressed down over the distant mountains. It looked as though they had shaved the tops of the peaks and ridges flat, and this made the hunting ground gloomier and more oppressive.

Banitul had chosen an *ukuk*[17] with sheer cliffs on either side to construct a shelter which consisted of only a roof. The nearby mountain walls would block the chilly wind. Looking up, you could see the pitch-black shadows of the trees frolicking like mischievous sprites. There was also a streak of softly lit night sky illuminated now and then by starlight. It was a warm, welcoming place to rest.

Experienced hunters all place their trust in the barren mountain cliffs. Because they are entirely bare, they can never give rise to sudden natural disasters. Banitul had cherished respect for the cliffs since his youth. Hunters must run about on top of the cliffs. Only by traversing them can they demonstrate their individual heroic abilities, and only if there are cliffs will the mountains inspire awe and fear. Perhaps bravery and majesty themselves are at base completely barren.

"Don't place your weapons where you can't lay your hands on them in case our enemies attack us by surprise." Although we had established a certain level of trust in our relations with other nations, memories of the slaughters of the past made it impossible for Banitul not to take precautions. Besides, monsters who can change their appearance lurk amid the beauty of the mountains.

In the mountain forest after dark the myriad creatures are like sweet infants sleeping soundly in the embrace of the earth. The radiance of the newly arisen moon shone in all directions, gradually dissolving the remaining hues of milky-white and bronze. Under the cold glow, the forest fell even more still. But this scene didn't last for long. Suddenly there appeared a bank of stiff black clouds that covered the full moon and the whole night sky. The mountain wind began to race around in the darkness of the canyons while the leaves and branches on the trees were stirred to mournful soughing cries. Layer after layer of black clouds stretched over the sky while waves of deep, muffled thunder carried from their depths.

"Off in the distance there must be a storm brewing. It might even be at our village. By the look of the sky tonight the weather tomorrow is going to be unbearable. What do you think?" Banitul was extremely concerned as he watched the sky grow darker and darker.

At dawn on the next day, although there was no cock crowing to prod them, one by one the men woke up more promptly than if they had been at home. Perhaps this was because they were in strange surroundings, or maybe it was the divine force of the hunting ritual that made them not want to be lax.

"Laung, you young guys go to the local stream and get water, then you can start cooking." Bukun was Laung's tama's brother. Faced with many miscellaneous tasks, he was naturally more than happy to order his younger relative around.

"No, on the hunting ground you can't make someone on their first hunt do odd jobs. If you do, you'll stir up a thunderstorm in the mountains. It's better to ask one of the experienced hunters to get water." Banitul's voice came from a corner of the shelter. The young men on their first hunt were pleased by such consideration.

After their bellies were filled with hot millet, Banitul immediately delegated a role in the hunting activities to each of the men. Then he asked for everyone's opinions and discussed those different opinions with the whole group. That way he was able to form a plan for the hunt that everyone was satisfied with.

"Tama Tulpus, it is appropriate that the relatively young men do the *mabuasu*[18] work. There is also no problem with the archery skills of the men doing the *mitala*.[19] As for the position of those waiting in ambush, would it be best for them to be directly in the escape path of the different types of game? I hope you can give us some help there." Before winding up the discussion, Banitul clasped his hands tightly together as a sign of sincerity and sought the ideas of those older than himself.

Tulpus was a short, skinny old man, but possessed a serious, thoughtful face burned black by the sun. He may not have been at all serious or thoughtful, but his deeply seated eyes and his thin, pointed chin gave his face a severe, grave expression. Men who are used to thinking serious matters over for themselves all have that kind of expression.

He had made more trips to the hunting area than anyone else. Therefore, when it came to the places where animals drink or the direction they go in search of food, he understood these things as well as he understood the habits of his friends. A lot of people believed that Tama Tulpus could find his way around the hunting ground with his eyes closed, except if there had been some natural disaster or manmade changes.

"As long as the dogs can sniff the game out of their hiding places, the positions that the leader has arranged for those waiting in ambush should be right for blocking the animals' escape routes and this hunt should bring back an abundant catch." It seemed as though Tama Tulpus was feeling cold. He spoke haltingly and was reluctant to open his mouth too wide. Suddenly, an idea flashed into his mind and his deep-set eyes began to sparkle. In a firm, forceful voice he explained sentence by sentence:

"From our experience over the past few years we know the escape routes of the animals like the backs of our hands. However...in the place where the sun sets behind the mountain there is a large tract of *tanapas*[20] that has become a new escape route for the mountain boars. Once the dogs were hard on the track of a sow with one piglet, but the clever sow went against all traditional hunting party reasoning and took her piglet into a brush bottle tree forest where there was nobody waiting in ambush. In the end, she disappeared without a trace. This made people wake up to the fact that the animals had long ago figured out how hunters think. Leader, I just want to make this one point to see what everybody thinks."

"Wuninan.[21] I will send someone to guard that area. Okay then. Everyone get your things ready and when it's light you can start doing the jobs I assigned to you." After Banitul thanked the elder he walked out of the shelter to check the conditions in the mountains. He knew very well that before beginning the battle with the quarry you need to listen to the language of the trees, the voices of the streams, and the clues of the wind. Then you must humbly accept their suggestions, because the wisdom to defeat the prey lies therein.

The overcast sky looked like the bottom of a cooking pot with a hole in it. A stream of weak clear light flickered down, illuminating the mountain peaks in the distance and slowing bringing the earth's wondrous forms to light. The mountain peaks before him were densely piled together and grew taller the further away they were. Some of the slopes were dotted with huge, protruding boulders that made him wonder what kind of magical power nature possessed after all. All of a sudden, a mass of black cloud rose from behind a tall mountain on the horizon and grew into a cloud bank that stretched even further than the mountain ranges. It then pressed toward the sky above Banitul at the exact speed of the wind. The dark shadow of the clouds was so immense that the entire sky seemed to be tilted in the direction that the cloud came from. In no time, what little light the dawn had brought to the forest had been stained pitch black by the black clouds so that it seemed that daylight had never come in the first place.

The bloated layers of cloud could no longer support their heavy load of rainwater and started to pour it down from mountain top to mid-slope. A flash of lightning jumped from one cloud into another, then one bolt after another swept toward the forest. Wild explosions of thunder pursued the lightning flashes creating a different sound on each of the mountain slopes. Even the little shelter began to rumble. This sent the crows in the tops of the trees into a frenzy of cawing. The timid mountain birds flew out of the woods in a panic in search of rocky crevices to hide away in. All creatures seemed to be responding to the signs of the storm's approach.

Large, dispersed raindrops began to fall. The wind became fiercer, whipping the trees in the forest into chaotic waves. The thinner, weaker trees were blown in all directions. Masses of leaves followed the powerful gusts and disappeared into the dim mountain gorges. Thrown about by the wind, the branches between the trees banged together and made loud creaking noises in response to the peals of thunder in the sky.

Banitul was so alarmed by the sudden onset of the storm that he was beside himself. When he pulled himself together, he quickly ducked into the shelter. Outside the shelter the heavens opened up and the rain started to bucket down. The swiftly moving mists and the curtain of raindrops almost completely obscured the forest scenery. Only in the bluish glow of the lightning flashes could you make out that the whole earth was trembling.

In all his life Banitul had never seen a storm like this one. It was almost life-threatening. The angry gods seemed to have dispatched their entire store of thunder and lightning to attack the mountain forest. The members of the hunting party were fearful and disquieted by Nature's bewildering display of force. They took refuge in the shelter feeling perplexed, but there was nothing that they could do.

"We must have done something wrong." Standing amid the wind and rain, Tama Tulpus's tone was reflective.

"It must have been that Bukun wanted to make the young men work on the hunting ground. That angered the gods and brought on this storm." The little shelter was extremely dark, and it was impossible to tell who was speaking.

"But…in the end Laung didn't go to draw water!" Bukun was agitated, wondering if it really was him who caused this calamity.

"Could it be that some family member broke a taboo? Do all your families know what rules they have to observe when the hunting party is in the mountains?" Banitul narrowed his eyes and tried to make out from the men's expressions which one hadn't reminded their families about following the traditional hunting taboos.

For Bunun people, hunting isn't so straightforward as it may outwardly seem. It is a sacred rite carried out by all the people in the village as a group. From the day that one of their members joins the hunting party, the whole family must observe a wide range of taboos. These include that they may not sweep the ground, because all the game animals will become like garbage that will be swept away and escape. They may not weave, because when the hunters are pursuing their quarry they will be easily tripped up by the string-like rattan vines. They may also not go into the mountains to work in the fields, because the soil that they turn has a rotten smell and that will make the game meat inedible because it tastes rank. People must not eat garlic, chilli pepper and other things with a strong aroma because the animals will easily scent the heavy smell and flee. They may not give fire to others or wash their clothes. That makes the abilities of the hunters disappear and their arrows will not hit their prey.

"Yes, I carefully told them several times." "Every time I go hunting, I tell them again. My family understand things extremely well." "Yes, I..." It was as if everyone spoke with the same voice in proclaiming their family's purity.

The mountain forests are the mountain forests, and the village is the village. Those who live in the village can't really grasp the true spirit of the forest. By the time noon approached, the storm had apparently run into difficulty and suddenly went quiet. The wild gales now dashed around forests in the distance. As things went quiet the dripping of rainwater sounded like hushed tears. The heavy storm clouds were now only thin cloudy mists gathering in the shady groves of the mountain hollows. In the darker quarters of the sky there were occasional flashes of lightning that squeezed out dainty thunderclaps that sounded like the burping of a baby after it drinks its fill of milk.

A dark brown mountain bird vigorously flapped its stubby wings as it flitted through the sky over the ravaged forest. When it was tired it alighted on a contorted, leafless tree branch. It looked left and right, surveying the surroundings, tweeting heartbreakingly, as if desperate to find a safe nest for her children. Mountain birds circled in the sky over the ruins of the forest and rested on the bare tree branches. Everyone knew that this behavior would continue for many days.

Banitul walked from the shelter and turned over a number of stones of different shapes. Small puddles immediately formed in the hollows beneath them and the stones in his hands dripped. Right away he realized that the forests were filled with too much rainwater and they could go soft at any time. If the ground was soft, then the pursuit dogs and the men would sink into the mud and their movements would be clumsy. They might even stumble into a canyon. A good leader should never push his people towards danger. Banitul furrowed his brow to survey the forest around him then settled on his decision.

"The rain has all hidden in the dirt. It's as if the whole mountain forest is floating in a stream like a piece of driftwood. That makes it very dangerous. Half of the afternoon is already gone. Before darkness comes, we need to strengthen our shelter so that we all have a safe place to take refuge for the time being." Banitul looked at the dispirited faces of his people but could only shrug his shoulders to indicate that he felt absolutely helpless.

"Umas, you young guys take care of the dogs. Don't let them go into the forest because they're too rambunctious and they'll make the animals wise and wary. Get to know the dogs. Let their eyes see into your souls so that tomorrow when you are out coursing with them, they'll listen to your directions and chase the quarry out without a fuss."

It was approaching dusk and the sun, absent the whole day, now struggled to escape from the entanglement of the storm clouds. It appeared over the back of the mountains to the west, its fresh evening red faded to a gloomy blood color that kept getting darker and darker. It was as if the day's storm had totally exhausted it. After the storm, even the mountain breeze slipped gently over from the canyon like a sickly old man. Something seemed to be weighing heavily on its mind and it had no way of telling anyone about it.

On the second day, all the men went off into the hunting ground to carry out the work assigned to them by the leader. They spent quite some time getting to the area that they were given. Before noon, the dogs easily chased a pair of adult mountain boars out of their den. The baying of the pursuing dogs and the shouts of the dog handlers shook the whole mountainside. Waiting in ambush, the hunters listened to the process of the pursuit, trying to determine the kind of game, and the number of animals. As soon as they heard the pursuit moving towards the area that they were responsible for they could draw their bows ready to shoot. But in the time that it takes an infant to take a shit the baying of the dogs became intermittent and lacked enthusiasm, as if they were just going through the motions. To the ears of the hunters their barking sounded completely forced, as if even the dogs knew that they were faking it. The forest fell silent again, and everyone realized that the clever animals had used their mysterious, natural-born powers to trick the quick-witted dogs into making a major mistake. That allowed them to disappear from the hunting ground without a trace, just like the air. When the hunters returned to the shelter in the evening to rest, their fatigue and disappointment transformed into a long list of complaints. Why hadn't anyone discovered the trail that the boar couple had used to escape on? Why couldn't people waiting in the area have been a little sharper and moved their ambush positions?

This continued until they saw Haisul lugging a fat mountain goat back to the cave. That made them temporarily forget the shame of having been made fools of by their quarry.

"Hu! It's a mountain goat. Haisul, how did you get it?" Banitul asked eagerly as he fixed his bow.

Haisul took the goat from his shoulders with a grunt then puffed out his chest and stretched his waist to shake off the fatigue. Or perhaps it was to show off a bit. He carefully stepped over some things strewn on the ground and found an open place to sit down. Pleased with himself, he kept rolling his eyes until he settled his enthusiastic gaze on his companions. Then very calmly, even a little disinterestedly, he said:

"As I was making my way back to the shelter my ears were drawn by the slight sound of dry leaves being crushed, so I stopped in my tracks and looked all around to find where the sound was coming from. Off in the direction of the small trail I saw a beautiful mountain goat munching on some tender shell-ginger sprouts. Without any hesitation I almost stopped breathing, slowly loaded an arrow and waited for the best opportunity to shoot. The clever goat must have smelled a dangerous scent and kept looking over in my direction. While he stared at me, I didn't dare move a muscle. Everyone knows that the animals in the forest have got perfect eyesight and hearing to prevent danger from getting near to them. As well, mountain goats have legs faster than the wind, so when I saw how alert he was, I thought to myself: this time the best I can hope for is an exchange of greetings."

Haisul shifted his body and took a breath then started speaking in a very ordinary tone of voice:

"With the help of the gods the beautiful goat lowered its head and continued munching on his ginger. He hadn't smelled my scent after all! I think it was a gift from the gods. Apart from the gods, who has the power to control all living things? Like a timid rat I gently shifted the bow in my hand. I was only concerned that the trees in the area might make some kind of noise. For example, what if the leaves in the surrounding trees all started to shake? Or what if some fruit fell from a tree and startled my quarry? Who knows what kinds of relationships exist between the creatures of the world? After all, they all live together in the mountain forests. But the gods had truly blessed me. With a 'swoosh', my arrow hit the space by the third rib behind its front leg. That's where a mountain goat's heart is. Woo, I had such good luck today, I thought it must be a dream."

"Haisul, you can notch the fact of shooting a mountain goat on your bow." Banitul stood up and, in front of everyone, he solemnly proclaimed Haisul's glory.

Hunters with great skills who have garnered people's respect have many impressive notches on their weapons. Every one of those notches were made after an all-out battle. They aren't something that a person can acquire freely like the air. After a hunter has shot an animal and it is verified before the other hunters he can carve a deep notch on his weapon. Aside from acknowledging that the animal has given their bodies to nourish the lives of the people, it also displays the glory of the hunter and their position of respect. True glory must be established by being recognized by others. Each notch is a story and a record of an individual's life.

Banitul invited a middle-aged man with deft hands to butcher the animal immediately. He also divided the fresh, warm *hadath*[22] into pieces for all members of the party to enjoy right away. Before they ate, Banitul prayed reverently:

"Hupikaunan! Ye gods! Please endow us with strength that can never be exhausted. Let us continue to hit whatever prey we shoot at. May our arrows always be straight and sharp so that the animals we target may not shake them off. With the blessing of the gods may we take down all quarry that appear before our eyes!"

"Tama Tulpus, the brains are for you in hopes that your wisdom will bring bountiful and peaceful results to this hunt." Banitul placed the entire, soft, slippery brain in the old man's hands.

"Husung, we'll use some of the head meat for dinner and then smoke-dry the rest to take back to the village. Those who can lend a hand should do so, especially the younger men so that they can see how their elders live in the mountain forest. We should get to bed early and hope that tomorrow we'll have more strength and better luck than we did today."

Although he wasn't entirely satisfied with the results of the day's hunt, Banitul firmly believed that the gods wouldn't let him down. So long as everyone prepared well, the gods must surely give them something to be joyful about.

The next day the dogs were in action only sporadically, and their hearts weren't really in it. Everyone knew that in the excitement of the moment certain dogs always pretended to be the first to pick up a scent. Other, less experienced, dogs barked and howled indiscriminately to cover up their anxiety.

Banitul hid in a clump of bushes in the ambush area, intently watching the animal trails for any movement. He was deathly afraid that if he lost concentration for even a moment the game would disappear out of sight. People find it hard to believe the speed with which animals can move about the forests.

Banitul was positioned at the highest point in the area. It was the last line of defence on the village's hunting ground and, aside from the fact that his position dictated that he had to take responsibility for defending it, Banitul could handle a hemp bowstring better than anyone else in the village.

The strong rays of the sun, and the humidity of the forest, made Banitul sweat profusely, soaking his entire body. The veins on his forehead and temples bulged. "Ooo, ooo" "Erh! erh!" The sound of monkeys romping happily in the dense forest canopy came from his left. He turned and saw a gang of comical looking monkeys in the tops of the trees. They were demonstrating how they play on the tree branches. Some were swinging freely from the branches with one hand, looking like abandoned beehives dangling in the breeze. Others were shaking the tree branches with all their might just to be provocative. Still others were even sticking their red buttocks out with the obvious intent of insulting the hunter down below. When he saw this, Banitul was so angry that he picked up a stone and was about to throw it, but when he remembered that lower down the mountain they had already let the dogs out and begun the hunt, he quickly put the stone back on the ground and breathed deeply to calm his anger.

"Why aren't the monkeys afraid of a hunter carrying a weapon?"

Banitul looked suspiciously around at the lie of the terrain. He noticed that on the ridge there were stacks of silvergrass and man-made piles of large stones. He was immediately filled with admiration for the monkeys' powers of discernment. This was the dividing line between two hunting grounds. In order to avoid misunderstandings, the people on both sides of this sensitive line avoided killing any game nearby. Possibly the monkeys had figured this out and used this dividing line as a safe place to rest. They knew that even if they saw a hunter with a weapon it did not represent any danger for them. Banitul then realized that the behavior of the monkeys was relaxed and graceful, as if they were intelligent people.

"I hope a mountain boar will try to flee along the trail in front of me." Although boars moved over a very wide range, like people, they liked to use their own trails. If you waited by the right trail you would get the opportunity to do battle with them.

Banitul hoped that the gods would grant him that opportunity. Unfortunately, all he could do was wait quietly for the gods to grant his wish.

Lower down the mountain a flock of startled birds flew from one grove of trees to another. Banitul thought that it was where the dogs and the dog handlers were situated, but he couldn't hear the calls of the handlers or the sounds of the dogs in pursuit. He exhaled lightly, partially to dispel some of the heat in his body and partially because he didn't know how else to deal with the long, tedious wait. He looked over the mountain forest extending out before him as silent as a village elder sunk in thought. Accompanied by a few chirrs from the cicadas, the forest and the sky were like a loving old couple gazing at each other in silence. With a look in their eyes as soft as water, they were expressing their gratitude for everything that the other had done the night before.

"Whop!" Banitul's huge right hand instinctively swatted his left arm. He saw a lot of black spots on his hand as he grabbed a dead mosquito and closely looked it over, then he looked at it again. He squinted and thought; it is said that only female mosquitoes enjoy drinking human blood, but how do you know it's a female? He couldn't see any *havis*[23] on the tiny insect, so he simply squashed it into a soggy mess.

Looking over the completely empty boar trail, he again tried placing an arrow in his bow, drawing it back and using the trunk of a maple tree on the other side of the trail as a target. Banitul was convinced that when any boars passed by that place, they would concentrate on getting by that tree quickly and not notice his presence. He was therefore satisfied with his choice of shooting position.

"Hoo-wah! The boars have bolted..." The dog handlers shouted to announce the start of the pursuit and the exuberant barking of dogs ripped through the stillness. Then the sound of the pursuit began to move quickly through the forest. The voices a men and dogs echoed in harmony over the slopes, making it seem as though the barking dogs were spread in all directions.

Just then, Banitul inwardly prayed that no wind would come up in the forest, because the wind is the animals' friend. It blows the scent of the hunters around so that the quarry have advance warning. That gives the animals plenty of time to change the direction of their flight so that they can avoid the shooting positions of the hunters.

"All the creatures in the forest must have a way of cooperating and helping each other so that they can continue to live in the forest."

The howls and baying of the hunting dogs continued to ring through the forest, bringing both excitement and relief to all the hunters. The longer that the quarry was on the run, the heavier the sweat on their bodies and the saliva dripping from their mouths became. Those smells drove the dogs into a frenzy of barking and made it easier for them to follow the tracks of the animals.

Suddenly, from the foot of the mountain there was an agonized yelp from one of the dogs. It was the kind of baleful cry produced out of extreme physical pain. Banitul was at once excited and anxious. He was anxious about the dog's safety, but excited that the quarry they had flushed was a boar large enough to counterattack a hunting dog.

"A large sow who has given birth to piglets." Banitul opened his eyes wider and increased his vigilance over the bend in the trail some distance from where he was positioned.

The heat from the sun's rays made the scenery before him appear distorted. Banitul used his hand to wipe away the sweat filling his eyes then tried to regain his focus. But soon his body was filled with a feeling of disappointment. The sound of the pursuit had crossed the stream in the canyon and was headed up the spine of the mountain opposite, further and further from his area.

Banitul looked at the sawtooth mountain range where the sunlight now fell. He knew that a clever boar would use the cover of the brush bottle trees and head quickly over the mountaintop toward the next mountain in the distance.

"It's a good thing that Tama Tulpus foresaw this situation, otherwise that boar would be snorting from its huge snout, feeling pleased with itself for escaping to another forest so easily. Let's hope that the hunters sent over there have chosen the best positions to ambush it." With a sense of great disappointment Banitul looked at the disused animal track before him.

Banitul treated elders like Tama Tulpus with great respect. Although they didn't have many days remaining to them, these old people were like the moon on a dark night. They led their people along the rugged mountain paths with their soft warm light, back to their loved ones. So only the hunter and the elders had the privilege of eating the head, tail, viscera and other tasty parts of game animals. The elders also were not required to do heavy labor in the fields. They were the wealth of the village because people only had to heed their instructions and all farm work would proceed smoothly. It didn't matter if they actually took part in the work or not.

"Oo-wah...oo-wah...hu!" A call that combined two long and one short call burst into the torrid air.

"Oo-wah...oo-wah...hu!" The coarse, long call rang out again.

This unique signal made all the hunters hidden in the bushes pop up like bamboo shoots after a spring rain. This call meant that a kill had been made.

The fathers and ancestors established a set of calls to send different messages through the broad, diverse mountain forests. One long call followed by one short one means that the prey captured is a mountain goat or a muntjac. Two long calls with one short one indicates a mountain boar. Three long calls followed by one short one means a mountain deer. Four long calls and one short one means that the prey is a black bear.

After the sound of calls had stopped, the forest once again fell into deep silence. Then a gust of wild wind suddenly started roaring madly through the trees. Then it swirled in a circle and raced off to another range of mountains, howling mournfully. It seemed to be grieving over the loss of a life. Those still waiting in ambush held onto their lofty fighting spirit as they continued their long vigil. Banitul was like a huge black rock just sitting there completely immobile. He didn't even dare reach out to chase away the mosquitoes flying in swarms in front of his eyes. Everyone hoped that the next time one of those unique signals was given, it would be their own.

"Leader! Banitul. Some of the dogs are so tired their legs have gone weak and they've lost their interest in the scent of game. What should we do now?" One of the dog handlers shouted out from the nearby stream.

Banitul looked up, squinted, and used his fingers to estimate the gap between the sun and the tops of the mountains. Seeing that the gap was only two fingers he determined that night would soon take over the path now occupied by the daylight, especially in the mountains.

"Men, the dogs need to rest earlier than usual so everyone should make their own way back to the work shed!" Banitul cupped his hands to form a megaphone and shouted into the deep, distant forest. Then he shook his legs hard because they had gone numb from kneeling for so long.

After he felt his legs reattach themselves to his body, Banitul looked in the probable direction of the shelter and started off down the mountain carrying his bow and arrows. As he walked along, he picked a few silvergrass shoots to chew on. Aside from quenching his thirst, the shoots helped pacify the rumbling in his stomach.

Striding quietly through the forest, Banitul's steps were softer than the breeze blowing through the tips of the tree branches. He began searching for an opening where he would have a wider line of sight in hopes of locating Hudas Aziman.

"Ha! Hudas Aziman is clearly standing over there." With a joyful expression, Banitul climbed up onto a tall rock, narrowed his eyes and stared at a place in the distance below the mountain.

In fact, Hudas Aziman was a gigantic old pine tree. Our people like to give names of ancestors to ancient, tall trees. This shows respect, but it also makes the trees into direction markers. It only takes a few large trees like this to serve as landmarks so that the hunters will never lose their way in the chaotic, mysterious mountain forests.

Not long after this, the sun set behind the mountains leaving behind a weak glow that only barely illuminated the earth.

NOTES

1. Chinaberry trees.
2. A string sack used when hunting.
3. A general name for the gods and spirits. Pantheism is a characteristic of Bunun religion.
4. The general name for game animals.
5. Female animals that are pregnant.
6. Alpinia zerumbet or shell ginger. (tr.)
7. Eurasian wrens.
8. Meaning "buttocks." This is often used as a swear word.
9. Duhasi means "brother." It is a form of address between equals.
10. A call to chase away ill fortune.
11. Mock strawberries; literally "snake strawberries" in Chinese.
12. *Schefflera arboricola Hayata*, commonly known as "dwarf umbrella tree."
13. Small goosefoot.
14. Masked palm civet, also known colloquially as "white-nosed heart."
15. Paper mulberry tree.
16. The clan hunting ground.
17. A gorge.
18. Leading the hunting dogs out to search for game.
19. Waiting in ambush for the quarry.
20. *Cyathea lepifera*, a large tree fern, known in Chinese as the "brush bottle tree."
21. Thank you.
22. Liver.
23. Female genitals.

CHAPTER 5

A HUNTER NAMED BLACK BEAR

"Why is the smell of arrow bamboo shoots so strong?" Banitul felt uneasy and stopped chewing so that he could hear better. Then he flared his nostrils to try to make out what message was being brought to him on the air.

"The smell of arrow bamboo shoots wouldn't be all over the place unless they'd been ripped up and chewed." Banitul scanned the surroundings and tightened his grip on his bow. He had noticed lots of moist, shiny, strip-shaped scat in the arrow bamboo grove, and they still smelled fresh.

Unnerved, he called out in a hushed voice, "There's a black bear in the area!"

Summoning all his powers, Banitul tried to calm himself. He squatted down a little and drew his bow as he surveyed the area, trying to locate the bear. He couldn't allow the bear to find him first. Suddenly, he heard a huge boulder toppling over in the grove of trees behind him. Banitul looked back with his bow drawn, ready to confront any emergency. Something that looked like an enormous black wooden pole flashed over him like lightning. He thought it was a large black bird flying past in front of him and spreading its wings over his face. Forcing his eyes as wide as he could he discovered that he was flying through the air in rapid descent. He finally came down heavily in a clump of silvergrass. The unbearable pain made him exceptionally alert and he was very aware that blood was dripping from his left arm, like rain from a roof, into the clump of grass. His bleeding arm felt cold and numb and that feeling was spreading over every part of his body. As he lay on the pile of silvergrass, limp and paralysed, his heartbeat wildly and his ears drummed, but he had no idea what to do because his mind was frozen.

Good things are like the sun. Bad things are like the stars that fill the sky. Lying there covered with blood, Banitul had no way of escaping his bad luck. All he saw was an enormous black object closing over him like the endless darkness of night. The V-shaped white fur on its chest was getting closer and closer, clearer and clearer, until it became a glaring beam of white light. From his many years of experience battling wild animals in the deep mountains, Banitul remembered that he had one last weapon in his chest bag—his *suhnun*.[1] He reached in and pulled his dagger from the bag and stood up to face his death. Gathering all his remaining strength and focussing it in the dagger, he plunged it directly into the bear's heart. The resistance of the bear's thick skin threw Banitul backwards into the clump of silvergrass again just as sharp claws slammed into the grass above his head. Momentum threw the bear's huge body forward and it dropped on top of Banitul, almost suffocating him.

"Black bears have such awesome strength!" Banitul no longer had the ability to strike back.

Ever so slowly, Banitul shifted himself around until he was facing the angry, wounded bear that stood there, flailing its paws wildly. Silently, he waited for the beast's third onslaught. In that moment he discovered that facing death is really very simple after all. Fear was completely superfluous. Although dazed, he could see the black figure of the bear roar and stand up. The pure white "V" on its chest was streaked with blood. It looked as though someone had chewed it to bits. The handle of the dagger flashed weakly amid the bright red of the blood.

"The dagger hit its heart!" Banitul lay there motionless, almost as though he wished for the bear's deadly charge.

He knew that animals have a lifeforce so strong and resilient that it is sometimes impossible for humans to comprehend. It would not have been difficult for the wounded bear to continue its onslaught, but the beast had apparently lost interest in the blood-soaked hunter. It wheeled around gracefully in the direction of a gigantic boulder. It slapped at the rock face with both its paws and let out a hair-raising roar. Fragments of rock flew in all directions. Banitul knew that it was his chance to run and take cover. But he found that he couldn't raise his left hand. In fact, he had almost no feeling in it at all. It felt as though most parts of his body had been nailed in place by the bushes around him making it impossible to move. The only parts of his body that could move freely were his eyes.

The bear's strange movements alarmed Banitul deeply. Just then, a bear cub crawled out from behind the boulder. Now he knew the reason why the bear had attacked its enemy: the most primal love—a mother's love. For the sake of the next generation all creatures will attack with utter disregard for their own lives.

The innocent little cub stood up on its hind legs and nuzzled against the mother bear's breast as if to lick the fresh blood from her, or as if it was asking about something. After it touched her it jumped back onto the ground, lowered its head and moaned sorrowfully. The mother pushed her cub with the top of her head, as if she was urging it to go someplace. Unable to resist the force of its mother's thrust the cub fell and slid down a steep slope to the bottom of a shady gorge. The mother bear panted heavily as she dragged her heavy body unsteadily off in the opposite direction. Banitul gritted his teeth and, ignoring the excruciating pain, sat upright. He grabbed a handful of *valu*[2] leaves from beside him then chewed them into a paste. He pressed the paste onto the bleeding gash in hopes that the green juice would seal the blood inside. He instinctively searched for his bow and arrows even though he knew that he no longer had the strength to draw the bow and shoot.

"Boom!" Something heavy crashed to the ground. Banitul was so frightened that the blood drained from his face. At that point he couldn't have withstood being kicked by a muntjac, let alone withstand the attack of a black bear...He stared stoically in the direction of the noise but all he could hear was the sound of deep breathing, like the breathing of an old man about to die. It was also like the sighs of someone who had cast away the love of their life. Eventually the breathing gradually slowed and became weaker until it disappeared into the tranquil mountain forest.

Banitul listened carefully to the entire process. When the sound of heavy breathing grew quiet his suffering and grief were replaced by the joy of rebirth...a rebirth after being spared by the black bear.

"Hu! The black bear has died. It was me...Hu! I killed a massively powerful bear! My dagger and I took down a ferocious black bear."

The glory of having killed a black bear made Banitul so proud that he forgot about his wounds. He tried several times to signal to the hunters in the area by making four calls to indicate that he had killed a bear. Unfortunately, all that came out of his throat was a series of hoarse jets of air and bloody mucus.

"Hoo wa..." The sound of a hunter's signal echoed through the valley. The hunting area was extremely broad, and it was impossible to make out what message was being sent from the distance. All that the hunters could do, aside from becoming more alert, was to make some wild guesses.

"Hoo wa..." "Hoo wa..." The hooting continued to ring through the forest. It sounded as though the man making the calls hardly took a breath between them and was obviously very distressed. Everyone began to feel as though something had gone amiss. The air filled with an inarticulate sense of disaster. They all set out as fast as they could for the top of the mountain where the sound was coming from.

"Our leader...Banitul is lying dead in a clump of grass." The hunter pointed a trembling finger at the dark figure in the silvergrass as he ran to greet the other hunters arriving on the scene.

"What? The leader is dead. Ai-ya...ai...May the gods save us!"

"Dead? How did he die?"

"Banitul! Banitul! What happened to you?" "Banitul! Get up, get up." They urgently slapped his wounded body hoping that the injured man would come to.

"Ai yo...ee. This mountain forest! This mountain forest! You are as vile as you are alluring, as gentle as you are heartless. Ai yo...yo." Overcome by grief, many of the men had no idea what to do.

"We have fallen into a trap set by the evil spirits. Quickly, take the leader back to the shelter. May the gods save us! Such a good man. Why would such a good man be treated this way? ...Oh gods! Open your eyes and look at his wounds. Don't make his family weep."

On the way back Banitul's arm swelled up badly and slowly turned purple. Someone took a length of hemp cord from their string bag and tied it above the gash. The wounded arm had swelled up to twice the size of the other arm and Banitul's face contorted with pain. The purple began to spread slowly into his forearm which was very unsettling.

Tama Tulpus instructed the men to lay a thick bed of pine needles in the corner of the shelter closest to the fire and least open to the wind. Banitul lay there with his eyes tightly shut. His face was completely drained of color and his chest slowly rose and fell with obvious difficulty. Everyone silently gathered around the wounded hunter. The hunting dogs walked back and forth in front of the shelter entrance whimpering sadly as if they had discovered a hostile power in the shadows waiting for a chance to attack.

"Husung, take a few men to find a large camphor tree and a pine tree with lots of pitch and bring them back here." Tama Tulpus frowned as he resolved to accept the heavy responsibility of saving the man's life.

"Umas, you and the younger men grind the charcoal from the fire into powder, the finer the better."

The shroud of night descended without anyone noticing and the mountain wind slowly came back to life in the blackness of the earth. It brought with it a chill from the depths of the forest. The hot air left behind by the daylight now transformed into hazy mist that lay motionless in the valleys like so many sinuous white snakes.

"Throw the pine wood into the fire. Banitul needs the strong flames. The fire must be strong all night long and we have to hope that the bed of pine needles will diffuse the heat from the big trees. The chill of nighttime could drown our leader as much as stream water could." Tama Tulpus sounded exhausted and his eyebrows hung low over his eyes. Many deep, stiff wrinkles were traced across his forehead and his lime-white lips were never at rest. One instant they were trembling, exposing an unfathomable terror, the next instant he pursed them into a tight purple ball...

"Umas, the charcoal powder? Give it to me."

Tama Tulpus used his dagger to cut away the uneven strands of flesh around the wound. Then he spread open the long gash with two fingers and filled it with the charcoal powder. The dry powder immediately soaked up all the dead blood inside the wound.

"Husung, Umas, come here. Banitul is your elder. I want to use the power of the *hidan-hidan*[3] that exists between the two of you to summon your far away ancestors. We will pray for them to return and help us, to battle to stop our suffering, to help us to pass through this difficulty." Light from the fire flashed over Tama Tulpus's face, illuminating his dignified profile.

Umas was very anxious to do something to help his tama. Unfortunately, since he first saw him collapsed in the grass there wasn't anything he could do. Up to that point, Umas had been like an unseen wind. All he could do was look at his tama lying on the ground suffering. When the elder asked him to do something for his tama, he stepped forward without the slightest hesitation. He desperately wanted to help, and he would do his utmost no matter what it was.

"Take these white ashes. When I'm doing the ceremony, you follow behind to sprinkle the ashes." Tama Tulpus gave two taro leaves full of ashes to Husung and Umas.

In his left hand he held four sections of reed tied in a knot. In his right hand he had pieces of meat from different parts of the bear's body stuck on thin bamboo skewers. He led Husung and Umas in front of the wounded man, raised his hands in the air and solemnly prayed:

"Ancestral spirits! Please open your eyes and see us. Please open your ears to hear us. Our crude, arrogant souls have led us into a trap set by demons. We now lie weeping in a pool of blood. We moan in our torment. Ancestral spirits! Please make use of our bodies and our souls as a medium for your power to chase away the evil ghosts. Ancestral spirits! Please make use of our bodies and our souls as a medium for your power to bring back Banitul's health and his pure soul."

Tama Tulpus asked the men behind him to start sprinkling the ashes. He lightly swept the knotted reeds and the meat on the bamboo skewers in front of, behind, to the left, to the right, and above the body of the wounded man. Then he addressed the demons hiding in a corner of the room where they could not be seen:

"You demons. Do not harm this man. We have game meat for you to eat. It is really fresh and delicious. This human's flesh has already gone bad. It is dirty and not good to eat. You demons. Once you have eaten the meat you must leave the place where we live and never return."

Tama Tulpus could see many evil ghosts roaming around, both inside and outside of the shelter. Outwardly they looked very much like dogs. There were brown ones and white ones, as well as striped ones. Sometimes they stood beside one of the hunters. Other times they squatted on people's shoulders, now large, now small. Some of them hid in the corners of the room growing long and thin like leaves so they fit there. Drawn by the aroma of the meat and Tama Tulpus's divine powers, the demons came out of all the corners and gathered in the open space between the wounded man and the fire. Tama Tulpus perceived that the time was right. He immediately grabbed a handful of ash from the hands of Husung and Umas then threw it at the demons. In that instant the ash turned into a jet of water like a waterfall that sprayed into the open space. The ash had come from the blazing fire and fire is the earthly manifestation of sunlight. Its power can destroy any living creature. Under the shower of ashes, the pernicious monsters were all melted into nothingness. Tama Tulpus left the shelter right away and walked to a place where the light of the fire did not reach. He stuck the reeds and the meat on the bamboo skewers into the ground. He hoped that the two kinds of magical objects would be enough to block the other demons hiding in the forest from entering the shelter to harm the lives of the stricken man and the other members of the hunting party.

When the ritual of healing and exorcizing ghosts was completed Tama Tulpus personally cut out the bear's heart. He cut it into several appropriately sized pieces and placed it in a pot to cook. It would be given to Banitul to fortify his strength. While he was doing this, he once again reminded the men that they could never let the fire go out.

Umas noticed that his tama's mouth kept trembling, as though he were mumbling some secrets to himself. He then gently wiped the beads of sweat as large as pigeon peas from his father's forehead. His tama's soul and physical body were locked in battle with the sickness demons. It was like when Talum had fought the evil spirits in a battle to the death so that his people could live in that "special stretch of mountain slope." Over and over again, Umas watched his tama's tortured expression and prayed tearfully to the gods of heaven and earth that his father would defeat the sickness demons.

In the mountain forests it is only those creatures that understand the dark night who still stand by amid the hubbub of the daytime. The songs of certain birds are rarely heard in the village. Their long, desolate chants sound as though they are thinking of good friends who live on distant mountain ranges. Some similar types of mountain birds gently warble and sing in harmony in another corner of the forest. They sing back and forth to each other in low, sad voices as if seeking a spirit so beautiful that it can never exist in this world.

As the moon climbed to the middle of the sky, Banitul's body began to twist and turn. Sitting at his side, Umas heaved a sigh of relief. He was convinced that now his father would not die. The ancestors had already travelled a long way to be with them, to watch over their descendants and to support them as they walked, step by step, away from the suffering that had beset them. Umas reached out to hold his Tama's hand. Its coarseness and warmth made him fall back into the years of his childhood. The lively little boy who loved to race around the mountain forests returned. He recalled the fondness hidden deep in the palm of that hand. In the darkest of dark nights this hand was there with him as he fell asleep. When he fell down or got into trouble, this hand was always there waving amiably before him. This is my turn to comfort you. Umas tightly clutched the limp, lifeless hand. His tama's sombre face was always before him. If it were possible, he would be willing to give his own life to relieve the suffering of the owner of that hand.

It was probably around daybreak when Banitul's breathing returned to a regular rhythm. As it rose and fell deeply and powerfully, his chest seemed more robust than ever, and his eyelashes twitched uneasily as his eyes moved beneath them. These changes greatly stirred everyone's spirits. Once again they could believe that no matter what corner of the forest it was, or what kind of danger, the ancestors would not easily abandon their descendants.

"That was the longest, most tiring night." Tama Tulpus clutched the whiskers on his chin as though he was afraid they would fall off.

The sky outside the shelter was gradually releasing pale rays of light. Still heavy with sleep, the mountain wind walked languidly and unsteadily toward the earth. It was preparing to wake the world's creature so that they could welcome the arrival of a new day. In the distance, the first beam of sunlight slowly illuminated the forest scenery. In the rays of morning light, the dewdrops on the leaves showed their limpid, crystalline little faces while the mischievous mountain birds teased the slumbering insects. The sublime voices of the streams in the gorges rang out, refreshing the souls of all the men.

"What time is it?" Banitul suddenly sat up on his bed of pine needles.

He looked down to find his son sleeping beside him then looked around at the strange stillness inside the shelter. A gloomy, deeply unsettled expression came over his face as though he was desperately trying to remember something but had grown frustrated because his memories were in such complete disarray.

"May the gods protect us. You're finally awake. Good, really great." Tama Tulpus put some dry wood on the fire then went over closer to Banitul. When he saw that the wound wasn't swollen or festered he shouted out of the shelter; "*Biahi!*[4] The leader has awakened. Everyone, come in."

"Thanks be to the gods. You have woken up." "Banitul, how are you? How do you feel?" "Leader, the gods slept with you all night..." "We were worried the whole night..." Everyone gathered around Banitul. Some were concerned and asked how he was. Others just stared at their leader who had seemingly died and come back to life as if they could hardly believe their eyes.

"All right! Don't be like little chicks trying to shelter under the mother hen's wings. I don't know if you mean what you say or if you're just covering up what you really think? What kind-hearted man is going to bring over the hot soup that's left in the pot?" Tama Tulpus had no qualms about making fun of the men crowded around their leader. He seemed to be joyfully welcoming the coming ritual.

"Ah ha ha ha...How could we not be saying what we really think? Ah ha ha ha..." Everyone laughed heartily, their white teeth and their eyes, filled with tears of joy, flashed through the gloom of the shelter.

Banitul raised the heavy pot with one hand and drained the thick soup in one gulp. After that he broke out into a sweat and then his spirit slowly began to revive as well.

"What time is it?"

"Dawn. The first light of the sun is still on the distant mountain peaks."

"Why don't I see you busy with the things you need to do before you go out hunting?" Banitul's memory also seemed to be returning to him, but when he saw everyone standing about idly, he couldn't make out what was going on.

"Banitul, when we saw that you had been wounded, aside from feeling anxious, everyone felt that we should follow village tradition and put a stop to the hunt. It might have been that your *itkula*[5] was the result of a curse from the evil spirits! Disaster is like a sky filled with storm clouds, it casts a shadow on the whole hunting party..., what we mean is that the curse might endanger the lives of other members of the hunting party. Sometimes halting the hunt is the only way of dispelling the curse, you must understand that."

"Who died badly? Who died accidentally? Me? My wounds are minor injuries that I got in a fight with a black bear. Did such minor injuries wipe out your determination to help your family members survive the winter?" Banitul's face flushed. The idea that his accident had impeded the hunt disturbed him and made him ashamed. He raised both his arms angrily and waved them in front of his chest as if to describe a beautiful circle. The charcoal powder that had hardened over his wound immediately peeled off and scattered over the ground. His worries were well-founded. It wasn't easy to obtain permission to go hunting, and it was the most important ritual for the village. They could not abandon it without very good reason.

When the members of the hunting party heard how angry their leader was, they just stood there, as immoveable as rocks in a stream. The faces of a few of them began to twitch involuntarily.

"So then...we understand what our leader means." Tulpus scratched the messy hair on his temples. His legs began to shake unconsciously as he racked his brains. Then, neurotically biting his lip, he said firmly but haltingly:

"However, if your body...if you are as healthy as a *hanvan*,[6] then we ask that you direct everyone what routes you want them to take today."

Banitul regarded the elder who was smiling faintly to show that he meant no offence, then he looked again at the men in the hunting party standing around him. Outwardly they were filthy and foul smelling, but they exuded the sense of great expectation that traditional hunters ought to have; the expectation of bring back abundant game and allowing their families to pass the severe winter in warmth and with full bellies. Banitul gave his right shoulder a slight shrug, secretly trying to determine how much his wound would affect him. A jolt of sheer pain shot through every part of his body like a lightning bolt. He grimaced and the veins on his temples bulged.

"Perhaps I am being punished by the gods because of something I did before. This injury seems to have stolen my ability to hunt. I need to stay here in the shelter and remain as still as muddy water so that all the defilements will precipitate out of my body and my soul can return to its originally clear state." Banitul took a deep breath and continued:

"Haisul, in the name of the village I turn all matters concerning the hunt over to you. You must respect your family's honor and protect the safety of all of the men."

"What? Wh...a..t....? There must be someone who can lead the hunting party?" The unexpected news brought beads of sweat to Haisul's face like dew in a time of drought. He kept shaking his head and looking around at the other men, hoping for some help.

"You have had really good luck. On the first day you easily brought down a mountain goat. Haisul, be the fierce Bunun hunter that we know you to be. Stand tall and say yes." Banitul reached out and grasped Haisul's hand.

If there are no dark days, then there will be no dark nights. The hunting party, now led by Haisul, seemed to be fully blessed by the gods. Like an old friend, the sun in the sky watched over everything that the hunting party did. It even used the power of its rays to make the game animals especially active. Deep green moss growing in the shady areas looked vigorous, sleek. The noses of the hunting dogs were also extra sensitive and easily discerned where the air had come into contact with game. Their eyes were sharper than hawks because they could make out animal tracks hidden under layers of fallen leaves. When panicked quarry fled, it always ran in the direction that the hunters had planned for, charging straight for the ambush positions. Then the magical bows discharge their arrows with precise accuracy into the hearts of the prey. The hunters' joyful shouts and the animals' calls to the death spirits constantly rang out from every area of the hunting ground. The mountain forest became a sacred space where a divine ritual unfolded, establishing a mysterious relationship between hunters and animals.

The long hunt finally came to its conclusion. Haisul continued to lead the whole hunting party. With the power of his spirit and the protection of the gods, Banitul's damaged life force and the abilities that had been wrested from him by the black bear returned to his body. His strength was at the same level as when he first entered the mountains. Haisul distributed the smoke-blackened, sour tasting meat from the various game to members of the hunting party according to their ability. Then, with joy in their steps everyone dragged their weary bodies and their heavy burden of game meat in the direction of the village.

Umas, Biung, Alang, Tiang and Pizing and the other young hunters who had been given permission to enter the mountains to take part in their first hunt prayed that they could grow wings to fly back to the village right away. For the first time they would receive the applause and respect of the villagers. For young hunters this was the moment that they had looked forward to day and night since they were born.

"Umas, hold on. When you young men walk in the forest you have to know how to steady your souls. Alang, slow down. You don't want to trip and fall in the forest." The experienced hunters deliberately slowed their pace until they moved like snails travelling abroad, bringing dark clouds to the faces of the impatient young men.

"Hu! Everyone stop and take a rest. You young guys on your first hunt go and find some dry kindling and weeds. We're going to make a fire here." When they arrived at the clearing at Tunkol,[7] Haisul ordered the party to rest.

"We want to get home. What's the point of making a fire and raising smoke? Won't the billows of white smoke give away our position and allow our enemies a chance to attack us?" Biung huffed into his hands clasped together in front of him.

"The thick cooking smoke lets our families know that the hunting party has returned safely. At the same time, it's a hint to the women at home that they can come out and help carry the game." His forehead glowing red and dripping with sweat, Tiang explained the reason for building a fire on the mountain ridge. He smiled slightly as if he felt a certain pride in his own cleverness.

"That's right. You scaredy-cat. Who's going to attack another nation's people in front of their own village, unless they're so foolish as to want to die. Biung, the rats would kill themselves laughing if they heard your sissy ideas. Ha, ha." Umas joined in the teasing. Sweat washed over his face giving him a complexion as smooth as a girl, but when he burst out laughing lots of wrinkles appeared.

The wisp of white smoke rising from the fire looked like a muscular arm reaching toward the pale, almost transparent halfmoon hung high in the sky. Approaching evening, the sun lay down shyly in a hollow in the mountains. The evening light grew richer, turning layer upon layer of emerald mountain slopes golden yellow. Fluffy white clouds that looked like wool drifted into the jewel-blue sky.

Since the beginning of the world, when a strong, fierce Bunun hunting party carries its bountiful store of game animals back to the village there is a mysterious force that emanates from the hunters and subdues all the chirping insects and singing birds in the mountain forest. Even the host of spirits in heaven and earth restrain themselves. That way, all is still as the hunting party follows the footsteps of the ancestors back home in peace.

"Banitul, during this hunt you killed a large black bear. That brings the highest merit, even though it cost you a nearly fatal injury to do it. We still believe that the power of your spirit can call back the souls of the men who went on their first hunt. Please now summon back the souls of the young men that still linger in the mountains." Haisul looked at Banitul more gently than he normally would have. Firm, even teeth flashed between his sincere, thin lips.

"After you started leading the hunting party the hunt was extremely good. Listen to me. You already possess abilities that others admire and fear. Go and call them here." Banitul rubbed the gash on his right arm under his coat. Then he sighed and said softly:

"When we first went to the hunting ground from the village the men's careful behavior and the mountain forest gave me a sign that foretold the strong protection and blessings of the gods. The gods took pity on us...but for some reason I alone was injured. Not only did that reduce the strength of the hunting party, it hobbled it. In my shame, do I still have the power to summon the souls of the younger generation? Haisul, I can see it on the faces of the gods. You should call the souls of the young men."

"Haisul, you do it. The women will soon be here to meet us." After Tama Tulpus, who was the oldest man among them, gave his support, the other men, each for reasons known only to themselves, stubbornly and resolutely affirmed this view. For some unknown reason the pack of dogs also grew restless. A female hunting dog who had been crippled by a mountain boar bite went straight over to Haisul and sniffed his bare feet. Then she lowered her skinny, wizened head and squatted at his side.

At first Haisul had given a hard, stone-cold refusal. But the men didn't hold back. In fact, they kept working to soften his resolve.

"All right then. In the name of the ancestors I will call upon the souls of the young men to descend the mountain as quickly as possible." After he spoke, Haisul turned in the direction of the hunting ground.

He raised his head and narrowed his dignified eyes then looked off to the high mountain that lay in the direction of the hunting ground. He tilted his head, placed his trembling hands on his hips and shrugged his shoulders slightly. After a fit of nervous coughing he began to call angrily toward the mountain forest. His voice was so loud that it startled people.

"Umas, if you hear my *mankauk*,[8] return immediately. We will go home together."

"Biung, if you hear my *mankauk*..."

"Tiang,..."

"Pizing..."

"Alang..."

The sounds of his cries were like flying spirits that soared through the sky over the mountains. They leapt from one sheer cliff to another even further sheer cliff. With the help of the mountain gorges his calls stirred up every corner of the mountain forest.

"Why do you have to call out our names? Obviously, we're right here." Umas was confused by the practice of calling names, but he kept his voice low when he asked.

"The spiritual power of those who go for the first time into the mountains to hunt is relatively weak and it could become the object of revenge by the spirits of the dead game. They want to grab your souls and rob you of the ability to obtain wisdom or pursue noble virtue in your future lives. The reason that we stop on the ridge closest to the village is not to rest but to call your souls back. We wait for your souls so that we can all return home together."

"Wait for our souls. Return home together." Umas rubbed his chest and begged his own soul to return quickly because he didn't want to live in a future without wisdom or virtue.

Several women bounded up and immediately started searching for their husbands. Some were speechless and just stared at their husbands who they hadn't seen for so long. Others looked their men over and over as if they were inspecting some object that they had lost and just found again. Still other women could only bow their heads and press themselves against their husband's chests like newly married virgins.

"Don't cry so loud...ah. Useless woman. You see a wound and it's as if your crying over a dead man. I'm fine, at the very least I'm better off than that bear. We can't do anything about things that have already happened...I'll take good care of myself. I won't let you become a widow. Okay then, don't cry...How bad can it be? Your son is already a courageous hunter and you're behaving like a little girl." Banitul's tone of voice went from reproachful to playful. Other people found it amusing but didn't know whether to laugh or cry.

"All you sincere, wise and kind women, thank you for coming to help us. We pursued the quarry with all our abilities and determination. We hope that you will not be disappointed and will continue to respect your husbands as you always have. You can take this roast meat to enjoy right away." Haisul gave out portions of meat of various sizes to the women who had joined them. The women then took over the work of carrying the game meat and tramped happily homeward into the night.

After a few days, every village in the mountain forests was singing the praises of Banitul and how he bravely stabbed a bear to death. His illustrious name had reached the ears of every Bunun. As a way of showing respect for his abilities the people especially added the title, "Bear," before his name—Tumath Banitul. This was to let later generations know that the Bunun people were capable of displaying their brave, fierce national character in the midst of the dangerous mountain forests.

NOTES

1. A dagger, these were often obtained from the Dutch in exchange for deer skins.
2. Taiwan kudzu vine.
3. Blood relations.
4. A summon to the group.
5. "Bad death," which means dying from accident or suicide.
6. A buffalo, here referring to a sambar, or water deer.
7. The mountain ridge closest to the village.
8. A call into the distance.

CHAPTER 6

CINA'S LOOM

In the season when the plum trees are bare all things become gloomy and languid. All that remain are a few colors, some visible, some hidden. The world is not only white and blue, you only need stop for a moment and look around, use you heart to understand things, and colors that you would ordinarily ignore appear before your eyes like departed souls. Light grey and dark brown shadows flicker from the bare, leafless trees, now mixed haphazardly, now arrayed in lines. Pristine twigs and branches draw infinitely changing figures over the cold sky. Then the breeze blows in and sets the patterns in motion, now gently rocking, now slightly trembling. The forest of fallen leaves brings a sense of loss, but it also possesses the most vivid colors. Look! The colors of the mountain forest change as the sun moves across the sky and its sunbeams change in intensity. It is just like our unstable lives where we use every possible means to resolve all the questions that confuse us before the arrival of death.

Not far from Umas there stood a small, distant hillock. It was a fresh, bright hillock perfect for weary people to pause and rest. It was also a good place for the forest spirits to study the play of children. The wind sweeping past Umas carried with it the random music that it creates as it glides through the forest. These are sublime melodies of praise that the myriad creatures sing to the earth. The wind will always blow, composing songs of the earth that live as one with the universe. It's just that too few ears know how to be still and listen to them. Umas casually threw a stone and pondered.

"Umas...Umas...where have you run off to?" A woman's voice exploded in the air.

"Cina, I'm here." Umas stood up from a patch of grass brushing away the dust.

"Come here and help me move something. The passing years have stolen the strength I had when I was young." Malas complained as she pulled at a mass of the sodden white ramie fibers.

"Cina, let me do it. You go and rest. Where do you want me to take it." The ramie fibers were bulky and fuzzy and Umas couldn't see the person hidden behind them.

"Take all the fibers on the ground out into the courtyard and put them beside the stove." A few days ago, Umas had gone with his tama, Tama Husung and Asulan to gather ramie that grew by the stream near the village. They pealed the stalks before they tied them into bundles and carried them home. There everyone continued the process by drawing the ramie through bamboo scrapers which they held tightly in their hands until the shaggy surface skin was completely removed. Then, after two more scrapings, they were left with a big pile of clean, pure white strips of ramie.

"Umas, divide the ramie strips in two then put half into the pot and leave the other half on the ground." Malas stirred the strips in the big pot as she poured in a large amount of white ash.

"What are you going to do with the other half?" Umas looked at the fiber on the ground.

"I'm going to dye that different colors to decorate the clothing."

"Which colors?"

"All kinds of colors...like the colors of nature."

"Cina, you're amazing." Umas leaned on her shoulder and spoke quietly into her ear.

Malas wiped her forehead with her hand, smiled uncomfortably, and said:

"It's really very simple. People learned how to do it long ago. If you add *utan-lukis*[1] juice to hot water you can dye fiber light brown; if you add ground-up crepe myrtle leaves you get black dye; if you pound tapioca root bulbs into a pulp and boil it you can make red ramie thread."

Malas could see that the ramie strips in the pot were now well blended with the ash, so she said to Umas:

"You watch the fire until the pot starts to boil."

Umas added wood to the fire in the stove while he played at grabbing the flames to warm himself. Once in a while he went over to the low stone wall to get some wood from the wood pile to feed the fire. After having eaten its fill of firewood, the fire loyally sent forth lively flames.

"Umas, has the water boiled yet?" For the past few days Hanagu had been struggling with an illness. Her face was bloated, and she looked exhausted and in pain. Her shoulders swayed and her listless bare feet made a slapping noise as she dragged them over the ground.

"It's boiling, it's boiled for a while now, Cina Hanagu."

"Use the wooden pole to lift the strips out of the pot and put them in the drainage trough. Then rinse them with clean spring water to remove any remaining ash." Hanagu pursed her thin, pale lips and peered into the pot with a gloomy, tired expression.

"Hanagu, go back into the house and rest. I can take care of this. I told you a long time ago that evil sickness demons changed the weather these few days and if you're not careful they can do you a lot of damage. You know what I mean? Don't try to be a hero." Malas walked over with a mix of different-colored dyes dripping from her hands.

"It doesn't take a lot of effort to treat the ramie. I can manage. Ai... I'm not really sick, it's just that...some of my joints seem to have been dragged off by evil spirits and I'm not as limber as I used to be." Hanagu had her hands on her back. She sighed helplessly as though someone had dowsed her with cold water.

"All right then. You do some of the easier things and Umas and I will take care of the rest." Malas's tone was even as she grasped Hanagu's hand. These two Husluman wives were both beautiful women. Their bodies were muscular, and their shoulders were strong and wide.

"Umas, bring the bamboo poles from beside the chicken coop."

Malas moved the ball of rinsed ramie from the drainage trough and started to rip the strips into finer threads. Hanagu also squatted down and helped out. She looked very determined, as if to tell all those who knew that she was ill that she could still work with her right hand even with her bleeding left hand behind her back. Seeing her sister-in-law in this state, Malas wanted to say something, but she couldn't bring herself to open her mouth. All she could do was wave her hand and make coughing sounds, that was all.

"Cina, Cina Malas, what are you doing?" Asulan was pulling Subali by the hand, or perhaps it would be better to say that Subali was hot on his heels, bent over, furious, panting, almost falling over.

"Subali, get away. If a bamboo pole hits you, you'll cry so loud the spirits will all run for cover. Crybaby, you'd better go off to one side." The bamboo poles were long, and there were a lot of them. It was hard work bringing them all over. This put Umas in a very bad mood. Amid all the cursing and scolding Subali stared at the adults with tears in his eyes as if to say, what have I done?

"Subali, be careful. Don't stand there. You'll get hit by a pole." When Malas saw the poles swinging over Subali's head she smiled a smile of concern and affection that only mothers are capable of.

"Cina, I...I want...I want to rip as well." Asulan tried to pull a soggy strip of ramie from Hanagu's hand as nonchalantly as if he were asking for a cup of water.

"Asulan, don't make trouble for no reason. Go play somewhere else. Play with the dogs, or the chicks. Damn kids! Children shouldn't get in the way of adults' work, ai! May the gods help us." Hanagu screamed with all her might.

"It's all right, sister. It's a happy thing if the whole family can work together. It makes your weariness run and hide where the rainbows go. The ants on the ground are like that. The whole family works together and they're so happy that they run around doing their work. I've never seen any ants slacking off and resting in the shade of a tree." Malas gave Asulan a strip of ramie and told him to sit beside her and work.

Everyone ripped the ramie strips into threads fine enough for weaving then arranged them neatly on the bamboo poles to dry. It didn't matter if it was raining because the rain would wash away any remaining ash. The dyed fiber couldn't be left outside to dry so they had to leave it inside where there was a draft so that the power of the wind would preserve the beautiful colors.

After a few days Malas saw that the ramie fibers were dancing lightly and freely in the breeze. As she felt the dancing fibers she looked up and squinted at the sky as if to thank the sun for helping out. Then she began pulling down the fiber one handful after another as if she were catch blossoms flying in the wind.

"Banitul, help me take down all this fiber. You use the wooden mortar to pound the wind-dried fiber and I'll crush it with my feet. After a few days Hanagu and I can start weaving." Malas's eyes were slightly downcast as she spoke to her husband.

Malas separated the thicker fibers and the thinner ones into two piles. She gave the thicker ones to Banitul to pound while she put the thinner ones into a winnow and used her feet to trample them. She also reminded Banitul to add some millet husks to the mortar to make the fibers soft and sleek. That way it was easier to weave, and the cloth would be shiny and beautiful.

"Isn't it better to use peanuts?" Banitul tilted his head to speak to his wife. He thought his idea was better, so he spoke quickly and gave his wife a keen look.

"Millet husks are leftovers, but peanuts are real food. If you use real food instead of leftovers that's a waste! What kind of behavior is that? Aren't you afraid that the gods will abandon our fields?" Malas gave her husband a look of astonishment. She couldn't understand where he got such stupid ideas.

Men and women who live together are all like this. To begin with, when they are young, or very, very early in their relationship, their conversations are all so amusing. In those wonderful times it's as if they both hold so many happy secrets in their hearts, and every one of those secrets are what their partner hopes for. They speak of their partner's fragrant scent, their warm bodies, and how their eyes are so gentle and loving. Even the slightest movements of their limbs reveal their affection. But now? All those secrets have faded to nothingness, and all their days are as if laid out in the palms of their hands. Everything is plain and predictable. They can even see their partner's thoughts as plainly as if they were spread out under the noontime sun. Aside from the work before them and how to get it done as quickly as possible, there isn't much they can talk about...to the point that they see everything about their partner as a major obstacle in their lives, something that they have to get rid of one way or another.

For several days it was as if the sun had forgotten that they existed. People felt like it had been a very long time since the sun had last come to visit them. The low-lying clouds were like a sharp knife blade that had lopped off the peaks of the mountains, dwarfing them and leaving only the wind to dart around between them.

"Hanagu, the ramie fiber that you made this time is much prettier than before." Having been conditioned with millet husk oil and dried in the wind and sun, the soft, strong ramie fiber looked especially clean. Malas couldn't resist running her fingers through it. When she remembered how her husband had suggested substituting peanuts, she looked down at the fiber in her hands again and the glow of victory on her face transformed into a smile of pride.

"Do you think we can get the weaving done before winter comes?" Hanagu asked, looking serious. She kept looking up at the sky as if she was afraid that the dark clouds might fall down on her head.

Hanagu's concerns were well founded. There were so many kinds of clothing and things for daily use that their family needed. Aside from the *patwaowan*,[2] *kulin*,[3] *kulin haul*[4] and *tapis*[5] for the men, they had to make *wulus*,[6] *halibanban*[7] and leggings for the women. There were also the *tapaa*[8] and *ililan*[9] for their beds, and *sithe*[10] and *gishut*[11] for accessories. Faced with this enormous task, Hanagu felt nervous and yet powerless. This was especially because when the women are weaving, other family members aren't allowed to go near them. That broke her heart and she didn't dare even think about it.

Because of the taboos and restrictions of traditional religious belief, weaving is a lonely, arduous process. The women have to hide away in the storage room or weaving room to do their weaving. During that time, they cannot eat together with their families, so they have to take their meals alone in those small rooms. The leftover food can't be disposed of or given to other family members to eat. If they violate the taboo and eat with their families, or if their food is eaten by someone outside the family, the new cloth that they weave will be easily ripped. In serious cases, the women themselves will lose their ability to weave.

"My sister, you are a good, hardworking, diligent woman. Diligent women are never alone because the gods work alongside them."

"Ai-ya, Sister, I have never been lazy. It's just that when I think about weaving all those different kinds of clothing and things for the household, I can't help getting anxious. No matter what I do, I can't get rid of that feeling." Hanagu averted her gaze as she spoke.

"It's not that much. It's really not that much. All we have to do is weave the cloth to make the clothing, that's all. The men's cloaks and the sheets and blankets are still useable. We'll take another look later."

"When do we start weaving?"

"After this night has passed." Malas put down the ramie fiber and said to Hanagu:

"So, we have to prepare all the things that we need for weaving before nightfall. We will let the sun tomorrow tell us when to begin our weaving."

There are a great many small components that go into the construction of a loom, including the *tuhlul*,[12] *papavu*,[13] *gigihgi*,[14] *isulu*,[15] and *matvai*.[16] Every year when people are confronted with these oddly shaped little parts it's like meeting a stranger for the first time and they rack their brains to remember how they all work. But when those two capable women worked together most of the problems were dispensed with as easily as a passing breeze.

Malas and Hanagu moved into the small room used especially for weaving. It was a small structure built outside of the stone courtyard wall. Normally the room was used to store the precious farming tools, and foodstuffs other than millet. During the season when the gods give their blessing, the room exudes the unique, heavy fragrances of *tai*,[17] *utan*,[18] *tsalad*,[19] *tsipul*,[20] *halidan*,[21] and *bahat*.[22]

Opposite the room the view was completely obscured by a grove of low, emerald green trees out of which a moist, fresh scent often wafted. Nobody knows when it started, but the villagers had a belief that in the deepest part of that green grove there lived a few fortunate people. When the weather was mild the painted eyebrow hwamei birds perched there and sang while the quails calmly and casually called back. The bamboo partridges for their part, constantly made terrified screeches as though some mischievous child had thrown a big rock and startled them.

"Hanagu, my sister, you ought to use the wooden shed sword to beat the threads. That way the new cloth will be stronger and more durable." Malas's voice was encouraging.

"Heavenly gods! I must be suffering the attack of malicious spirits. Look, the whole piece of fabric has been ruined by one tiny thread... No matter how closely I look at it, I can't make out which way it goes. Sometimes it goes off that way, and other times it slides off the other... Cursed thread...why are you so set on destroying my work." In her anger and anxiety Hanagu cursed, raising her voice to a pitch normally only used in singing.

"Don't get all worked up. Ramie thread is very fine, and we have to be even more careful in guiding it in the direction we want it to go. Take it slow, don't get worked up. Streams that flow the slowest are the most graceful and make the most gentle and beautiful sounds."

At night, under the milky white glow, light flickered from the fire in the weaving room like fireflies descending into the mountain forest. Her sweat-covered face hidden in the darkness, Malas closed her eyes and began to sing a traditional melody that sounded like the murmuring of a stream. At first her voice was a soft as a whisper, then suddenly she called out in a resonant, emotion-filled tone:

> Kuisa tama? Sithan tu tangavat
> Where have all the adults gone?
> They've gone to gather garlic chives.
> Athah sisitha? Hushus tu busul
> Why have they gone to gather garlic chives?
> Because they want to clean their guns.

As Malas's chime-like soprano voice slowly softened, Hanagu continued, sounding as gentle and distant as dandelion fluff in the wind;

> Athah hushushuson? Papanah tu sakut
> Why do they clean their guns?
> Because they want to shoot a muntjac.
> Athah papanahun? Is-kapandian mas china
> Why do they want to shoot a muntjac?
> Because they want to give it to their cinas to eat.
> Athah kapandian? China hi chichindun
> Why do they want to give it to their cinas to eat?
> Because they want to ask their cinas to weave cloth.

Malas's pitch again rose higher, phrase by phrase, until people were speechless, while Hanagu's deep voice became as rich and intoxicating as the millet wine her people brewed. Singing in very different registers, the two women moved with precise, even steps, through the traditional song. Their harmonious, tremulous voices were melodious yet sorrowful, like the mountain sparrows that chase the wind through the cold night sky:

> Athah chichindun? Papainuk tu uvath
> Why do they want their cinas to weave them cloth?
> Because they want clothing for their children.
> Athah papainukan? Siahal thautu sisit
> Why do they want clothing for their children?
> Because the children are shivering from cold.

The white sky and the forest stood coldly above the earth. Malas's son, Subali, and Hanagu's son, Asulan, were lying on the top of the icy-cold stone wall quietly gazing into the little room. Their eyes were laboring as if they were trying to see through the walls. Or perhaps they had some great expectation hidden in their hearts. The clicking and clacking of the looms was an irresistible force that held them enthralled for a very, very, very long time.

"Asulan, let's go into the room and see our cinas." Subali suggested innocently.

"No, they'll get mad." Asulan whispered back hesitantly. He only knew the sacred nature of weaving and not the reason behind it.

"Then let's just take a peek through the hole in the wall, okay?"

"No way. They say it will make the new cloth look really horrible and give children nightmares." Asulan looked down at little Subali, then abruptly looked up and declared confidently, just like the adults do when they are imparting ancient wisdom.

When strains of singing started to intersperse with the sound of weaving coming from the room, the boys were soothed and just leaned on the wall quietly listening. When the singing stopped it unsettled the boys and they craned their necks as if they were trying to retrieve the lost songs.

"Asulan, let's sing to let our cinas know that we're here, okay?"

"Okay, that's a smart idea. But you have to sing too, right?" Asulan gave his little friend a respectful pat on the head. Then he reared his head, raised his chest to take a deep breath, and started singing in a naïve, guileless voice:

> Sima iskadaitha atha-atha minanual
> There was a silly nutcase who came from afar.
> Katu tupan a ulan
> Don't make fun of others.

Subali knew the adults sang this song to teach children to be nice to people. He had learned it, but he couldn't remember it very well, so he put one finger in his mouth to follow the melody as it drifted higher. This made the veins on his neck stand out as he screeched:

> Msiala Malka bunun
> You have to treat others well
> Nasauhabas malinakal
> If you want perpetual happiness.

Asulan sang one children's song after another as if he wanted to reconnect with that time when he would sometimes sit by his mother learning how to sing the songs. Subali frowned while doing his best to hum along. In the end, Asulan took Subali's little hand and started to dance and spin around like a sprocket wheel until their little bare feet had left dusty imprints all over the soft black soil.

During the time of weaving the cinas' songs accompanied the sound of their looms that flowed constantly from the little room. The songs of the children answered back like echoes in a mountain valley. The resonant, moving voices were not only filled with the feelings of family members, they also warmed the fallen leaves in the mountain forest.

Notes

1. Tapioca.
2. Shirts.
3. Chest bags.
4. Long chest bags.
5. Loin cloths.
6. Robes with narrow sleeves.
7. One-piece skirts.
8. Sheets.
9. Blankets.
10. Belts.
11. Cloaks.
12. The warp beam, made from a hollowed-out log.
13. Shed sticks made from two thin bamboo sticks.
14. Shed sword. A wooden stick carved into a knife shape used to tighten the weft.
15. Shuttle. Used to pass the thread back and forth.
16. Heddle. Used to keep the threads separate.
17. Taro.
18. Sugar cane.
19. Barnyard millet.
20. Maize.
21. Pigeon peas.
22. Squash.

CHAPTER 7

THE LOST VILLAGE OF WOMEN

Standing beside the bonfire, Laung kept coughing because of the smoke, but he was very determined to tell his strange yet thrilling story. Umas, Biung, Alang, Pizing and a lot of others were all listening with rapt attention. This elder who so often drew an audience with his fluid, mellifluous voice was Pizing's tama.

"It was a mysterious place. A place the you couldn't find by using the sun or large trees." Laung was medium height and very thin. His eyes crowded too close to his bulbous nose, but they sparkled with a glint of slyness. When he told his stories he always smiled slightly, but his smile, like the bandana around his head, was always tight and trim.

"Was there really such a place?" Someone slapped their thigh, shot Laung a glance and poked the tip of his tongue into his cheek to indicate that he didn't believe it. The people beside him also curled their lips and shook their heads.

"There was. There was just such an amazing place in the mountain forest. Not only that...there weren't just women there, it was a whole tribe of women."

"It must have been a dreadful place. If women don't have their men it's as if they don't have the sun, the moon, or the stars, and everything is shrouded in darkness. How could women ever survive in a place like that?" Aziman laughed coldly, his face was completely expressionless. He was quite old, but he joined the village late and for that reason his land allotment was relatively small. He had a lot of problems in his life and this made his face as tough and severe as a rocky cliff. His skin was dark brown, and people couldn't help but notice how his skinny he was, although his belly was round as a drum. Ordinarily his face was expressionless like that of an old pine tree. He wasn't so much kind-hearted as he was plain and uncomplicated.

"Was it all women? Was it really all women there?" Biung was like a bashful child, but that big nose swaying on his face let slip an innate impulsiveness that he had hoped to keep hidden.

"There's no need to doubt it. This is something that our ancestors had personal experience of." Laung kept sweeping his eyes over the crowd as if to tell everyone that there were absolutely no grounds for questioning his story.

"So, hurry up and tell us. Don't be like the *hanum*[1] that just curls up and lies stock still, or like one of those faceless underworld spirits that make people feel very uncomfortable."

"But that would be no good. Don't forget, we came over to help fix the house." Laung pointed at the black rock surrounded with burning wood. It was only then that everyone knew the reason they had been gathered there.

During the last storm the slate slabs on the roof of the shaman, Bisazu's, house had been blown out of place. That meant that the sunlight and the rainwater could just come straight into the house and steal eggs without needing to turn any corners. It was the custom of the village for all everyday problems to be dealt with through cooperative effort. Besides, Bisazu's contributions to the village were greater than others. That's why people wanted to help him through this difficulty. With the urging of his family members, Umas had come over to help with the work.

"If we don't use the fire to split the stone there's no way of breaking it into slabs. Tell us the story now while we're waiting. Otherwise...it's okay if you don't tell it." Someone was playing the simplest psychological game of all.

The blood of adventurous, indominable hunters flows in the veins of our people. It is an ancient, stubborn blood. All it takes is an insulting glance or a flippant comment and we take matters very seriously, ready to put our lives on the line to persuade others of their error, or to refute their ideas altogether. This quality is like a leach fixed firmly to our skulls and it drains us of all sense of reason. It doesn't matter if the other person intended to make fun or not.

"Ha, ha. Okay, I'll tell you then. In any case, it's going to take some time before that stone splits." Sitting in the midst of the thick smoke, Laung not only showed that he possessed that ancient stubbornness, he started to tell his story

> It was in my old village...long, long ago, so naturally I wasn't there to see these things for myself. There was once a kind-hearted, friendly man called Bukun. His ancestors were the fiercest clan in the Takis-todo community. No other nations dared to follow in their tracks because they had traversed the most dangerous territory. It would simply have been foolish to try to imitate them. But the brave, fierce martial spirit of his ancestors had not been passed down to Bukun himself.

"Why would that be?" Someone asked quietly, putting their hands over their eyes to block out the thick smoke so that they could look more closely at Laung.

> I heard, at least someone said, that Bukun's wife always ordered him around and that led him to develop the virtues of being hardworking and patient. He was used to being humble and

accepting wherever he went. Everyone should know that one fiery rebuke from a woman is more effective than the repeated and earnest exhortations of the elders. If you really think about it, sometimes if a woman has the spirit of a mountain boar in bed, she may actually be able to help and support a man's moral character with a force as irresistible as a waterfall.

Although Bukun was in an unenviable situation, most of his friends and relatives had a very good impression of him. Every time he had a fight at home lots of his relatives would sympathize with him completely. When they saw his face covered with red welts people became very emotional and said how unjust it was, as if the welts had been on their own faces. Whenever the children saw him walking by, they shouted happily, as if they'd just discovered a bird's nest, because he always had the patience to play with them. As well, he often made simple toys for them and told them lots of stories about spirits and ghosts and those trivial things that make children laugh. That's why the kids all liked to gather around him, some pulling at his clothes, some climbing all over him. The more mischievous children were always finding ways to play tricks on him. All in all, because of his very deferential nature, even the hunting dogs that the villagers raised couldn't be bothered to bark at him.

Even though he had the sympathy and high regard of the people, his wife had never shown him any respect. She spent the whole day complaining that he was lazy and let people down. It was so bad that Bukun only had to stretch his stiff muscles to bring on a string of rebukes like a swarm of bees. As far as his wife was concerned, there wasn't anything good about the way Bukun looked, and one glance at him gave a person the urge to hurl unwarranted abuse. Every time he was faced with this kind of abuse, Bukun could only shrug his shoulders, shake his head and gaze off into the distance to take stock of the situation: Ah, it must be about time for the sun to set. Nonetheless, in his wife's mind his seeming lack of concern congealed like pork fat that fed the fire of her anger. In the end, Bukun's only recourse was to escape the house. Of his had very limited resources, outside the house was the safest place. It was a little piece of heaven where he could find some short-lived happiness.

The villagers didn't have any strong opinions about Bukun's wife's appearance, but they couldn't but notice the vicious look in her eye. They were even more in awe of her skill at unleashing a steady torrent of abuse. But nobody could imagine how she had developed this skill.

The hunting dog that was closest to Bukun had the same feeling. Although its bravery during the hunt as well known in the village and had become the reason that the bitches wanted to mate with him, it was still no match for the overwhelming shouting and yelling of that woman. So, the dog's domestic habits were virtually identical to its master's. When it walked through the door it hung its head abjectly, dragging its tail on the ground, or holding it between its hind legs. It tiptoed around like a child that had done something terribly wrong and any casual behavior would bring earthshaking fury. When indoors, the dog secretly kept an eye on the position and movements of its female master. All it took was for her to raise the object in her hand even slightly and the dog instinctively dashed outside yelping frantically.

Nobody could tell if Bukun was simple in the head, or if his thinking was too unsophisticated, but he had an attitude of thorough unconcern about everything. So long as he wasn't on the verge of starvation, he could pass his days in complete contentment. He had the same attitude about raising his own children. So long as they weren't injured on land or drowning in the stream he was too lazy to even cast his eyes in their direction. Nor would he take the initiative to ask the children how they were. He had two children; one daughter and one son who was skinnier, weaker and sicklier than the daughter. Due to the situation with their parents, they grew up without proper guidance and this meant that the two children had no mutual understanding and felt very estranged from each other. Because they were so very different, outsiders couldn't tell that they came from the same parentage. The boy was withdrawn and listless. He went around with a melancholy look that was much too serious for a child. The elder sister was always running between villages and grew up among women who were daring and wanton. Very early on she saw the ugly side of life. She eventually grew curious about some of those women and wanted to imitate their behavior. Although the children's shared blood didn't have the power to draw them together, factors in their environment meant that they both drifted about like wild animals wearing ragged, dirty clothing.

On a day filled with bright sunlight the small birds were hopping and twittering around in the woods while an eagle stroked its wings to whirl through the fresh, clear sky. As usual, Bukun was out trying to escape his wife's chiding. He took his dog and walked into the forest with no particular objective in mind, although he thought he might catch a few unfortunate *puthudas*[2] along the way. That season, the squirrels were especially numerous, as numerous as Bukun's troubles. His arrows brought a constant stream of anguished cries from the squirrels. Those cries rang all over that strange land where none of our people would ever go. Real hunters weren't interested in going there just to bother the squirrels.

Night gradually painted the forest in its own colors. Bukun was breathing hard, feeling extremely tired, so he lay down to rest on the top of a grassy green hillock above a cliff. He folded his hands to make a pillow and lay there motionless like a drop of rainwater that had forgotten to slide down into the stream. As he stared at the sky, many random thoughts began to swirl around in his mind, assaulting him, but he couldn't grasp their meaning. He tried to escape all those unpleasant thoughts by turning on his side and looking down on the silent, majestic forest. Here and there were deep gorges filled with a chaos of bushes. In the fading light of evening he could vaguely make out deep piles of leaves, branches and fragments of rock that had fallen into the shady gorge from the cliffs above. Elsewhere he could see a towering sheer cliff face from which hung a waterfall cascading into a broad, deep lake, spraying water droplets everywhere. The lake water was pitch black, as if it had been muddied by the waterfall. The trees around its shore were tall and straight.

The evening sun followed the path it had taken for a million years as it slowly sank into the depths of a mountain hollow. The crowd of mountain peaks began to cast their long blue shadows over the nearby valleys. Bukun knew that he should return to the village, otherwise it would be too dark to make out the twists and turns of the mountain trails. But when he remembered that returning home meant being subjected to his wife's unprovoked abuse, he heaved a heavy sigh and set the grass by his head in motion as if blown by the wind.

He was about to get up and head down the mountain when he suddenly heard a sound coming from the distance. All he could see were a few *a-ak*[3] standing on a bare branch. They looked left and right suspiciously, as if they were about to launch some evil plan. He thought he must have been hearing things, so he decided to strike out done the trail, but again that sound rang through the tranquil forest. He wondered if it might be the early signs of one of those thunderstorms on the distant slopes so often heard in the mountains. But when he stopped to listen more carefully, he was almost certain that it was the sound of the hooves of a large herd of animals stampeding through the forest. The noise then set upon him with an indescribable terror. In the same instant, as if it had just caught the most terrifying scent of its entire life, the dog at his side cast the friendship they had developed over many years into some deep canyon and shot into the dense bushes like a frightened rabbit with its tail between its legs. Bukun stood stock still, his hair standing on end.

All of a sudden, a crowd of strangely dressed human forms swept around him like the wind. Some were wearing tight-fitting jackets while others were naked, their thick, exposed chest muscles jiggling up and down. They had sharp bamboo arrows dangling from their waists and most wore unusually wide skirts. A small number had only a small cloth tied between their thighs. All had long hair hanging over their shoulders, and large square faces that made them look extremely ferocious, although their eyes were tiny, like pigs.

One of them seemed to be the leader. She was a tall, stocky elder with the look of someone who had experienced much during her life. She wore a long-sleeved jacket and had a long plaited red cloth wrapped around her head. There were two *tulkuk-hanitu*[4] plumes tied behind her head and she carried a bow as long as she was tall. Bukun fell over backward from fright. All he could think about was how to escape attack. But, just like his fate in general, things didn't go the way he hoped. A heavy object fell over his body squashing him flat. The pain made him gasp for breath. He wanted to sit up and see what had happened, but after squirming a little, everything went still again. An idea took hold of Bukun's mind, one that he had never had before: Since there was no way to survive, he might as well lie still and bravely accept his death. In any case, death wouldn't be as bad as he had imagined. He had experienced many worse things during his lifetime. In times of extreme disillusionment people always accept this sanguine view. Bukun began to feel dizzy and his eyes went black. Eventually, without realizing it, he fell into the most comfortable, satisfying slumber.

When he woke up, Bukun discovered that he was lying on a bamboo bed just like every other morning. That made him wonder exactly what had happened to him. He remembered the green little hillock, the gorge filled with so many bushes, and that group of strange looking people. "Could it just have been a dream? Could it be that I returned home long ago?" He began to get anxious. "What about the squirrels that I caught? Those were my hard-won booty." He remembered that he had caught several small squirrels and went to look for them. In the end he couldn't find so much the smell of their farts.

He heard a commotion outside the house, and this frightened him. He thought that he must have been missing for a long time and he had dreamed a lot of inexplicable dreams. Most importantly, the game that he had caught in his dreams had been lost. Now he didn't even have enough to make a meal for his family. He hung his head in disappointment because he had absolutely no way of explaining these things to his wife. All he could do was to await severe punishment with a heavy heart in the same way that he would wait to return to live in the eternal home of the ancestors.

But things weren't quite as he had imagined because the person who came through the door wasn't his wife but an entirely different group of people. The leader of the group was an imposing figure and all of them looked extremely severe, yet they remained mysteriously silent.

"Who are you? How did you get into my house?" Bukun asked cautiously. "It was you who captured us and brought us here." These people could speak after all, and they had women's voices. This situation startled Bukun so much that he didn't even dare blink. Usually it was a single husky woman who brought him endless suffering. Now he was surrounded by husky women. His face screwed up into a terrified ball and it was a long time before he came to his senses. He didn't dare believe it. How could there be so many women as big and husky as his wife?

"My wife is waiting at home for me and I have to get back right away. She's a very gallant woman." After he spoke, Bukun felt a little like he was making fun of himself. He never imagined that his wife's fierce, malicious nature would end up being his final resort. Nonetheless, this reasoning made him considerably bolder. He stuck out his chest and stepped forward intending to push aside the crowd and go out the door. At that point the leader with the feather headdress appeared from behind and gave him a solid punch to the throat. This sent Bukun reeling back and forth, but he was eventually able to regain his balance and stand straight.

The next moment that gang of women with murderous looks in their eyes surged at Bukun like big beans pouring out of a winnow. This set the whole house creaking and groaning with the sound of wrestling. After a flurry of flying fists and feet, Bukun was left bent over with his hands on the ground. He struggled to straighten up and reason with his opponents. In the end, someone in a red robe dove onto his back like a hawk. Bukun could only crawl around on his hands and knees like a big prawn desperately trying to scurry off. The women standing around him started to trample him, then they tried to pick him up so they could throw him back onto the ground...One group burst in crazed laughter. Their arched, black eyebrows arched even more when they laughed. Bukun lay on the ground with his legs stretched out straight. His head rested in a pool of gradually congealing black blood. Blood soaked hair hung coldly over his face. Then, all his fright, pain, weakness and helplessness transformed into a series of hoarse screams: "Ah...ah...ah...ah...' 'Woo...woo...woo' 'Ah yah yah...ah yah yah...ah yah yah..."

In most cases, heart-piercing, bone crushing pain grinds down a person's resolve. In this respect, humans and dogs are alike. Bukun realized that from now on he would be a *pais*[5] for the women.

After the incident, Bukun became the busiest, and the only, man in the village of women. As he worked diligently and obediently the fierce women slowly began to reveal their gentler side. Occasionally, when Bukun was half dead from fatigue, they even cast him a disdainful smile.

Bukun had one major fault. He had an irresistible hatred of doing his own housework. He also lacked persistence and patience. Yet, his neighbours only needed to come looking for his help and no matter how onerous or heavy the work, he would never refuse. He treated it as something that he would have done as a matter of course anyway. Any time the village was making preparations for a traditional ritual he would be the first one there. Even if it meant waiting there by himself smoking his pipe, he wouldn't complain. The women also often asked him to help with their work, asking him to do odd jobs that their own men couldn't be bothered with. In other words, so long as it wasn't his own chores, Bukun would exert himself to the utmost to do any task for any person. Now this quality allowed him to face his role as a slave without resistance. Not only that, he felt he should simply accept this fate and be a man who obeyed women for the rest of his life. So, you might say that, from a certain point of view, having a vicious wife at home was a blessing after all.

Yet, a slave is still a slave. It is a lowly position lacking any respect. At night the women locked Bukun in a special chamber. It was a very sturdily built structure. Because it had been filled with the breath of so many people, as well as their sweat and their sighs, every night the room would start to reek. And every night, three or four women came to visit. Aside from his hectic schedule during the day, Bukun's work as a slave included being responsible for procreation or helping the women vent their lust. As far as these women were concerned, this was a continuation of the punishment that he received during the daytime. It had nothing to do with being anyone's soulmate.

The village of women formed a very long time ago. To begin with, they were the same as our ancestors, living alongside men. Afterwards, the men started to get lazy about showing their affection and sometimes didn't even share game meat or other food with them. So, the women in the village gathered together, left their husbands behind and went to live in a secret place. Since they had no husbands, they relied on a unique method of producing further generations. If they wanted to have children, they climbed up on their rooftops and got pregnant by allowing the wind to blow into their genitals. Or else they would go to the side of a stream and wait for waves to form. Then they took foam from the waves and put it into their private place in order to conceive. Later, if they gave birth to a baby boy, they killed it. If they had a baby girl, they did everything in their power to raise it well.

Because their resentment for men had accumulated over many years, they harbored an urge to use hunting techniques to capture men. They saw men not only as tools of labor, they saw them as living toys for venting their primal desires. Bukun had a little bit of experience in the arts of love, but every night he had to do the work of replacing the mountain wind and the foam from the waves far too often. His legs became so weak that he couldn't stand up. Even if the torrid skin of the strange women did bring some temporary pleasure, most of the time in the thrall of passion he couldn't help just wanting to take a shit. In his dalliance with many different women he always thought of his own wife. These thoughts made him painfully ashamed, and that made him less and less enthusiastic until he lost interest altogether. He was extremely lonely and only wanted to weep. Unfortunately, the women were angered at what they took for his deliberate snubs. This made him long for his own wife all the more. It also meant that when the room creaked and groaned it was the result of the women's anger, rather than their lust. In the end, in order to escape the suffering and take back some control of his life, Bukun could only gather what little strength that remained to him after lovemaking and take pleasure in the feeling of being completely limp.

Good things are easy to forget; bad things are easily inflated. It seemed like bad luck was Bukun's all. During his harrowing days in the women's village he came down with some serious unknown disease. In fact, aside from the fact that he was chronically overworked, his strange symptoms had even more to do with being forced to smell the sweat of so many different women. His cheeks began to slacken, the corners of his mouth sank and his whole body exuded an air of death. Every time he lay there, emaciated and naked, waiting for a woman to come and visit him, the phosphorescence glow of his bones almost shone through his coarse skin. Worse still, every so often he let out a fetid, sour smelling jet of flatulence potent enough to kill a flower.

"You look like hell, and smell like it too." The situation in bed repulsed a lot of women. Furthermore, Bukun's vileness awakened in them memories of a primal hatred towards men that lay in the depths of their hearts. Now those memories were like seeds after the rain, quickly sprouting and growing strong.

"Men are just useless. We should throw him into the darkest of dark canyons, otherwise his weird diseased body is going to destroy our whole village."

"Right. Throw him in the river and drown him. Let the river carry him off to the ends of the earth. We don't need this bother, we just need to wipe him out, and wipe him out now!" Their loathing expression and their exaggerated tone of voice made it seem like they were discussing some stupid crow that had crashed into a tree and fallen into their courtyard.

In a half-waking state, Bukun became aware that there were big sheets of something crashing onto his body. It turned out to be the splashing of a waterfall. He gazed up at the sky floating above the pool created by the waterfall. The cold mountain spring water and the gushing sound of the waterfall roused him from his stupor. He felt a piercing wet pain in his lower back and in his legs. The frigid water was pouring into his clothing and his shoulder blades were freezing. He tried to move and walk to shore to rest, but his whole body was weak and numb. When he regained full consciousness, he realized that he was shaking violently and his arms and legs were cramping. His viscera were also burning and trembling...and it was all getting more and more intense with the force of the waterfall. The waves of shuddering grew ever more intense and heat from all over his body gnawed away at the deepest parts of his soul. Then a suffocating pain prodded him to sit up and see what was going on, but after a few twists and turns he fell still again. The waterfall cascaded down with boundless energy, but in this battle with the cold and the pain Bukun unexpectedly gained the most important victory of his entire life. Or perhaps we can say that he obtained the mercy and protection that only the gods can provide. The power of the spring water washed his strange illness away as if it were washing dirt from clothing. He regained the modicum of health and strength that once was his.

In the village, there were different stories about Bukun's disappearance. Some said that he had been the subject of a curse by evil spirits in the mountains. Some thought that an enemy people had captured him as a warning against any future incursions on their hunting grounds. Regardless of the theories, because of what happened to Bukun the entire village fell into a state of panic. The village shaman used his powerful magic to engage in a long distance, unfamiliar battle of resistance against the evil spirits. The village leader led the village braves to the nearest enemy village with the intention of finding some trace of Bukun. However, from Bukun's perspective, none of these things had any noticeable effect. They may as well not have happened. In the end, with dishevelled hair and wearing the strange clothing of the women's village, Bukun dragged his exhausted body back home step by painful step. His reappearance immediately got the attention of the villagers. They circled around to look at him, inspecting him carefully from head to toe as though he were a newborn infant.

"Bukun, where have you been these days?" Somebody asked. The children also gathered around and stared at him like the adults. Bukun told the story of being captured by a gang of women as quickly as he could. When it came to the matters of losing his masculine pride and being humiliated, he used his peerless narration skills to cover up and embellish them. One villager who considered himself clever firmly resisted the idea of women becoming pregnant from the wind or foam as if he were fighting off evil spirits. He added emphasis to his objections by constantly shaking his head gravely, trying to get others to take his side.

But the village elders all believed him without hesitation. One elder stood up and vouched for the truth of Bukun's story. He also declared to the people in all seriousness that according to the experience of his ancestors, strange people and things really do exist in the depths of the mountain forest. Then he stated resolutely that if you listen intently in the deepest forest you will hear a group of women shouting happily or crying in fear about one thing or another.

After he returned home, Bukun went back to his old ways. He lay around the house all day, but because of his traumatic experience his body and mind aged prematurely, giving people around him the mistaken impression that he had already arrived at the age when he could rightfully enjoy retirement. From that time onwards, everyone respected him as one of the village elders and someone who provided testament to the truth of the ancient legends. This brought him much satisfaction and he always enjoyed telling his unique story to others. Every time he told the story the details changed. This was no doubt a product of his natural penchant for telling lies. But in the end, he always let others know the part about having been the only male slave in the village of women, and about being their plaything in bed. All the same, kindhearted women still pitied his fate as they had done before and complained about the injustice he had suffered. They treated his misadventure like yet another case of his wife's abuse. Some of the men doubted the truth of the story out of jealousy. They didn't think that Bukun was capable of living together with a lot of women and accused him of being a crazy liar. They especially found his claim to have entertained so many women every night absurd to the point of being deranged.

Whatever the case, Bukun and the story of the village of women has become like a pair of *taistusan*[6] that will always live in the hearts of the people. Because of Bukun's legend people also formed the habit of not making a lot of noise while in the forest. This way they don't disturb the lives of the forest animals, and lots of men can maintain their fantasy of hearing the mysterious women shouting happily or crying in fear.

There was no question of Laung's ability to draw a crowd with his stories. Everyone in the audience listened to him with rapt attention. All the men imagined that they were Bukun as they progressed through the story then returned to the fireside after their adventures in the village of women.

Tama Ulang stood up. He was wearing an old pair of deerskin shoes and he paced back and forth with his hands clasped behind his back. He sized up the men squatting beside the fire and then said in a quiet, very measured tone:

"When you go to help someone, you shouldn't move like a snail. Have you forgotten the teachings of the ancients? We came here today to help our fellow villager repair his house, but instead you all hide under the ground listening to stories like *sunsun*.[7] Laung, at our age we ought to behave with respect. All right. Let's get moving. Today only comes once and we don't want to waste it."

"*Tuhas*[8] is right. The fire has split the rock. Let's get to work." Laung knew his mistake and started ordering people around in earnest, as if he were doing his own housework. Some of the men stood on the roof and piled the slabs of slate, others passed the slabs up from below. Everyone carried out the repair work in a methodical and orderly way. Yet in the quiet atmosphere it seemed that their thoughts were still filled with fantasies about the village of women.

Can a man live together with so many women? Umas wondered as he carried a slab of rock still warm from the fire.

Notes

1. Pangolin, or scaly ant-eater.
2. Squirrels.
3. Crows.
4. Taiwan pheasant.
5. A captive or a slave.
6. Twins.
7. Shrew.
8. General term for elder brothers.

CHAPTER 8

THE WOMAN WHO
CAME FROM AFAR

Spikey green millet shoots sprouted and grew by the day, following the footsteps of the sun and moon. With the blessing of the gods the clumps of millet grew so thick that you couldn't even see the heads of the squirrels hiding underneath. Suckling at the earth's bosom, the grain grew exquisite buds which then exuberantly spit forth tiny flowers. After that, the heads formed in layers of lustrous golden-brown kernels bursting with fragrance. When the masters of the fields came and saw their crops filled with sweet milky nectar they were elated and stood there admiring them for a long, long, long time.

That is exactly how Umas felt the first time that he set eyes on Abus. He savored that golden color, the cascading fragrance and the lovely, sweet milky nectar.

On that day, after the cock crowed a second time, Umas, a water flask on his back, went to the river with Asulan to *munsulan*.[1] The trail to the river was difficult because it was hung along a very steep slope. The calls of countless birds rang from the bushes on both sides of the path and they could see freshwater prawns pretending to be rocks, lying motionless in the shallows of the stream. It was only when the prawns gave their neighbors an occasional nudge that Umas even realized that they were there. The river water flowed down the stony black precipice and came to rest in a pool below. The opposite bank was uneven and jagged, as though someone had gnawed away at it. From the bank you could see branches of driftwood reaching out from the depths of the pool. Whirlpools formed around the branches as the river chased the brown colored foam downstream. The dawn moonlight spread obliquely across the surface of the water forming a path that no one could travel. Thick mist rose from the river's surface vaguely diffusing its moist, fetid breath. The sky was still filled with stars.

Having drawn water, Umas led Asulan back along the trail home, water dripping from the bamboo flasks in their string bags. Once they made it across the steep slope Umas stopped on a grassy mesa where the trees thinned out. He looked off in the direction of the rising sun. The darkness of night was already disappearing from the mountain peaks, gradually allowing the sweet, gentle glow of dawn to appear. It all brought him a sense of carefree freedom.

"Umas, there is so much plump, beautiful *samah.*"[2] Asulan pointed to the clumps of green beside the trail. Piles of wild rattan lay beside the duck greens. They reached their long tendrils over the stocks of the greens like ghostly claws, as if they would launch a murderous assault at any time.

"We should pick some and take it home." Umas leaned his bag on the bank beside the trail. People like to cook the tender shoots of duck greens with their meals. You can add ground peanuts to make *labainu*[3] that everyone likes.

"Who's there?" Suddenly they heard a voice. Asulan looked around fearfully, hoping to find its source.

"Who are you?" A tall, slim woman dressed in a cream-colored traditional robe popped up from behind a tangled wild peony thicket and then pushed out from the bushes covering a narrow side path. She was holding a handful of fat, tender wild duck greens.

"We are the grandsons of Talum. I am called Umas. Are you gathering duck greens?" Umas gave a nervous cough.

"Talum? Hudas Talum? Is the old man well?" The woman looked down at her own bare legs and quickly brought them together.

Umas silently studied her heart-shaped lips. They were so red it looked as though she had just eaten strawberries. She smiled shyly from under the shadow of her eyelashes, as if she had been put upon. The dawn light illuminated her cream-colored ramie skirt allowing Umas to make out the vague outline two plump legs and the decorated border. Her calves were satiny white which startled him a little. Only her nicely rounded heels were lightly tanned.

"Are you from our village?" Umas stood there with one foot extended. He gazed intently at the girl's hair that was parted in two and fell in an arc over the contours of her fair shoulders.

"Yes, my home is at the top of the village...near the foot of the mountain." The girl sized up the person before her with restless, playful eyes.

"Which family is that?"

"I'm from the Istanda family, the eldest daughter of Paian." The girl looked down and rubbed the waistband of her skirt with her darkly tanned fingers.

Umas swept the hair from his forehead and asked cautiously;

"May I know your name?"

"Abus." She raised her crystal-clear eyes slightly and glanced shyly into Umas' eyes, then she immediately dropped her head again. Her voice was so soft that he could hardly hear it, but the smile on her lips and the shallow dimples on her cheeks betrayed her pleasure.

"I don't think I've seen you around." Umas looked confused. In his mind he desperately ran through the faces of villagers, but the pretty face before him did not appear.

"When we moved to the village...it was the season when you wrestled with your father. By that time my parents had judged from the changes in my body that I had left the world of childhood behind. They insisted that my only friends would be the weaving loom and kitchen chores." Abus's eyes clouded as she stared off into the wilderness. It was as if she could see her joy-filled childhood years lying just beyond the grassy mesa.

"Do you have a husband?" Umas let slip a faint smile. His tone was mischievous.

"Why do you ask?" Abus's face appeared to flush with anger although she still played nonchalantly with the duck greens in her hand.

"No reason. I was just curious." Umas kept nodding his head by way of a general apology for himself.

"No. I face the moon at night alone."

Umas's eyes flew urgently to the girl's body. Her clear, daring eyes flashed from beneath her greyish-black woven headband. There was a shallow dimple on one of her supple cheeks. Umas turned his eyes back to her hands. They were rough, large hands accustomed to hard work. Her strong, erect torso was wrapped tightly in a black blouse and her large, firm virginal breasts bulged with the awkwardness of youth from her thin chest. Two peanut-sized upturned nipples pointed slightly outward from under her blouse.

"Why are your eyes so like an owl's?" Abus looked down at her own dusty toes.

"Like.....an owl?" Umas squirmed uncomfortably, as though he had fallen into some mud.

"Exactly. Your eyes are even bigger than an owl's."

"Everyone in my family has eyes like this. There's nothing I can do about it."

"Umas, are you married?"

"No." Umas didn't like this question. It made him itch as if he was entangled in rattan vines."

"Why haven't your parents killed a boar and found a good woman for you?"

Umas pressed his lips together in embarrassment, but then immediately gained control of himself. He sensed a tone of mocking in her words, but he couldn't quite put his finger on. Then he got it, and a mischievous glint flashed into his eyes.

"My woman has only just grown up and she spends all her time hidden away in the kitchen. At most she might come to the river to draw water and pick some duck greens to take home for dinner."

Abus's raised her eyebrows in amazement. The duck greens dropped from her hand and she blushed while her toes dug into the ground uneasily. In that instant, a mysterious swell rose between their two souls. What had begun as very simple thoughts were now released into a much larger space. A light also came over their faces, a light sustained without the aid of rational thought.

Hudas Talum had been in the village longer than anyone else. Because of his straightforward, generous, hospitable nature, and his willingness to help others, he had gained the universal respect of the villagers. Now, thanks to the kindness and filial piety of his family, he was able to live out his years without care or concern. He liked to wile away his days in reminiscence of bygone times, but now his well-intended wish to avoid interfering in the affairs of his children and grandchildren had actually become a matter of concern for his family.

From sunrise to sunset he sat on a raised dirt platform beneath the eaves of his house. Sometimes he looked off to the furthest mountain ranges, remaining silent for a very long time. Nor could anyone guess what he was thinking. Other times he walked along with his head bowed, inscribing endless lines in the dirt as he dragged his walking stick along with him. He wanted to reconstruct the vague memories of past events and past thoughts that remained in his memory into fresh new patterns in his life. But those things that had been stored for so long had long ago broken into dozens of faded fragments.

The old animal-skin hat the he wore was now cracked and bare. It made the wrinkles on his face seem deeper and more pronounced. His unkempt beard gave off a greyish-white sheen and the hands that clutched his walking stick were covered with prominent purple veins filled with slow-flowing black blood.

"What's wrong, Hudas? The sun is too strong. You should go inside and rest." When Umas got home, he happened to notice the old man's wrinkled neck and asked out of concern.

"What can I do about that, my child? The sun may be extremely hot, but my blood is chilly and cold, like leaves rotting under a dead tree." Our blood grows cooler year by year. Talum shook his head firmly yet helplessly.

Umas imagined that the blood flowing in the old man's veins was no longer fresh and red, but purple slurry; slurry that laid in a mountain gorge and never saw the sun from one year to the next.

"Hudas, are you afraid to die?" Even though older people often talk about death, Umas was careful about asking.

Talum turned his wrinkly neck, rubbed his beard, and with a trembling voice said:

"Aging and death are just the way of heaven and earth. I'm not afraid of a death that I have never seen. Death is just when an individual's soul moves to a different place. It is the necessary process of is-an[4] leaving the material world, changing into *malantangus*[5] and walking toward

Maiasan.[6] Once you pass the valley of death you gain much greater power to continue protecting your descendants. I could never be afraid of that. I will walk toward the eternal resting place of the ancestral spirits without the slightest fear. I await that day with fervent hope, just as if I were waiting for my best friend."

"Have you ever felt regret about the past?"

"Never. I lived every day to the fullest. When I was young, I used all of my spiritual powers and the wisdom of the ancestors to lead my people in a successful migration. We walked through grassy green plateaus, crossed the coldest ice and snow and found a place blessed by the gods. For the sake of our livelihood I led our people in performing solemn rituals asking for the protection of the gods. For the sake of food, I led our people into the mountains to kill fierce game animals." The old man opened his mouth, now filled with yellowed teeth, and took a labored breath before continuing:

"Many dances of love have drifted across the stage of my life. With the protection of my father and mother my life spirit changed from soft and weak to strong and hard. The love of our people has dried my tears in the darkest times. I have never strayed from the instructions of the elders. Because of the support of my family, I have never lamented when faced with reversals. I know for certain that during the time that I have lived on this earth I have stood before the gods and acted out the sacred play of life perfectly and without fault."

"Hudas, you are the most perfect Bunun." Umas smiled as he stroked the old man's hand.

"However..." The old man suddenly sighed and shifted his attention to something else. With that sigh it seemed that all those positive things had become nothing but an illusion.

"However what?" Umas' mouth dropped open. He was disquieted by the old man's distress.

"Umas, sit down." The old man pulled at the corner of Umas' coat with his thin, withered hand.

"You have taken part in the coming of age rites and you have gone into the mountains to hunt several times. It's time that you began to live as an adult."

"Right. I live very well." Umas replied casually.

"Ah...My child, you still don't understand what it really means to live as an adult. Your soul should not live alone. You need a soul that brings you joy as you welcome the coming of every day together."

"Hudas, what are you talking about?" Umas looked up at the sky, but the sun was too strong and he couldn't look at it directly. He thought that maybe the old man had been out in the sun too long and become confused. Why else would he say such completely illogical things?

From the time he learned how to think, Umas had been very satisfied with his life in the mountain forests. When it came to the demands of traditional religion and customs, he had always been very respectful and followed carefully in the footsteps of his parents. With the guidance and protection of the ancestral spirits he could already point to many, many delightful memories. Since he was able to enjoy such abundant, peaceful days Umas would have been happy to remain a child, relying on his parents and nurtured by their ancient wisdom.

"What I mean is, is there a girl that you like?" The stern look in the old man's eye conveyed heavy expectation. It made Umas feel as though he was in the presence of a second, small sun.

"What girl? Why should I like a girl?" Umas stood up and wiped his forehead with the back of his hand. He looked left and right hoping that someone would come along to interrupt their conversation.

"You need to find a girl of average build, not to fat or too thin, one with fair skin and glossy, jet-black hair. Her breasts should be ample, and her buttocks should be firm. Her personality should be gentle and diligent." The old man's withered hands suddenly grew stronger and his old fingernails sank into Umas' forearm.

"Oh...Abus." The inescapable pain in his arm made him think of the girl standing on the mountain slope with wild greens in her hand.

"Who's that? Whose family does she belong to? Does she have a husband?" If he had the strength, Talum would have been jumping up and down like a child. Unfortunately, he didn't even have the energy to stand up.

"She's Paian's daughter." Umas sighed as he rubbed his arm. He kept wondering how the old man had conjured so much strength.

"Oh....oh..." The old man grew silent, as if he was trying to grasp something in his thoughts.

That evening, Talum and Banitul were sitting together in the courtyard. The mountain wind sweeping through the warm, dark night was filled with sweet fragrances. In that season, countless gorgeous wildflowers came into bloom. Some grew by the side of the pathways, others sprouted from the narrow cracks between the rocks. You couldn't smell their aroma during the daytime, but at night they all woke up and filled the wind that blew through the darkness, carrying their scent in every direction over the mountain side. Initially, the air outside the house brought an unexpected freshness to their faces and made Talum feel dizzy. It was as if he was walking through a dream. His mind was muddled and unclear, his body numb. But he found this sensation relaxing, especially since the night air was filled the balmy fragrance of wildflowers. He breathed easily, filled with fresh, cool sensations, tranquil and incomparably happy.

"Tama, over the last few days I finished plowing the land on the slope beside our field. We're just waiting to do the planting." Even though the old man spent his days cooped up inside, resting and wiling away his time, Banitul still let him know what was going on with the family's labors and the situation of the fields, always seeking his opinion. In the hopes of growing a little more food, Banitul had plowed and prepared part of the steep slope that ran down into the valley.

"It's very dangerous working on that steep slope....besides, that section of land is too small. You just have to spit hard and you can spit all the way to the other side of it. It isn't worth the trouble."

"But it's important not to waste land." Banitul explained patiently.

The moon had come up and the earth was bathed in soft moonbeams. Silver radiance shimmered from the towering mountain peaks and hazy mist lay over the slopes, obscuring their view of the forest. All the stars were swimming around in the heavenly ocean stirring up ripples.

"Banitul, do you know a man called Paian?" Talum's eyes widened and he leaned meaningfully towards Banitul, as if he wanted to squash him flat. Banitul tried to back away.

"I know him. He came to the village later, but it was still you who gave them their land allotment."

"Oh, is that right. No, what I mean is, do you know what kind of family they are?"

"Ah..." Banitul finally figured out what the old man was trying to say.

"Umas likes his daughter."

"Really? Is that right? The little dog..." Coming out of the blue like that the news flustered Banitul and he was at a loss for words.

"Umas is grown up now. He can't continue to live alone, especially not here in the vastness of the mountain forest." Talum's expression had that gravity possessed by all the elders.

"Do Paian and his daughter have any connections of blood over the last five generations with you or your departed cina?"

During the course of his life Talum had absorbed the essentials of traditional religion, customs, and taboos. He knew that marriage taboos were especially strict and that the restrictions on who could marry whom absolutely could not be violated. That was because those who joined in incestuous marriages not only died young, they could lead their entire clan into decline. Even after thousands of years, stories of weird births resulting from violations of marriage taboos still circulated around the village. He was afraid that these two healthy children might give birth to an animal or plant because their blood relationship was too close.[7]

"Paian is a member of the village hunting party. We have often battled shoulder to shoulder in the forest. If he has dealt with me in the spirit of honesty, then there are no blood relationships between our two families."

"Banitul, take gifts that will please the girl's family and *masinhav*.[8] Don't let me go to the eternal resting place of the ancestors still worried about this matter." Having established new direction in this important affair, Talum straightened himself up and cast his gaze somewhere into the pitch-black distance.

The morning air had cloaked the mountain wilderness in a frigid robe. Banitul walked out into the courtyard, shivering. Contrary to his responsible habits, he inadvertently looked up suddenly to survey the surroundings. Then a prayer slipped into his mind. It was a private, silent prayer. The kind of sorrowful prayer that people in need of help make to the gods:

"Oh, ye host of gods, help me!" Then he turned and looked at his busy family members, speaking to them nervously and rapidly:

"Husung, check the gifts again. We don't want to neglect anything."

"I know. I'm in the process of checking things right now." Husung turned his string backpack over and could see the stoneware pot, a hoe, ramie cloth and dried mountain goat skin all firmly pack inside.

"Malas, what nonsense are you messing with now? Go and call Hanagu and Umas right away." Banitul shouted at his wife.

Malas was a short, dignified woman. She was wearing radiant, greyish-white robes and a round headdress with colorful ornaments suspended from it. She tried to hide her concerns as a cina. Glancing at Umas, she turned to husband and said:

"Davi,[9] did you have an auspicious dream last night? Today we won't return with heads bowed, will we? I don't want our son to be humiliated."

"You have such a big head, and it's full of questions that make people angry. Or are you thinking some of your muddled thoughts again? My good wife, it doesn't do any good to get yourself all in a tizzy. The ancestors said: if you work hard in the fields you will definitely get some crops. We just have to do the things to hand conscientiously. As for the results...that is up to the gods to decide."

Sternly, and with an air of dignity, Banitul walked toward the upper levels of the village. Because of the weight of their backpacks, Husung and Umas made their way with their heads bowed by the effort. With their skirts swishing, Malas and a tight-mouthed Hanagu followed behind them. Their neighbors hurried to the roadside to see them off. Then, as if searching for prey, they watched for a very long time as they disappear up the slope.

The wide courtyard of Paian's house came into view. A hunting dog leapt over the low stone wall that was not yet covered by moss. It circled their legs sniffing and bounding like an enthusiastic host.

Paying no attention to the dog, Talum quickly strode into the courtyard, deathly afraid that he would lose the courage that he had built up on the way there. He knocked on the door frame then tilted his head and shouted inside:

"Mihumisan!"

An old man came out from an inner room. He was not very tall, and his back bore the weight of many years. His face was firm, emaciated, and covered with wrinkles, but like so many elders, it revealed a spirit of reserve and directness.

"How are you! Elder Paian." The guest again offered his sincere greetings.

"Very well, very well." The host bowed politely as he replied then turned to direct the guests into the living room.

"Buni, come out and speak with our guests."

An elderly woman came out from the kitchen wearing a snug ramie blouse that highlighted her broad, flat, boney figure. Her single skirt was grey and only reached to the middle of her calves which were wrapped in black *tavi*.[10] She waved lazily from above the bench then retreated to sit before the guests.

"Recently we have welcomed so many guests. The things we ought to be doing are starting to grow moss." The hostess drawled, as if talking to herself.

"Everyone, please sit down. It's easier to talk when we're all seated." The host spread his hands and pointed hospitably toward the bench.

"We have a very important matter, otherwise we would not trouble you elders." Banitul got right to the heart of the things.

"Speak. What kind of great matter could warrant so many people coming to visit?" Paian was somewhat confused by the exaggerated behavior of his guests.

Umas just stood there, not blinking an eye or moving a muscle.

"My child, why don't you sit down. Sit down, sit..." The host kept pointing at the bench. When he suddenly noticed all the presents in the backpacks, he looked surprised. Finally, he understood what this great matter was.

"There is a beautiful girl in your family and our family has a good-hearted boy. Can we adults allow them to live together? We are anxious to know if you are planning to marry her now. Perhaps we can become *mavala*."[11] Banitul nervously pulled at the earlobe beside his sideburn. He was so flustered he almost pulled it off.

"Well...who knows....well..." Paian was at a loss and scratched his bald pate. After he gathered his thoughts he continued:

"To tell the truth, I have never been in this situation before. It's a difficult question...however...at the moment so many things have come upon us like flood waters. We need our daughter to help out, besides... she's still so young...she's still so young...right, Buni?"

"That's true." Buni replied calmly, as if she had seen through their guests' intentions as soon as they came in the door.

"I have seen your daughter. She is a lovely as a flower. Why do you keep her in the house? ...Do you really want her to just slowly wither away?" Seeing that things were not unfolding as smoothly as they had imagined, in her role as an elder, Hanagu made this interjection. Husung, who had maintained his silence since they had entered the house, stared at his wife admiringly. This bolstered his own courage, but not enough that he dared open his mouth to speak.

"A lot of people have been here before you to seek our daughter's hand in marriage. Our daughter won't just wither away at home. I can assure you that the child we have raised will never anger the gods. She is a child beloved of the gods. In all things, whether it's laboring in the fields or working in the kitchen...she always devotes herself wholeheartedly. She would never be like the thieving sparrows who hide away in some dark corner as soon as they hear the grass discussion private matters." The hostess was fond of drawing out her words, very fond indeed.

"If there's a good young man you should marry her off." Malas also offered her thoughts, glancing towards her son as though she was hoping he would do something extraordinary right on the spot.

"Young people these days...huh, women weave all night long... they're all no good. They're all useless dolts." Buni's mouth curled into a derisive smile. Then she cast a sideways glance at Umas who continued to sit with his chest forward. Umas shifted uncomfortably towards his tama and seemed to whisper something into his parent's ear.

"Ai, ai, young people today even criticize their elders behind their backs..."

"I would never criticize my elders." The unwarranted rebuke and deliberate ridicule didn't sit well with Umas.

"There's no problem with marrying off our daughter." The hostess began to cluck like a mother hen watching the shadow of a hawk descending towards her. "However, we would never recklessly give her away to someone with a temper like a boulder dangling from a mountain cliff. There's no way I would let my dear child spend her days worrying when the boulder might fall and crush her."

From the tone of her voice and what she said, Banitul thought that their proposal had already been rejected, so he anxiously took a deep breath;

"Of course, this is entirely a private matter for your family...A groom is like a field. All you have to do is pray sincerely and the gods will grant you a fertile tract of land. If...you are not favorably impressed by us, that is of course a completely different matter. Please forgive me for speaking thus."

It seemed that things had taken a turn for the worse. Hanagu interjected again, earnestly and sincerely reeling off a stream of pleasing, finely considered words. It was like sprinkling medicinal herbs on torn skin and having the skin immediately healing over.

"What are we? We are good friends! Since we're talking about the important matter of our son and daughter's wedding, we should approach things with wise and temperate consideration. That way we can ensure the happiness of our children...Abus is an exceptional girl. Not only can she weave and take care of household chores, she is very capable at all that she does." She waved her hands up and down creating lovely flying images. Then she looked at Paian and the unfriendly-looking Buni and said:

"Umas is also an exceptional young man. His healthy body and excellent hunting skills allow him to move freely about the mountain forests. From his family he has inherited a hardworking nature, and that means the millet that he cultivates will receive the best care. Elder Paian...I invite you to travel all over the mountain forests belonging to the Bunun people and make enquiries...They are a clan with a reputation as fine as a rainbow. Nobody would dare to slight them. Let us think it over carefully. We are not the enemies of our children, nor are we evil spirits that intend to harm them, is that not right? As with all elders we want to love them, to protect them and bless them..."

Hanagu's words were like gently flowing water that streamed lightly and easily into the ears of Paian and Buni. Husung had been listening intently. In his heart he praised her:

"Hu, my beautiful and clever wife speaks admirably! When she speaks it is just like when she weaves, she thinks of ways to solve the problems as she works. The power of her words is just like the mountain wind, all things must bow their heads to listen and then submit to her ideas unconditionally. It's awesome, truly awesome."

There was no questioning the ability of Hanagu's mouth to spout a burbling stream of words. She kept praising the girl and her family from their most distant ancestors on down. Then she took the pot, hoe, ramie cloth and dried mountain goat skin out of the bags to show them off. The pot was made with the same technique as their ancestors use to make a shell for the great crab. It was not only sturdy, but bold. The skin had come from an extra-large goat, and could be used in place of two average skins...

"What else can I say? What mother and father want their child to suffer?"

"We certainly want her to marry, but I still think that Abus is too young." The host smiled, refusing with a studiously good-natured expression.

"She is now fully grown! She's really grown up!" Banitul spread his arms forcefully as if wanting to take his host's gradually softening heart into his hands.

"Whether sooner or later, eventually all mothers and daughters must part..." At that point Buni, who had been so contemptuous, began to weep.

"Buni, call our daughter out and let everyone see her."

"Abus!"

Abus stood timidly in the doorway playing mechanically with her wide skirt.

"Come here, come here! Don't be so shy." Buni waved her over, smiling with tears in her eyes.

Umas quickly looked her over from the top of her head to the toenails on her bare feet just like he would look over a freshly harvested millet field. He thought to himself: "What a beautiful girl!"

Abus was also casting glances toward Umas so that their eyes met. Her innocent, bashful but honest regard seemed to be saying, "All that I am is before your eyes, think whatever you want."

"She's a beautiful girl." Umas responded silently with a smile and a gentle gaze.

"That's good. Go back into your room." Paian waved his hand.

As Abus walked back to her room she turned to look back at Umas. She did nothing to hide the smile on her face and the curiosity in her heart.

"How about this, my friend, Banitul..." After exchanging looks with his wife Paian said,

"We should all go and discuss the matter amongst ourselves, then we can decide how to deal with this matter."

As they walked out into the courtyard Banitul's voice had a conclusive ring:

"We will return in two days."

As the host sent them off his mind seemed to be in turmoil. He was silent, and apart from the wind, there was no other sound.

"He really is a handsome, capable young man..." During the night by her husband's pillow, Buni lightly stroked Paian's labor scarred hands and his arms covered with stiff black hair, "Paian, your daughter wants to marry. Just looking at her...it's as if she has already departed with him."

Paian impatiently turned over so that his back faced his wife's flat, chilly breast. He snorted and said:

"You're so sick that you can't think properly. When they were here your words were like a fire intended to burn them alive. You made them so mad that their faces turned red and their necks stiffened. Now it seems like you'd be happy to see your daughter married off."

"I already supported this marriage and that's why I used insults and ridicule to express the joy in my heart. If they didn't understand that, it's not my problem. Besides, our ancestors have instructed us that scolding and ridicule can lead the two families to live more prosperously. And besides, old man, I also wanted to let them know that before they try to bully our daughter, they had better think about her ferocious cina."

"Of course, they'll never find a girl like ours. Abus is an obedient, filial daughter. She wouldn't dare do anything even the slightest bit wrong." Paian turned over in bed and snorted with pride.

"You don't want to let her go?" Buni asked quietly. She pressed against her husband's muscular back and affectionately massaged his shoulders.

"It isn't a matter of wanting to let go or not. Aiyo, move over a little, okay! I don't have any room to sleep. What's with you today, massaging me as if you're stroking a pregnant ewe? As far as Abus getting married or not, I leave it to you."

"You should cherish your own daughter. They are a hardworking and frugal family. They live in prosperous circumstances. You have to tell me what you think, too..." Paian's wife spoke hoarsely into his ear.

He turned over and slid up to the bamboo wall then started making snoring sounds as if he had fallen asleep.

On a physical and spiritual level this marriage had presented Banitul with the biggest test of his life. Although the village was gradually expanding, the people moving in were increasingly diverse. But, in the end, the gods protected them all! In the paths that ran through the village there seemed to be an ancient strength that bound every family tightly together. All things were carried out in a communal fashion with everyone helping each other.

Banitul and Paian lived in the same village together. Their friends and relatives also lived in one place. So, when it came to making preparations for the wedding everyone in the village stopped work and took part. Some began early by brewing the wine. Others went up the mountain to cut firewood to cook food for the wedding banquet. Others helped by weaving new clothing for the wedding couple. Still others brought out their dry-roasted mountain boar meat, along with all of their wooden bowls, wooden chopsticks, and wooden spoons to be used at the banquet. As to whether they would be able to get them back afterwards, they didn't seem overly concerned.

When the bride was sent off from her home a woman suddenly started tugging at her skirt and wouldn't let her go. This made it extremely awkward for groom's side who were at a loss to know what to do with this busybody. When she realized that everyone had noticed her efforts she started to bawl and explain how hard it is to be a daughter-in-law, as if it were her own daughter who was getting married.

Abus stepped through the door of her husband's house accompanied by Paian, Buni and the family elders. She sat down on a woven shell ginger mat in the livingroom. Aged Talum took the head of a pig slaughtered for the wedding in his hands, raised it over the head of the bride and moved it in a circle. All the while he prayed:

"Hupikaunan! I pray to the heavens with complete sincerity. Today our family welcomes a daughter-in-law. Preserve her health so that she will seldom suffer illness. After we join in alliance with her family their power will ensure that we always have food to eat, the pigs we raise will always be fat, our chickens will multiply, and our goats will give birth to kids every year. Today our family welcomes a daughter-in-law. Henceforth when we enter the mountains to hunt, we will always capture all manner of game. The crops that we cultivate will be as abundant as the spring water. Today our family welcomes a daughter-in-law. Henceforth our family's descendants will fly around the forests like swarms of honeybees. All members of this family will live in love and peace. Hu! Hu! Hu!"

After the blessing was completed Umas and Abus were sent off into the grain storeroom at the rear of the house. That would be the new world for the newlyweds. From time to time, the cina of the bride could come to observe their lives there, but all others were prohibited from entering. In the storeroom was food harvested that year and provisions stored up from previous years, but there was no other furniture except for a sturdy, brand new bamboo bed.

After watching his daughter peacefully and perfectly enter the storeroom of the groom's family, Paian led his relatives back home. As they walked out the main door he seemed to go crazy and started violently kicking the doorframe. Then he shouted angrily,

"My most beloved daughter has entered through this door and become your daughter-in-law. You must teach her well and guide her conscientiously. If in future I hear that she has done anything to damage the family name or transgressed against the feelings of husband and wife I will come back and kick down your door posts."

That evening the two families invited their friends and relations to separate banquets in their own houses. This demonstrated the prosperity of the families and also prevented mischievous footsteps from finding their way into the storeroom by offering the temptation of good food and wine.

"Come here." At nightfall Umas reached out lovingly.

Abus sat on the edge of the bed covered with cold sweat. She felt as though her insides were all tied in knots. Umas touched her heel with a callused finger, then he touched her calf, and finally he stroked her thigh, all the while mumbling meaningless nothings. Suddenly, he took her by the waist with alarming strength and embraced her tightly. Then he pressed her onto the bed like an eagle taking control of a small bird. With two or three thrusts he penetrated her deepest, most private place. It took almost superhuman forbearance for Abus not to die then and there. In her heart she thanked the gods for allowing her to endure the exquisite pain. But from amid the pain came pleasure, and the new life that she had sought so long was born. The two of them rolled about in the blazing hot bamboo bed while the cloth pad on the bed soaked up the drops of blood that they shed.

Lying on top of Abus, Umas' body, followed newfound, primal lust towards new potential. He discovered new resources there that satisfied his heart's wildest demands. Everything was for the first time, but it became more and more familiar, as if he had done it all thousands of years before. Their movements grew feverish yet meticulous and skilled. It felt more amazing and sublime than anything they had ever experienced in their lives. In the end, they entered a world of ecstasy together. It seemed that every time that they finished Umas came to life once again, his body producing an entirely new kind of strength. Even the sweat in his armpits seemed more excited and impulsive.

In those early days of their marriage they especially loved that lonely bamboo bed. It burned like fire. It was filled with the sweetest honey. They howled and screamed deliriously under the moonlight, calling out each other's names until their voices went hoarse and they fell exhausted.

NOTES

1. To draw water.
2. "Duck greens" or Cyanotis cristata which Bunun people eat.
3. A traditional Bunun delicacy.
4. The heart or the soul.
5. The general term for ancestral spirits.
6. The eternal resting place of the ancestral spirits.
7. According to mythology, people who make incestuous marriages always give birth to animals or plants.
8. Propose a marriage.
9. A pet name used between husbands and wives.
10. Leggings.
11. Relatives.

CHAPTER 9

THE SEASON FOR TYING SOGON GRASS KNOTS

Wind lightly caressed the fire ravaged face of the mountain slope in the ancient valley. The huge trees strewn over the ground were like fallen warriors stubbornly supporting their shattered bodies, spitting out white smoke as they recounted all their lifetime struggles.

In the fields on those slopes the villagers were silently pulling out the weeds and tree roots that clung to the ground like leaches. From time to time some of them straightened up and coughed dramatically on the choking smoke, then took the opportunity to enjoy a bit of a break from their labor.

A rattan vine in his hand, Umas wiped the sweat from his forehead. The jet-black soil on his hand made his already dark complexion even darker. When he looked at Abus working beside him he felt a twinge of guilt. He knew what it meant last night in bed when she tapped his toes with her toes, but everyone was sleeping together on the same platform and the others would noticed every intimate little movement, so he had no choice but to pretend to be as stiff as a dead rat, then he shifted his feet away, turning back to give his wife's ear a light pinch.

For many nights after the ritual slaughter of the pig which allowed the souls of this man and his wife to be so tightly conjoined, they often used this gesture as a signal to their beloved to be as still as the night while they drifted off into dreamland. How often in the depth's night had Umas heard the urgent breathing of his parents issuing from every corner of the wooden house only for those sounds to be transformed into long, disappointed sighs after an elder had coughed to warn them. Suspended high in the sky, the moon, teased and prodded by the dark clouds, made faces to mock the predicament of these ardent couples.

"Umas, when we finish work we can go and pick up some wood to take home." The trunk of a mulberry tree clung to the earth like an infant suckling at the breast. Abus tried to pull it out, but she only succeeded in making the veins on her neck stand out even further.

When his wife finally broke her silence Umas was relieved of the huge stone in his heart. He casually asked her;

"Didn't Tama Husung and Cina Hanagu take a big bundle back yesterday?"

"Why do you have to quibble over household matters?" Abus finally managed to yank the mulberry out, sending the soil from its roots spraying in all directions like a swarm of angry bees."

"Aiyo!" Umas cried out, grabbing his right eye.

"What's the matter?"

"What happened?" One after the other, people who had been lost in their labor straightened up and looked over at Umas squatting on the ground, more curious than concerned.

With everyone watching, Abus immediately squatted in front of Umas and asked with alarm:

"What's the matter? Move your hand and let me take a look!"

Abus straddled her husband's thighs so that he wouldn't fall backwards. Then she forced his eye open with her fingers and looked into his flickering black pupil. Apparently finding something, she shouted like an excited child;

"Ah! There's a bit of dirt in there. Look up...Good. Now don't move, I'll blow it out."

Abus blew hard into Umas' eye. The blast of air on his eye combined with a lot of spit made Umas feel extremely uncomfortable. He pushed his wife's hands away and continued to rub his now chilly eye. He teetered on the verge of falling over and his legs just naturally fell on either side of his wife's thighs. He said:

"All right! All right! My eye doesn't hurt anymore."

All of a sudden, they heard a powerful male voice intoning the strong, clear strains of an ancient song:

> You are a gentle vine
> I am a strong pine
> You are going to climb
> All over my body.
> You are a waiting trap
> I, an amorous muntjac
> You are out to capture
> My soul.

"Ha, ha." One of the old men was upset. "That's not the way it's supposed to be sung. You troublemakers can't just change the meaning for your own purposes."

Then another man continued the song in his clear, resonant tone:

> Everyone has passed by there,
> Many people have passed by there,
> The vine is buried on the pine tree's body

Everyone has passed by there
Many people have passed by there,
The little muntjac holds the trigger in her embrace.

"What a mess, what a big mess. You good-for-nothings have made a mess of that old song." The old man gave an agitated smile.

As Abus listened wide-eyed, she was overcome with girlish bashfulness. She couldn't bear the taunting looks in the eyes of the others. Flustered, she pushed her husband away and went straight back to her work area. Umas was left sitting on the ground not knowing whether to rub his eye or use his hand to steady himself.

"How could the woman who lies naked in my arms be so embarrassed. Ai...it makes me embarrassed too." Umas followed her back to the work area. He bent down and started pulling up thorny weeds. The sting of embarrassment made him forget all about the thorns pricking his hands.

The amusement over, several disappointed-looking men unconsciously rubbed their eyes then bent over to continue their work.

As the partridges cried to bid the daytime goodbye the villagers, exhausted yet exhilarated, headed back to the village along the narrow mountain trail. Abus stopped in her tracks and pointed into the depths of the forest, then she turned and said to her husband:

"Umas, there's bound to be lots of good hard firewood in there. Let's chop some and take it home."

Not far below the path there lay a beech tree that had been struck by lightning. Because of the lightning strike, the surrounding weeds had all retreated to live some distance away, creating a broad open clearing. As Umas prepared to chop the log into lengths suitable for carrying home Abus stepped nimbly over to the log, looked down and asked softly:

"Have you ever tied sogon grass knots to mark a path?"

"Well...uh, I didn't see any big clumps of sogon grass, so I don't know how we can use it for markers." For a time Umas stood there confused, then following his wife's meaningful glances, he sheathed his knife and ran toward a small path. Looking back at his wife who was twisting her eyebrows into knots, he said:

"I'll tie sogon grass knots along the path right away."

"It's getting dark! Do it quickly." Abus bowed her head and started plucking the miscanthus grass seeds from her skirt.

After tying bright green sogon grass around the old, dried-up clumps of sogon grass Umas smiled foolishly as though he couldn't guess what his wife had in mind. Sogon grass knots along a path could protect the secrets of a husband and wife, as well as prevent others from carelessly creating awkward situations.

He had forgotten when it was, but once Umas had gone by himself to check on how the millet was growing in a newly opened field. On his way home he noticed that the position of the sun was still quite a long way from the depression in the mountains where it set. Then he spotted a deep, deep forest and he thought to himself; "I should go in and see what kinds of game live there."

His plan was to determine what kinds of animals lived in the area from their tracks. While he was at it he could check to see how the shell ginger shoots were growing. If the shell ginger shoots were showing above the ground, it was the start of the hunting season.

It took him a while to get accustomed to the darkness of the forest. Suddenly, he heard the sound of rhythmic panting coming from a gully formed by rainwater runoff. Umas carefully craned his neck to take a look. He saw Tahai from the village lying on his back on top of a rock. His long hair was spread out on the rock and his wife was busily chopping at it with a sharp stone shard. Apparently Tahai had seen him coming long ago and said to him casually:

"Umas, are you checking out the situation of the game animals, or looking for places to put traps?" All villagers are natural hunters and they understand why someone would go into the forest by themselves.

"Right! I was seeing what this forest was like and thought I'd get the animals' opinions. Having your hair cut?" Umas looked left and right, like a game animal that had exposed it's tracks.

"It's too hot. It's more convenient to have my hair short." Tahai sat up.

"You carry on then! I'm going somewhere else to have a look around." In his haste Umas couldn't make out the trail that he had come along but from the sound of the couple's heavy breathing he knew what had been going on. Unfortunately, he had forgotten to tie sogon grass knots along his trail and he ended up looking like a bit of an idiot.

Umas lightly picked away the bits of leaf stuck to Abus's face. Then he said:

"We'd better move fast, otherwise the others will think that we've been up to something again."

His wife opened her eyes and languidly replied:

"Really? They've all done it...they can think what they want. What other people think is like storm clouds on the horizon. We can't control whether they rain or not."

"It's always better to get back home sooner."

"You do the chopping first and leave the rest to me."

With a practiced hand Abus sorted the wood according to thickness and length, then she tied it into one large compact bundle with rattan vines. After that she used the ramie cord extending from her head strap of woven rattan to secure it. Finally, she placed her head in the head strap and said:

"Umas, give me a boost and we can go home!"

"Let me carry it." Umas felt a little badly.

"Carrying wood isn't that hard. You can follow me and take a break."

Umas followed behind, occasionally brushing weeds from Abus's buttocks and thinking to himself; getting married is so much easier nowadays. If it was still as the ancestors described, it would be like trying to catch those quick-witted monkeys. You would seldom succeed, and it would just make you depressed. Umas had once heard this ancient tale:

In highest antiquity Bunun people could freely marry their blood relations. But this incestuous behavior angered the sun and the moon, whereupon all manner of disasters befell the lives of the ancestors.

There was a brother and his younger sister who, upon hearing the clear, beguiling song of an oriole became confused and began to embrace each other. One of their neighbors was an impetuous fellow who walked in on them without warning, hoping to borrow tinder. Only then did the brother and sister come to their senses, but they couldn't pull themselves apart no matter what they did. The brother was ashamed and took his knife and cut off his penis. Then he dragged has sister off to commit suicide together. In death they turned into blossoming cherry trees with interlocking branches. That is the reason that our people have passed down the prohibition against burning cherry wood under any circumstances.

After this incident, the ancestors not only placed a strict taboo on marriages between blood relations or siblings, they also realized that the human penis is really not conveniently made. So, they decided to exchange their penises with the hunting dogs in hopes of avoiding trouble when men and woman spend too much time entwined together.

"The poor dogs!" Umas thought of how children throw cold water over hunting dogs that have just finished mating.

Spring water flowing from the bamboo pipe pounded onto the ground with great determination. Soaked by this clear, clean water the plants in the area grew lush, green, and easy. There was a woman kneeling bent over before the bamboo pipe, as if doing exaggerated prostrations.

"Aren't these the kind of leaves that you feed to pigs? Why are you using them to wash your hair?" Umas looked at the green plants growing everywhere.

Abus quickly pulled her head out from under the stream of cool water sending water from her hair spraying in all directions and forcing Umas to retreat several steps. She squinted as she blew away the water dripping around her mouth and replied:

"When I was little my cina told me that if you use these leaves to wash your hair it makes your hair grow black and shiny."

Umas looked at his wife's hair full of leaves. The patches of green looked a lot like millet mixed with wild black nightshade. It was gorgeous. Abus squeezed the water out of her long hair by twisting it as hard as she could. She said:

"Can you take me to the village on the other side of the mountain tomorrow to see Hudas Mua?"

"What do you want to go for?" Umas cast a sidelong glance at his wife thinking that she looked rather comical that way.

"Don't you have ears? Every night the owl comes to hoot outside of our house. It makes me shiver all over every time because I think it is letting me know that I'm pregnant." Having experienced much of life in the mountain forest, Abus could now guess the secret meaning of the owl's call.

Hudas Mua was the only *patus-uvath*[1] in that region of the mountains. She knew how to let an infant pass safely from a woman's belly. Her hands had a divine power. The people respected her because she could tell whether a woman was pregnant just by feeling her belly.

In seasons when they weren't busy with farming work many people who wished for children personally took gifts of smoked meat and pounded millet to her. They respected her magical powers and also empathized with her pain at not having children of her own.

"Perhaps all good people have nothing!" Umas sympathized, but also thought it was strange.

"If I'm really pregnant we can ask her to perform a spell in advance to prevent the fetus from being in the wrong position." Whether from anxiety or because she really wanted her hair to dry quickly, Abus had practically pulled her hair out from wringing it.

All midwives have mysterious powers. The fetus not only can hear every word that they say, they always obey them. So, a midwife always tells the fetus to sleep in the bellies of their mothers in a position most suitable for "falling on the earth and becoming a person." However, she will also warn women who are carrying twins or multiple fetuses that this violates the taboos established by the ancestors. The children will bring the curses of the gods into the world and will cause irreversible disasters. For that reason, they must use medicinal herbs that have had sorcery performed on them to make the twins return back to the world of the gods.

The next day, Umas and Abus took a pair of small chickens and some fine cloth to visit the place where Hudas Mua lived. These were gifts for the midwife to ask that she give them her blessings.

As the sun rose in the sky a drowsy hawk flew very low over the mountains. The windless valley looked lovely and generous as clouds of mist of various sizes gathering in some areas. The air was gentle and still, manifesting an indescribable purity. Dew sparkled brightly on the emerald green shrubbery. Through the silence they could hear the constant high-pitched twittering of sparrows and the deep buzzing of the bees. The air was full of the fragrance of wildflowers that wafted to their nostrils in waves. It made them feel that this was truly a land blessed by the gods.

Sparse clumps of dried grass were dispersed over the small hillocks where Umas and Abus came to a stop to gaze wide-eyed at this incomparable scenery. Two huge *sausauvath*[2] intertwined enthusiastically and violently, now rising erect, now falling back to the ground together. The way they rose up and fell back down, combined with their hissing and the crisp sound they made when they hit the ground, made Umas and Abus think it was a sacred ritual for worshipping the gods, so they didn't dare disturb them. Umas remained where he was, watching solemnly and thinking to himself: "The gods are fair. They allow all creatures to perpetuate their kind on this vibrant green patch of ground in their own unique ways."

"The snakes do a dance to make the owls hoot." Abus's eyes lit up with excitement thinking of how she had also acted out this exquisite play.

It was an extremely simple courtyard, spacious, comfortable and convenient. However, that isn't how Umas remembered it. Now he really loved the courtyard's cool, tranquility.

"Such a quiet, secluded house." He sighed in admiration.

When they entered, Hudas Mua was in front of her house sorting *utan*.[3] She was an older woman and was wearing the simplest of traditional garb including a turban. Her face was covered with wrinkles and her body was withered and hunched. But just like a young woman she insisted on doing everything for herself, apparently unaware of the meaning of fatigue.

"Mihumisan, Hudas Mua. How have you been these days?" Umas stood bowed before her. Abus stood silently at his side.

"I've been quite well, just a little *bulu*,[4] otherwise I'd have to say that my days pass very pleasantly. Have you two been well? Where are you coming from?"

"We're from Red Village. I am Banitul's eldest son. My wife is Paian's eldest daughter."

Umas had seen how industriously the old woman worked. Her hard fingers covered with purple veins looked like a crab's pincers as she pulled a freshly unearthed yam from her string bag, quickly turned it over and cut off any lumps or fine roots with the other hand. When the yam was clean and round, she threw it into a rattan colander. Two rather bold old hens walked into the room one behind the other. They went over and pecked at the pieces of yam beneath her skirt then made an urgent retreat with it in their mouths.

"Ah, yes. Wonderful people. The gods will protect good-hearted people. You are very lucky children." Hudas Mua looked cheerfully and serenely at the two young people who had been raised by good people.

Umas appeared to feel awkward. He was hesitant and uneasy, wavering like a clever hunting dog who suddenly comes upon two good things to eat. His words were on the tip of his tongue, but he couldn't get them out. Finally, he swallowed hard and brazened it out:

"Hudas Mua, I want..."

"Have you come to me with some important matter?"

"The owl wanted us to come here."

The old woman stopped what she was doing. Her eyes shone from under her wrinkled eyelids as she fixed her stare on the beautiful young wife.

"Come in then. Let me have a look."

"Creeeeeak!" The door screeched as though it was being torn apart. A warm moldy smell spread from inside the room, bringing a pleasant sensation to the blood in their veins.

Abus lay on her back on the bed exposing her slightly protruding belly for Hudas Mua to examine. Her slow probing motions and heavy breathing unnerved Umas, especially when he saw the pain that the emotional and physical pressure gave Abus. The beads of cold sweat on her forehead made him regret that he had brought her here.

"Thanks be to the gods! Your virtue is as pristine as the spring waters and your behavior, as gentle as moonlight, has please the gods and moved them to bestow a perfect little life upon you. The legs of the child sleeping in your belly lie straight, not crossed. It is a healthy boy baby." The midwife finally spoke.

Umas immediately rushed forward and helped his frightened wife up, at the same time telling her:

"Hudas Mua says that it's a boy..and it's healthy...you can..."

"I heard." Abus interrupted him. "Help me up."

Hudas Mua was a very considerate woman. Past experience told her that it helped people when she revealed her secrets. She told Umas and Abus:

"Our descendants are all spirits in the eyes of the heavenly gods. They are precious spirits that will extend the lifeline of the Bunun people. Before they take on physical form they are called Is-ang.[5]

With the passionate nightly summons of the husband and the gentle expectations of the wife, the spirit brings the blessings of the gods into the warm, moist belly of the mother. The good mother then greets the spirit with the *logbo*[6] representative of our people. After ten months, the spirit moves from the left side of the mother's belly to the right side, and then to the middle. Then finally the spirit enters the world as a Bunun[7] to begin their long and wonderful life in the village with their family."

In order to avoid bringing shame to the midwife for personally accepting things from other people, before they left, Umas placed the gifts that they had brought behind the door. Then, holding his wife's hand tightly in his own, he stepped joyfully out onto the road home.

From the time that they determined her pregnancy, Umas discovered that Abus was much weaker than before. Walking under a large tree he quietly said to her:

"You must be tired. Let's rest." As he spoke, he considerately moved some rocks out of the way so that Abus could sit down more comfortably.

"Do we really have a child? Are we going to be able to raise it? Can we give him a happy life?" Abus knew that the days ahead wouldn't unfold as she imagined.

"Have you ever seen any of our people starving to death in this part of the mountain forest? Don't worry. This land will sustain our child, and it will continue to sustain our children's children's children...so long as it exists."

There were a lot of very old sogon grass knots beside the big tree. Umas teased his wife:

"Abus, how many sogon knots have you tied?"

"Don't be stupid! You tied all of these." Abus laughed as she slapped her husband lightly on the shoulder.

"Is that right? I tied them all? You mean that you don't like tying sogon grass knots?"

Abus bashfully picked up a stone from the ground and threw it at him. The sound of their laughter frightened away the little birds looking for food in the tree.

"Umas! Look!" Abus pointed to a fresh, bright green sogon grass knot beside a dying, partially withered clump of grass. It was as if a pair of loving souls were soaring and singing together deep inside that knot. After staring at it for a while they smiled and shook their heads, knowing what the other was thinking.

There was a bunch of sogon grass lying across the path. Umas lightly moved it to the side, not wanting to damage it because when the new mortal soul grew up, he would definitely want to use this grass to tie a beautiful, loving knot.

Before they entered the village, Umas and Abus looked back at the path they had just walked along. They saw a mountainside covered with bright green sogon grass knots and bowed their heads shyly in the breeze.

NOTES

1. A midwife.
2. Brocade snakes.
3. Yams.
4. Gout.
5. Here meaning the human spirit.
6. Physical characteristics.
7. Literally, 'person', but here meaning Bunun person.

Chapter 10

The Ritual of Birth

Moonlight shrouded the cold mountain forest like a heavy cotton quilt. Looking at it from a great distance, the earth emanated a pristine silver radiance like the bottom of a clean-scrubbed pot. The night wind floated and swirled following the contours of the mountain slopes, playfully blowing the moonlight slowly towards the peaks of mountains standing opposite the village. Beneath the Chinaberry trees, myriad fragments of light flashed in all directions on the wind. It seemed that the fireflies were busy enacting a ritual all their own.

Umas was a tall, robust village brave with abundant life experience, but it was the pride so evident in the way he held his head under that fringe of hair, and the way he raised his black eyebrows that people especially noticed. That was how his spirit of fearless independence truly showed itself. Yet these days you could no longer discern the high-spirited heroism of former days on his young, handsome face. His eyes were narrowed from fatigue, and the tips of his black whiskers were already a little yellowed. Prematurely grey hair grew from his temples, and his forehead was etched with thick lines. Even in his hand gestures and the way he moved his body you could sense a kind of excessive irascibility. This sometimes played out as a deliberate letting loose. And it was all the result of the constant stress of knowing that his wife was about to give birth. The stress ravaged him both physically and emotionally, so it was inevitable that it would leave behind scars.

A dejected expression on his face, Umas took his languid body into the kitchen to wait. A large pile of scarlet coals blazed in the traditional stone stove, silently illuminating the kitchen, and warming the black night air.

"Umas, aren't you tired? You should go and rest." Banitul looked up at his son leaning against the wall.

"I can't sleep. Abus was crying so loudly. Tama, do you think she's in any danger?" It may have been because the smoke in the kitchen was too thick, or perhaps he was just really tired, but Umas' eyes looked bloodshot as he spoke.

"No way. Abus isn't in any danger. The gods are standing by our side. Your wife is just crying as loud as she can to call the child out of her belly. Besides, she's the bravest woman in the village, she's not going to have any trouble. You can relax." Banitul smiled and looked optimistically at his son. Yet anyone could see that this was forced, and the smile quickly disappeared from his face.

"Poor Abus, she started crying in the evening along with the partridges. Now the partridges are tired, and they've stopped, but she's still wailing in pain. Tama, we must have done something wrong if she's suffering like this." Umas bowed his head. Because he was so anxious and at a loss, his teeth knocked together, making his shoulders tremble uncontrollably.

"What's that matter with you? Faced with a little bit of adversity you've gone so pathetic. That's the stupidity of people, I tell you. That kind of inborn stupidity will always be our biggest stumbling block! It's worse than hatred. Umas, you have to break up those stumbling blocks in the face of adversity. Ugh! Uh! The old man started to choke and gasp in the smoke. He stopped for a moment then started to cough. The sound of his coughing rumbled deep and congested, as if it were coming from a huge grain barrel. But he kept on talking, ignoring the coughing:

"The men in our family aren't allowed to cry. We would be ridiculed by the spirits of nature and our family would be disgraced! Throw away your tears like a brave Bunun man."

At dusk, the mountain forests rang with Machilumah[1] melodies. The sound of the tunes was forceful and resonant, setting off rumbling echoes in the vastness of the forests. Aside from letting family members at home know that the laborers were returning home with heavy burdens, the songs helped to dispel all the fatigue and sorrow of the day. That's what our people are like. They love to sing to give vent to their heartfelt emotions and their secrets.

Just then, a form suddenly appeared from the distance. He was different from everyone else and he flew in from the direction of the village. His appearance made the men stop singing. The chime-like laughter of the women stopped as well and faded away.

Umas, it's your Subali." Someone with sharp eyes shouted out.

"Oh no! Something must have happened to Abus." Umas once imagined that he could foresee the future clearly, and now he saw Subali running and shouting himself hoarse. It confirmed his sense that if something had happened, it must be to do with his wife.

"Abus might be about to give birth. Yesterday I saw her belly and it was bulging like a pumpkin that was about to burst." Aping was a tall woman with big black eyes beneath her wide eyebrows. The look in her eyes made people think that they had to believe her.

When Umas arrived at his house, Abus was sitting on the dirt floor of the living room waiting to give birth to her child, as was the custom of all the village women. Our people believe that humans must rely upon the earth to live, so the first thing that any newborn must do is to make contact with nature so that they can mutually begin to build their intimate relationship.

The village midwife took along two or three women to assist her. They were all respected elders and they were going to use their accumulated wisdom and experience to protect the lives of mother and child.

"Umas, after you knew that the gods were going to give you a baby, did you and Abus respect all the taboos established by the ancestors? For example, as soon as you got up in the morning, did you fold up your quilt then open the windows and doors and that sort of thing, as the ancestors require?" Because Abus was suffering more than other women, Banitul found it hard not to suspect that someone in the family had incited the anger of the gods.

"Tama, you can see with your own eyes that I am a man whose faith is strong and whose behavior is honest. In the days since becoming pregnant, my wife and I have observed all of the traditional taboos. Even when we carried yams home from the fields, we immediately dumped them straight on the floor. When we took millet to the fields to eat, as soon as we arrived at our destination, we opened the wrapping cloth and displayed the millet before the gods. We did all these things in hopes of gaining the pleasure of the gods so that they would allow our baby to be born without incident, and that there would be no harm to the parents." Umas also couldn't understand why Abus was being submitted to more suffering than others. "And so that the baby does not become a thief whom people hate and try to drive away when he grows up and enters adulthood, I even told Abus not to eat the meat of flying squirrels while she was pregnant. We have constantly followed in the footsteps of the ancestors. Could it be that the gods did not observe our spirit of reverence?"

"Anana-kai! Anana-kai!"[2] Abus's troubling moans still reverberated through the air.

"Tama, let's go...we'll see if there is any way that we can help." The moaning tore at Umas' heart, goading him to rise to his feet.

"Ai! My poor child. Everyone's abilities have their limits. There are some things that we just aren't equipped to deal with. It's like the animals in the forest; some can fly, some can jump, some can climb, and some can run as fast as the wind. Our gods hoped that people with different abilities could learn to help each other. When it comes to giving birth, only the midwife can ensure that your child will appear before us quickly. Only the midwife can dispel the pain that giving birth brings to a woman. Come! What we can do is learn from hunters who wait for their prey. We will wait for the best possible results in solitude and apprehension." Banitul's voice was filled with warmth and sympathy.

In the living room several elderly women were gathered around Abus. Some were sitting on the ground with her, supporting her upper body. Others were wiping the sweat from her face, while still others were pressing down on her legs that writhed from pain. In all, the living room was almost reminiscent of a scene with a group of hunters trying to tie up some small, weak animal. Because her powers had gained the recognition of those in the village, the midwife, Hudas Ibu, had become the elder solely charged with the responsibility of welcoming little living beings. After a night of struggle, aside from showing the age that one would expect in her face, Hudas Ibu's eyes were drawn into narrow slits from fatigue.

"The child is clinging to his mother's belly like a leach. This won't be good for the mother if it continues. Who can grab the other end of the ramie cord for me? We're going to have to squeeze the child out of the belly with a length of cloth." This was the first idea that sprang from Hudas Ibu's mind.

"Harder! We have to squeeze hard in the direction of her toes. Quickly! Come on now!" The midwife urged them on loudly. The other women felt anxious or fearful. The sound of footsteps like scurrying mice, as well as banging noises that shook the mud walls, constantly issued from the living room. Along with all the other random noises, it made people wonder if these elders really did have the ability to protect mother and child.

"Anana-kai! Anana-kai!" Cina's screams began again, but by now they were becoming hoarse and weak.

Then suddenly, "Wa! Wa!" The squalling of an infant that they had waited for all night finally cut through the night sky over the village. At the same time, the joyful sighs of the elder women pealed from the living room like silver bells. Even the mountain forest outside of the house began to rustle with "Sha! Sha! Sha!" sounds in the wind.

The cries of the little creature made the family by the fireside all tilt their heads in unison to listen. Among traditional rituals, that is what the ceremony to give thanks to the gods is like. In the stone stove, charcoal on the verge of turning to ashes suddenly collapsed when it heard the infant's cries. This sent shockwaves through the cinders that had long been piling up around the fire.

"Abus, do you have enough strength to give thanks to the gods?" Hudas Ibu looked at Abus's body covered with sweat and blood.

Abus raised her eyebrows, placed her feeble hands on the bloody ground, and struggled to sit up, but the weight of the sweat on her forehead was enough to send her tumbling back into the arms of the woman sitting beside her.

"You have given your blood in exchange for the safety of your child. All your strength has been used up. Let me do the ritual to thank the gods in your name." The midwife placed the infant beside Abus then took hold of her right hand to stroke the palm of the infant's right hand. Then she solemnly pronounced a prayer to the heavens:

"Hu...Hu, Hu! In Abus's name I extend deepest gratitude to the most powerful gods in heaven. The life of this infant comes from your pleasure. Tell us how we can refuse the seductions of the evil spirits. Oh, Heavenly Gods! If I ate taboo or unclean foods while my child was still in my belly do not make my child suffer the consequences of your curses. In the name of Abus, I pray that in future this child can live a healthy, peaceful life. After the child grows to adulthood, may his voice be as resonant as a waterfall, and his behavior as clean as pure water. Hu...Hu, Hu!"

After she had finished the prayer the midwife used a piece of bamboo that had been sharpened like a knife to cut the umbilical cord joining mother and child. Then she took some *gan*[3] that she had ground in advance from her bag and spread it on the umbilical cord while she ordered the other women to clean up both mother and child. After the baby had been safely born, the sound of footsteps in the living room suddenly became joyful and relaxed. In the midst of all the activity you could also sometimes hear the light, mischievous sound of laughter.

Abus looked pale and drawn, but amid the sound of laughter she finally smiled with that smile that a mother who has just given birth should have. It was a satisfied smile like the lilies blossoming all over the mountain slopes. The baby who had just arrived in the village kept his eyes closed and his lips tightly pursed. His cheeks were flushed as red as autumn maple leaves as he fell soundly asleep on the cloth brought over by the village women. Even the gecko on the ceiling chirped away in approval at the child's pleasing appearance. The women helped Abus up onto the bed to rest. Although her eyes kept twitching from all the excitement, Abus kept her eyes closed and pretended to sleep. The whole time her lips, now purple from exhaustion, were drawn into a smile that only new mothers smile.

"Whew! The frightening part is over. Once again Ibu with her strong powers has protected the lives of a mother and her child. There's no way the evil spirits can control the situation here now." After Banitul heaved a sigh of relief, he leaned his exhausted body against the wooden post beside him, closed his eyes and tried to cover up the expression of alarm that he had worn all night long. His ears were still trained on all the movements in the living room.

"Such a long dark night." Umas heaved a sigh as well.

The stillness of dawn and the blue mists shrouded the sky above the mountains. The dew was heavy and weighed the grasses to the ground. Tree frogs croaked in the mountain streams, and in a dense grove of maple trees not far from the reed house several birds sang their song, "Jigulasi, jigulasi."

"Umas, this is the baby's *binainuk*.[4] You personally have to bury it beneath a large tree outside the house." A woman walked into the kitchen carrying a red cloth bag.

"Thank you all for leading my wife and son through their life's most dangerous chasm. I will never forget everything that you have done here tonight. In future, if you have any kind of difficulty at all, I give you permission to call upon my family." Umas bowed deeply, then, with hands trembling from excitement, he accepted the beautiful red bag.

"Umas, I'm going to the storehouse to get a hoe." As Banitul spoke he strode from the kitchen filled with energy.

Umas carried the red cloth bag towards a large camphor tree outside. Banitul followed closely behind him, shouldering a hoe.

"Umas, you have to bless your child personally." Banitul spoke softly as he stopped not far away.

"All right. Where's the hoe?"

Umas placed the red bag on top of the thick roots of the tree, then dug a deep hole in the space between two raised roots.

"Tama, does the child's placenta have to be buried beneath a big tree?" This first experience made Umas curious, even a little bit incredulous.

"The placenta has used its great power to protect the feeble little being for a long time. We must respect and thank it. By burying it beneath a large tree it expresses the hope that the child will grow as strong as the tree and will be able to stand proudly on the earth."

"You mean that every tree with a placenta buried beneath has a special relationship with a particular person's future? Does that make them 'trees of life'?" With a graceful motion Umas shrugged his shoulders, as if he didn't fully believe what he was hearing.

"Of course. Our ancestors have always done this." Banitul spoke cheerfully, his face glowing in the shade of the tree. "That's why our ancestors never considered that climbing trees was something you did for fun. If they had to climb a tree, they would be sure not to break any branches, nor would they pick any of the leaves unless they had good reason, just like they would never harm physically another person."

"Why is that?"

"If you break a branch, the person whose placenta is buried beneath the tree will also be injured. For example, their hands or feet might be harmed, making it difficult for them to move around, or their eyes might be damaged, making them blind, or their ears could be hurt so that they wouldn't be able to hear sound. If a tree loses most of its leaves, the spiritual power of the person will be weakened and in the future they will suffer constant illness leading to their death." Banitul brushed the black dirt from his hands and continued to explain:

"Umas, think about it: if you were to damage a 'tree of life' that represented one of your own family, that would be the same as you harming your own family member. That kind of behavior would lead to you being punished by the gods."

"Tama, where is my 'tree of life'?" Umas opened his eyes wide.

"It's also this strong camphor tree. This is our clan's 'tree of life.' It will lead our family towards a peaceful future." The two looked up at the same time to see the great camphor tree reaching high into the sky.

The village finally roused itself, and strands of white smoke rose from each of the thatched rooves. The smoke swirled and danced with the morning breeze. The air itself was absolutely still, clear and fresh. The mountain peaks, short and tall, that extended into the distance, stood out so clearly where they drew close to the sky. It was as though some kindly god had deliberately washed them clean with spring water...

Abus reclined at an angle, feeding the baby from an especially prominent, milk-filed breast. As she looked down at the tiny creature that had hidden away in her belly for ten months, the pain of her night-long ordeal turned to crystal tears that flashed brightly in the corners of her eyes. All those anxious feelings had changed to gentle motherly love. Feeling so moved, she softly began to sing a lullaby to the baby, a tune that had been passed down by the ancestors:

> Cina returns from the fields with a smile,
> Tama gives her ramie to make a new dress
> She splashes water on the greedy puppies
> Who grab the ramie and scamper about.

"You still haven't drunk any hot soup. How can you nurse the baby? If you're not careful, you'll lose the strength the fight off the disease demons." Umas brought in a bowl full of hot broth made from fresh ginger and green beans. He was all smiles as he stepped nimbly into the bedroom. "Abus, I have to take the child out now to welcome the sun for the time in his life, and to let him see the world. It's really important for his life. I also have to pray to the gods to allow him to grow into a brave, skilled Bunun hunter."

"Is the sun almost up? Have you got the weapons, knife and animal skin that you need for the ritual all ready?"

"Everything is ready. Come! Let me hold the child."

"Be careful, he's still very small. Don't hurt him."

It was just there, under the eaves to the left of the main door. Banitul was there in the gradually increasing morning light, busily setting the pile of rags and dry kindling wood on fire. The bluish smoke wafted about in the courtyard on the morning breeze. The hunting dogs, chasing around and practicing their attacking skills in front of the courtyard, thought that there was a fog coming in, so they all scrambled under the eaves to lie down on their mats, then closed their eyes to rest. A few of the younger, more playful dogs were restless and looked angrily at this blue smoke-mist.

"Tama, why did you make a fire in front of the main door?" Umas walked out of the house.

"Abus has just completed her birthing. Her body is as weak as dandelion fluff. One gust of wind and she could be blown a long, long way away. I think that the evil spirits may take advantage of this and try to harm her, and that would leave us to weep for days on end. The evil spirits enjoy making people fall into months of despair, weeping, shame and disaster. Our ancestors all used this method to combat them." Banitul kneeled on the ground with his eyes closed as he continued to blow into the flames with all his might until his face turned red.

"What else can you do by making the fire?"

"The gods know that our powers are weak, so in order to protect our people they transform themselves into warm flames and come to live with us, protecting our lives every moment of the day. From now on, in order to protect Abus, anytime an outsider enters the house they have to cross over the fire. That allows the power of the gods to chase away any evil spirits that people may bring from outside." Banitul changed his tone and continued to speak:

"If you notice that the flames are dying down and are about to go out, you must quickly add wood so that it continues to burn strongly. You have to do that until Abus recovers her health. Do you understand?"

The flames began to look as strong as they were supposed to, and the ever-decreasing smoke was carried on the wind up into the blue, blue sky. The hunting dogs returned to the courtyard to play at attacking and chasing each other, stirring up clouds of dust in the process. Swarms of flies and mosquitoes that had been waiting for a chance to fly into the house had long ago been chased into the clumps of bushes in the distance by the smoke.

In his left hand Umas held a bow and arrows as well as a piece of dried animal skin. Carrying the baby in a *tavuk*,[5] he faced Banitul standing by the fire and said:

"Tama, I want to take this child to perform Duhumis."[6]

"Go then! Take him to welcome his first sunrise." Looking at the adorable tiny creature, Banitul nodded his head with satisfaction.

After he walked out of the courtyard, Umas stood in front of the woods to the left. The distant mountain range was tinged golden yellow by the rays of the sun so bright that it was impossible to look at it directly. The valley looked like a long, narrow fissure extending from beneath his feet. The inexhaustible stream that flowed perpetually through it flashed with a cold glint, like a dagger that hunters use in close combat with ferocious prey.

Under pressure from the fierce beams of morning sunlight, the fragments of nighttime darkness still remaining at dawn retreated, step by step into the mountain valleys. Slowly, the birds soaring in the sky, the slumbering village, the shadowy forest, and the people preparing to go out and cultivate their fields, all appeared crystal clear in the golden light reflecting from the mountain slopes.

"Swish!" Umas dispatched an arrow, straight, violent and swift, in the direction of the forest.

"Hu! May the beautiful, kind-hearted infant at my side grow to be an able, strong Bunun hunter. May his life be like the mountain ranges and reach beyond where the eye can see. When the villagers are cursed by the evil spirits and become ill, may my child remain healthy and strong. When my child grows up and enters the mountains to hunt, may he not be confused by the steep cliffs and deep canyons and fall to his death. He will have eyes provided by the gods so that whatever he aims at, he will strike. When he pulls his bow to shoot at game, he will hit it every time. This child also carries with him inexhaustible good luck. From this time forward, the millet that our family grows in the fields will be as fat and beautiful as strings of pearls. The pigs, chickens and other livestock that we raise will be as numerous and boisterous as a swarm of bees. The evil spirits that surround us will flee in shame into the darkest mountain canyons. Hu! Hu! Hu!" The sound of Umas' resonant, sincere prayers reverberated back and forth through the tranquil ravine for a long, long time.

Umas followed the sounds as he gazed up at the uneven mountain peaks. Surrounding the tallest of those peaks there was a white cloud, incomparably clean. It looked like an old man with grey hair and a compassionate face. He had a smile on his face as he stared down at the earth with a satisfied expression.

"My child, you are going to spend your life in Nature's blissful domain. It will bring you a joyful and prosperous future." Tama happily patted the infant on his back then turned and walked back home.

After Umas returned the baby to Abus, he immediately hung the ceremonial piece of animal skin on a cross-shaped bamboo frame.

"Tama, do you mind holding the other side of this frame. I'm afraid that I'll pull the skin crooked." Umas worked with his head bowed.

"This represents the first time that the child shoots a game animal, and it also symbolizes that when he eventually goes into the mountains to hunt, he will bring back much game, and that he absolutely will not return empty-handed. Umas, when you get the skin tied securely you have to keep it in the storeroom so that the evil spirits won't find it and damage it. That wouldn't be good for the child's future."

Umas noticed that as Abus busied herself around the kitchen she often stopped to wave away the smoke that got into her eyes. Her feet moved lightly over the earthen floor as if she was afraid to hurt the floor, or perhaps she was worried that she would harm her own wounds. Umas gazed from a distance as she drifted back and forth in the kitchen along with the smoke.

"Abus, you should go and rest. Let me do it." Umas grasped one of her hands.

"I'm already able to work. You just go and bring in some more wood. Today we are inviting the midwife to come and eat with us."

"Wow, so much food! I'm already getting hungry."

"I made it to thank the midwife for her help. Tama says that we have to learn how to make others happy."

Flames shot from the stove formed from three stones. Their light flashed and leaped all around the kitchen like mischievous sprites. Banitul, Husung, Hanagu, Umas, Abus and the midwife all squatted around the round pot and wooden plates which all brimmed with food. The children all sensed that this had to do with giving thanks, so they very thoughtfully played outside.

"Hudas Ibu, thank you for allowing our child to arrive safely in the village. This disobedient rooster wasn't as strong and beautiful as other people's roosters. I'm not sure what you will find to chew on aside from his dry, hard bone. I risked ridicule and shame by inviting you here to eat with us." With his wooden spoon, Banitul scooped a lot of meat from the iron pot and placed it in a wooden bowl. This he placed in the quickly disappearing space in front of Hudas Ibu. The earthenware pot that had originally been filled with chunks of meat had suddenly become just a watery pool. Waves of light still issued from the flames in the stove. This transformation made everyone so nervous that they couldn't sit still. Everyone bowed their heads trying to hide the expressions of regret on their faces.

"The gods in heaven have surely witnessed your sincere behavior and that is why you have received a healthy infant." Hudas Ibu's voice was low and hoarse.

"Where is the baby? We should all bless the frail, delicate child."

"Right! Our ancestors have told us: 'Children are our greatest asset.' Praying for the baby's health and safety is the most important thing." Banitul nodded his head in agreement.

Abus carefully passed the baby to the midwife. The midwife stroked the baby's forehead with the palm of her right hand then pronounced a blessing for the child in a pious tone:

"Hapikaunan! The family of this child are especially hospitable. They have been very good to me, inviting me to eat this sumptuous feast and drink the most fragrant millet wine. I pray that all the children in the village may live in peace and that they will not shatter the compassionate feelings of their mothers. I pray that this family's children will be as adorable as a string of pearls. Hu! Hu! Hu!" The midwife sprinkled a few drops of wine on the infant with her fingers. When she finished her prayer, she returned the baby to Abus.

"Abus can get out of bed and walk. From today on people who come to visit mother and child no longer need to step across the bonfire. That fire that was there to stop evil spirits from entering the house can now be extinguished." Hudas Ibu's expression was extremely solemn, and this made the wrinkles on her face stand out more clearly.

The last light of the evening sun glowed through the grasses and green trees, making the ripe plums shine like gorgeous crimson jewels. An old man sat in the courtyard quietly gazing at the plums growing on the mountain slope. Because he was old, his life had become more difficult and melancholic. His eyes had lost their former vigor.

Recently, Talum had been aging quickly. His breath smelled like some sort of rotting wood, and everything in his life had been disrupted by feelings of death, this despite the fact that he could foresee his own death. Most of the time, Talum lurched about in his room like a ghost, muttering to himself about his memories of things of the past. The old man had already lost his sight and hearing and now it seemed that he had trouble making out who it was that was speaking to him. Sometimes he imagined that he was discussing bygone times with people he knew long ago. He talked about strange, incomprehensible things. It became impossible for those around him to continue communicating with him because nobody could understand what he was trying to say.

He started the habit of spending his days in solitude. But recently Talum had become lucid again, and his usual confusion had disappeared. This unusual turn of events actually made his family worry all the more. His life was once again filled with enthusiasm. He would even follow the sound of the baby's crying and go up to the child and start talking to himself:

"Have all the adults died? Why do they let you cry all by yourself?" His gentle regard was the same as when he had seen a child weeping in the courtyard because they had bloodied their knee.

"Hudas, come and eat." Umas brought over a wooden plate full of food and placed it before the old man. Talum usually couldn't remember where the kitchen was, so when it came time to eat, the family just brought his food to him where he happened to be.

"Umas, tomorrow the moon will be in the same stage that it was in when the child was first born. You should give him a name." The old man raised his eyebrows and looked at Umas with that same old powerful look of his.

"Hudas, you know who I am! You know that Abus gave birth to a child!" Umas' eyes grew red and he embraced the decrepit old body.

"I hear the baby crying every day. I am very aware of everything that happens in the household." Talum was as proud of himself as a child that had won an important game without really trying.

"Everything is ready. Tomorrow we will perform Pagingan[7] for our child. All the people in the village will come and celebrate with us."

When he thought about how they were going to introduce their child to the whole village, Umas felt especially good. That was because, after the ritual of naming and feasting, the child would officially become part of the village. Not only would this bring vitality to the life of the village, it meant that the child would enjoy the protection of the entire village.

"Don't allow Subali, Asulan and the other children to take part in the infant naming ritual."

"Why?" Umas fed a piece of tender, fat meat into the mouth of the old man.

"The ability of children to control their physical spirits is limited. They often sneeze or fart during rituals, and that ruins things."

"It isn't as though we are going out to hunt. Will those things violate the taboos of the naming ceremony?" Umas kept feeding food into the old man's mouth.

"Of course. The sound of sneezing summons the evil spirits, and that is not at all good for the naming ritual. The smell of flatulence in the ritual area displeases the elders, and that kind of unfilial behavior is not permitted by the gods." There was too much in his mouth, so the old man spit the whole works out onto the ground, although he kept making chewing motions.

"All right. I will make note of that."

Umas was considering whether to feed the rest of the food on the plate to the old man when the latter suddenly opened his eyes and said angrily:

"Why are you stealing my food?"

"I just want to help you...ah...Hudas, have you forgotten who I am again?" Not knowing what to do, Umas just patted the old man on the shoulder.

"Davi! Today everyone in the village is coming to see the child. Does he have new clothes? Is the millet wine good? Did you wash my clothes?"

Umas babbled on like a mother hen who had just laid an egg, and he was making a lot of noise as well.

"Subali, you children can't take part in today's naming ceremony." Umas continued on like a mother hen.

"Why not?"

"It has been prohibited by the ancestors."

"So what are we supposed to do?" Subali pouted, feeling hard done by.

Tama Ilung was now old, but when he had been younger his hunting skills and bravery had brought him respect. His honest behavior and spirit of loving and protecting others had made him a model when people instructed their children. For those reasons Umas had very politely invited him to preside over the naming ceremony. Umas hoped that after he had gone through with the naming, his baby would be endowed with Tama Ilung's abilities and virtue.

Abus was wearing a close-fitting traditional costume as she smiled and greeted the people who came to offer their congratulations.

After all the people were assembled, Tama Ilung, who was presiding over the ceremony, entered carrying a gourd ladle full of millet wine and walked in front of the infant. With an air of gravity, he called out: "Hupikaunan!" All the people watched in silence as the sacred ritual began to unfold.

"Hu! The child is to be named Banitul. He will inherit his grandfather's illustrious name. This name will bring the child eternal health and strength surpassing all others. Disease-bearing evil spirits will not be able to violate his body. His movements will be as vigorous as an eagle, and when he grows up, his deportment will be a pure and clean as the moon. His reputation will be as majestic as Savah.[8] All the evil spirits will be fearful of the name that is given to him today, and they will not dare enter our village. Hu! Hu! Hu!"

In traditional times, aside from naming each infant in the presence of the gods, it was imperative that the ancestors' rules for naming be strictly observed. The eldest son inherited the grandfather's name. The second son inherited the great grandfather's name. The third son took the grandfather's younger brother's name, while the fourth and fifth sons took the paternal uncles' names. The eldest daughter inherited the grandmother's name, the second daughter took the great grandmother's name, and from the third daughter on down they all inherited the paternal aunts' names. This venerable traditional custom not only commemorated the grace of the ancestors, it also created an unassailable solidarity in the family.

After Tama Ilung finished his prayer he wet his finger with wine and dabbed it on the baby's mouth. Once the ritual was over, all the other people came over and gently shook the baby's tiny hand as they pronounced their sincerest blessings. Shaking the infant's hand represents that all the people of the village acknowledge the child as a part of the village. It is also a promise that while the baby is growing up, if he runs into any difficulties, the people will all do everything in their power to ensure that he continues his progress towards a peaceful future.

When all the people had finished giving their blessings, they all reverently said; "Mihumisan."[9] Little Banitul apparently was moved by the blessings of the adults, and he started to smile happily as he lay there in Abus's arms.

With everyone's help, a lavish feast was neatly laid out on the ground in the courtyard. Umas and Abus served as enthusiastic hosts.

With a little help from the millet wine, those people who were by nature reserved began to talk and laugh more loudly and with more abandon. It didn't take very long before everyone was as happy as can be. It seemed as though the entire village was joyful because of the arrival of this tiny new creature. Even the tall tree where the infant's placenta had been buried began to dance, while countless birds hopped and danced freely about in its branches. The tree's thick leaves also soughed a deep song in the mountain wind.

The people then started to sing the praises of the host of gods in their fine singing voices. All the creatures in the area of the village began to dance to the tune of those ritual songs; some swung their thin waists, some rocked back and forth. The creatures of the world all dancing in unison was a dazzling sight. The resonant sounds of the ritual songs and the blessings echoed about in the mountain valleys, they floated off toward the mountain forest, rushed toward the heart of the heavens, and penetrated the deepest depths of the earth...

NOTES

1. Songs of those carrying heavy burdens. These were ancient melodies.
2. A cry of pain.
3. A kind of high-mountain herb that is fragrant and piquant.
4. Literally, 'clothing', but here meaning placenta.
5. A length of cloth for carrying a baby.
6. The "wish-granting ritual" in which adults pray for the future of the baby.
7. A child's naming ceremony.
8. Jade Mountain, the highest mountain in the minds of the people.
9. In the Bunun language this means, "Live well." It is the most solemn blessing among our people.

About the Author
and the Translator

About the Author
Husluman Vava (1958–2007), was born in the Indigenous Bunun village of Takimi (Longquan), Taitung County in southeastern Taiwan. As a university student he studied the myths and legends of his people. Then, as a schoolteacher in a Bunun community, he participated in many traditional cultural activities. His early writing explores traditional Bunun culture and mythology, while in his later work he takes a greater interest in cultural and religious values. *The Spirit of Jade Mountain*, for which Vava won the Taiwan Literature Award, is his most important work. It follows a Bunun boy's growth to maturity, and his quest for meaning in the cultural and religious customs of his village.

About the Translator
Terence Russell is a senior scholar of Chinese in the Asian Studies Centre at the University of Manitoba. He received his PhD in classical Chinese from Australian National University and his MA and BA in Chinese from the University of British Columbia. Dr. Russell has translated the works of numerous Indigenous and ethnic Chinese writers. He also has rendered two full-length novels by the Shandong writer Zhang Wei: *September Fable (Jiuyue yuyan)* and *Seven Kinds of Mushrooms (Mogu qizhong)*. He is currently coeditor of Taiwan Literature: English Translation Series.

www.ingramcontent.com/pod-product-compliance
Lightning Source LLC
Chambersburg PA
CBHW030331120726
47901CB00007B/1753